THE
FIGHTING
TEMERAIRE

THE
FIGHTING
TEMERAIRE

Sam Willis

Quercus

First published in Great Britain in 2009 by
Quercus
21 Bloomsbury Square
London
WC1A 2NS

A CIP catalogue record for this book is available
from the British Library

ISBN 978 1 84724 998 2

Text and plates designed and typeset by Helen Ewing
Printed in the UK by CPI William Clowes Beccles NR34 7TL

THE HEARTS OF OAK TRILOGY

This is the first book of the *Hearts of Oak* trilogy, which explores three of the most iconic and yet largely unexplored stories of the 'Great Age of Sail'. *The Fighting Temeraire, Admiral Benbow* and *The Glorious First of June* are the biographies of a ship, a man and a battle that will splice together to form a narrative of an era that stretches from the English Civil War of the 1640s to the coming of steam two centuries later. This 'Great Age of Sail' was once written about in heroic terms but many of those legends have since been overlooked. The details of the stories themselves have become confused and the reasons behind the formation of those legends ignored. With more than a century of professional naval history to draw from together with new access to previously restricted archives, now is the time to look afresh at those stories of heroism from the perspective of the modern historian; now is the time to understand how and why *The Fighting Temeraire, Admiral Benbow* and *The Glorious First of June* became legends.

> Heart of oak are our ships, jolly tars are our men,
> We always are ready; Steady, boys, steady!
> We'll fight and we'll conquer again and again.

D. GARRICK, *Heart of Oak* (1759

Acknowledgements

This book could not have been produced without the help of a number of people. I am particularly grateful to Professor Sam Smiles, a world-renowned Turner scholar who is so generous with his knowledge and time. Jeremy Michell, Doug McArthy and Alex Fullerlove at the National Maritime Museum along with the staff of the Caird Library were also very helpful. Emma Strouts at Christie's has, once again, helped me gain access to some little-known images and objects. My grandfather, Commander Derek Willis, read this through in draft and made many valuable comments, as did Andrew Bond, who continues to be a guiding light. And of course there is Torsy; always there and always certain.

For Tors
'Nothing could be finer.'*

*Admiral Collingwood to Captain Harvey
of the *Temeraire*, 28 October 1805

The fighting *Temeraire*
Built of a thousand trees,
Lunging out her lightenings,
And beetling o'er the seas

HERMAN MELVILLE, *The Temeraire*, 1866

A Journal

of the Proceedings of
H. M Ship

Téméraire

Contents

List of Illustrations

LIST OF MAPS

LOG BOOK IMAGES
(The National Archives, Kew)

Maps

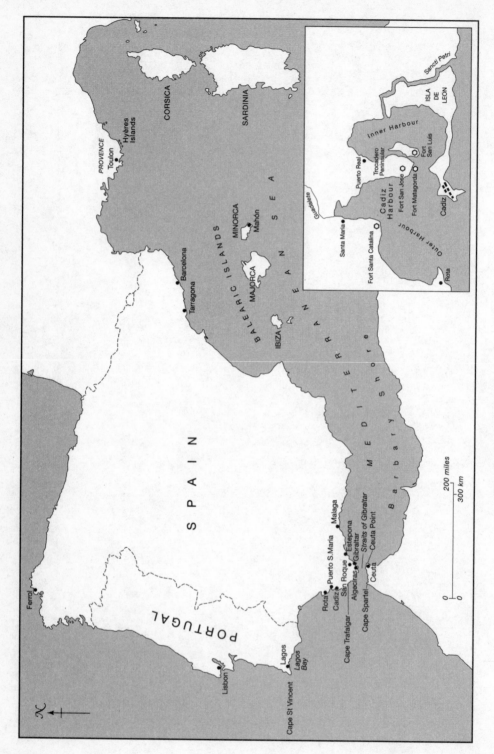

The Western Mediterranean and Cadiz

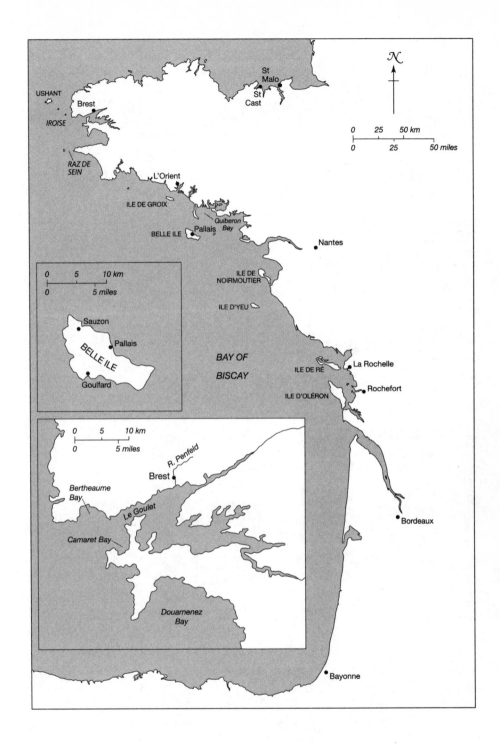

USHANT

Brest

IROISE

RAZ DE
SEIN

L'Orient

ILE DE GROIX

Quiberon
Bay

BELLE ILE   Pallais

St
Malo

St
Cast

N

| 0 | 25 | 50 km |
| 0 | 25 | 50 miles |

Nantes

ILE DE
NOIRMOUTIER

ILE D'YEU

| 0 | 5 | 10 km |
| 0 | 5 miles | |

Sauzon

Pallais

BELLE ILE

Goulfard

BAY OF

BISCAY

ILE DE RÉ   La Rochelle

Rochefort

ILE D'OLÉRON

| 0 | 5 | 10 km |
| 0 | 5 miles | |

R. Penfeld

Brest

Bertheaume
Bay

Le Goulet

Camaret Bay

Bordeaux

Douarnenez
Bay

Bayonne

Western France

xxiii

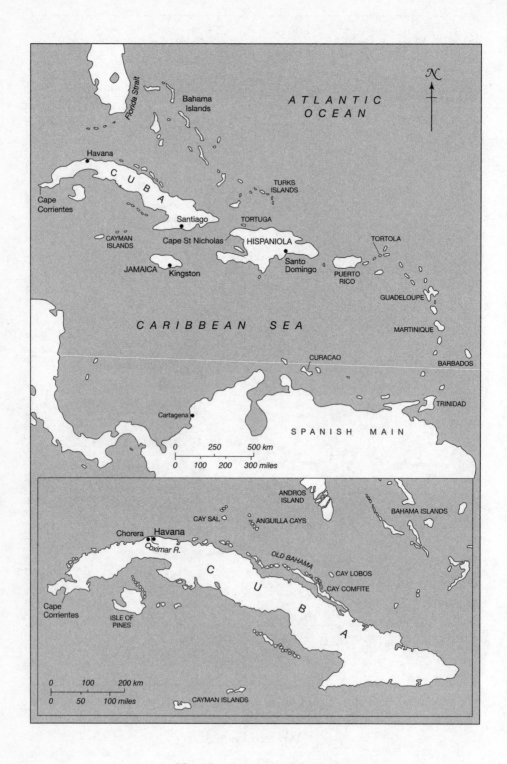

The Caribbean and Cuba

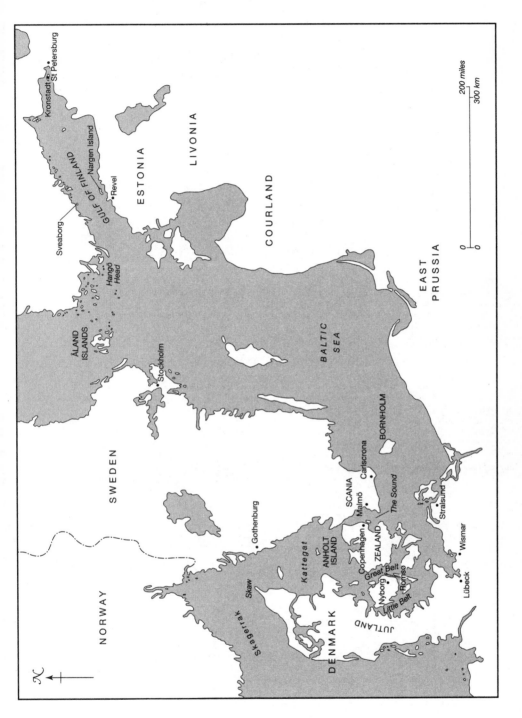

The Baltic

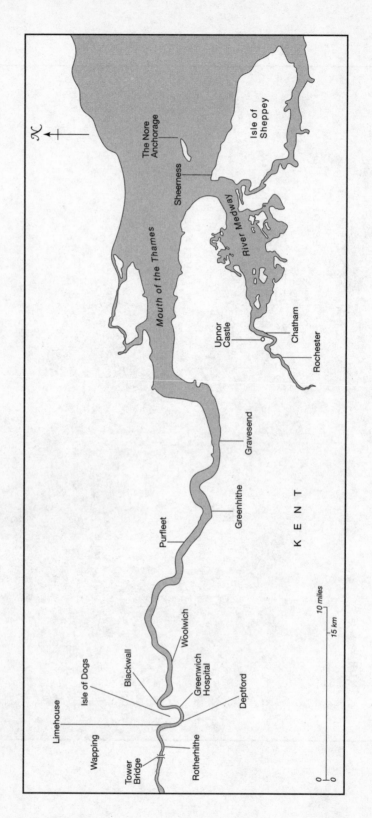

The Thames

Preface

In August 2005, BBC Radio 4 ran a poll to find the nation's favourite painting. It was won by Turner's *The Fighting Temeraire Tugged To Her Last Berth To Be Broken Up, 1838*, and it was won by a landslide: it received over a quarter of all votes cast, fighting off Constable's *The Hay Wain* and other equally well-known works by Manet, Hockney and Van Gogh. Turner was a genius whose techniques revolutionized art history, and *The Fighting Temeraire* is his masterpiece. It is one of the most iconic images of the ages of both sail and steam, and is one of the greatest works of art ever created by a Western artist.

For some it is popular quite simply because it is familiar, but for others much of its allure lies in the story that it tells. Today it hangs in the National Gallery in Trafalgar Square, only yards from Nelson's Column, a monument that commemorates Nelson's death at the Battle of Trafalgar in 1805. Both the painting and the statue are less than a mile from St Paul's Cathedral, where Turner and Nelson are buried within feet of each other: Britain's most famous artist and Britain's most famous admiral are intimately linked in both past and present by this painting, a painting whose significance grips the nation as surely in the twenty-first century as it did when it was painted in 1838. It is a story that unites the art of war as practised by Nelson with the art of war as depicted by Turner and, as such, it ranges across British cultural history in ways that other stories do not. And yet the story behind the painting has only ever been partially told.[1]

To tell it properly, one must go back as far as the Seven Years War, fought at sea between Britain and France between 1756 and 1763, for the full story of the *Temeraire* is the story not of one ship, but of two. The *Temeraire* in Turner's painting was actually the second ship in the Royal Navy to carry that name, but it is impossible to tell her story satisfactorily without explaining how the name came to be British at all, and how and why it was chosen for the prestigious three-decked 98-gun warship built at Chatham in 1793. It is also important to distinguish between the two as there was some confusion over which *Temeraire* is depicted in Turner's painting: she was mistakenly identified by some of the earliest reviewers as the first ship, the French *Téméraire* which was captured in 1759. She was startlingly different from her successor in appearance, but on paper can only be distinguished by the accents in her name.

The result is a detailed picture of British maritime power at two of its most significant peaks in the age of sail, the climaxes of both the Seven Years War and the Napoleonic Wars. It takes us from the Mediterranean to the Channel; from the Western Approaches to the Caribbean; and from the Baltic to the Atlantic Iberian coast. It covers every conceivable aspect of life in the sailing navy, with particular emphasis on amphibious warfare, disease, victualling, blockade, mutiny and, of course, fleet battle, for it was at Trafalgar that the *Temeraire* really won her fame. She broke through the French and Spanish line directly astern of Nelson's flagship, HMS *Victory*, and, for more than three hours, had two of the enemy's line-of-battle ships lashed to her. She saved the *Victory* at a crucial moment in the battle, and fought until her sides ran 'wet with the long runlets of English blood . . . those pale masts that stayed themselves up against the war-ruin, shaking out their ensigns through the thunder, till sail and ensign dropped.'[2] For her bravery, she was the only British ship singled out for praise by Vice-Admiral Cuthbert Collingwood after the battle. Turner's painting is a memorial to this magnificent ship in the poignant final hours of her life afloat. 'Never more', wrote the contemporary art critic John Ruskin, 'shall sunset lay golden robe on her, nor starlight tremble on the waves that part at her gliding.'[3] This was the poetry of the moment that inspired Turner.

Alfred Thayer Mahan, the most influential naval historian the world has ever seen, declared that 'distinguished ships have a personality only less vivid than that of the men who fought them'. They do indeed. Each has a story to tell and many believe that of the *Temeraire* to be the finest of them all. It ends today in Room 34 of the National Gallery in Trafalgar Square, where a steady stream of visitors gazes at her beauty on Turner's canvas. But it must begin over a thousand miles away and two hundred and fifty years ago, in the dining room of a Spanish palace, on a hot and dusty evening in August 1759, where Admiral Edward Boscawen was having his dinner.

I.

The Escaping *Téméraire*

AUGUST 1759

Moor'd in Gibralter Bay.

It was August 1759, and Admiral of the Blue Edward Boscawen had been invited to dinner by Francisco Bucareli y Ursua, Governor of San Roque, a small Spanish town with a monastery at its heart no more than five kilometres from Gibraltar. The Rock had been captured by the Royal Navy in 1704 and had been the home of the British Mediterranean Fleet since the island of Minorca had been taken by the French in 1756. One hundred and nine metres above sea level, San Roque is an eyrie from which it is possible to see down to Gibraltar Bay and, on a clear day, even across to North Africa. There are few more dramatic locations on the whole Atlantic seaboard of Europe. A vast expanse of sky meets the swirling waters and uncertain winds that characterize the convergence of two oceans and the division of two continents. To the east lies the Mediterranean; to the west, the Atlantic; to the north, the Iberian Peninsula; and to the south, Africa. For the Romans and Greeks this was the very edge of the world, the Pillars of Hercules, but by the 1750s Gibraltar had become the centre of a world encompassed, and contested, by European navies. Today it is still a strategic key to the Mediterranean, Africa and Asia. It is one of the most emotive places on earth and drips with weight of history. It is particularly fitting, therefore, that the events that were to follow would live up to the drama of their location.

Boscawen and his fellow officers were pulled ashore from their warships in a flotilla of longboats, leaving wakes that reached from their mother-ships like the tentacles of a sea creature projecting British sea power ashore. Once they had landed, the men wound their way up the dusty track that led to the settlement perching at the top of the hill. As his men filed in to the evening party, Boscawen posted a sentry to keep watch over the British fleet lying in the calm of Gibraltar Bay. For despite the genial surroundings and the hospitality of their Spanish host, the British officers were uneasy.

Their purpose in the Mediterranean had recently taken a decisive turn. Britain had been at war with France for three years. They had failed to come to any peaceful agreement over the extent and location of the boundaries between British and French possessions in North America and along the banks of the Ohio River, tension had spilled over into armed conflict. The war that followed, known as the Seven Years War, was the first conflict in human history to be fought around the globe. By the summer of 1759 both sides had had successes, but British expertise in amphibious operations had begun to turn the tide. In the first few weeks of the war, however, the French had besieged and captured the island of Minorca, the only British naval base deep in the Mediterranean, from where the Royal Navy had been able to monitor closely the activities of the French Mediterranean Fleet at Toulon. The loss of Minorca was a terrible blow to the British, both practically and psychologically, and a tide of professional and public outrage at the political and military lethargy that had led to its surrender erupted in the winter of 1756: the government fell and was replaced by a new administration under William Pitt, and George Byng, the admiral held responsible for failing to relieve the besieged garrison at Minorca, was court-martialled and shot on his own quarterdeck.

Since then, British troops had enjoyed great success in Canada, capturing the Louisbourg fortress on Cape Breton Island and Quebec itself in 1759. In the Caribbean the important French sugar island of Guadeloupe was captured, and the French had been driven from the valuable Coromandel Coast of India by a combined British naval and army force. Together, these British successes drove the French to one final desperate measure which would solve all their problems at a stroke by giving them sufficient bargaining power to reclaim their lost territories and end the war with some dignity. In early 1759 the French Foreign Minister, the duc de Choiseul, drew up plans to invade Britain. However, the French navy would first have to unite its Atlantic and Mediterranean Fleets, and this became the central focus of the war in the coming weeks. Once united, the ships from Brest and Toulon would give the French numerical superiority over the British Channel Fleet and Western Squadron and would, in theory at least, enable them to seize control of the Channel or distract the British long enough to launch the invasion.

There were, in fact, two separate plans. Either the main French force would come into the Channel and 'distract' the British Channel Fleet while a smaller force escorted the invading armies to their appointed destinations, or the entire combined Brest and Toulon Squadrons would act as the escort. In both instances, the French armies, collected in two significant forces at either end of the Channel, would have to be landed. The force to the west, now encamped around the shores of the inland sea in southern Brittany known as the Morbihan, was commanded by the duc d'Aiguillon, whose force was to be embarked and then escorted around Ireland to land in the Clyde estuary in Scotland. The naval escort would then sail to the other major French force, based at Ostend, and would land it in Essex, by the mouths of the Crouch and the Blackwater. Meanwhile, a final and smaller force based at Dunkirk would be transported to Ireland.

It was an extremely complex and hopelessly unrealistic plan, devised by government administrators who neither understood the sea nor sought the advice of those who did. The crucial questions of wind, tide, weather and sea conditions were simply ignored. Nevertheless, the threat felt by the British was very real. There was no escaping the fact that the French intended to invade and her armies glowered over the horizon. The British, moreover, were well aware that their armies were already stretched to the limit, with the majority of their troops stationed abroad and very few left to protect the coasts. Both the French and the British knew that if Britain's maritime defences could be breached, she would be found to be more or less defence-less. The reaction of the British government was swift. As soon as they appreciated the extent of the French plan and understood its full implica-tions, the Western Squadron, now a formidable fleet of twenty-five sail of the line under the command of the energetic and resolute Admiral Edward Hawke, was ordered to cruise off Brest with no respite, and emergency orders were sent to Boscawen at Gibraltar.

Hitherto, the aims of the Royal Navy in the Mediterranean had been threefold: to annoy the French, to protect British trade and to maintain the security of Gibraltar. Boscawen had taken over command of the Mediterranean Fleet in April and he had executed his orders with great success. He had kept a close blockade of both Toulon and Marseilles and had deployed his cruisers at the well-known focal points of Mediterranean trade to protect British interests. Indeed, so dominant had the British naval presence been, that the Toulon fleet had been forced to retire into the inner road of Toulon harbour to seek the protection of its fort's guns from the sniping of British cruisers and the threat of their fireships. That was no place from which to exercise naval power, and the British enjoyed absolute control of the seas. So powerful was their position that the French believed Boscawen would launch raids and possibly even attack Marseilles or Toulon. A full ten battalions of regular infantry, together with militia, were stationed between Toulon and Marseilles to defend the coast from amphibious assault. While the French languished in port, the British sailors became fit and strong and their officers' confidence grew both in their own ability and that of their men.

On 3 August, Boscawen received fresh orders from the Admiralty. England herself was under threat. Intelligence had shown that the French were amassing huge flotillas of invasion craft in southern Brittany – preparations so vast that they had cost the French government thirty million livres on flat-boats alone, enough to build thirty Third Rates like the *Téméraire*.[1] With French war strategy now tipped towards a final desperate throw of the dice, Boscawen was ordered to keep the French fleet bottled up in the Mediterranean. If they were somehow to escape, he was to follow them wherever they went and bring them to battle. If they could not be discovered, part of his fleet was to head at full speed to the Solent to join the Channel Fleet, leaving a smaller squadron in Gibraltar to defend British interests in the Mediterranean.[2]

These new orders came at a particularly bad time for Boscawen. The challenge of maintaining a powerful presence in the Mediterranean was formidable, particularly with the wonderful natural harbour of Port Mahón in Minorca now denied to the Royal Navy. Boscawen's ships were forced to keep the sea for months at a time and constantly fight the northerly winds which blew the ships away from the coast. By the end of July, after three months of continual operations and ceaseless vigilance, many of the ships were so foul and weather-beaten that they were quite unfit for prolonged operations.[3] Broken masts that had been temporarily fished needed to be unstepped and replaced with fresh timber; patched and torn sails had to be replaced by fresh bolts of canvas; standing and running rigging had to be surveyed and the frayed lines had to be protected and if necessary replaced; the blocks, tackles and other moving parts of the standing rigging had to be given a new coat of tallow; and the standing rigging had to be wormed, parcelled, served and then coated in tar. Only then, with four protective coatings, was it sufficiently protected from the weather, the sea and the sailors themselves, whose continual presence aloft gradually wore it down as surely as the sails that flogged themselves against it. The ships' bottoms were also coated in weed and barnacles and the timber of their hulls pocked by *Teredo navalis* – the shipworm which bored holes in timber as surely as any drill.

As it was, Boscawen's ships were falling apart, but above all his men needed water. In the heat of the Mediterranean summer a continual supply of diluted wine or spirits quenched the men's thirst and was crucial in the recovery of those with fever. Fresh water was also used to wash clothes, to steep the salted provisions and boil the food. In the Mediterranean summer a large ship of the line might use up to three tons of water per day. It was the need for water that finally forced Boscawen's hand and, in July, he reluctantly lifted the blockade of Toulon and took some of his fleet to Salou Bay, close to Tarragona, which he knew as the best watering place in the Mediterranean and also a fine source of fresh vegetables at a reasonable price. Today the area around Salou is still scattered with sweet fresh-water springs where the locals fill huge jugs of water which is valued for its mineral properties, although at Cala Font Beach the natural spring which used to pour into the cove has long ago dried up. The rest of the British fleet returned to Gibraltar, where they scraped their bottoms clean, took their masts and yards down, completely overhauled their rigging and received fresh victuals and stores. It was at this point, with his vigilance impaired and his fighting capability compromised, that Boscawen received his new orders. The Gibraltar Squadron was now the front line in the defence of Britain itself. So it was with a troubled mind that Boscawen sat down to dinner with the Spanish governor at San Roque. He knew that his absence from Toulon would quickly be noted by the French. Just when he needed to pin them down more closely than ever before, events had conspired against him. The time was ripe for a French sortie and Boscawen knew it only too well.

Until his ships and men were sufficiently refortified to regain their place directly off Toulon, Boscawen's only comfort lay in the narrowness of the straits that he had to defend. The Straits of Gibraltar are only eight miles wide at the narrowest point and yet sailing warships, with masts over 150 feet tall, could see each other up to twenty-one miles away. At such extreme distances only the masts and perhaps only the tops of those masts were visible, but it was possible to signal by setting, furling, raising or lowering the sails. Indeed the sails were used in this way to communicate quite detailed information over long distances. If two ships could see each other clearly at a conservative estimate of fifteen miles and a chain of such ships stretched back to a main fleet, or as in this case, to a naval base, the number, speed and direction of an enemy fleet perhaps as much as thirty miles distant could be known very quickly.

The ability to communicate in this way was, of course, threatened at night, but lights could be used in a similar way, albeit over far shorter distances. At night, however, the main problem would be the initial discovery of the enemy fleet. Ships in company usually carried lights at their stern and in their rigging to aid station-keeping and to prevent collision, but a ship or fleet wishing to remain elusive, as the French surely would in their escape from the Mediterranean, would extinguish their lights. Boscawen could only hope that if the French tried to escape, he would hear of it before nightfall. Station-keeping at night was notoriously difficult and ships in company would cut their speed to reduce the likelihood of collision, particularly if they were sailing with their lights extinguished. Boscawen could reasonably hope, therefore, that a fleet could not get far in the short nights of the Mediterranean summer.

Nevertheless, it was crucial to make contact with the enemy before they passed through the straits. If the French sneaked through under cover of night, it would take time to react to an alarm, however quickly it was made, and by then they could have disappeared deep into the vastness of the Atlantic, bound for the Caribbean to threaten Britain's trade or her colonies. Alternatively, they could have darted back to a Spanish or Portuguese harbour – to Cadiz, Lisbon, Vigo or Ferrol. Most worrying of all, they could have crossed Biscay and made it to the French harbours of Rochefort or even Brest. The options were almost too numerous to consider. No doubt intelligence from fishing boats and cruisers would eventually pinpoint their location, but such a network of communication took weeks if not months to bear fruit, and by then it could all be too late: Boscawen's best hope was to spot the French on their approach to Gibraltar and to follow them. To that end, as soon as the first two frigates had completed their repairs and were ready for sea, he immediately ordered them to search for the French; the

Lyme to cruise off Malaga, and the *Gibraltar* across the mouth of the Straits, from Estepona to Ceuta Point.

At Toulon, the French had made ready for sea, but it had taken them months to do so. The original invasion had been intended for early summer, but it was not until August that the Toulon Squadron was sufficiently manned to mount a sortie. A lack of willing men to serve in the French navy and particularly at Toulon was just one of the many problems that beset the French in these years. The sailors were disillusioned after years of broken promises, their pay was long overdue and the ships were ill-provisioned, all the result of a king who failed to value his navy.[4] Finally, however, the ships were manned, the stores loaded and the sails bent, and Rear-Admiral Jean François de La Clue-Sabran weighed anchor on 5 August. Much as Boscawen suspected and exactly as he feared, La Clue was relying on the coming night to cloak his ships as they flitted through the straits and burst into the Atlantic. There was a distinct possibility that the moon might reflect on the bleached canvas of their sails, signalling their ghostly presence to prying eyes, but with luck the night sky would be thick with cloud and the darkness impenetrable.

La Clue had gambled, correctly, that Boscawen would not know of his intended destination. Only two months previously the British had captured the important French sugar island of Guadeloupe in the Windward Islands and a reprisal was expected. It was considered therefore just as likely that La Clue would cross the Atlantic to attack Guadeloupe as it was that he would head north and rendezvous with the Brest fleet in home waters. Historians are still unsure exactly which destination was intended but we do know that La Clue's initial destination was the Spanish port of Cadiz, a little over a hundred miles west of Gibraltar. There he planned to reassemble his ships, which he fully expected to have been scattered in the night-time escape from their Mediterranean prison. The first stage of the operation was nothing more than a quick dash past the bulldogs at the gates.

La Clue's fleet crept out of Toulon unobserved and then crossed to the southern shore of the Mediterranean where they hugged the Barbary Coast and prepared themselves for the challenge of the coming night. By noon on the 15th they were already only twelve leagues to the south-east of Gibraltar.

Now all that was needed was a strong easterly breeze to carry them past Gibraltar under full sail. While Boscawen and his officers sat down to a magnificent dinner in the Palace at San Roque, out at sea the clouds gathered and white horses began to race across the tops of the waves as the wind picked up. As it blew steadily from the east and night began to fall, La Clue was ready and everything was in place.

Aboard his magnificent new 80-gun flagship *L'Océan*, the sailors swarmed up the masts and the young and agile topmen danced across the yards. The footropes under the yards on which they stood stretched with their weight and the sails were released. Down on deck the sheets were hauled tight by lines of men working in unison. In this period signalling systems were unsophisticated and the easiest way to communicate ideas was to demonstrate the admiral's intent through action – his sails, in effect, were his signal flags. So as the great sails of the flagship billowed out in the freshening breeze and the yards groaned and bent to their load, all the ships of La Clue's fleet followed suit, heeling together with the wind and punching their bows into the swell. The waves slapped the hulls, the spray spattered the decks and the rigging whistled in the wind. Everywhere was the sound of sail.

With the enemy so close, and in such strength, it was vital that the fleet retained cohesion. It was not possible for each ship to sail at the very best of her ability; rather, they all had to sail at the speed of the slowest. La Clue drew up his ships in two lines. It is unclear exactly why he did so, but by forming into two parallel divisions his fleet became shorter, would take less time to pass through the straits and was therefore less likely to be seen. All the French needed now was a little luck. Perhaps Boscawen would be unable to order frigates to sea as scouts; perhaps the scouts would be damaged or their lookouts blinded by a squall. Perhaps they would look in the wrong direction for the crucial minutes it would take to pass them or perhaps they would see the French, but be unable to signal their discovery. Whatever happened, the French were under no illusion. In the past few months Boscawen's force had demonstrated time and again that they were resolute and skilled, while the French knew themselves to be undermanned and unpractised. They knew that their only hope was escape. It is easy to imagine their chagrin, therefore, when an officer aboard *L'Océan* glanced to starboard and saw a tiny speck lying silhouetted against the northern horizon.

For many years it has been believed by historians that La Clue passed through the Straits of Gibraltar unaware that he had been spotted, but a translated account of the action by a French officer, held in the archives of the National Maritime Museum, leaves us in no doubt that the French knew that they had been seen.[5] As the strange ship came closer it was clear that she was not a fishing vessel, as she had three masts; nor was she a merchantman, as her masts were too high and her hull too fine. She was evidently a warship, and a fast one. She came towards the French fleet under full sail, but once close enough to reconnoitre them, establish how many there were and upon what course they were sailing, how well they were handled and how fast they sailed, she swiftly tacked and headed at full speed to the north with her precious cargo of intelligence. The ship the Frenchmen had seen was the British frigate *Gibraltar*. Her log records that the wind was strong from the east, and that she was cruising twenty-five leagues from Cape Spartel.[6] At half-past five she started to make out a body of ships and by six she had counted a total of fourteen men of war creeping along the Barbary Coast and heading for the Straits. Everyone aboard knew that there were no other British forces of such a size in the area since all British warships of any size were refitting in Gibraltar Bay. This mysterious fleet could only be French and they could only have come from Toulon. As she headed back to the fleet, the *Gibraltar* frantically began firing cannon – thirty-two shot in all – and lighting lanterns and burning false fires to alert the British in the bay that something significant was afoot. Her efforts were repeated by signal guns on the Rock itself and also at Europa Point. It was a decisive moment in the war, perhaps the most important so far. When the French heard the cannon blasts they knew the game was up. They were immediately and extremely concerned, as they assumed that the British fleet was ready to sail. The reality, that the majority of the fleet was in the middle of re-fitting, the flagship herself had no sails bent to her yards and most of the officers were not in Gibraltar at all, but dining at the governor's palace at San Roque, was completely unknown to them. Their dash for the Atlantic had become a desperate race, but they still had every chance of escape.

It was at this point that the sentry keeping watch on the Bay from outside the governor's palace in San Roque saw the huge form of the 90-gun *Namur* start to move. She should have been stationary at anchor, and this was not just any ship; this was Boscawen's flagship, and she had set sail without him. We do not know if this had been prearranged or if an enterprising junior officer had taken the momentous decision of assuming command of the flagship by himself but, either way, the *Namur* slipping her anchor and heading for open sea was the clearest possible signal that the French had been sighted. A stampede ensued.

In the summer of 1759 there were few things that would galvanize British sailors in European waters more than the discovery that the French were at sea. Rumours of the invasion plans were rife, but the sailors had been frustrated at the inactivity of the French navy and shamed by British naval capitulation at the Battle of Minorca in 1756. Minorca had been besieged by a hundred and twenty thousand French troops, and every French soldier there was sustained by maritime supply lines protected by the French navy. If the French could have been driven from the sea, the besieging army would have been forced to surrender and Minorca would have been saved. Moreover, in the battle that followed, the British had one more ship than the French; a slight but not insignificant advantage. Nevertheless, the initial attack of the British fleet, commanded by Vice-Admiral John Byng, was easily repulsed by the faster and more skilfully handled French and, after successive feeble and failed attempts to bring the French to action or at least to force them clear of Minorca, Byng failed to renew the engagement and Minorca fell. Boscawen in particular was so badly affected by what he described as the 'disgrace' in the Mediterranean that he was unable to sleep when he heard the news. To prove the point he got out of bed and wrote a letter to his wife at five o'clock in the morning.[7]

The only significant British naval success in the Mediterranean had come nearly two years later, and a full eighteen months before La Clue attempted his escape with the Toulon fleet. Off Cartagena in February 1758, a small squadron of French ships was chased; two were captured and one was driven ashore. Of those that were captured, one was particularly significant. The *Foudroyant* was the beautiful flagship of Admiral Duquesne, but had previously been the flagship of Admiral La Galissonière, commander of the French fleet at the Battle of Minorca. The British humiliation at that battle had largely been orchestrated from her decks, from where Galissonière had handled his ships with consummate skill. The capture of the *Foudroyant*, therefore, was both a boost to British morale and a balm to disgraced honour. And it was made even more significant by the fact that Byng's flag-captain at Minorca, Captain Arthur Gardiner, whose personal reputation had been badly damaged by his standing by Byng's actions, commanded the ship that first engaged the *Foudroyant*. He fought closely, bravely and tenaciously and he died for his valour.

Since then the Royal Navy had enjoyed no significant success in European waters. In fact the only real confrontation with the enemy at all had occurred in June when two French frigates were chased into a heavily defended bay near Toulon. Boscawen would not rest until an attempt had been made to cut them out or destroy them where they lay and he sent in a force of three ships. Once inside the confines of the bay, however, the fickle Mediterranean breezes died and the three British warships lay becalmed under the combined guns of the bay's forts and the frigates themselves. The British ships acquitted themselves with honour, but the operation became a desperate fight for survival. Twenty-six British sailors died, forty-five were wounded and the ships were badly cut up. The frigates, meanwhile, remained in French hands.

This lack of clear opportunities to engage the French on their own terms was all the more galling to British sailors because of the growing belief in the Royal Navy that they were superior to their foe. Certainly the poor result at the Battle of Minorca had been a major blow, but in that battle the much faster French ships had repeatedly drifted out of range of the cumbersome British and the British sailors had simply been unable to fight the fierce and close engagements that they desired. Indeed, the success of the French at Minorca must be attributed more to French skill and guile than to a lack of courage or skill in the crews of the British ships. On the contrary, in 1756 and right through until 1759, the navy rode the crest of a wave of self-belief that had been built on the swell of naval success that had characterized the previous war, the War of the Austrian Succession. Successive devastating naval victories in 1747 at the First and Second Battles of Finisterre, the former under the command of the innovative and inspiring Admiral George Anson and the latter under the dogged and aggressive Admiral Edward Hawke, had demonstrated in no uncertain terms that British seamanship, carefully nurtured by a generation of officers committed to the professionalization of the service, would triumph. The facts spoke for themselves: at the First Battle of Finisterre the entire French fighting force of six ships of the line was taken, along with eighteen of the thirty-eight merchantmen they were escorting. At the Second Battle, five months later, six of the eight French ships of the line were captured, and they were so badly mauled that only two masts remained standing on all six of them. Almost four thousand French sailors were killed or wounded. Admiral Sir Peter Warren, who had fought in the First Battle of Finisterre, summed up the mood of success in these years, claiming that by the winter of 1747 there were more French ships in British ports than in the ports of France.[8]

A further boost to British motivation, if any was needed, was provided by the evident reluctance of the French to fight. Their ships had not been designed for the rigours of blockade and large scale fleet-battle, but for transatlantic trade protection and privateering, and French naval strategy reflected this policy. Whereas British squadrons were instructed to take every opportunity to destroy enemy shipping, French ships were instructed to avoid battle if at all possible. Nothing could be more indicative of this to British sailors than the French fleet trying to sneak through the Straits of Gibraltar in the middle of the night. Here was an excellent opportunity for a bold attack by the French on a weakened and ill-prepared enemy lying at anchor in Gibraltar Bay, but they chose instead to run. A visibly fleeing enemy was undeniable proof that they did not want to fight. An immediate and powerful fillip, no other action could give such a significant psychological advantage so powerfully and so completely to the enemy. The French, meanwhile, were now cursed with the insecurity of continually looking over their shoulders to the horizon. A creeping sense of dread could unsettle the minds of the chased as surely as a growing sense of self-belief would swell the hearts of the chasers. This is what had so inspired the British crews to victory at the two Battles of Finisterre, it is what inspired them now and it is what would ultimately lead the Royal Navy to dominate the world's oceans by the end of the war.

British motives in fighting the French did not of course rest only on the abstract concepts of courage, revenge or perceived personal and national superiority: battle was an unmistakable opportunity to get rich. The value of any prize or prizes was distributed amongst the squadron, the commander-in-chief receiving an eighth, the captain of the victorious ship a quarter, an eighth going to the master and lieutenants, another eighth to the warrant officers and another to the inferior and petty officers. The final quarter was divided between the seamen and marines. We know from a letter written by Boscawen to his wife in 1756 how his men were affected by the prospect of prize money from just a single ship: 'you can't think how keen our men are', he wrote, 'the hope of prize money makes them happy, and a signal for sail brings them all on deck'.9 And yet here was the possibility of capturing *fourteen* enemy ships. For the officers this was an opportunity to acquire staggering wealth in just a few short hours. The prizes captured at the First Battle of Finisterre, for example, were valued at £300,000. Indeed so much money could be made and so confident was Boscawen in making it that he built his magnificent house in Hatchlands in Surrey, which can still be viewed today and is owned by the National Trust, in part on the promise of riches alone. 'I flatter myself to make the French pay for this building this summer', he wrote to his wife, 'I have got at least one-fifth of it already and another trip to the southward will bring three or four sugar ships more in our way.' Boscawen was particularly concerned about the size of his chimneys and the roaring fires they would service, 'for I have no opinion of a damp house'.10 Here, then, was an opportunity for Boscawen to pay for his house in one glorious action, and never worry about the size of his chimneys again.

In short, therefore, not only did those British sailors who heard the guns of the *Gibraltar* signal the presence of the French fleet and saw the great *Namur* slip her cable on that summer evening in Gibraltar in August 1759 see a rare opportunity to vent their frustration on their elusive enemy, but the hope of glory, wealth and promotion was no pipe-dream; it was both a possibility and a necessity. And the sailors knew that the responsibility for the defence of England had fallen to them. 'Never before', wrote Sir Geoffrey Callender, one of the earliest historians of the navy, 'was battle like the battle of Lagos; never was one that counted more to the growing British Empire.'11 It is reasonable to believe from the subsequent rush to get to sea that the sailors knew that they were making history.

Very few sources survive that describe that frantic rush to get the British fleet to sea. We know from the journal of Boscawen's flag-captain, Captain Buckle, that as soon as they saw the *Gibraltar* firing guns to alert the fleet, they sent the *Namur*'s barge to meet her and, when they finally made sail, they did so in such a rush that they rammed and sank the ship's long-boat, which had been moored to the anchor cable by the bow.[12] We also know that Boscawen's dinner party broke up immediately and that he and his officers ran back to their boats, which surprisingly had been hauled clear of the waterline and took some time to re-launch. To those who attended the dinner party, there was more than a whiff of treachery in the air. One young midshipman commented:

> They found their barges hauled up upon the beach; done either by, or
> at the instigation of the Spaniards, to delay as much as possible the
> Admiral's return on board; the enemy's fleet at that very instant
> making the best of their way through the Gut: whether premeditated
> or not, is uncertain; but the circumstance was singular.[13]

While most of the fleet's officers were hurrying back to their ships, the few lieutenants who had remained in the squadron were sent from ship to ship with orders for the crews not to wait for the return of their captains, but to bend their sails as quickly as possible, to weigh anchor and to head for the open sea behind the *Namur*. In almost every instance, ships had large parties of officers and sailors ashore and many were left behind in the confusion. For those who were lucky enough to make it to a ship there was little choice about which to board. When the *Namur* finally cleared Gibraltar Bay, she did so with the captains of two other ships aboard her; the *Edgar* carried men from the *Active*; and Robert Harland of *Princess Louisa* and William Lloyd of the *Conqueror* swapped ships with each other.[14] The noise, hurry and confusion everywhere were remarkable. Not only did the majority of the ships have to bend their sails to the masts and some even re-step their top-masts which had been struck for repair, but every ship also had to be prepared for the coming battle. The *Prince* had to clear her middle gun deck, which was blocked with casks, and without sufficient time to weigh anchor, they simply cut the cable, leaving the anchor embedded in the seabed. The decks of the *America* were so encumbered with clutter that much of it was simply thrown overboard. Most of this had to be done with strange crews on strange ships, and with very few officers to orchestrate it.[15]

Nevertheless from a state of almost complete dislocation and within three hours of receiving the signal that La Clue was racing through the straits, the flagship and seven other ships of the British fleet had cleared one of the world's most notorious harbours, which is still renowned today for the eddies and willie-waws which beset it in an easterly wind. It is an achievement that has stunned naval historians ever since and is one of the finest of all examples of the professionalism, belief and discipline which characterized the Royal Navy in the Seven Years War. By 10 p.m. Boscawen was at sea. Ahead of him lay the vastness of the Atlantic, but somewhere tantalizingly close lay the promise of glory. By then the French were well clear of the Straits, and were sailing in line to the north-west. Boscawen ordered the *Gibraltar* to catch up with them and track them through the night.

As darkness fell on the night of 17 August the situation was precarious for both sides. La Clue knew that he had been sighted on his approach to the Straits, and Boscawen knew that La Clue would have broken into the Atlantic by the time he had cleared Gibraltar Bay. Boscawen led the vanguard of the British force; more ships under Vice-Admiral Thomas Brodrick would catch up as soon as they were able to leave Gibraltar. By 11 p.m. Boscawen was clear of Cabrita Point, where he brought-to to hoist in his boats. He now had to decide where to go. It was quite possible the French fleet had headed directly west for the Caribbean, but Boscawen's primary concern was that they had headed north-west, to rendezvous at Cadiz or to weather Cape St Vincent and make for the west coast of France. That is the route that he chose. Aboard the *Namur* the helm was put over and the yards trimmed to take the wind over her starboard quarter. The other ships of the squadron followed his example and they raced to the north-west. Although unprepared for such a rapid departure, Boscawen's ships were nevertheless freshly scraped, the sails were perfect and their rigging strong. They tore great rents in the sea as they picked up speed, carrying every stitch of canvas possible. Most of the logs record sails splitting and booms breaking under the strain imposed by the eager crews. We know from a letter written by Boscawen to the Admiralty that his ships noticeably out-sailed the French during the chase.[16] It is not surprising; in such condition and crewed by such eager men they would have been a match for any warship. But would the dawn reveal an empty horizon or one decorated with the lines of masts and the shapes of sails? Only the rising sun would tell and it was still eight and a half hours away.

La Clue was also faced with a tricky decision. He knew that if his fleet rendezvoused at daylight in the anchorage of Rota, on the north-western edge of Cadiz Bay, they would be vulnerable to a British attack as Rota was entirely unprotected by shore fortifications. The strong north-easterly wind would also make it difficult to reach the safety of Cadiz; and even if they did make it to safety, the British could as easily blockade them in Cadiz as they had done all summer in Toulon. Their only alternative was to run for the open sea in the hope that the British would suspect that they had headed to Rota or Cadiz, and use the time won by the British detour to escape. This was fine in theory, but in practice it was far from easy. The course required to make Cadiz from the French location off Cape Spartel was perhaps north-north-west, while that required to weather Cape St Vincent was west-north-west; a difference of four points of the compass or a full 45° to the south. Unfortunately for La Clue, he had not envisaged such a change of course before embarking and all of his captains knew only that they were to sail through the Straits, at which point they were allowed to open their sealed orders.[17] Those orders specified Cadiz as their destination. None of his captains had any orders whatsoever regarding an alternative, nor did the French navy at this stage have night-compass signals. In fact it was not until 1832 that the French navy had anything resembling detailed signals for changes of course at night, and the most appropriate signal in August 1759 was 'sail large on the starboard or port tack'. All La Clue could do, therefore, was to change course and shorten sail in the hope that this would give his ships enough time to observe this, and in the time-honoured tradition of station-keeping in fleets, follow their leader. La Clue would then extinguish his lights and disappear into the Atlantic, hopefully copied, and then followed, by his fleet.[18] To do so would, ideally, have required him to fire guns or rockets to draw his fleet's attention to his change of course, but fearful that the British were hot on his heels it is possible that he omitted to do this. It was a recipe for disaster. The extinction of his lights would necessarily cause a real or perceived lack of cohesion. If the instantaneous act of extinguishing his lights was missed on a very dark night such as this, there was no telling whether the admiral had indeed extinguished his lights and was still there, invisible in the darkness, or whether the ships had parted company.

La Clue's change of course was either not seen, or was deliberately disregarded, by eight of his fleet. As so often in the history of warfare in the age of sail, the motivation of the fleet captains remains obscure. Perhaps they knew very well that La Clue had changed course and extinguished his lights, but chose instead the guaranteed safety of Cadiz harbour. Perhaps they genuinely believed themselves to have lost contact, and in the morning feared isolation in the face of the entire British fleet. Either way, by dawn, La Clue's force had been reduced by three line-of-battle ships, two 50-gunners and all of his three frigates. He now had no fast ships to act as lookouts and provide early warning of an enemy presence, and he had only seven ships strong enough to lie in a line of battle if he was attacked. La Clue was in serious trouble. With the French fleet thus dogged with uncertainty and confusion, the British relentlessly chased the horizon as the rising sun on their backs illuminated ever more of the Atlantic, and while they did so they cleared for battle.

When dawn broke, the French were now thirty or forty miles east-south-east of Cape St Vincent, and when La Clue counted his ships and found that there were eight missing, he does not at first appear to have been surprised, nor overly concerned, putting their absence down to the difficulty of station-keeping at night. Indeed, so confident was he that his missing ships would soon broach the horizon that he hove-to to await their arrival.

The first ships that appeared, three ships and two smaller trading vessels, were clearly not La Clue's missing squadron. The French sailors hoped they were British and chased, but they soon turned out to be harmless Swedish merchantmen who had passed the British an hour or so earlier. Soon afterwards, the horizon was once again cut by the cruciform masts of square-rigged ships, and this time there were clearly eight ships; the number that had gone missing at night. La Clue sat patiently awaiting their arrival, unaware that the vanguard of the British fleet that had left Gibraltar, and which had sailed through the night to the north-west, also consisted of eight ships. Unfortunately for La Clue, they were still too distant for the national characteristics of their rigging and hull shape to be distinguished, and so, rather hopefully, he made the private signal in the belief that they were his fellow-countrymen. The lookouts in the British fleet, meanwhile, were not so confused; the frigate *Gibraltar*, the eyes of the fleet, had been sent ahead to reconnoitre the strangers and confirm that they were French.[19] The French private signals were seen and ignored; the signal for 'general chase' was made and the British fleet prepared physically and psychologically for battle.

The French realized their mistake when the British rearguard, which had been marshalled by Brodrick at Gibraltar and had then chased in Boscawen's wake through the night, broke the horizon. The unthreatening fleet of eight men of war instantly and unquestionably became the British fleet of seventeen. The French were outnumbered and out-gunned but, worst of all, they were trapped. La Clue realized that for the British to have got so close in a matter of hours, they must have ships that sailed significantly faster than even the finest of the French and now they had got too close. To attempt escape now would merely postpone the inevitable. There was going to be a fight whether he liked it or not.

The French ships fled before the wind, the point of sail which most separated them from Boscawen's chasing ships, but to maintain cohesion they travelled at the speed of the slowest ship, the *Souverain*, which had been placed at the centre of the squadron for her protection. Gradually but relentlessly they were overhauled by the faster British ships. The wind, moreover, was variable, and the British enjoyed a fine easterly breeze while the French lay almost becalmed. It was not long before the French sailors were able to make out clearly Admiral Boscawen's flag aboard the *Namur*.[20]

Edward Boscawen had been waiting a long time for this moment. The third of five sons, he had entered the navy in 1726 at the age of fourteen. Six years later he was promoted to lieutenant and, at thirty-one, he became a captain in 1742. By 1759 he was a talented commander at the peak of his powers who had faced the French at Anson's victorious First Battle of Finisterre in 1747 and he carried a scar on his shoulder where he was shot by a French marksman as a permanent reminder of that day. The courage he showed in that battle led directly to his promotion to flag rank. He had also served in the Caribbean in the previous war, and had been present at the sieges of Portobello in 1739 and Cartagena in 1741. In the Seven Years War, Boscawen had been present at the capture of Louisbourg in 1758. His first-hand experience of the sickness that could ravage British crews if they campaigned at the wrong time of year and with insufficient supply lines, particularly in India and the Caribbean, haunted him for the rest of his life and he was constantly preoccupied by the health of his crews.

His fighting career was particularly distinguished by the capture of the same French officer, Captain Hocquart, three times in fourteen years: in 1741, 1747 and 1755. He wrote to his wife with no small measure of pride and humour in his achievement when he captured him for the final time in the summer of 1755. She replied:

> Ah! *Pour la troisième fois Monsieur Hocquart—quel bonheur!* Mr J. Cleveland [the Secretary to the Admiralty] himself came hither with your letters, and I think I have never been happier than when I received them. I could neither eat nor sleep for 3 days and yet lived so well upon joy that I have grown fat ever since.

The letters between Boscawen and his wife are among the hidden gems of naval history. They are thoughtful, eloquent and detailed, and were exchanged by lovers. The letter to her long-distant husband finishes:

> Come then, dearest love, and let me make it the business of life to try if I cannot make some amends for the fogs and ice with which your great and noble designs have been over-clouded and chilled. God grant you may meet with no clouds on shore; with me you shall have nothing but sunshine . . . Adieu, my dearest love. God grant you all blessings, and to me that of receiving you in my arms![21]

If Boscawen's private life was marked by emotional devotion to his wife and six children, his working life was marked by a corresponding professional devotion to duty. Confident in his own fighting record, Boscawen had been a harsh critic of Byng's failure to drive the French from Minorca in 1756 and, although he did not sit on the court, he has been noted as having a share in the responsibility for the verdict at Byng's trial, the death sentence which accompanied it and the subsequent execution. The politician and writer Horace Walpole called him 'the most obstinate of an obstinate family',[22] and his style of command mirrored this mixture of doggedness, courage and experience. He trained his men relentlessly at gunnery for the day they would meet the French, but was keenly aware of the unreality of training, and that only the experience of war itself could sharpen the men's minds. In June 1756 he wrote to his wife: 'we are at this minute practising firing, it being calm and many of the fellows hit the mark, *note nobody is firing at them.*'[23]

This was the first and only occasion that Boscawen had commanded a fleet in the presence of the enemy and he was not going to pass up the opportunity. It was said that while serving on the *Dreadnought*, the officer of the watch called him one night, saying, 'There are two large ships, Sir, which look like Frenchmen, bearing down on us. What are we to do?' 'Do?' answered Boscawen, turning out and going on deck in his nightshirt. 'Do? Damn 'em, fight 'em.'[24] The same desire to get at the enemy, a foreshadow of the aggression that was to characterize Nelson's greatest successes, is visible in the journal of Boscawen's flag-captain as they chased the French. Eager to get at them but anxious not to lose cohesion in so doing and thus leave ships of his van division vulnerable to defeat in detail by the compact French squadron, Boscawen repeatedly signalled to the rear division to make more sail. He then picked out the *America* for special attention and signalled to her specifically. Ten minutes later, with no response, he signalled again and then once more after half an hour of chasing when the *America*, for an unknown reason, hove-to and hauled up her mainsail. Shortly after, it was the turn of the *Guernsey* for special attention, and once again the signal was made: '*Make more sail!*'

The life of the French admiral, Rear-Admiral Jean François de Bertet de La Clue-Sabran, is a little more obscure. He was openly recognized as a protégé of the comte de Toulouse, Louis XIV's bastard son who had been made Admiral of France at the age of twenty without any seafaring experience. La Clue owed his promotions and appointments to his benefactor, for his career had already been littered with errors of judgement which did not deserve reward. As a result, he did not enjoy the full support, and more importantly, the unquestioning respect, of his men. Nothing illustrates this better perhaps than an incident which had occurred at the end of the previous year. La Clue was awaiting reinforcements in Cartagena harbour from where he would cross the Atlantic to the West Indies and then sail on to Louisbourg. When they arrived, he ordered them to anchor in a nearby bay; but instead of obeying his orders, the man who received them, Rear-Admiral Duquesne de Menneville, replied that he would 'prefer' to cruise just offshore. Casually, La Clue did not press the point, but that night a strong and sudden change in the wind blew Duquesne and his ships straight into the path of a British squadron while La Clue was embayed and unable to help. Two French ships were taken, including Duquesne's flagship. The resulting reduction in naval power in the West Indies and

Canada had a devastating effect on the ability of the French to fight in those waters. Louisbourg fell months later and, shortly afterwards, Canada itself. La Clue nevertheless remained in favour and was promoted to command the Mediterranean Fleet after the death of Admiral de la Galissonière.[25]

Our understanding of the engagement that followed between these two men is in many ways typical of our understanding of eighteenth-century sea battles. Terse, dry descriptions of engagements survive in the ships' logbooks, and although the master and the captain kept separate logs, the information is usually duplicated, with observations of wind, weather conditions and damage to the ship being the prime concern. Occasionally there is a description of battle, but it is never written in any detail and never is any action explained or justified. The commander of any ship or squadron that had engaged the enemy wrote a formal report to the Admiralty, but again, the actual detail of the engagement was usually sketchy unless there was any particularly controversial behaviour which needed to be addressed. In the heat of battle, moreover, there was no time to take notes or write as events unfolded. There was also much to be done after a battle. The ships had to be repaired; the wounded cared for; the prisoners guarded; and the prizes secured, repaired and taken to safety. The logbooks were written at the end of a very testing day, and the lengthier reports perhaps a day or two later. In every case, they are written after a period in which the author has been under extreme stress, has had little or no sleep and is possibly wounded. More than one logbook is stained with blood. In every case the most detailed descriptions are written after the event occurred, usually after a delay of several days, but in many cases several years or even decades have gone by before the event is immortalized in ink.

More often than not, however, somewhere on one of the ships involved, an interested, educated man or woman, often a sailor with an intuitive grasp of the events unfolding and endowed with impressive powers of observation and description, witnesses the action and records it in a private journal or perhaps a letter home. Then, through a series of curious twists of fate, that letter or journal survives intact and legible more than a quarter of a millennium later. This is exactly what happened at this battle, which became known as the Battle of Lagos. We are particularly fortunate in this instance, moreover, because the man who witnessed the battle between La Clue and

Boscawen was not a civilian but an experienced sailor. Not only that but he was a slave; and not only was he a slave, but an educated slave; and not only was he an educated slave, but a talented writer. Recorded through the eyes of this extraordinary witness, our understanding of the Battle of Lagos is unique.

That important witness was Olaudah Equiano, one of the eighteenth century's most colourful characters. Born in 1745 in a village east of the Niger River in what is now Nigeria, Equiano was captured at the age of ten by slave-traders and taken to what are now the southern states of America. After these events and by the age of twenty-one he had earned enough money to buy his freedom and went on to take part in Phipps' expedition to the Arctic in 1773 in which the young Horatio Nelson served as a midshipman on HMS *Carcass*. In 1789 he published his memoirs, *The Interesting Narrative of the Life of Olaudah Equiano*, and in doing so invented an entire literary genre, the slave narrative. His book remains one of the most important of all of the narratives written by slaves in the eighteenth century and he went on to become an ardent member of the Movement for the Abolition of Slavery.

It was not uncommon for black sailors to work in the navy, but they have left very little trace in the historical record, and even fewer descriptions of battle. Much the same can be said of slaves serving aboard British ships, but they were far less common, and in many examples it is a practice which seems to have been carried out subversively by disguising their names and registering them as sailors. In this instance, however, Equiano appears to have been serving openly aboard Boscawen's flagship the *Namur*, having been brought aboard by his master, Michael Pascal, the *Namur's* sixth lieutenant. Pascal had bought him from a planter in the West Indies after a business visit to the plantation. 'While he was at my master's house', wrote Equiano, 'it happened that he liked me so well that he made a purchase of me. I think I have often heard him say he gave thirty or forty pounds sterling for me, but I do not remember which.'[26]

Equiano was then taken on horseback to the docks, an experience he found profoundly disturbing, and there, together with Pascal, boarded a merchantman for England. They arrived in Falmouth and woke the next day, to Equiano's astonishment, to a ship covered in snow: he thought it was salt. Equiano stayed there for some months with friends of Pascal, but was eventually reunited with his master, who had been appointed to the *Namur*. Pascal sent for Equiano, who sailed from Falmouth to London, and boarded the *Namur* at the Nore. Thus the fourteen-year-old slave Equiano learned to sail a warship. Although at first startled by the noise, commotion and guns of the warship, he wrote, 'I was so far from being afraid of anything new which I saw that, after I had been some time in this ship, I even began to long for battle.' Now was his chance. At 1 p.m. the French hoisted their colours and formed into line. The ship leading the French line was a particularly beautiful specimen of a French 74-gunner, and her name was *Téméraire*.

2.

The Captured *Téméraire*

AUGUST 1759 – FEBRUARY 1760

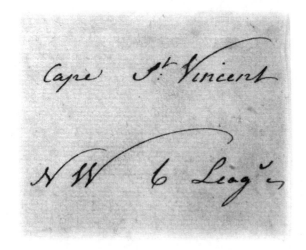

Boscawen's fleet bore down rapidly on the French in the teeth of a fine breeze. The question remaining was when to open fire, and in such a chase this was not a straightforward decision. Gunnery at sea in any situation was exceptionally difficult. A ship moved with the sea in a number of dimensions at once. The bows could rise and fall; the ship could roll unpredictably to port or starboard; she might be pushed from her course by a wave, a gust of wind or a mistake by the helmsman; she might simply rise and fall as the swell passed underneath her, and all these motions could affect the target ship as well. Moreover, not only were both ships moving with the sea, they were also moving along their chosen course, and they never did so at exactly the same speed. The best way to be certain of a successful hit, therefore, was to get as close to the enemy as possible before opening fire.

The pressures of chase, however, did not always make this practicable. Sailors knew that a lucky hit in the enemy's rigging might stop her dead in the water. If a mast lost the strength of the web of its support, for example, it would not be able to carry the heavy press of sail required in a chase. The captain would be forced to reduce the canvas on the stricken mast or even strike the mast itself to prevent further damage to the ship. In either case her ability to escape would be drastically and immediately reduced. More often than not in chase, therefore, the longest-barrelled guns which fired the furthest would be used to take pot-shots at the enemy in the hope of causing some lucky damage.

To open fire in this way also helped to ease the tension amongst the crew: it must not be forgotten that the build-up to naval battle was excruciatingly slow. Even in the most mismatched of chases between warships, the difference in speed was never more than two or perhaps three knots – that is two or three nautical miles *per hour*. If two ships or fleets therefore first saw each other on the horizon fifteen miles away, it would be at least five hours, and perhaps seven or eight, before they met. In this case the log of the *Namur* records that they first saw the French at dawn (about 7.30 a.m. at Cadiz in August) but the first British ships did not open fire until 2.30 p.m., and the *Namur* not until 4 p.m. – that is eight and a half hours after first contact. Those hours of waiting were long indeed. Certainly the ships were prepared for battle: the decks cleared, the rigging secured, the most important lines 'doubled-up' to provide extra security in case they were damaged, and the men were fed and encouraged. But to begin firing at the greatest possible range was the simplest way of easing the tension aboard: finally the men could take some positive action against their enemy, or at least witness one or perhaps two gun crews doing so. Largely symbolic, but a powerful symbol indeed, it declared that the battle had begun.

There was, however, an alternative philosophy which had been nurtured in the previous war by aggressive British admirals such as Anson and Hawke, the decisive victors of the First and Second Battles of Finisterre in 1747. Three years before those battles, Hawke had fought as the young and inexperienced captain of the *Berwick* at the inconclusive Battle of Toulon in 1744. Then, as the British fleet, still at some distance from their enemy, bore down on the combined French and Spanish fleet, some British ships began firing. It was suggested to Hawke by a number of his officers that this was too soon. 'Upon my word gentlemen I can not give an opinion', he replied. 'I dare not venture to do so, as I have never yet been in action. But when my turn comes I will try to prove to you how I think we ought to behave on these occasions.' Hawke then withheld his fire until he was alongside his opponent in the enemy line, the *Poder*, and poured in such a well-directed fire that she struck her colours in a quarter of an hour. The *Poder* had two hundred dead or wounded to the *Berwick*'s six.[1] At the First and Second Battles of Finisterre, both Anson and Hawke adopted this philosophy to great effect, witnessed and to a great extent brought about at the First Battle of Finisterre by Boscawen, then captain of the *Namur*. Then, the fastest British ships, similarly led by Boscawen, chased a French squadron and gradually overhauled their rear. The British withheld their fire until they were right alongside and only then began to engage. The resulting slaughter on the French ships was immense.

To engage in this way both reduced the wasted shot inevitable in long-distance engagements and kept the gun crews fresh for as long as possible. Gunnery was exhausting, both physically and psychologically. The heaviest cannon and their associated carriage and shot weighed over three tons and had to be manhandled by a team of seven men. Each gun had to be run in, cleaned, primed, loaded, run out and then aimed by physically shifting it towards bow or stern and raising or lowering its barrel as required. The noise of the explosions and the stress of working with explosive material further burdened the senses. But to engage close gave the sailors the added psychological boost that every shot would tell, and that the engagement, although fiercer, would be far shorter. It was also more likely to end in a decision one way or the other. Finally, for the ship about to be engaged, the steady approach of a silent aggressor was ominous indeed. The silence was deafening. These men were not trigger-happy and their silence spoke of confidence, discipline and courage; it spoke of determination, a desire for success and strong leadership. Even before the ships engaged, therefore, the psychological effect of this tactic was profound.

This then was the tactic used by Boscawen. As the French fired at a distance from their stern chase guns in a vain attempt to injure their pursuers and thus secure their own escape, the shot sailed past the British masts and rigging, or caused only minor damage by passing through the sails. Aboard the *Namur*, meanwhile, the sailors were ordered to lie flat as they steadily drew up with the French fleet. Boscawen had only one target in mind. He did not engage the first ship he came up with, nor indeed the second or the third, but sailed imperiously past them all, his ship being battered by French cannon. Only when he drew alongside *L'Océan*, La Clue's magnificent flagship, did he engage and he did so ferociously, firing all three tiers of his guns into her at once.[2]

Boscawen's approach blended the long-established and unwritten rule of sailing warfare, that the commander should engage his opposite number, and the tactics of Anson and Hawke at the two Battles of Finisterre (1747). In those actions the British fleets had caught up with the French from the rear but, as they began to overlap and engage, the British ships did not stop to engage only the enemy rear as they came up, but continued up the French line, passing the British ships that were already engaged. This is exactly what

Boscawen had in mind; as he sailed up the French line towards *L'Océan* he expected the ships following him to do the same, engaging the French ships as they passed.

In this Boscawen was disappointed. He flew the signal for the line of battle, the ships to engage as they came up, and sure enough the British ships astern of him fiercely engaged the rearmost ship of the enemy, the *Centaur*. But as more British ships came up, those who had first engaged the *Centaur* did not move quickly on to make space for the new arrivals. By the end of the battle the French line had only been engaged as far as the *Souverain*, the fourth rearmost ship of the fleet. The *Centaur* was engaged by five separate British ships, each fresh for the fight, each with their fire withheld until it was certain to strike. In the face of such overwhelming odds, her crew fought with distinction, and in effect engaged as the escort to a convoy of merchantmen. By holding up the British ships she gave the rest of the French fleet a better chance of escape. The *Centaur* was mauled by the British, but did not surrender until two hundred French sailors were dead, her captain de Sabran Grammont had been wounded in nine places, she had lost her fore and main topmasts and had received a great deal of other damage to rigging and hull.

Despite the overwhelming numbers, this action at the rear of the French fleet was certainly not a one-sided affair. A midshipman from the *Guernsey* later recalled that a large shot had gone clean through the mainmast, while down below

> where the wounded are always carried (I) was there witness to a
> scene shocking to humanity. I ascended precipitately, and endeav-
> oured to banish from my mind the melancholy impression of the
> sight; but this was extremely difficult . . . a heavy shot, from an
> enemy's lower gun, penetrated the side of our ship just between wind
> and water, abaft the main chains; forced its way through the purser's
> store-room into the cockpit; and, having there taken off the leg of
> our surgeon, Mr. Beckley; another from Mr. Evans, surgeon's mate;
> another from John Bull, a marine, who was assisting them; and lastly
> the leg of a chair; made its way through the cockpit deck, and lodged
> itself in the brandy-room.[3]

This was one of the worst possible scenarios aboard a warship in battle. The surgeon, usually the only qualified medical man aboard, the surgeon's mate and their assistant, always a man chosen for his strong stomach and experience of dealing with wounded, were all incapacitated by a single shot. Aboard the *Guernsey* there was now little immediate respite for the wounded, and it is likely that the surgeon would have had to direct another assistant in his own operation to stop the bleeding of his legless stump. In that he was successful, however, for the midshipman who witnessed the carnage later recalled that he bumped into Mr Beckley, the unfortunate surgeon, many years later at the Royal Exchange in London, where he was hobbling about on a wooden leg. The sprightly Mr Beckley, delighted to see an old shipmate, even claimed that he had recovered the culpable cannon ball, which was still in his possession.[4]

Meanwhile, at the head of the British line, and halfway down the French line, Boscawen had engaged the French flagship *L'Océan*. Although the first British ships at the rear began firing at 2.30, the breeze died shortly afterwards and it was not until 4 p.m. that Boscawen came alongside his enemy and unleashed a hailstorm of iron. Twenty-five French sailors were killed on the spot and forty more badly wounded. One man was caught in the mouth by a splinter which broke his jaw and knocked out most of his teeth. Within three hours, eighty-six were dead and more than a hundred wounded aboard *L'Océan*. The ship itself was also mauled. None of the masts actually fell but they were badly damaged in the web of rigging that supported them and in the timber itself. Within minutes the sails were so full of holes that one French witness compared them to a sieve. Down below, water poured in where British shot had burst through the French hull and carpenters worked frantically to plug the holes with bungs of timber lined with tar and tallow. An hour and a half after the firing began, one officer saw La Clue stagger as he exhorted his sailors to fight. He was quickly surrounded and supported. He had one leg broken and the other badly injured by a piece of iron, but otherwise his injuries were minor cuts and grazes. Now leaning on the shoulders of his officers and covered in blood, he nevertheless remained on the quarterdeck to direct the fight. The French fleet may well have been manned by disaffected sailors resentful of their superiors and commanded by officers with specific instructions to avoid battle at all costs, but once forced to fight, they fought well.

After the initial onslaught from the *Namur*, the crew of *L'Océan* fought fiercely in response and by the end of the day that ship alone had fired more than two and a half thousand shot in reply. As the British had chosen to engage so close, it was difficult indeed for many of those French shot to miss their target. La Clue wrote 'my shot were so well aimed that his mizzen-mast was carried away, his maintopsail yard came in two upon the deck, the sprite-sail yard and the jack-staff were cut away, all his sails were torn . . . never was such a fire seen as my squadron kept up.' By the evening she had lost her entire mizzen-mast, which had fallen overboard throwing all of the men in the mizzen-top into the sea. Her fore and maintopsail yards had also fallen. These were the sails that were always used in battle. Captains always wanted to protect as much of their canvas as possible, but at the same time maintain sufficient steerage way to control their ships and take advantage of situations as they arose, juggling their speed to keep alongside the enemy. This was not straightforward. An enemy that wished to remain elusive and not tied down to a broadside duel might shoot forward or astern, or yaw to port or starboard with little warning, and an attacking captain had to react. Without these sails the *Namur* was crippled. She could neither control her speed nor hold her position: she was merely a floating battery. In the course of a 'formal' fleet action in which both sides were determined to fight it out this was not necessarily a handicap, but in a chase action such as this, to be disabled was a major blow, and could not be hidden from the French. Certainly *L'Océan*'s rigging and sails were badly and visibly damaged, but one French sailor estimated that she could still make a league and a half an hour. This may not seem much on its own, but the *Namur* was clearly disabled and there was no hiding the extent of the damage with the remains of her main- and foretopsail yards lying smashed on the deck and their rigging hanging over the side. As the ships drifted apart, La Clue took his chance and fled.

If he wished to continue the fight, Boscawen's only option was to shift his flag; the *Namur* was clearly going to be out of action for many hours – in fact it was three days before she was ready to sail again and numerous carpenters from around the fleet had to be drafted in to assist with the repairs. He boarded one of the *Namur*'s broken boats, the only one to have survived the battle, and left her for the *Newark*, a 90-gun ship. Such a momentous action is noted rather matter-of-factly in the captain's log, in between a description of damage to the rigging and the report of the deaths of seamen Thomas Quinnell, Thomas Cattness and John Williams, who died of their wounds at 10 p.m. Similarly, no historian then or since has ever made a great deal of the decision, but it was extremely rare for a British commander to shift his flag in the eighteenth century. Indeed, it was so significant that La Clue made it a matter of triumph in his letter to the French Ambassador in Lisbon and claimed that he had beaten off his assailant.[5]

Amidst all of this chaos, the young Equiano experienced his first and only sea battle. He survived, but only just. He was stationed on the middle deck, where he worked as a powder monkey with another boy, specifically assigned to bring powder from the magazine to the aftermost gun of the deck. There would have been more than thirty such boys under the age of eighteen aboard a ship the size of the *Namur*. Depending on their rating, they acted as servants for the officers, as young seamen in training to be future topmen or as young gentlemen gaining experience before being rated as midshipmen. In action they were used, regardless of their rating, as powder monkeys. It was a hazardous job that required a great deal of care and initiative. It was essential that only the requisite amount of gunpowder was brought to the gun; the powder monkeys had to work at the same speed as their gun crews. If they worked too slowly, the gun crews would be unable to fire; too quickly and there would be a dangerous build-up of powder behind the gun which could easily ignite from a stray spark. Two years after this action HMS *Thunderer* suffered thirty dead and fifty wounded when powder ignited in exactly this way.

Even if the boys worked in harmony with their gun crews, however, there was still the opportunity for costly error. The powder was packed into individual flannel cartridges by the gunner and his mates in the filling room, a room separate from the magazine and lit from an external lantern through a pane of glass. The cartridge itself was then placed in a leather pouch with a close-fitting lid before being carried to the respective gun. For Equiano and his friend, this was a hazardous journey indeed, as, working on the aftermost gun of the deck, they had to travel the length of the entire gun deck carrying the explosive charge. It was on these regular journeys through the blizzard of splinters that Equiano witnessed 'the dreadful fate of many of my companions who, in the twinkling of an eye, were dashed to pieces and launched into eternity.' Equiano was badly affected by such carnage, and readily expected every moment to be his last. His first reaction was to wait for the French to reload before making his trip to and from the magazine, but soon realized that such precautions were fruitless; he was equally vulnerable anywhere on the ship. 'Cheering myself with the reflection that there was a time allotted for me to die as well as to be born, I instantly cast off all fear or thought whatever of death.' He merely hoped to survive so that he could tell his new-found English friends of his experience.

When, and if, the boys arrived at their appointed gun, they carefully opened the lid of the leather pouch and took out the cartridge, which was placed to the rear of the gun crew, but still within easy reach. It was at this final stage of the operation that Equiano realized that he, and the entire ship, was in danger of immediate destruction, for the cartridges were rotten. The main powder magazine was always in the forward part of the hold in British ships, specifically so that the bilge water would run to the ship's centre, and therefore away from the powder store, but still all cartridges were vulnerable to damp and rats, and those that had been affected either failed to explode, or as in this case disintegrated before they were loaded into the gun. It was common practice, therefore, not to prepare too many cartridges before an action, but to make them up as they were required. Equiano, it seems, had been very unlucky. He had been transporting pre-made cartridges which had been sitting on the shelves in the magazine, slowly rotting. As he took the cartridges out of their leather pouches, the bottoms failed to bear the weight of the powder and fell out, pouring the gunpowder onto the deck. This was catastrophe enough, but Equiano had been working near the match-tub, a small wooden keg holding a slow-burning match, used to ignite the gun. The boys desperately sought the half-barrels of water kept near each gun crew to dampen the sponge and douse any dangerous sparks, and they drenched the loose powder. There was only just enough left. The ship was saved but Equiano was badly shaken.[6]

At this stage of the battle, three of the French fleet in the van were as yet untouched, the French admiral had escaped, the British admiral had been forced to move to another ship and most of the British captains were clustered around one ship at the French rear. This was not working out as Boscawen had planned. However, the momentum of the day gradually turned as the *Centaur* finally surrendered. In holding up the British warships she had acted impeccably, and the French report of the battle singles out her crew for defending her colours with the greatest bravery.[7] It was still not much of a victory, however, and it had been won at great cost to British ships and crews. Fifty-six British sailors had died, a hundred and ninety-six more had been badly wounded and one ship was disabled.[8] As night fell, everything still hung in the balance.

The French fled into the setting sun, with the British, now led by Boscawen in the *Newark*, racing after them. The French began to despair. In the bright light of the moon the silhouettes of the chasing British ships could clearly be made out and, although they were only being chased by the least damaged of Boscawen's squadron, the French knew that by morning the rest would be back under way and shortly rejoining the main British force. This was too much for the captains of the *Guerrier* and the *Souverain*, the two fastest ships of the French fleet, both of which had been blooded in the previous day's battle. One headed to the north-west, made it clear around Cape St Vincent and fled to Rochefort on the west coast of France; the other headed south-west to the safety of the Canary Islands.[9] When dawn broke on the morning of the 19th, therefore, yet again La Clue discovered that he had been abandoned in the night.

There were now only four French ships left: the battered flagship *L'Océan* and three fine 74-gunners, *Modeste*, *Redoutable* and *Téméraire*, all of them unscarred. There was, however, no escaping the fact that La Clue was now outnumbered, he himself was severely injured and the British ships were faster than his. His only hope lay in the protection of the neutral shore of Portugal, now only a few miles away. He took his ships to a tiny creek in between Lagos and Cape St Vincent that was guarded by the twin forts of Exavier and Lago, where he sought protection under the Portuguese guns. There the British were legally forbidden to engage the French and La Clue could make good his escape overland.

There is today no sense of the drama that took place in that little bay two hundred and fifty years ago. *L'Océan*, one of the largest ships in the French navy, but now bearing the scars of her battle with Boscawen, her sails cut to shreds and her hull peppered with cannon shot, came over the southern horizon under full sail, in company with three ships, and chased by an entire British fleet. As the French ships came closer to shore, two took in sail and anchored cautiously in the shallows under the guns of the fort but *L'Océan* took no such precautions. Injured and defeated though she was, her admiral would not surrender. Her course remained true and her sails remained set. The closer she came to shore the more unnatural her element seemed. It was not unusual to see these ships at anchor off the beaches of southern Spain and Portugal, but they were only ever manoeuvred under minimal canvas to allow their captains to work their ships surely and precisely. Here was a mighty flagship of the French navy under full sail, her wounded masts and yards creaking with the effort of escape, driving her to her own destruction.

She never stopped but ran onshore with such speed that all her masts were taken over the side by her momentum and there she lay, stranded in the surf: a dismasted, battered hulk after an act that won La Clue great respect from the British sailors.[10] In an instant a magisterial sight had become pitiful; a ship had become a shipwreck. Her sails, which moments before were full of wind, were now full of water, and they pulled the masts and rigging deep into the sea. Her hull, designed only for the freedom of the seas, was savagely forced into unnatural shapes by the unforgiving sand and her back was broken in an instant. Worse was still to come. The captain of *La Redoutable* followed his admiral's bold example and he too ran his ship ashore. And there they lay, *L'Océan*, *La Redoutable* and perhaps fifteen hundred French sailors, stranded upon their beached warships, while the British bore down and the bewildered Portuguese looked on.

The French had very little time. They did not know if they could rely on the Portuguese to enforce their neutral rights, and they were even more uncertain if the feeble guns of a single fort could deter an entire British battle squadron aflame with bloodlust. The crew of *L'Océan* quickly prepared to abandon ship, but one witness estimated that the ships lay two musket shots – some 360 metres – from shore. The very best swimmers might make it ashore, but the majority of the crew could not swim and the injured would need help. Their only chance of escape was with the ship's boats. But as had happened aboard the *Namur*, these had all been badly damaged in the battle and could not be floated without at least some basic repairs. The carpenters and seamen bent to their task, patching, caulking and rigging with desperation as the British ships drew closer. Finally, those that had been made seaworthy were hoisted over the sides of the leaning hulks of *L'Océan* and *La Redoutable*.

The injured La Clue was the first to be taken ashore, along with the ship's money chest and a number of other seriously wounded men. However, the tide was nearing its full height, and the beaches of the Algarve slope with astonishing abruptness into the sea. At high tide the waves can rise up four or five feet even in the height of summer with very little ground swell. It would have been very difficult to land a ship's boat on such a shore even if it was crewed with fit and healthy men. But these boats' crews were exhausted from battle, scared of capture, and the boats themselves were loaded with injured sailors who were unable to help. Of the four boats that left *L'Océan*, three were overset and broken to pieces on the shore. Only one remained, and there were still seven hundred people aboard that ship alone. They began to make rafts.

The Portuguese, meanwhile, saw that the British intended to pursue the French right into their territorial waters, and opened fire from the fort. It forced Boscawen's squadron to heave-to just out of range and await instructions. Boscawen was faced with a delicate situation that could easily erupt into a diplomatic storm, but he did not see it in those terms. His enemy was the French, and they were escaping. The Portuguese had no navy to speak of and Britain could, at a push, risk a temporary disruption of diplomatic relations with the Portuguese court. As it was, the British public were terrified of invasion, La Clue's ships were the means by which that invasion would occur and he had them within his grasp. He selected a number of captains and signalled for them to board the *Newark*. There, in the words of a midshipman from the *Guernsey*, one of the ships selected for the operation, they were ordered 'to proceed at the hazard of our ship and our lives to destroy the French ship without any regard to the laws of neutrality.'[11]

Boscawen's primary objective was to secure the French flagship, in case La Clue was still aboard, and he first ordered the *Intrepid* and *America* to bring out *L'Océan*. Captain Pratten of the *Intrepid*, however, had already anchored and so Captain Kirk of the *America* bore down to the stricken flagship alone. Once more withholding fire until point-blank range, he fired into the French ship and ordered her to strike. There was no fight left in the men remaining aboard and they quickly complied. Kirk's officers climbed aboard to assess the damage, but found her so badly broken by gunfire and her hull so stricken that she could not be moved. The remnants of her crew were taken aboard the *America*. A few hours later, around midnight, she exploded. Equiano, still alert to the unfolding drama, wrote: 'I never beheld a more awful scene, in less than a minute the midnight for a certain space seemed turned into day by the blaze, which was attended with a noise louder and more terrible than thunder, that seemed to reveal every element around us.'[12] *L'Océan* had blazed her final defiance to the British fleet.

The *Guernsey*, *Prince* and *St Albans*, all ships from Brodrick's rear squadron, which had now caught up, were then sent in against the stricken *Redoutable*, which had been beached far closer to shore than *L'Océan*. The *Prince* anchored nearby and opened fire, savaging the static ship with a series of broadsides. The few Frenchmen left aboard ran for the rails in a desperate attempt to escape ashore while armed boats from the British ships rapidly pulled across. Much like *L'Océan*, *La Redoutable* was discovered to be too badly damaged to be hauled free, and she was burned. Some hours later, she too exploded. One witness recorded, 'We were at the distance of a few miles but the report was tremendous; the sight however was but for a moment and all was dark and still.'[13]

On seeing the British cross the invisible line into Portuguese waters, the crews of *La Modeste* and *La Téméraire*, the two ships anchored in the shallows under the guns of the fort, also began to abandon ship and make for shore. The *Jersey* went in under fire from the Portuguese forts and brought out *La Modeste* very little damaged. Captain John Bentley of the *Warspite* was the man given the honour of capturing *La Téméraire*. By now there was very little wind but a great swell, and as only a few men of the *Téméraire* had been able to get ashore, her decks were still packed with humanity when the *Warspite* opened fire. The battle was over and her crew had seen *L'Océan*, *La Redoutable* and *La Modeste* strike, but much to the surprise of Captain Bentley the crew of the *Téméraire* would not surrender without a fight. At 2.45 they fired a few shots at her, but there was no call for quarter from the Frenchmen and so the *Warspite* manoeuvred under her vulnerable and beautiful stern. At the stern there were no oak walls three feet thick, but flimsy panes of glass and decorative mouldings. Inside the hull there were no transverse bulkheads running athwart ship to protect the men from gunfire. The shot from the *Warspite* tore through the officers and crew of the *Téméraire* and although the futility of their situation was clear they withstood a number of broadsides before her captain, M. de Castillon, lowered her colours, a full hour after the British had begun to engage. 'We sent an officer on board and took possession of our prize which proved to be the *Téméraire* of 74 guns and 716 men; at a quarter before five we cut her cable and carried her down to the admiral,' wrote Bentley. He sent aboard seven petty officers and fifty-three men, took out a hundred and thirty-three prisoners and then sailed her out of range of the Portuguese fort's guns to join the British fleet. On their way they fell in with the *Culloden* whose captain donated them a further midshipman and ten more men and took another hundred and thirty-one prisoners out of the *Téméraire*.[14] It did not take long for the prize crew to establish that *La Téméraire* was a fast ship, a powerful ship and a beautiful ship. And now she was a British ship.

The Battle of Lagos was a wonderful victory for the Royal Navy in material, strategic and psychological terms. The French had lost five ships – three captured and two destroyed, including a flagship – and they had lost almost five hundred sailors, killed, wounded or taken prisoner. The British fleet, in contrast, lost none of their ships, only fifty-six dead and a hundred and ninety-six wounded. And yet still Boscawen did not rest. He sent the captured and heavily damaged *Centaur* back to Gibraltar for repairs, but took the rest of his ships to cruise off Cape St Vincent in the hope of intercepting the stray Frenchmen who had abandoned La Clue during the chase. In Cadiz, Brodrick soon discovered the eight French ships that had fled on the first night of the chase. He blockaded them there so successfully that the French were ridiculed by their Spanish allies, who are said to have put up a notice advertising the French fleet for sale: 'For particulars apply to Vice-Admiral Brodrick'.[15] Thus reassured, Boscawen headed back to Spithead, puffed with the pride of an admiral returning with a fleet swollen by ships of the enemy, and comforted by the knowledge that the rest were easily contained. He arrived home on 1 September 1759.

Strategically the battle was also a clear success. Upon hearing the news, the Prime Minister, the Duke of Newcastle, wrote to the Earl of Hardwicke: 'I own I was afraid of invasion till now.'[16] The cloud of fear that had hung over the southern shores of Britain was lifted, temporarily at least. The French army was still massed in Brittany and Ostend, and the French fleet at Brest was still a significant force, but without the added numbers of the Toulon fleet it was no match for the British Channel Fleet, the Western Squadron and now most of the Mediterranean Squadron combined. Faced with such formidable logistical problems, the invasion plans should have been dropped immediately, but so much money had been spent in getting the scheme to this late stage that it was decided to continue. While the broad strategic situation had not altered, therefore, and Britain was still under threat of invasion, the balance and focus of the naval war had shifted dramatically. The Mediterranean was no longer the fulcrum of the war; that had shifted to the north-west coast of France, where the Brest fleet lay at anchor.

The psychological impact of the battle was also significant. The shame of the Battle of Minorca in 1756 which had hung around the necks of the sailors of the Mediterranean Fleet had been removed. Dramatically different from Byng, Boscawen had shown no self-doubt and no lack of belief in the ability of his men. Nor had he raged against the injustice of the hand which he had been dealt; he had used the resources at his disposal and he had done his duty. Boscawen acknowledged that the victory 'was well, but it might have been a great deal better',[17] but such regret was very much the norm among naval commanders of the day. Boscawen's particular gripe was that, while he had pressed on to engage the French flagship, those that had followed him had engaged the rearmost of the French line without continuing up to their headmost ships. This was his tactical plan, but it had not been enacted as he had wished.

There are three possible explanations for this, each important to the way that we understand how and why fleet battles evolved as they did in the age of sail. Firstly, it is possible that Boscawen had been unable to transmit his ideas effectively to his fleet captains, either by refusing to share his ideas, by being unable to make himself understood, or, as is most likely in this case, by having no time to call a council of war before battle was joined. Secondly, it is possible that he *had* made his plans clear at some stage in the preceding weeks of blockade, but that he did not wield sufficient authority for his wishes to be enacted. This frequently happened in battle. Fleet cohesion was achieved more through the complex social relationship between a commander and his officers than by orders alone. Fleet captains ignored their fleet commander time and again and would continue to do so up to, during and after the Battle of Trafalgar.

The final possible explanation for their behaviour lies in the practical restrictions of sailing warfare. Many of the British ships were damaged in the rigging as they approached the French and, when the two fleets finally joined, the fine easterly breeze which had blown the British ships up to their enemy suddenly dropped, and both fleets were beset by light and variable winds. It is perfectly reasonable to suppose, therefore, that many of the ships may have wished to continue up the French line as Boscawen had desired but were simply unable to do so. This type of incapacity was fully expected in fleet battle. All in all, therefore, the battle may not have gone exactly as the commander had intended, but that is not to say that the fleet necessarily misbehaved; it is, indeed, significant that none of Boscawen's captains was tried by court martial after the battle, as was usually the case throughout the century. The root of Boscawen's concern was that an attack according to his tactical plan may well have prevented the escape of the *Souverain* and *Guerrier* – only two ships of the original force of fourteen.

The details of the battle were published in the popular broadsheets and Boscawen was universally applauded. His arrival at Portsmouth was received with wild scenes of popular rejoicing, he was given a public ovation on arrival in London, and he was summoned immediately to the King, who received him with every possible measure of esteem. His actions in defying Portuguese neutrality, although they roused a diplomatic storm, were fully approved of by the British government, and Lord Knowles was sent out to make a humble apology in the presence of the diplomatic corps.[18] Boscawen, meanwhile, was sworn a member of the Privy Council and was made a general of marines with an annual salary of £3,000. Two of his captains were knighted, one of them Captain Bentley of the *Warspite* who brought out the *Téméraire*. Matthew Buckle, who had been given the honour of returning to Britain with news of the victory, was given a prize of £500 by the King to buy a sword when he returned with the despatches. Booksellers nationwide sold tracts and poems extolling Boscawen's success, in which poets were forced to meet the formidable challenge of rhyming something – anything – with 'Boscawen'. This is one commendable solution:

That day, then, jolly buck, we'll set the taps a-flowin'
And drink rest and good luck to Admiral Boscawen.[19]

For the crews of the British ships the success was a welcome return to the heady days of 1747 and the two similar British victories over fleeing

French squadrons. Once again they had proved themselves in battle; once again they had chased and caught an escaping French squadron that had fought fiercely and bravely; and once again they had overcome. The setback of the Battle of Minorca had been defied; the Battle of Lagos marked the moment when the wind of British success began to blow with reassuring consistency. Battle by battle, the Royal Navy was building a portfolio of victories that would infuse British crews with battle-winning confidence for a generation and more. The combined result of all of these factors was that, in September 1759, confident, well-manned, well-fed and well-trained British crews manned British ships that patrolled the Western Approaches to the Channel, waiting for the French to make the next move.

In all of these ways, therefore, the Battle of Lagos was a turning point in British maritime history. So often that turning point is associated with the far more spectacular Battle of Quiberon Bay that followed only three months later. Then, the French fleet finally made the bold decision to leave Brest in an attempt to unite with the force of invasion craft grouped around the Morbihan in southern Brittany. They were intercepted by Edward Hawke on their way south as the sun set on a stormy winter's night. The British squadron crowded sail from the west, forcing the French to seek sanctuary in the inshore waters of Quiberon Bay, which they did willingly in the belief that Hawke, with no local knowledge and no pilots to guide him, would be forced to stand off in the deep water and wait for the storm to abate. Hawke, however, was not a man to be taken lightly. Much like Boscawen had in the summer, Hawke understood the precarious political and military situation. The British Isles were still under threat of an invasion and needed a victory at all costs. He was also a veteran of conflict with the French and a talented fighter. More importantly, perhaps, he was also a talented seaman, which could not be said for all officers in the eighteenth-century navy. He was far less afraid of the inshore waters of Quiberon Bay than the French admiral, the marquis de Conflans, suspected. Indeed, Hawke reasoned that where Conflans could take his ships, he could too, and he sent his fleet headlong into the bay after the French. There, the French were destroyed. Seven of their ships were sunk or captured, two and a half thousand men were lost, and with them went all possibility of launching an invasion.

The year 1759 was the peak of British military success and was celebrated nationwide in poem and song:

Blow the trumpet, strike the lyre
British hearts with joy inspire,
Voice with instruments combine
To praise the glorious Fifty-nine![20]

Purely in naval terms, however, the tide of British glory that flowed from 1759 must not be measured from the success at Quiberon in November 1759, but from the early spring of 1758 with the capture of the stunning *Foudroyant* (80) on 28 February, the *Raisonable* (64) on 29 May, the *Bienfaisant* (64) on 25 July and then with Boscawen's victory at Lagos in August. Between the spring of 1758 and December 1759 the French navy lost nearly half its total fighting strength.[21] The captured *Téméraire* was symbolic of those heady, summer days of British maritime success. She had been taken violently from the French and in defiance of Portuguese neutrality. The tree of British sea power had reached its full height: its roots were deep, its canopy wide and the *Téméraire* was its fruit.

She had been built to a joint design by Pierre-Blaise Coulomb and his son François in Toulon in 1749, a two-decked 74-gun ship of 1,685 tons, almost a hundred and seventy feet long, a fraction over forty-eight feet wide and nearly twenty-one feet deep. She was armed with twenty-eight 36-pounder cannon on her lower gun deck, thirty 18-pounders on her upper deck and sixteen 9-pounders on her quarterdeck and forecastle – a total of 1,692 livres, the French equivalent of the British pound weight. Fully fitted she might have cost somewhere in the region of 800,000–900,000 livres. She was certainly eye-catching and her design, with a distinctive straight-sided stern profile, a large projecting balcony and elaborate carving, harked back to a much earlier age of warship design, in the reigns of William III and Louis XIV (fig. 3).

La *Téméraire* was a significant physical force, but perhaps as importantly, her name was an established part of French naval tradition. This *Téméraire* had fought as La Clue's flagship of the rear division at the successful Battle of Minorca in 1756, and an earlier French *Téméraire* had fought at the great French victory of the Battle of Beachy Head in 1690. She was one of a fleet of ships ordered by Louis XV in 1748 in response to French losses in the War of the Austrian Succession, and by 1758 the French navy had built fifty-two ships of 64 guns or more. Crucially, almost all of them were powerful two-deckers, like the *Téméraire*. In November 1754, forty-five of the fifty-five French ships of the line were 64- or 74-gunners, all arranged on two decks, and all designated as Third Rates. In fact, the French navy had no First Rates at the time, and the largest of the powerful two-deckers, 80-gunners such as La Clue's *L'Océan*, acted as flagships.[22]

The situation was very different in Britain. The Seven Years War was an important time in the history of British warship design, which had stagnated during the previous war and had reached its lowest ebb with the production of a class of eighty-gun three-deckers in the 1740s, designated as Third Rates. To accommodate three tiers of guns, but still retain their class as Third Rate ships of the line, these ships were built short but high. As a result, their centre of gravity was raised and they pitched and rolled heavily in the smallest of seas. Indeed it was frequently found impossible to open the lowest tier of gunports in anything but the smoothest of seas. As a result, an enemy ship of nominally equal or even lesser strength but better design and able to use her full complement of guns was frequently more than a match for them. In 1744, a future admiral, Charles Knowles, had written: 'I have never seen or heard since my knowledge of things that one of our ships alone or singly opposed to one of the enemy ships of equal force has taken her.'[23] Foremost in his mind must have been the battle in April 1740 in which the beautiful Spanish 70-gun *Princesa* was taken, when it took three British ships of nominally equal strength to subdue the Spanish monster.

Although never so extreme as the infamous 80-gunners, most British-built ships of the line shared the same basic characteristics: they were short and high, but they were all strong and they were designed with a strategy in mind. These were ships built to patrol close to shore in the Western Approaches, the Channel and the North Sea in all weathers and at all times of year. They were also designed to fight. This may seem an obvious requirement but it is a crucial point. French ships of the same period were not designed to stand and fight in line like the British. They were long, loose and fast and designed purely for the protection of the transatlantic and Levant trade, the centrepiece of French maritime policy developed during the preceding war. Large two-decked ships provided the perfect combination of firepower and mobility to execute that strategy.

In comparison with the British warships they were, however, massive for their class. The first of these powerful French two-deckers to come into

British hands was the 74-gun *Invincible*, captured at the First Battle of
Finisterre. Most British two-decked ships of the same period carried only
sixty-eight guns, and were generally considered pretty useful, but in terms of
tonnage, the *Invincible* was fifty per cent larger than an equivalent British
70-gunner and she fired a broadside seventy-five per cent heavier. Indeed,
the French livre weight of 489.5 grams was eight per cent heavier than the
British pound and the heaviest French gun, the 36-pounder, fired a ball more
than one-fifth heavier than the largest British naval gun for two-deckers,
the 32-pounder. A little over a decade later, in 1758, *Le Foudroyant* was
captured. Again she was a two-decker, but carried even more guns, a total of
eighty-four. These ships were so powerful that the Royal Navy rated the
French twin-decked 80-gun ships as equivalent to their own three-decked
90-gunners.[24]

The impact on British ship designers of these captured ships was profound. The solution to the design problems of the mid-sized warships was
plain: the answer was not to make large First or Second Rate three-deckers
smaller, as they had in the 1740s, but to make two-deckers larger. After 1758
no three-decked ship of less than ninety guns was ever built again in Britain,
and in the mid-1750s the Admiralty began to order its own two-decked 74-
gunners, which were designed by Sir Thomas Slade, appointed Surveyor of
the Navy in 1755. It was accepted then and is accepted now that he was the
greatest naval architect of the century. By the time that Boscawen fought the
Battle of Lagos in August 1759, ten of Slade's two-decked 74s were in service
in the Royal Navy, and one of them was the *Warspite*, the very ship that cut
out the *Téméraire*. The *Warspite* was typical of Slade's designs. She was a
fraction shorter, narrower and shallower than the *Téméraire* and 106 tons
lighter but, unlike the previous generation of British two-deckers, she was a
match for her enemy.

By September 1759, Slade's ten British-built 74s were augmented by a
further ten captured ships of similar dimensions, and so the disparity
between the size of the British and French ships that met in battle began to
change. In November 1759, when Hawke's fleet chased Conflans into
Quiberon Bay, four of the seven ships in the van division, the ships that took
the greatest risks and met the first and fiercest broadsides of resistance, were
two-decked 74-gunners. The Admiralty then reacted to the news of
Quiberon Bay by ordering three new 74s. The result was that British ship

design caught up with the French. In terms of single-ship engagements, the turning point came in 1761 when the British *Bellona*, a new 74-gunner, captured the French 74 *Courageux* in a single-ship action off Vigo. In subsequent years it was taken for granted that in single-ship engagements any British ship could match a French ship of the same size. Indeed some believed that any British ship could match any French ship of up to fifty per cent greater gun power.

The newly captured *Téméraire*, therefore, was both a sign of the times and a symbol of the future. Her fine lines and size distinguished her as French, but her design as a powerful two-decker also fitted very neatly into the new British battle fleet that was to dominate the world's oceans for a generation. By the 1790s, entire squadrons were made up of 74-gun ships. At the Battle of the Glorious First of June in 1794, sixteen of the twenty-five British ships and nineteen of the twenty-six French were 74s, and at the Battle of the Nile in 1798, nine of the thirteen French and all bar one of the fourteen British ships were 74s. They were large enough and strong enough to provide the backbone of the battle fleet and fight in the line, but they were also fast and highly manoeuvrable. Such homogeneity was a great advantage in fleet manoeuvre. In practice, it was impossible to get two-decked ships to sail on parity with those of one deck, or three-decked ships to sail on parity with those of two.

Upon her arrival in England, the *Téméraire* would have been handed over to the Surveyor of the Navy who would have taken her lines and determined how she would be re-fitted. This was standard practice. French warships were built and fitted with French strategy in mind; they lacked the large holds and magazines of British warships designed for sustained cruising and battle. In fact her first captain, Matthew Barton, was astonished at how few stores would fit into her when she was equipped for her first expedition. He complained that she could only take in four and a half months' worth of bread in the bread room and hardly anything in the fish room; and that two hundred tons of water entirely filled the hold.[25] The internal arrangements of British ships, moreover, conformed to established arrangements and measurements and, in effect, the whole interior of a prize ship was ripped out and rebuilt to conform to those standards. This made the process of maintenance and repair of a battle fleet far simpler. During this process British shipwrights would also replace inferior French technology with superior British designs. The ship's pumps are one such example. They were essential for pumping out water from a leaking ship but also for providing salt water for everyday use and fire-fighting. Those requirements were common to every warship but the British pumps were far superior to any on foreign warships. The British design was known as the chain pump and comprised an endless belt of S-shaped links which carried water from the well, in the bottom of the hold, to the gun deck, where they discharged into a large cistern before returning downwards again. The water which had collected in the cistern was then routed overboard through a series of wooden tubes. These pumps were usually fitted as a group of four at the points of a square around the mainmast, and when used in unison they could remove vast quantities of water. A single British chain pump could pump out a ton of water in only 43.5 seconds. The major advantage over pumps operated by levers was that, having a revolving motion, they could be operated by large numbers of men, thus substantially increasing their output.[26]

French anchors were also far inferior to their British counterparts, as were French capstans. In the rigging the one major difference lay in the quality of the blocks. Again, British blocks were far superior to French and this in turn allowed smaller crews to move the largest yards, and hoist boats, guns and stores with tackles secured to the yards. British rigs were simply far more efficient than the French. The size and shape of the sails were also likely to change, particularly for ships such as the *Téméraire* that had been built in Toulon by Mediterranean shipwrights for service in the Mediterranean. Her masts would have been tall, her yards long, her sails light and her ropes thin; she would simply not have withstood the winter blockade duty in the Western Approaches that the Royal Navy would require of her.

Captured ships were also dramatically altered externally. It was common to replace the most decorative parts – the stern carvings around the windows which lit the officers' quarters and the figurehead – as these had highly distinctive national characteristics and it was of the utmost importance that the nationality of a ship could be identified from her appearance. The most experienced officers could identify specific ships from their silhouettes alone, but at a far more basic level it was an essential skill to be able to identify a warship's nationality, or at the very least to be able to identify a stranger. To make that task easier, therefore, the Admiralty did their best to standardize decoration on British warships whilst maintaining an acceptable quantity of individual characteristics for each ship's decoration, to keep each distinctive within the British fleet.

Finally, of course, the armament would be changed as French cannon were not built to the same calibre as British. The *Téméraire* was rearmed, with twenty-eight 32-pounders on her lower deck, thirty 18-pounders on her upper deck, ten 9-pounders on her quarterdeck and six 9-pounders on her forecastle.

What was retained was her name. Téméraire means nothing in English; an indistinct mix of rash and reckless, it carries none of the undertones of foolhardiness that those words imply in English. She was one of a number of ships renamed by Louis XIV in 1671 to emphasize the inherent superior personality traits of French royalty in general and Louis in particular. She thus formed a fleet that consisted of ships such as *Foudroyant* (devastating or stunning), *Glorieux* (glorious or proud), *Magnanime* (magnanimous or noble), *Victorieux* (victorious or triumphant), *Courageux* (brave), *Florissant* (flourishing or blooming), and the jewel of them all, the name which so neatly sums up Louis' perception of himself and French royalty – *Sans Pareil* – without equal.[27] In spite of the difficulties of translation, the political and symbolic significance of retaining a captured ship's name were powerful, as was the sailors' belief that to change the name of a ship was unlucky. British sailors were unable or unwilling to pronounce *Téméraire* properly, and so she became to them *Timmera*.

Shortly after her return with Boscawen's Mediterranean squadron, she was surveyed at Portsmouth in February 1760 and purchased by the Admiralty in March for £11,175 19s 9¾d, with £9,693 4s 3½d allotted for the hull at £5 15s per ton, plus £32 19s for masts and yards, and a further £1,449 16s 6¼d for furniture and stores. She was officially named that same month before being refitted at Portsmouth, a process so thorough that it took nine months to complete and cost £11,574 13s 7d.[28] Thus the French *La Téméraire* was transformed into an almost unrecognizable warship that shared her name, albeit without the accents, and her French skeleton, but her soul was now British. HMS *Temeraire* had been born.

3.

The Amphibious *Temeraire*

OCTOBER 1760 – OCTOBER 1762

The Admiralty was obsessive about monitoring the performance of all of its ships, and the new captain of the *Temeraire*, like all captains, was required to fill out a report which detailed the specific characteristics of his vessel. From this report, we know that the *Temeraire* had a draught of 25 feet at her bows and 24 feet at her stern. Fully stowed her lowest gunports were an acceptable 5 feet 7½ inches above the waterline and she could make a full ten knots in a good breeze with all sail set up to her topgallants. She steered very well and tacked as well as most other ships. She made very little leeway, only half a point when sailing close-hauled, which was truly exceptional for the time, but she sailed best with the wind a point or two abaft the beam. In a head sea she was next to useless, and although she made little leeway when close-hauled, she only travelled slowly; no more than three knots at best.[1] She was, in short, a classic example of French marine architecture. Fast off the wind and slow sailing into the wind, she had been designed to cruise between the Mediterranean and the West Indies in light, predictable winds. She may not have been naturally designed to fit into British naval strategy, therefore, but there was always room for a fast ship.

The immediate question for the Admiralty was what to do with her: 1760 had come and gone and with it a narrow window to negotiate a peace. At the end of the year Britain had conquered Canada, her avowed intention at the very start of the war, and the French navy had been all but destroyed between the spring of 1758 and the winter of 1759. Meanwhile the French government was penniless and in disarray and Marshal Belleisle, a strong advocate for peace within the French court, had died and been replaced by the combative duc de Choiseul. Even before Choiseul took over as naval minister, he had been involved in a subtle game with the Spanish court, for the only saving grace of the French war effort in 1760 was the formation of an alliance with Spain. With the resulting access to the Spanish navy combined with the riches from Spanish silver and emerald mines in the New World, France would be able to continue the war or, at the very least, negotiate a much more satisfactory end to it from a position of power.

At the same time, the British government was deeply divided between those who sought peace and those who followed the energetic minister William Pitt. Pitt believed that France should be driven even further into the ground, so that she would be unable to resuscitate her navy for generations. This, he believed, was the surest way of safeguarding British interests. He was also alert to the possibility of a French alliance with Spain, and at no stage halted his future plans for the war. After the defeat of the French Mediterranean and Atlantic fleets, Pitt, advised by George Anson (First Lord of the Admiralty) and Lord Ligonier (Commander-in-Chief of the Army), believed that the way to secure a decisive victory over the French was through surprise amphibious operations launched against French possessions worldwide. By the end of 1760, Pitt's gaze had settled on the Indian Ocean, where French warships and privateers continued to harass British trade with great success from their island base at Mauritius. At exactly the same time, the first overtures for a peace between Britain and France were being proposed by the king of Prussia Frederick the Great.

It is unclear exactly when the plan to attack Mauritius changed, but it is known that in the three weeks after the first proposals for peace were received, some highly confidential dispatches between Spain and France were intercepted by the British. They were written in code, but the code was quickly broken, and the intelligence was sufficient to forewarn the British government of an alliance between France and Spain. An operation in the Indian Ocean now seemed far from sensible; thousands of British troops and large numbers of warships would be of little use fighting on an island on the other side of the world if the formidable Spanish navy decided to combine with the French army to launch an invasion across the Channel. Moreover, if the tabled peace negotiations did, in fact, gain any momentum, any victory at Mauritius would have no bearing on the result: it would be almost a year before the news of a victory would make it back to Britain. With the preparations for the Mauritius attack so far advanced, however, it was far simpler to change the destination than to abort the mission altogether. What was needed was a valuable French possession within spitting distance of British waters, from which the troops and ships could be recalled in an emergency. The obvious answer was to attack Belle Isle, a tiny island fifteen miles south-west of Quiberon Bay.

It was the obvious answer because it was not a new idea. Detailed preparations for an attack on Belle Isle had already been drawn up, but they had been postponed indefinitely in December 1760 as the season was too late to launch an amphibious operation in Biscay. Indeed, the weather is so appalling in Biscay in the winter months that it was a severe challenge simply to maintain a squadron of warships in the Western Approaches. British blockading squadrons were frequently blown back to the safety of Plymouth or Torbay. To venture to the rocky, foggy and lee shore of north-western France in December with a fleet of cumbersome troop transports was therefore unthinkable. Indeed when Anson was sounded out on the advisability of such a scheme, he responded that he was 'extremely against it'. That was in contrast to the King, George II, who was 'violently for it', but it was Anson's advice that was taken.[2]

Anson's main concern was the time of year, but another significant problem was whether the warships could get sufficiently close to shore to protect the troops during the landing. In fact Captain Hotham, the officer charged with sounding the waters around the island, had learned that no large vessel could get within two miles of the main fortification at Pallais except at one point, which was dominated by inaccessible French batteries built high into the cliffs. Those cliffs, an officer said, were a 'chain of rock forming irregular precipices and exhibiting steep rising ground from the tops of the cliffs . . . small bays and narrow valleys or ravines with sides very steep and difficult of access penetrate deep into the heart of the island . . .' The fortifications of the citadel itself were begun in 1658 and then improved in the 1680s. Although they were by now nearly eighty years old, the citadel on Belle Isle was one of the finest fortresses in all of France. The general in charge of the army, Studholme-Hodgson, summed it up: 'the whole island is a fortification, the little nature had left undone had been amply supply'd by art . . .'[3] There were three thousand troops on the island and a further four thousand two hundred that could be called up from the militia. There are three ports on the island of Belle Isle – they are Pallais, Sauzon and Goulfard, but they scarcely deserved the name of harbours, being either too exposed, too shallow or otherwise dangerous at the entrance. By March, however, the weather had improved sufficiently to launch the operation and it was simply hoped that close reconnaissance would reveal a suitable landing spot.

Aside from the proximity of Belle Isle to British shores, an invasion had both military and diplomatic advantages, the one stemming from the other. Belle Isle is a windswept and ugly island, approximately thirty-three miles square and surrounded by high cliffs. From its physical description one might consider it a possession of little value but, in the age of sail, it was exactly those characteristics that made it so important. The transatlantic voyage from west to east posed one very major problem – how to approach the coast of France safely. In this era in which the greatest minds of the day were still struggling with the problem of calculating longitude at sea, the safest way for a navigator to approach a foreign shore was to run along a parallel of latitude to a known and easy landfall. These tended to be high islands, visible from a long distance and surrounded by deep water – in short, Belle Isle. Here was landfall just proud of the hazardous Breton coastline that navigators could easily locate and then run on the prevailing south-westerly winds north or south to access easily the French ports of L'Orient, Nantes, Rochefort, La Rochelle, Bayonne, Brest and Bordeaux. To occupy Belle Isle, therefore, was to occupy a base which the great majority of French warships and merchantmen, homeward-bound from the rich Americas, would be forced to approach. It was also crucial because the largest of all French naval dockyards, that at Brest, was entirely reliant on seaborne supply for the materiel to keep the French navy operational. *Everything* that was needed for the building, repairing and fitting-out of ships had to be imported to Brest, past Belle Isle.

Crucially, the island itself provided a large and safe lee from the prevailing winds. The largest fleet of warships could ride out the worst Atlantic storms in safety between Belle Isle and the French coast. It also potentially provided a valuable base from which blockading ships in the Western Approaches could be re-armed and re-victualled rather than having to return to the relatively distant shores of south Devon. In a future war against the combined forces of France and Spain, the likelihood of which was now increasing daily, Belle Isle would also provide the British fleet with the incalculable advantage of a base interposed between the fleets of France and Spain, serving in a similar manner to the way Gibraltar divided the French fleets at Brest and Toulon. Moreover with Belle Isle so close to the French mainland, approximately the same distance as the Isle of Wight is to Portsmouth, the French government would be forced to maintain a high concentration of troops there to discourage or oppose a British descent onto mainland France and to discourage further British attacks on the nearby islands of Yeu, Ré and Oléron to the south and Ushant and Groix to the north.

For a British force to occupy Belle Isle, therefore, would be unendurable for the French crown, and no price would be too high for its restoration in any subsequent peace negotiations. For the British, this was a possible key to the reclamation by negotiation of Minorca, that most valued Mediterranean possession lost so carelessly by Byng in 1756. Pitt knew, moreover, that Spain might demand Minorca as the price of an alliance with France, but as long as the British held Belle Isle, the French would be in no position to grant it. Diplomatically, therefore, and particularly in the eyes of Pitt, this was the true value of the operation, although he alone seems to have appreciated it in these terms.[4] In the short term, meanwhile, it would be certain to divert French troops from Germany, where the war on land had reached a critical stage.

With the destination of the attack settled on Belle Isle, troops and war-ships steadily built up at Portsmouth, and one of the ships ordered to join the growing fleet was the *Temeraire*. Before she could go, however, *Temeraire* needed a captain, and a young man named Matthew Barton was commissioned into her in October 1760. It was a significant appointment as both Barton and the *Temeraire* were, in their own way, quite famous. A great deal of public interest was always associated with prizes of war and the *Temeraire* had been mentioned by name in the published despatches that described Boscawen's victory off Lagos. Barton, however, was famous for an altogether different reason.

He had fought at the most famous action of the preceding war, when the enormous and beautiful Spanish 70-gun *Princesa* was captured in April 1740. Far more than a simple engagement, the *Princesa* action became notorious because it took three British ships, each with a nominally equal armament, to subdue her. It was the first incident when the extraordinary disparity between British ship design and that of the French and Spanish became clear. Barton had then fought at the siege of Cartagena under Admiral Vernon in 1741 and at the Battle of Toulon in 1744, and had sailed to North

America under Boscawen where he served in the attacks on Halifax and Louisbourg at the start of the Seven Years War. Since then he had captured a French warship in 1756 and had successfully escorted a fleet of a hundred sail from the West Indies back to Britain. This young man, therefore, was a skilled sailor with considerable experience of battle both at sea and on land and, by 1760, had gained a glowing reputation as a talented leader. He was a natural choice for the forthcoming attack of Belle Isle.

This was, without doubt, a glittering career, but Barton's fame was due not only from his successes, but from an unrelated disaster. In November 1758, his ship, the 50-gun *Litchfield*, was wrecked on the north coast of Africa, and the hundred or so survivors were all washed ashore, quite naked, on the coast of Morocco. There they survived on drowned sheep washed ashore from the wreck, until they were found, captured and enslaved by the Sultan of Morocco. They were housed in a dark and vermin-infested hovel, although the officers had the comfort of blankets, and were forced to work in slavery for eighteen months until they were ransomed by the British crown. Such a remarkable story did not escape the attention of contemporary publishing entrepreneurs and an account written by a lieutenant of the expedition was published in 1760. With Barton in command on her first commission, therefore, the *Temeraire* already enjoyed a greater share of the limelight than many of her sister ships.

The *Temeraire* was also to play a leading role both literally and figuratively in the forthcoming operations. On the voyage to Belle Isle, she was ordered to lead the line of battle when on the port tack. To lead any line of battle required a great deal of initiative and no little bravery; it was, in the words of Captain Graham Moore, 'The post of honour and peril'.[5] Most of the time it was the leading ship which instigated any manoeuvre and her actions were mirrored down the fleet. This could be something as simple as a change of course by one or two degrees or as complicated as a tack or wear or even the assumption of an entirely new formation. In battle the lead ship would usually be the first to engage and to be engaged and it was at the very beginning of an action, when opposing crews were fresh and quivering with nervous energy, that the broadsides were the most destructive. A ship which assumed that position, therefore, had to be nimble, captained by a responsible, brave and thoughtful captain and crewed by the finest and most disciplined men. In a forthcoming action, her seamanship and endurance would be tested more than any other. So while no specific evidence survives relating to the reputation of Barton and the *Temeraire* in 1760, her location at the very front of the line sent to attack Belle Isle tells us all that we need to know. The *Temeraire* was already one of the finest ships in the navy. Moreover, if any further proof was needed, she formed part of the division led by Augustus Hervey and, in a memorandum to the fleet issued days before they set off, it was made clear that, in the event that something happened to him, command of the rear division would fall to Barton and the *Temeraire*.[6]

This role for the *Temeraire* was not the only post of distinction for ships or officers who had been involved in Boscawen's action at Lagos. Command of the Belle Isle expedition could quite plausibly have been given to Boscawen himself, particularly in view of his substantial experience of amphibious assaults, but he died suddenly in early 1761 from typhoid fever, aged only forty-nine. Command of the expedition was therefore awarded to Augustus Keppel, a man whom Boscawen himself had held in the highest regard: 'there is no better seaman than Keppel', he wrote, 'few so good and not a better officer.'[7] Keppel was an obvious candidate not only for his abundant talent, but for his recent success in an amphibious operation against Goree, a strategically significant French settlement on the western coast of Africa.

Although the attack could not be led by Boscawen, the squadron was infused with the influence of his success. Not only did the *Temeraire* lead the line, captained by Barton who had fought with Boscawen at Louisbourg, but the entire fleet was commanded by Matthew Buckle, Boscawen's most trusted aid and flag-captain, and the man who had been given the honour of returning to the King with the despatches of the victory at Lagos. The *Swiftsure*, moreover, was commanded by Thomas Stanhope, who had been knighted for his conduct at the Battle of Lagos. Both Stanhope and Buckle had also been present at the Battle of Quiberon Bay. Thus the strands of experience and reward permeated British fleets in these years. As success was added to success, so the fleet became imbued with the spirit of veterans of conflict who had tasted success and who had acquired the habit of victory. This process, typified by the presence of these men and the *Temeraire* on the Belle Isle expedition, was one of the central underlying reasons for the steady growth of British maritime superiority that was to create an empire that stretched further than ever by the end of the war.

We are fortunate that a great deal of paperwork survives from the Belle Isle expedition, because the letters of Samuel Barrington, captain of the *Achilles*, were carefully preserved. These papers, which include all official correspondence between an admiral and one of his captains, offer the most valuable insights into the specifics of the expedition and to naval warfare in the mid-eighteenth century in general. A missive of particular interest for its rarity is a highly detailed order to the fleet which explains the steps to be taken in case of separation. Keppel issued a private signal or code by which British ships might recognize each other by day or by night. They are not, as one might assume, relatively simple, but are staggeringly complicated. The order reads in part:

> The Ship that first makes the Signal shall hoist a Dutch Pendant at the Maintopgallant mast head, and an English Pendant at the Foretopgallant mast head, to be answered by an English Pendant at the same place, and a French Pendant at the Mizentopmast head.

And by night:

> The Ship that first makes the Signal shall hoist two Lights of equal height in the Mizen Shrouds and four Lights of equal height in the fore Shrouds. To be answered by three Lights one above another in the fore Shrouds, and one Light in the main Shrouds. Then the Ship that made the first Signal, shall burn three false fires; and the other shall reply by burning two false fires.

And then, when within hail:

> He who hails first shall ask *What Ship's that?* And he who is hailed shall answer *The King*. The other who hailed first shall reply *Unanimity*. Then he who [was] first hailed shall answer *His Glory*.[8]

These orders are a powerful reminder that, although the French *Téméraire* was originally part of a fleet that had largely been destroyed in 1758–59, there was still a potent threat to British ships entering French waters. Station-keeping was all but impossible at night, and in the fogs of the Channel it would be easy to become separated from the fleet and to find oneself confronted by a French or Spanish privateer or a lone cruising warship. This powerful warship, therefore, was armed with elaborate codes to protect her as surely as the shot and powder of her guns.

She sailed from Portsmouth on 29 March at the head of an armada that consisted of eleven ships of the line, eight frigates, two fireships, three bomb-ketches, sixty-four transports, four store and baggage ships, four hospital ships, five ordnance ships, three bomb tenders, fifteen victuallers and fifty flat-bottom boats known as flat-boats – the landing craft of their day. We know from her first muster book that she was manned with exactly six hundred and fifty men.[9] Together, they transported approximately seven thousand troops. As they set sail, almost immediately this most prestigious of ships ran aground not once but twice. She was hauled off the sandbank on both occasions, first with her sheet anchor and then with the kedge anchor, but for fear of being left behind by the convoy she was supposed to be protecting, she was forced to leave behind both anchors along with the ship's longboat and, no doubt, a fair measure of pride.[10]

Once arrived off Belle Isle, a force of eighty marines, made up of four officers, four sergeants, two drummers and seventy rank and file, was kept in constant readiness aboard the *Temeraire* to assist in the landing, with each man allocated three days' ration of bread and cheese.[11] Eighty men were a drop in the ocean of such a mighty invasion force, but the valuable role of the *Temeraire* did not lie necessarily in the fate of these men, but in that of her captain. Matthew Barton had been ordered – and honoured – to command the fleet of flat-bottomed boats that was to land the invasion force itself and then to take command of the naval troops ashore. Once the plan of attack had been settled upon by the combined commanders, Commodore Keppel and Major-General Hodgson, the invasion itself would, for a time at least, be the sole responsibility of the captain of the *Temeraire*.

Up to 1761, British forces had enjoyed mixed success in amphibious assaults on French soil. At the start of the war they had only very vague ideas about how to conduct an amphibious landing, but by the time the Belle Isle operation was conceived many lessons had been learned. There had been a highly successful attack on Cherbourg in 1758, but a contrasting disaster at St Malo, where eight hundred British troops had been massacred on the beach at the bay of St Cast. Right from the inception of the Belle Isle assault, government ministers and military planners had harboured grave concerns about the prospect of attacking such a formidable natural fortress. To make matters worse, the British had been openly reconnoitring the island for almost six months. They had been unopposed throughout and had reported a 'perfect state of tranquillity'[12] on the island. In reality, however, the French knew that something was afoot and had taken great care to augment the island's natural defences. They had constructed formidable redoubts and had built batteries high into the cliffs. By the time that the British fleet sailed majestically around the south of the island on 7 April and began a detailed search for an appropriate landing place, the French were watching, quietly confident that every beach that could accommodate the landing force was a death trap.

Ignorant of the quality of the French preparations, the British drew up their plans. Six frigates were sent to cruise in the gap between the island and the mainland to sever any communications, while thirteen of the line and three frigates were despatched to cruise off Brest to prevent any sortie by the remnants of the French fleet. The *Temeraire*, so central to the forthcoming invasion itself, anchored a little distance away from the rest of the fleet and hoisted a blue pendant, the signal that she was the rendezvous point for all of the transports and the flat-bottomed boats.[13] Keppel and Hodgson, meanwhile, had been taking a closer look at the shore in a cutter and had settled on an inlet midway along the south-eastern shore as the focus of their attack.

The next morning the wind was favourable and Keppel made the signal to disembark the main force while a feint was made further north, near the village of Sauzon. The main invasion force gathered in their flat-boats around the *Temeraire* and were led inshore by Matthew Barton. Three British warships, the *Prince of Orange*, *Dragon* and *Achilles*, together with two bomb ships, opened fire on the great four-gun battery that commanded the little bay, and succeeded in silencing it. Then, in the words of Keppel, recorded with a measure of pride, the troops were 'pushed towards the landing with great briskness and spirited behaviour at three different places near each other by Captain Barton.'[14]

Things were looking up and the invasion force passed the line of battleships that had anchored nearer the shore to cover their descent. It was only when they had landed and had fought their way to the back of the beach, however, that the full extent of the French preparations became clear. French troops were deeply entrenched high up in the cliffs, which formed a natural amphitheatre, and, in the months before the attack, had scarped away the bottom of the cliff, which was now vertical and could not be climbed without scaling ladders. One flat-boat, laden with sixty grenadiers, managed to land a little further up the coast on some rocks, from which they climbed up to the French positions. No sooner had they formed up, however, they were attacked by a far larger body of French troops and forced to fight their way back to the rocks. Only twenty of those grenadiers survived to be picked up by another flat-boat and taken to safety.

This miniature withdrawal was then repeated by the entire force. Under continual fire, the flat-boats were once again manned and the invasion force taken off with heavy loss, some dead, some captured. The weather then worsened, driving the flat-bottom boats against the unforgiving hulls of the warships and troop transports so that twenty were destroyed. Many of the transports also ran foul of each other and were damaged. It was not an auspicious start, but the invasion force, at least, had been led courageously and well by Matthew Barton of the *Temeraire*. News of the failed attack and the French defences was met with grim resolution in Britain. Pitt simply ordered four more battalions and a fresh supply of flat-boats and military stores, escorted by five more ships of the line to Belle Isle.

Sustained bad weather at Belle Isle, meanwhile, had given the British force time to recuperate while it awaited its reinforcements, and by 22 April they were set for another attempt. This time, however, it would be at a different location, and there would be two feints, at St Foy and Sauzon, designed to distract the enemy from the main descent. The commanders of the feints were nevertheless instructed to make a good go of it and to hold their ground if they could, rather than simply creating a diversion. Brigadier-General Hamilton Lambart led one of these forces and chose a spot that was so high, so steep and so threatening that the French had made no effort at all to augment the natural defences. They had not even posted sentries to watch over it. When Lambart succeeded in landing his troops on the rocks and they then found a route to the top of the cliffs, his tiny force was unopposed. A message was quickly sent back to the fleet while Lambart prepared to hold his ground, and the entire landing force, destined for the main assault at Fort d'Arsic, was diverted to Lambart's defended cliff top.

After a brief skirmish in which the British dominated, a great fire was seen burning at the highest point of the island, the signal for all French troops and native inhabitants to retreat to the fortress of Pallais. The beaches were left clear for the British landing.

The army advanced while the navy steadily unloaded the tons of stores that would be needed to besiege Pallais and to keep the British army in the field. This was a stern challenge and no time could be lost since the army had to be made secure, and it had to be done within three days, when the soldiers' provisions would run out. On hearing that the troops had landed and held their ground, Keppel ordered that the sailors involved in getting the cannon, provisions and necessaries for the army ashore all be given double allowance of wine or spirits. They were also read a message sent direct from the King as soon as he had learned that British forces were ashore:

> The Commodore has it in command from His Majesty to express
> His most gracious satisfaction of the behaviour of His Officers and
> Seamen upon the present service; and has firm reliance on the con-
> tinuance of the same spirit and vigour on the further operations
> towards the complete reduction of Belle Isle.[15]

Those ashore, meanwhile, soon discovered that the great cliffs were only their first challenge: one soldier remarked that the redoubts that surrounded Pallais were 'perhaps the best constructed that ever were seen', and he believed that the challenge of taking Belle Isle was as great as the more famous attack at Quebec in 1759, which was only taken after Wolfe's madcap assault of the Heights of Abraham.[16] Pallais withstood the British siege for a further seven weeks, but finally surrendered on 7 June. The British losses were 282 dead and 494 wounded, and they had used up 11,926 shells and at least 15,522 shot in the attack.[17] News of the success was sent back to England, by none other than Matthew Barton of the *Temeraire*, who had also been publicly thanked for his services by General Hodgson. Upon his arrival, as was then the common practice, Barton was presented with £500 by the King.

Detailed plans were immediately drawn up by the French to recapture Belle Isle with a huge force of fourteen ships of the line, two frigates, a dozen *prâmes* (another type of landing craft), a dozen gunboats and fifty-four flat-boats. What the French lacked, however, was enough sailors to man their ships, and enough supplies to meet the naval minister's demands. Such an attack could never become a reality. Belle Isle stayed firmly in British hands. It remained a valuable card in the negotiations at the end of the war which saw Minorca returned to British hands and the relinquishment of Canada by the French. The entirety of Nova Scotia itself was exchanged directly for Belle Isle.

The fate of Belle Isle and the inability of the French to do anything about it highlighted the wider problem of France's inability to continue the war from any position of strength, and it was not long before she allied with Spain. An agreement known as the 'Family Compact' was signed on 15 August 1761, but war was not openly declared by Spain until January 1762. Within days the British government had decided to attack Havana, the Cuban jewel of the Spanish West Indies. A magnificent city, Havana was also the main focus of Spanish naval power in the Americas. It was home to a large, permanent naval squadron, which enjoyed sophisticated dockyard facilities far superior to anywhere else in the Caribbean. And these were not just facilities to maintain and repair ships; by the 1750s the shipyard at Havana produced almost a third of the Spanish navy's ships, using its unparalleled access to the tropical hardwoods of the South American rain forests. Unlike British ships built of oak, Spanish ships were built of teak and mahogany. These ships were the finest afloat, as tropical hardwood is almost impervious to rot and extremely strong. Finally, Havana was one of the crucial staging posts between the riches of South America and Europe. It was the rendezvous point for the homeward-bound *flota*, the annual convoy which transported the treasure to Europe. The warehouses of Havana were packed with valuable tobacco and her vaults with silver and jewels.

A successful assault, therefore, would drastically deplete the Spanish navy and deprive those ships not based at Havana of her dockyard facilities. The immediate loss of revenue in the taking of Havana would be a fearful blow to the Spanish and French war effort, as would the longer effect of the interruption of trade between South America to Europe. Finally, the psychological impact would be profound. The Spanish believed Havana to be impregnable, and with good reason. The city's fine natural harbour was protected by a narrow and easily defendable entrance, not unlike Portsmouth in Britain. The approaches to the harbour were defended by one of the world's most formidable fortresses, El Morro. The fortress was surrounded by an enormous ditch, 65 feet deep at its deepest, 105 feet wide at its widest, and 43 feet long at its longest, and it was cut out of solid rock. It was also built on a promontory overlooking the harbour; there was no fresh water anywhere nearby, and besieging forces would be forced to carry it overland in the Caribbean heat. El Morro had a powerful arsenal and other batteries commanded those areas that the guns of the fortress could not target. Inside the harbour, moreover, was a force of twelve Spanish ships of the line, all heavily armed. These ships could be anchored in position to rake any vessel foolish enough to force the harbour entrance, and lucky enough to survive the guns of El Morro.

Ultimately, Havana was protected by geography. The nearest British naval base was at Jamaica, five hundred miles south-east from Cuba's north-western point. The north coast of Cuba was protected by a series of reefs and small islands sandwiched against the coast of Cuba by the Great Bahama Bank, a large, treacherous and unpredictable sandbank and the graveyard of countless ships. To approach Havana, therefore, a large force of deep-sea ships would have to approach Cuba from the south, and then pass round the north-western tip of the island before making their way two hundred miles along the north coast into the teeth of the prevailing wind. Sailing warships could make ground dead to windward but it was exceptionally difficult and took a very long time. The Spanish, therefore, rested in full confidence that no large force would be able to approach them without revealing their intention weeks in advance, and even if they did make it to Havana, the defences were formidable and the city adequately, if not well-garrisoned. Any offensive operation would, by necessity, be large and slow-moving and thousands would die of disease before the city fell. This was no casual assumption, but a certainty; the climate had already accounted for at least one significant amphibious assault on Spanish soil in the West Indies: the expedition of Vernon to Cartagena in 1741. To take Havana, therefore, was an opportunity to humble, if not humiliate the Spanish. They had dared to declare war on Britain, and the British were determined to show what they were capable of in the first exchanges of the war. The full might of British military planning in foreign waters, now honed after nearly six years of warfare, during which British forces had driven the French with relentless success from India and Canada, and with the capture of Belle Isle had occupied the soil of France itself, was now turned towards the island of Cuba, and the city of Havana.

As Anson and Ligonier planned the assault on Havana in London, British forces in the Caribbean were already amassing for an assault on the French island of Martinique, an important prelude to the descent on Havana. Warships and troop transports were sent from Britain and America to bolster the forces already there. With the siege of Belle Isle successfully concluded it was clear that the French were unable to launch a relief operation, and warships and troops were freed from their service at Belle Isle, although not before time. Many of the ships had been there since April and their crews were starting to feel the effects of scurvy. The first lieutenant of the *Achilles* and her captain of marines were so ill that the former had remained confined to his cabin for a full month and the latter's fingernails were coming off, the skin peeling from his hands.[18] Those who were ill were sent home to recover, but for the rest a new challenge awaited. After a brief stay at home they were ordered to the Caribbean, to the certain horrors of thirst and disease but the possibility of unimaginable riches. The *Temeraire* thus turned her stern galleries to the barren and windswept rock of Belle Isle and on 16 October 1761 headed west and south in search of more glory as flagship of the convoy.

The prospect of new climes had concerned Matthew Barton a great deal, particularly because the *Temeraire* had been loaded with a quantity of white wine to augment the beer or spirits that were usually served to the sailors. In every instance alcohol lasted longer than fresh water and diluted alcohol was an important part of every sailor's diet. In home waters where they had access to it, beer was the sailor's principal drink, but on foreign stations wine, brandy, rum or even arrack in the East Indies were the drinks of choice. In this instance, however, the wine with which the *Temeraire* had been provided was relatively weak, and this was a grave concern, for weak wine quickly turned sour in a hot climate. Barton wrote specifically to his admiral for the forthcoming Martinique expedition, George Rodney, and he was one of eight captains to do so. It is unclear how the issue was resolved, but it is certain that Rodney empathized with their concerns, for he forwarded their letters to the Admiralty Secretary.[19]

The passage to the Caribbean was uneventful – in fact the only interesting event was that they opened a barrel of beef that was two pieces short – and the *Temeraire* and her charge of three thousand troops arrived at Barbados on 14 December. There they met up with the rest of the invasion force, which had been further boosted by 7,600 hardened veterans of the war in America, and on 5 January 1762, almost 14,00 troops, thirteen ships of the line and twenty-four smaller warships set sail for Martinique. Two days later they arrived.[20]

It was never going to be an easy assault. Martinique is thirty-five miles long and only thirteen miles wide, but it is cut by great ravines and is thick with forest. The coast is surrounded by hidden rocks and shoals, with few landing places open and large enough to support an invasion force. In the days before the main attack the *Raisonable* had been lost on one of these rocks at the entrance to St Anne's Bay, where Rodney planned to land his force. The grounding had been witnessed by the *Temeraire*, who sent a boat to help, but they could only take off her crew.[21] The *Raisonable* now rested high and dry, an unmistakable signal of British intent and a reminder of the obstacles they must first overcome. Rodney did not change his plan, however; although the *Raisonable* was stranded and it was clear where the British intended to land, they had silenced the battery commanding the bay. The *Raisonable*, moreover, now marked the edge of the shoal upon which she was stranded.

There was, in truth, little choice over their landing site. In between the few coves and beaches, the cliffs of Martinique are high and steep. The main fortification and administrative centre was at Fort Royal, set high up on the cliffs and surrounded by three heavily defended hills from which hostile warships could be targeted with heavy and plunging fire as they struggled in the lee of the huge cliffs. This was the key to the entire operation, but there were few stronger bases anywhere in the Leeward Islands. A force had succeeded in landing on Martinique near Fort Royal two years earlier, but had been forced to retreat. Now Rodney landed his men a full three miles from their target, and they began to cut a road through the forest and to drag the besieging cannon into position. It was appallingly heavy work, and it was led by sailors including men from the *Temeraire*. Perhaps unsurprisingly, there was disciplinary trouble among those sailors who had been left behind to continue the tedious day-to-day maintenance of the ship in the sweltering

1. Admiral Boscawen's report of the killed and wounded at the Battle of Lagos, 20 August 1759.

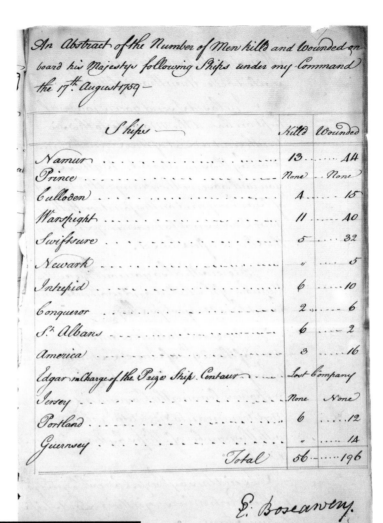

An Abstract of the Number of Men killd and Wounded on board his Majestys following Ships under my Command the 17th August 1759 —

Ships	Killd	Wounded
Namur	13	14
Prince	None	None
Culloden	4	15
Warspight	11	40
Swiftsure	5	32
Newark	"	5
Intrepid	6	10
Conqueror	2	6
St. Albans	6	2
America	3	16
Edgar in charge of the Prize Ship Centaur	Lost Company	
Jersey	None	None
Portland	6	12
Guernsey	"	14
Total	56	196

E. Boscawen.

2. Admiral Edward Boscawen by Joshua Reynolds, *c.*1755.

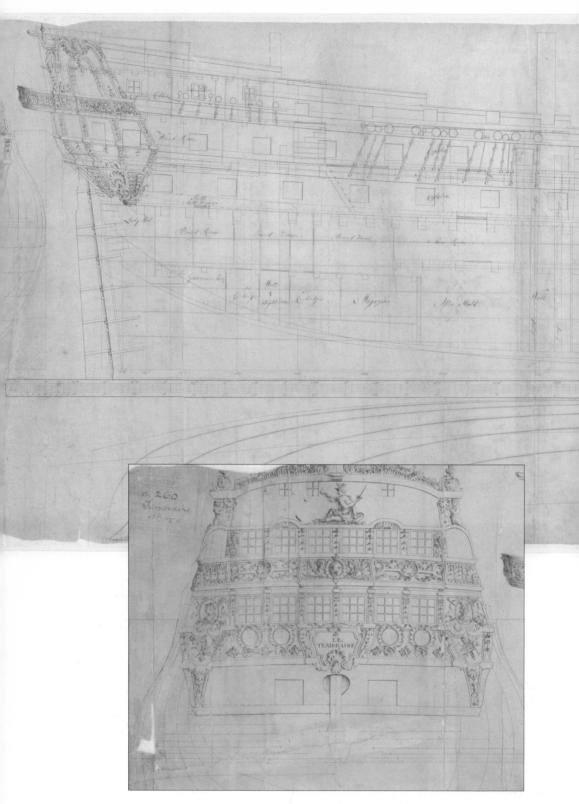

3. Admiralty draught of the captured *La Téméraire*, 1759.

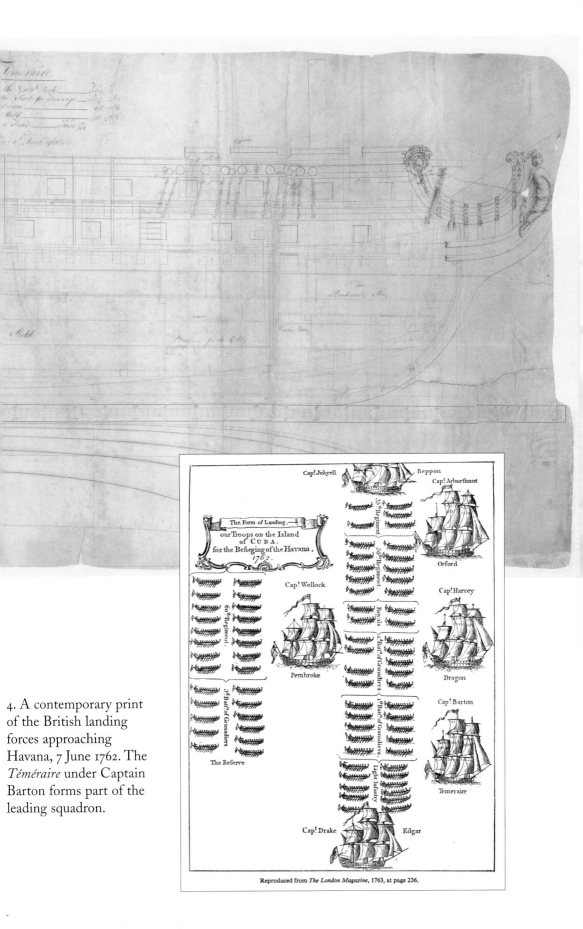

4. A contemporary print of the British landing forces approaching Havana, 7 June 1762. The *Téméraire* under Captain Barton forms part of the leading squadron.

The Form of Landing our Troops on the Island of CUBA for the Besieging of the Havana, 1762.

Cap.t Jekyell   Reppon   Cap.t Arburthnot

35.th Regiment.

50.th Regiment.

Orford

Cap.t Wellock   Cap.t Harvey

Royals

Batt.n of Grenadiers

Pembroke   Dragon

1.st Batt.n of Grenadiers

2.d Batt.n of Grenadiers

60.th Regiment.   Cap.t Barton

Light Infantry

3.d Batt.n of Grenadiers

The Reserve   Temeraire

Cap.t Drake   Edgar

5. *The Capture of Havana* by Dominic Serres (1770–5).
Although no contemporary images of the *Temeraire* at
Havana survive, this is a fair representation of her on duty
outside El Morro fortress in 1762 by an artist who was
actually present during the siege. Flatboats under
Temeraire's command are depicted landing prior to the
storming of the fortress on 31 July.

6. Chatham Dockyard by Joseph Farrington, 1785–94.

7. The launch of HMS *Temeraire*,
11 September 1798, from the original,
now lost, by Philip Burgoyne.

8. Figures of Atlas from the quarter
gallery of HMS *Temeraire*.

9. The prisoner-of-war model of HMS *Temeraire*,
kept in the Wool House museum, Southampton.

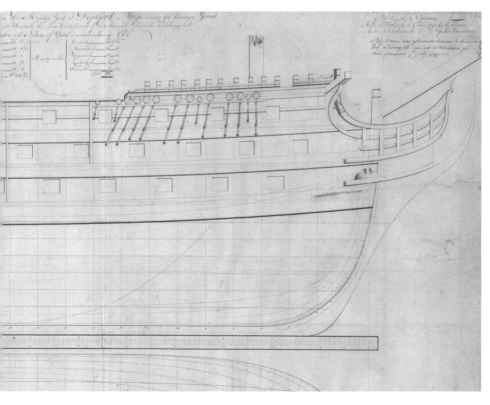

10. Admiralty draught of HMS *Temeraire*, 1798.

11. HMS *Temeraire* by Geoff Hunt.

Caribbean heat. The captain's log, which since their departure from England had been relatively free from punishment, begins to record lashes handed out for drunkenness, mutinous behaviour and insolence.[22]

For those who served ashore with the army, however, there was the excitement and fear of taming a wilderness, defeating the French and, most importantly perhaps, of showing up the army. An infantry officer who witnessed the assault later wrote of the British sailors:

> You may fancy you know the spirit of these fellows but to see them
> in action exceeds any idea that can be formed of them. A hundred or
> two of them, with ropes and pullies, will do more than all your dray-
> horses in London. Let but their tackle hold and they will draw you a
> cannon or mortar on its proper carriage up to any height, though the
> weight never be so great. It is droll enough to see them tugging along
> with a good 24-pounder at their heels; on they go, huzzaing and hul-
> looing, sometime up hill, sometimes down hill; now sticking fast in
> the brakes, presently floundering in the mud and mire; swearing,
> blasting, damning, sinking in and careless of everything but the
> matter committed to their charge as if death or danger had nothing
> to do with them. We had a thousand of these brave fellows sent to
> our assistance by the Admiral; and the service they did us, both
> onshore and on the water, is incredible.[23]

The army reciprocated in kind with a fantastic effort of its own and Fort Royal was bombarded by both land and sea. Through extraordinary combined efforts Martinique fell on 4 February and French power in the West Indies was broken. General Monckton, commander-in-chief of the land forces, acknowledged in his first despatch the 'harmony that exists between the fleet and the army' and Rodney noted the 'eager and cheerful activity of the officers and seamen who contributed everything in their power.' He later glowed with pride as he sent news of the island's capture back to the Admiralty: 'I can only repeat in this public manner my entire approbation of the conduct of all the Officers and Seamen of that part of His Majesty's fleet which I have the honour to command, all having exerted themselves in their proper stations with an ardour and resolution becoming British seamen.'[24] The success at Belle Isle, which had rested so surely on the cooperation between the navy and the army, had clearly transposed itself with great success to the Caribbean. The British amphibious forces were on a roll and now the greatest prize of all lay in their sights.

The officer charged with the responsibility for the naval side of the Havana expedition, Vice-Admiral Sir George Pocock, had left Spithead on 5 March in company with the Duke of Albemarle (the brother of Augustus Keppel), who was to command the land forces. They headed for Martinique, where they were ordered to rendezvous with Rodney's already considerable army.

Shortly before Pocock arrived, however, Rodney received a letter from the Governor of Jamaica requesting immediate assistance. Secret letters intercepted aboard a French merchantman had suggested that a French squadron under the command of Rear-Admiral the comte de Blénac was preparing to invade Jamaica, possibly with the help of Spanish ships and troops from Havana. The British also knew from a separate source that a force of eight ships of the line carrying three thousand troops had escaped from Brest at the end of January. Only four days after Rodney received the cry for help from Jamaica, Blénac was spotted off Martinique, which he did not know had fallen to the British. Blénac escaped and Rodney was faced with a serious dilemma. His orders were explicit: he was to make every warship available to Pocock for the Havana expedition. Pocock was due to arrive any day and yet the threat to Jamaica was real enough for immediate action to be taken. Rodney despatched Sir James Douglas (previously Commander-in-Chief of the Leeward Islands and now Rodney's second in command) to Jamaica, almost a thousand miles away, with the majority of his fleet: two bomb ships and twelve of the line, of which one was the *Temeraire*.

Although sending these ships hundreds of miles away from Pocock and Albemarle at first appeared entirely to undermine the viability of the Havana campaign, in fact their role now proved vital. By the time Douglas arrived in Jamaica, it was clear that the threat to the island had passed. Blénac, in fact, had been to Havana in an attempt to raise Spanish forces to join him in attacking Jamaica, but had found a quiet city slumbering in its own security and entirely unaware that war had even been declared. The Governor of Havana was not prepared to take a French admiral's word that

Spain and Britain were at war and contribute troops from his precious garrison, so Blénac had left empty-handed with the French plans for a combined assault on Jamaica in ruins.

Blénac now lay at Cape François, on the northern shore of St Domingue (western Hispaniola), off the south-eastern tip of Cuba. There he was ideally situated to interfere with the British attack on Havana, as the cumbersome troop transports would have to pass him close by. Douglas now saw his opportunity. A convoy from New York was expected daily, and, ostensibly to protect their arrival, he ordered a number of warships, including the *Temeraire*, to cruise between Cape François and the island of Tortue (Tortuga). In doing so they not only protected the convoy, but also blockaded the French in Cape François and thus prevented them from uniting with the Spanish ships at Havana, or interfering with Pocock's preparations for the Havana attack. Indeed, by now Blénac had heard of the British intentions towards Havana and planned to return to reinforce the garrison. However, upon seeing the powerful British squadron cruising offshore, he stayed where he was, leaving the British preparations to go ahead unopposed.

Once the convoy had safely passed by St Domingue, and Pocock had gathered the majority of his force at Cape St Nicholas, the *Temeraire* and the other ships blockading Blénac were ordered to join the main invasion force. They arrived on 25 May: nineteen ships of the line, three 50-gunners, nineteen frigates or lesser warships, a hundred and sixty troop transports, victuallers, ordnance vessels, hospital ships and 12,600 men. If it was a stunning achievement to have united such a vast invasion force safely, at a single point in seas thousands of miles from home, and with two hostile fleets in the vicinity, the next challenge was more formidable still: this fleet now had to get to Havana, and ideally it had to do so entirely unobserved.

The plan for the British assault rested on the Spanish assumption that all attacking ships would be forced to approach Havana from the south-east, that the Old Bahama Channel to the north was impassable by a large fleet. The man behind the scheme was George Anson, a man who had circumnavigated the world between 1740 and 1744, and to whom navigational hazards were particular challenges. Moreover, somewhere on his travels Anson had stolen, captured or otherwise acquired an accurate Spanish-drawn map of the Old Bahama Channel and he was sure that, with adequate care and preparation, it could be navigated. If he was right, the Spanish would be taken totally by surprise. The prevailing winds blew straight down the channel, so the fleet could travel very quickly to its destination. Indeed, so poor were communications on Cuba that the British ships could travel considerably faster than a message could be carried on horseback from one end of the island to the other: surprise was not just hoped for, it could almost be guaranteed.

To assist in this extraordinary venture, Pocock had found ten Spanish pilots, all of whom claimed to know the channel, but upon close examination, nine of them were found to have no significant knowledge of the waters at all and the only one who did was extremely old and almost blind. Neither Pocock nor Anson was prepared to undertake such a venture on the strength of Anson's mysterious map alone, and now, without pilots, there was only one sensible option: the channel would have to be surveyed. The frigate *Richmond* was ordered to sound and survey its entire length of almost five hundred miles and to produce detailed sketches of the land on each side from a number of specific locations. While she was doing so, the *Richmond*'s captain was given specific orders to kidnap any Spanish pilots he came across.[25]

The survey was uneventful and once the *Richmond* had returned, without any kidnapped Spanish pilots but with detailed sailing directions and confirmation that Anson's chart was indeed accurate, the fleet set sail. There was no stopping: on 3 June a boy fell overboard from the *Temeraire*, but no effort was made to save him, and he was left to be picked up by a troop transport.[26] The armada was preceded by a number of small vessels which took soundings along the way, and marked every significant cay or reef with a buoy, by lighting a fire or anchoring a ship's boat near it. This was so effective that the narrowest and most dangerous part of the channel, between Cay Lobos and Cay Comfite, was actually passed at night. To protect the vulnerable transports a novel fleet formation was adopted, the great fleet being divided into seven divisions. Each division was protected by three warships, one on the left flank, one in the centre, and one on the right. Behind the centre guard-ship lay the huge mass of transports, further protected by extra warships to their right and left. The *Temeraire* led the fourth division, and sailed at its front, in the centre. Behind her came a full twenty-four storeships, four of which were loaded with fascines (bundles of brushwood) for the coming siege, two with negroes to provide manpower to build the batteries, three with horses, and six with the baggage of the general officers.[27] Everything proceeded smoothly until a number of Spanish ships were met at the far western end of the channel, but with so much at stake they were mercilessly hunted down by British frigates. Some were captured while others were driven inshore where they could pose no threat to the secret mission. Only a week after they had left Cape St Nicholas, the entire fleet of almost two hundred sail was clear of the channel and less than a hundred miles from Havana. To put this success into context, a delayed squadron attempted to navigate the channel and join up with the British forces at Havana at the end of July, but one warship and five transport ships were wrecked at the entrance; they did not even make it in, let alone navigate its whole length safely.

In Havana, meanwhile, the Spanish were confident if increasingly unsettled. They had met Blénac but had still not received official word from Madrid that Spain was at war with Britain. Attacks by British privateers on Spanish merchantmen were a certain sign that hostilities had been declared, but it was not the definitive proof that the Governor of Havana sought. Only the most rudimentary precautions were taken for Havana's defence. Spanish merchantmen were told of the potential hostility of the British, the Havana garrison was placed on alert and three warships were recalled from Mexico. However, with no British naval concentration reported at Jamaica the Spanish still considered themselves safe. The twelve beautiful ships of the line lying inside Havana harbour remained without their sails bent, as if laid up for winter. If united with the remaining seven Spanish ships in the Caribbean, they would form a force to match the British and, if combined with Blénac, would outnumber them by far. Nevertheless, no long-range reconnaissance patrols were ordered to ascertain the reality of the situation and the Spanish governor even jokingly wrote to the Minister of the Indies that he requested a transfer to Florida, as otherwise he would have no opportunity to distinguish himself in the coming war. It is a letter of stunning ignorance: he knew neither that he already was at war nor that a huge British invasion force was bearing down on him along the invisible north shore of Cuba.

Even when the British fleet appeared over the western horizon, and the alarm was raised from the watchtower of the great El Morro fortress, the governor declared that the fleet was a Florida-bound convoy of harmless merchantmen, and he returned home, having ordered the garrison to stand down. Then he went to church. Meanwhile the strange fleet did not disappear over the horizon, but came closer. And the closer they came, the more it became apparent that the fleet consisted of numerous warships, all of which were towing flat-boats, and that they were intent on Havana. The governor was not summoned again until he had finished Mass. This was, after all, Pentecost, one of the major festivals of the Catholic Church, and to disturb a service with wild claims of a British fleet approaching would be unseemly and might cause panic. When he once more mounted the steps at El Morro, however, the situation was unmistakable. A vast fleet lay silhouetted against a thunderous sky: Havana was going to be attacked, and very soon. Even as he watched, a number of fleet auxiliaries started to probe the shoreline for suitable places to land.[28]

The very next morning the British landed, demonstrating the lightning speed at which their amphibious forces could now work. The enemy had been taken by complete surprise and given no time to recover. In a similar fashion to the attack on Belle Isle, a feint was launched while the main force landed elsewhere. In this case Pocock himself led the feint with a formidable force of twelve of the line, several frigates, ordnance ships, victuallers and storeships. Their boats were filled with the ships' marines and were rowed ashore near Chorera, four miles west of Havana. Meanwhile, Albemarle's army was embarked into the flat-boats at dawn. At 9 a.m. they began to move towards the shore at Coximar, six miles east of Havana. Once again the *Temeraire* was in the thick of the action, her captain and crew honoured with the protection of the main fighting force. A contemporary image gives an imaginary impression of how the ships lined up that day to embark the troops and escort the fireships (fig. 4). Arranged in three divisions, the centre was commanded by Augustus Hervey, the right wing by Captain Barton of the *Temeraire* and Captain Drake, and the left wing by Captains Arbuthnot and Jekyll.[29]

Three ships bombarded a small fort that guarded the landing site, and two small warships raked the beach and forest with a hailstorm of lead to clear the way for the troops. In the first wave alone, 3,963 infantry landed, together with light infantry, grenadiers and artillery. There was no opposition. For the next two days the army established a foothold and there were a number of skirmishes, particularly when the British crossed the Coximar

River. By 9 June the army needed to establish a route by which food, water, cannon, shot, powder, ball and building materials to construct batteries could be transported to the front line. As at Martinique, this was where the seamen excelled and a strong naval force of six lieutenants, twenty-four midshipmen and a hundred and eighty seamen from six ships of the line were landed at Coximar to cut a road through the woods and begin moving ships' cannon to the front line. One lieutenant, four midshipmen and thirty seamen from the *Temeraire* made up a sixth of that force, and the entire shore party of sailors was placed under the command of Matthew Barton of the *Temeraire*. Time was of the essence and, as at Belle Isle, each man only carried three days' worth of provisions with him.[30]

Once the road had been cut, tons of supplies and stores had to be landed in the surf and transported over the log-laid road through the thick forest. To make matters worse, gallons of fresh water had to be brought by boat from Chorera on the other side of the bay, landed and then carried overland, all under fire from the Spanish warships in the harbour and the guns of El Morro itself. The exact role of the *Temeraire* in these tasks, all of which were entrusted to British sailors, remains unclear, but it is certain that by 15 July she had landed *all* of the cartridges she had for her 32lb guns, with the exception of only forty, which were retained for the few guns she still had aboard. Over the next two days she sent ashore five hundred 32lb shot. Not surprisingly, therefore, in undertaking such hot and thirsty work the crew of the *Temeraire* drank the ship dry of her rum, and she had to be supplied with more from another ship, the *Temple*. Food for those lucky enough to be aboard was regularly augmented with fresh fish, caught by the *Temeraire*'s pinnace.[31] Onshore the soldiers and sailors suffered appallingly from thirst: 'The bad water brought on disorders which were mortal,' wrote one, 'you would see the men's tongues, hanging out parched like mad dog's, a dollar was frequently given for a quart of water.'[32] To ease the sufferings of those fighting, great teams of sailors carried water ashore while others worked in shifts sewing sandbags out of old sails or making blinds to protect troops in the batteries from snipers.

Nevertheless, through extraordinary exertion, by 1 July four great batteries had opened fire on the fortress of El Morro. The sailors then distinguished themselves in their gunnery, and some of the guns were serviced by ship's crews. There was even one battery, known as the 'sea battery', manned exclusively by sailors from Keppel's flagship, the *Valiant*. Their efficiency and accuracy stunned the army. One soldier wrote: 'our sea folks begin a new kind of fire unknown, or at all events unpractised by artillery people. The greatest fire from one piece of cannon is reckoned by them from 80 to 90 times in 24 hours, but our people went on the sea system, firing extremely quick and with the best direction ever seen and in sixteen hours fired their guns 149 times.'[33] For those who had built the batteries it was heartbreaking that, shortly after the commencement of the bombardment, the largest, which had taken six hundred men seventeen days to build, caught fire and was completely destroyed. Despite the setback it was swiftly rebuilt by a dedicated force of five hundred sailors and fifteen hundred negroes.[34]

The Spanish reaction to the attack made their situation far worse than it might have been. Taken so completely by surprise, they did not even have their log-boom ready, which should have protected the harbour. Their response was to sink three of their fine warships, *El Neptuno*, *El Asia* and *La Europa*, across the harbour mouth. This certainly prevented the British from entering the harbour, but the guns of El Morro and the large fleet of anchored Spanish ships inside the harbour were deterrent enough. By blocking the harbour mouth the Spanish had bottled up their entire fleet and granted Pocock absolute local control of the sea. With the French blockaded in Cape François, Pocock could do as he wished off Havana, unthreatened and unchallenged for the present and foreseeable future. That was one of the main reasons why warships like the *Temeraire* could unload their guns, cartridges and shot, and send their sailors ashore to help the army with such confidence; there was simply no possibility of any attack at sea, and the full resources of the British squadron could be focused on the reduction of El Morro, for this was Albemarle's plan.

That plan has come under a great deal of criticism ever since. The city of Havana was crowded with civilians and poorly protected – it could have been taken quickly and relatively easily, and speed in this operation was of the essence. The hurricane season was only a few weeks away and the men were already dying in their hundreds from yellow fever, which some claimed had been brought to Havana by the ships, like the *Temeraire*, which had served at Martinique. Whether or not this is true, the *Temeraire* was certainly suffering, and her crew was very sickly including her captain.

Nevertheless, Albemarle opted instead for a traditional siege of El Morro, the strongest part of the defences. He was a man who did things by the book, and this was the way that he had been taught. Batteries were therefore raised against El Morro and it was bombarded night and day for six weeks.

Little progress was made at first and it was decided to augment the landward attack by a seaborne bombardment of the fortress. Four ships were chosen for this dangerous task, and they were led by the incorrigible Augustus Hervey. Scouting missions at night had determined that the water was deep enough for the ships to approach quite close, but shallow enough for them to anchor. It remained unclear, however, whether once the ships were in position their guns could be brought to bear on the fortress. On the other hand, it was obvious to everyone that those ships could easily be targeted from the heights of the fortress. Nevertheless, Hervey took the ships in, slowly and steadily in the light winds, and the gunners in the fortress massed on the seaward side. The prospect was too much for the captain of the *Stirling Castle*, who fell behind, despite repeated signalling from Hervey. Once the ships had anchored, the gunners of El Morro fell on their motionless prey and they were savaged. In return, the ships' fire inflicted almost no damage on the fortress, the cannon simply blasting away ineffectively at the heavy rock foundations. It was in the midst of the carnage on the British ships that Hervey, who had now run aground and was unable to retreat, calmly sat down to write an official report to Keppel.

> I am unluckily aground, but my guns bear. I cannot perceive their fire
> to slacken ... I am afraid they are too high to do the execution we
> wished. I have many men out of combat now, and officers wounded;
> my masts and rigging much cut about, and only one anchor. I shall
> stay here as long as I can and await your orders ...

Shortly after he scribbled a private message to Keppel asking for help, and he signed off, in one of the perfect understatements in military history, 'often duller, and ever yours, A. Hervey'.[35]

Hervey's ship was eventually refloated and the squadron recalled, but by then over two hundred sailors and the captain of the *Cambridge* were dead. It was not a complete disaster, however, as the batteries had taken their opportunity to bombard El Morro on its landward side while the garrison focused on the threat of the warships. All but two guns on the landward side of the fortress had been dismounted and it was even considered possible that a 'practicable breach' could be made. They were wrong: the Spanish soon remounted their guns and focused once more on the British batteries. A full month passed, the British troops succumbing now in shocking numbers to disease, before El Morro finally fell. Army engineers, assisted by West Country sailors who had once been tin-miners, mined the great fortress's walls, and when they were sprung on 31 July a slender breach was made. It was rushed by a small force and taken with only fourteen killed and twenty-eight wounded. Spanish prisoners were sent out to the waiting British ships, and the *Temeraire* received her quota.[36] Meanwhile the fighting continued around Havana but, with El Morro taken, the city itself soon surrendered. That, however, was not before the British had expended all of their ammunition, and been forced to beg of the Governor of Jamaica as much as he could spare.

The taking of Havana was one of the richest successes in history. Aside from the warehouses full of trade goods and other valuables, there was an entire fleet of fourteen sail of the line, each worth a small fortune. It has been estimated that the total money seized was in excess of £3,000,000. £737,000 was paid out to British troops as prize money, although the division of the loot, which had been agreed between Pocock and Albemarle before the attack, was strikingly unfair. The money was divided between two flag officers, forty-two captains, 183 lieutenants, 363 warrant officers, 1,302 petty officers and 12,607 seamen. Pocock and Albemarle each received over £122,000, while the lowliest seamen, the men who had made all of this possible, received only £3 14s 9¾d. That share was even less than an army private, who received £4 1s 8½d.[37]

Because so many Spanish ships were also taken, representing nearly a third of the entire Spanish navy, the capture of Havana was as much a naval victory as it was a traditional army conquest. Spanish power in the West Indies was broken, the myth of Havana's impregnability destroyed and the lines between Old and New Spain severed. It had been won at great cost, however. Between 7 June and the middle of October, 5,366 soldiers and more than 1,200 British sailors died: only 744 had died from enemy action; the rest had been killed by disease. Of the navy's dead 93 per cent were killed by disease and many hundreds more were too badly weakened to fight. Only 560 of the army's dead were killed by the enemy.[38] In the last few weeks of the siege barely a day passed by without a death being recorded in the *Temeraire*'s log. One of those struck by the fever was her captain, the heroic Matthew Barton. He was so enfeebled that he was ordered home aboard another ship, and thus the *Temeraire* was separated from her first, but by no means her last, charismatic and highly successful captain. Barton arrived home in March 1763 and was paid off, but his constitution was broken and he never served afloat again. A contemporary biographer declared that 'as a husband, he was faithful and affectionate; as a master kind and forebearing; as a friend, unshaken and disinterested'.[39]

Men like Barton fighting in operations like those against Belle Isle, Martinique and Havana took British maritime success to a new level. Every one was a masterpiece of planning, amphibious warfare and naval prowess, and they were all characterized by cooperation between navy and army. One witness at Havana wrote: 'Such was the resolution of our people, and such the happy consequences of that happy and perfect unanimity which subsisted between the land and sea-services, that no difficulties, no hardships, slackened for a moment the operations.'[40] In all three operations there are no particular instances in which the *Temeraire* stood out or covered herself in glory more than other ships, but that is entirely characteristic of this period of British amphibious success. Indeed, her lack of distinction marks her out as a particularly smooth operator. She was strong, steady and reliable; so much so that she was trusted time and again with significant responsibility, and her captain with command of the landing forces themselves. Her role was not prominent, therefore, but it was central to the fall of Belle Isle, Martinique and Havana, and by 1762 the *Temeraire*'s association with British naval success had established her reputation with such force that her name had already become immortal in the Royal Navy. Worn down by prolonged service in the Western Approaches and the Caribbean, she was already starting to age, but as her remaining days in active service fell, so her star rose.

4.

The New *Temeraire*

JULY 1793 – JUNE 1799

His Majestys Ship Temeraire Chatham

The next twenty years of the *Temeraire*'s life were remarkably undistinguished in comparison to the previous five. She stayed at Havana until October 1762, before sailing to the Jamaica station. As she left she ran foul of one of the Spanish warships deliberately sunk, but as soon as she was clear things started to look up. On 28 October the British fell in with a French convoy and the *Temeraire* won for herself a prize – the 20-gun French frigate *Volunteer*. The rest of the British fleet mopped up two more frigates and five of the merchantmen, laden with sugar, coffee and indigo. It was a valuable haul in itself, but only the day before, the British prize agent had come aboard and paid the men their monies owed from the reduction of Havana, and now out at sea the sickness that had bedevilled the British besieging forces lifted as quickly as it had arrived.[1] Once at Jamaica, the *Temeraire* was briefly under the command of yet another distinguished sailor, Adam Duncan, a towering man in both charisma and stature who more than thirty years later distinguished himself against the Dutch at the Battle of Camperdown in October 1797, one of the hardest fought of the age of sail. By 1763 the *Temeraire*'s captain had changed once more, and she was commanded by Richard Bickerton, who had made his name as a frigate captain aboard the 20-gun *Glasgow*. To be given command of the 74-gun *Temeraire* was quite a promotion, but it would have been particularly welcome because he was present as captain of the *Ætna* fireship at the Battle of Lagos, when the *Temeraire* was first taken. There was little immediate prospect of glory, however, as in the year when Bickerton became captain of the *Temeraire*, the Treaty of Paris was signed, bringing to an end the Seven Years War. The *Temeraire* was ordered back to British shores and paid off in August. A month later she was surveyed, and after a small repair was fitted as a guardship and sent to Plymouth, where she remained for eight peaceful years. She then made a brief and perhaps nostalgic return to the site of her capture, when she transported a regiment to Gibraltar and returned with troops who were due leave. Upon her return she was posted as a guardship at Plymouth once more, and there she remained, her active-service life over.

While the *Temeraire* slowly rotted in Plymouth, an event of great significance to the outcome of this story occurred in Maiden Lane, Covent Garden. On 23 April 1775, Mary Marshall, daughter of a family of artisans and tradesmen and wife to a barber, gave birth to a son. Three weeks later the babe was baptized, and named Joseph Mallord William Turner. Perhaps nothing is more appropriate to the astonishing life of this child than that he was born on St George's Day, the feast day of the patron saint of England, for he was to become the best loved of all British painters.

That he began to sketch when he was young and was prodigiously gifted in youth is certain; the earliest known paintings by Turner are of Margate, made when he was only twelve. His father is believed to have encouraged his talents and even advertised his son's paintings for sale in the window of his barber's shop. Turner appears to have been painting professionally, or at least being paid and commissioned to produce paintings, by the age of fifteen, shortly after he had been entered as a student at the Royal Academy, in 1789. He exhibited his first work at the Royal Academy in 1790 and won the Society of Arts prize for landscape drawing in 1793. A year later one of his sketches was engraved for the first time. It was a distant view of the bridge and city of Rochester in Kent, an ancient city dominated by a castle and within spitting distance of Chatham dockyard, one of the greatest naval dockyards in Britain. Turner did not know it then, but he was less than a mile from the newly formed hull of the ship that would forever be associated with his name and which would raise him to the pantheon of the world's greatest artists.

The original *Temeraire*, once magnificent and her timbers scarred with glory, had long since disintegrated beyond further use in the still waters of the Hamoaze in Plymouth, and had been sold for £550 in 1784.[2] But this was not to be her inglorious end, for the Royal Navy, ever conscious of its heritage and the political value of history, made it a practice to preserve the names of particularly glorious ships. No one in the Admiralty had forgotten how the *Temeraire* had been captured from the French in 1759 or what she had achieved in the climax of the Seven Years War. So when a new and powerful three-decker of 98 guns was ordered to be built at Chatham, it was determined to name her *Temeraire*, in honour of her illustrious forebear.

That keel was laid in July 1793, four years after the fall of the Bastille and five months after Revolutionary France declared war on Britain. In the four years since the start of the Revolution, France had pursued a vigorous foreign policy, and in November 1792 she offered assistance to revolutionaries everywhere. French naval power was something of a muddle in these years, however. On the one hand, the French navy enjoyed an unprecedented level of prestige after the war of American Independence in 1775–1783. It was beaten badly at the Battle of the Saints by Rodney in 1782, but had played a significant role in stretching the resources of the Royal Navy, and had fought skilfully and well at the Battle of Ushant in 1778. Most significantly of all, however, it was the Battle of the Chesapeake in 1781 that had sealed the fate of the American Colonies. The British general, Earl Cornwallis, had fortified himself in the seaport of Yorktown, but was blockaded there by the French admiral, the comte de Grasse. The British fleet under Thomas Graves sailed to confront the French, but were unable to bring about a decisive battle, and the French returned to the Chesapeake while George Washington marched towards Cornwallis from the north. There was no hope of relief, and six weeks after the Battle of the Chesapeake, Cornwallis surrendered, along with his entire army. Britain sued for peace soon afterwards and the American states won their independence. They had been greatly aided in doing so by French sea power.

Not only had the French ships been effective, but their number and size had been growing during the war. A large building programme centred on three-deckers had begun in 1778, immediately after the Battle of Ushant in which the largest French ships had clearly demonstrated their worth. By 1783 they had five afloat and two more on the stocks. One of those, the *Commerce de Marseilles*, had 118 guns – much bigger than anything that had ever been built in Britain.[3] While these ships were being built, however, the navy itself began to disintegrate under the influence of the Revolution. Many of the officers who had served with success and gained experience in the American War were from aristocratic backgrounds with royalist sympathies, and they were ruthlessly cut out of the navy like rot from their own ships. They were replaced by seamen, many of whom had a great deal of experience of the sea but no experience of command. The new ships gleamed, therefore, but the navy was plagued by mutiny, disorder and fear.

The British, however, could take no comfort from this internal disorder, for the French had demonstrated that they had the infrastructure to man and equip a navy, albeit with difficulty, and they could certainly do so again. Indeed, after the American war an entirely new system of manning the navy was adopted with a future war against Britain in mind.[4] The fervour of the Revolution, moreover, gripped many of those sailors, and their courage and tenacity at this early stage in the Revolutionary War was not to be doubted or underestimated. The British were forced to respond to this French building programme, therefore, and in the decade between 1783 and 1793 a remarkable programme of shipbuilding, superintended by Charles Middleton, Comptroller of the Navy, and personally supported by the Prime Minister, William Pitt, saw thirty ships of the line built and eighty-four more repaired. When war finally broke out in 1793, British strength was equal to that of France and Spain combined.[5]

The new *Temeraire* was part of that building programme. She was a Second Rate, a uniquely British design: cheaper than First Rates, but still capable of providing the power and prestige of a three-decked ship of the line. It did not, however, make her necessarily smaller than First Rates. The ships of the British navy, as with any navy, were never all of a uniform class or age, but there was a continual process of overlap which saw new ships serve alongside old ships, and in this age of rapid improvement in ship design, new ships tended to be significantly larger than old. The *Temeraire*, for example, was part of the new *Dreadnought* class of Second Rates designed by Sir John Henslow in 1788, which were the largest Second Rate ships yet built. The *Temeraire*, furthermore, was the largest ship of that class, and was in fact so big that she was actually a foot longer than HMS *Victory*, the quintessential 100-gun First Rate of the Royal Navy. Indeed, the *Dreadnought* class of Second Rates were so large that they were re-classed in 1817 as First Rates of 104 guns. The *Temeraire* was also unusually armed for a Second Rate. It was normal for these ships to be armed with 32-pounders on the lowest deck, 18-pounders on the gun deck and 12-pounders on the upper deck, but the *Temeraire* was armed with 18-pounders on both top decks, and her sheer draught bears a note to the effect that the Lords Commissioners of the Admiralty had approved the departure from custom.[6]

Although she was classed as a Second Rate, therefore, in the fleets in which she first served, the *Temeraire* stood out as one of the largest and most powerful ships afloat. Unlike so many of the smaller ships of the line and frigates which were contracted out to private shipbuilders, all of these prestigious three-deckers, both First Rates and Second Rates, were built at the Royal Dockyards. The honour of constructing the *Temeraire* went to Chatham, the very yard where HMS *Victory* herself had been built almost forty years earlier. It was the first coincidence that was to splice the fate of these ships together.

Chatham dockyard lies ten miles up the winding River Medway, on its southern shore, and was one of the most important of the Royal Dockyards. Deptford, Woolwich and Portsmouth were all older, but Chatham could still trace its royal heritage to Edward VI, who wintered his ships in the Medway in the late 1540s. A little over sixty years later, Chatham received its first dry dock and began to expand rapidly. The first ship built there was the 56-ton pinnace *Sunne* in 1586, and nearly five hundred ships followed her into the Medway before the shipyard was shut down in 1984.

Chatham's location made the dockyard's success. It was close enough to London to be easily reached by naval administrators and for the yard to access the naval stores imported to London. It also had wonderful access to the oak forests of the south-east, particularly around the Weald of Kent. As with all dockyards, however, the principal advantages of Chatham's location become especially clear when it is approached from the sea. The Medway provided an anchorage for the entire British fleet, an anchorage which was relatively safe from attack as it lies so far upriver, but which nevertheless lay close enough to the capital and reinforcements in case of attack. Finally, and crucially, the mouth of the Medway does not open onto the English Channel, but to the southern extremities of the North Sea, making it strategically perfect for a naval war with the Dutch. Thus Chatham grew throughout the seventeenth century to become an important shipbuilding yard and a naval base in its own right: it was where the fleet was built, repaired, fitted, armed and laid up. An immense infrastructure developed around Chatham, and it became a defended town with a formidable gatehouse and surrounding ditches and walls, designed to prevent goods being taken out as much as to stop invading armies breaking in. The river itself was protected by forts along its length at Gillingham and Cookham Wood.

By the late eighteenth century, however, Chatham's star had started to fade. The focus for the last fifty years had been on wars not with the Dutch, but with France, Spain and America, and the navy needed yards that gave easy access to the Western Approaches, to the Atlantic and beyond. As a result Portsmouth and Plymouth had become the main naval bases while the fortunes of Chatham, facing east, declined. To make matters worse, the Medway had been steadily silting up, and without a favourable wind it could take ships as much as six weeks to reach the open sea. Once they were at sea a squadron still faced the formidable challenge of sailing the wrong way up the English Channel, directly into the prevailing wind. Naval forces at Chatham were simply unable to respond quickly enough to the continually shifting strategic situation in the global wars of the mid- to late eighteenth century. However, while Chatham lost its role as major naval base in the 1770s, it still retained a great deal of importance as a shipbuilding yard. The infrastructure was all in place and, hidden so far up the English Channel and with no French or Spanish naval bases in sight, it was completely safe.

As an industrial complex, Chatham dwarfed all others in England and covered almost seventy acres. Even the individual buildings such as the sail loft were larger than the largest buildings of the private firms. The Royal Dockyards were also the focus of the largest skilled communities in the country. Nowhere else could one find such a variety of trades as that which united to build these warships. They were then some of the most sophisticated single structures created by man, representing an achievement which has been compared by some historians with the construction of the medieval cathedrals. Everywhere were buildings designed and built for a different purpose. Dotted around the base in the formal pattern of rigid Georgian planning were wharves and jetties, slips, storehouses, mast and plank houses, seasoning sheds, saw pits, carpenters, joiners', smiths' and painters' shops, rigging houses, officers' houses, open spaces for stacks of timber, mast ponds, a ropery, a hemp house, a tarring house, a hatchelling house, a sail shed, a sail loft, a chest room, a kiln, a treenail house, a beam house, a capstan house, a plank house and a boat house, and that is not all. Chatham had four single docks and six slips, more than anywhere else apart from Portsmouth, and was the only yard apart from Plymouth that could accommodate three First Rates on slips. In 1790, just three years before work on the *Temeraire* began, 1,589 men were employed there.[7]

We are particularly fortunate that so much of the dockyard at Chatham survives today. Many of the original buildings at Portsmouth or Plymouth were badly bombed in the Second World War, and the interiors of most of those that survived have been dramatically changed, but at Chatham the majority of the site is as it was when it was built, making it easily the best preserved of the Georgian dockyards. Indeed, if one visits Chatham today, it is not too difficult to imagine the yard in full flow in 1793 when the *Temeraire* was laid down. The great gatehouse survives; the sailmakers' loft, built in the 1720s, is partly constructed of beams from a seventeenth-century warship; the ropery, an extraordinary building 1,135 feet or nearly a quarter of a mile long, still makes rope today on the site where rope has been made since 1618.

We are also particularly fortunate in being able to create an image of the landscape in which the *Temeraire* was built because Daniel Defoe visited Chatham in the early eighteenth century, when the dockyard had already reached its height and employed as many men as in 1793. Defoe is famous for his works of fiction, particularly *Robinson Crusoe* and *Moll Flanders*, but few know that his output was exceptional in both its quantity and its quality. Samuel Johnson once named *Robinson Crusoe* as one of only three books readers ever wished longer, but historians must say the same for his extraordinary work *A Tour thro' the Whole Island of Great Britain* (1724–7), which is considered one of the most important books on eighteenth-century Britain ever written. He visited all the most significant places, and many unknown spots too, and he was careful to go to Chatham. 'The buildings here are indeed like the ships themselves', he wrote, 'surprisingly large, and in their several kinds, beautiful: the warehouses, or rather, streets of warehouses and storehouses for laying up naval treasure are the largest in dimension and the most in number, that are anywhere to be seen in the world.'

Defoe carries on in fine style, describing the buildings, the different stores and the extensive storehouses, the whole appearing to him,

> like a well-ordered city . . . and though you see the whole place as it
> were in the utmost hurry, yet you see no confusion, every man knows
> his own business . . . The expedition that has been sometimes used
> here in fitting out men of war is very great, and as the workmen
> relate it, 'tis indeed incredible; particularly, they told us, that the
> *Royal Sovereign*, a first rate of 106 guns, was riding at her moorings,

entirely unrigged, and nothing but her three masts standing . . . and
that she was completely rigged, all her masts up, her yards put to, her
sails bent, anchors and cables on board, and the ship sailed down to
Blake-Stakes in three days . . . I do not vouch the thing, but when I
consider first that everything lay ready in her storehouses . . . a thousand or fifteen hundred men to be employed in it and more if they
wanted; and every man knows his business perfectly well . . . it might
be done in one day if it was tried; certain it is, the dexterity of
English sailors in those things is not to be matched by the world.[8]

This is the world into which the *Temeraire* was born; an ancient heart of
British shipbuilding and sea power, and testament to the British commitment to the sea as the way to secure her present and future.

The very bones of the *Temeraire* were British as well: she was built in
Britain and she was built of Britain. In the eighteenth century there was no
finer material in Britain for the construction of ships' hulls than English oak,
and there was no finer oak in the entire country, with the possible exception
of the Forest of Dean, than that found in the south-east. There were a
number of reasons for this; this was not blinkered nationalism, but based on
considered expertise gained from centuries of shipbuilding. Firstly, English
oak trees are of the correct species – *Quercus robur*, which grows thick, strong
and gnarled. Secondly, the British climate is sufficiently mild for the oak to
grow at a sedate pace, and the slower a tree grows, the stronger it is. Finally,
English oaks did not grow in the great, dense oak forests of Europe in which
trees grow straight to compete for light, but in patchier woodland or in isolated hedgerows: the ideal conditions for the twisted forms that are ideal for
shipbuilding.

It is from such distorted trees that the finest shipbuilding timbers come.
The skeleton of the ship is made of curved pieces of timber that provide it
with its complex underwater shape, and each section of these curved timbers
must come from a single piece of wood, with the grain following the curve of
the intended part. In particular and most important are the timbers which
provide the wine-glass shape of the hull, known as the 'futtocks', and those
which support the decks from underneath at either end, just like a modern
shelf-support and which are known as the 'knees'. The best wood, moreover,
came from the clayey soil and the mild climate of the south-east, and so

Chatham was especially blessed with the resources required. We know that most of the timber that built the *Temeraire* came from Hainault forest in Essex, augmented by supplies from Kent, Sussex and Surrey. In total, she was built of 5,760 'loads' of timber, each load consisting approximately of the timber from a substantial tree, or some fifty cubic feet. All in all, over 288,000 cubic feet of timber were used to build the hull of the *Temeraire*.[9]

The masts and spars, however, were another matter entirely. The ideal timber for the rigging was of uniform girth, cylindrically straight, supple and strong and almost elastic in its properties. If one visits a modern mast-making shop, and sees a mast being made of the finest mast timber, one should be able to twist the chips that come from it without them breaking. Unlike deciduous trees, conifers secrete a sap which keeps the timber supple as long as it stays in the tree. Once the tree has been cut, it is necessary to block the outside air entirely from the freshly cut log, to prevent the sap from drying out. To this end, huge mast ponds were built at the largest dockyards, in which the timbers were kept submerged until selected by the shipwrights. The great oak, on the other hand, was laid out in huge piles in the dockyard, specifically so that it *could* dry out: tough oak was dry oak.

For the masts, therefore, pines and firs were ideal, and the best of all was *Pinus sylvestris*, but as with oak it was not enough simply to find this species of tree; it also had to be grown in a specific climate, one with short hot summers and long cold winters. The British Isles, even in the far north of Scotland, was unable to produce anything approaching the quality required. The nearest landscapes that met those requirements were the mountain slopes of northern Russia and the Baltic, and it was from there that the masts and spars came. A large quantity of planking also came from those shores, as in 1793, when the *Temeraire* was built, mechanical sawmills had yet to be introduced into Britain. Indeed, the sawpits where sawyers worked together to cut and shape timber survived at Chatham until very recently. Abroad, however, machines were used to cut the tall trees from the dense European forests into the long planks that were ideal for shipbuilding. Danzig in particular was the centre of this trade. The logs were floated down the Vistula from the mountains and once near the shore were cut into planks using windmill-powered saws.

The other major sources of British shipbuilding materials at the end of the eighteenth century were the forests of North America, although access had of course been greatly restricted by the loss of the American colonies in the previous war. Elsewhere, the extraordinary teak forests of India and Africa were beginning to show their worth. Thus, although one might consider a warship such as the *Temeraire* to be a 'heart of oak', it was more than possible that she could be built from a variety of timber from six different continents.[10]

Nevertheless, in terms of the type of wood required, the new *Temeraire* would have differed only slightly from the old. Oak, albeit French rather than English, would have been used for the latter's hull and pine or fir for her masts and spars. But the new *Temeraire* differed from her predecessor in two very important ways. Firstly, she was British built. This was important because the French tradition of building warships was markedly different. The business of ship design and shipbuilding is always a compromise between speed, manoeuvrability, storage space, strength and size. The French tended to sacrifice inherent strength to achieve speed. Their ships were long and relatively loose; often the timber was fastened with iron nails rather than the timber pegs known as 'treenails' that were used by the British. The second major difference was in the rate of ship. The old *Téméraire* was a Third Rate, two-decked, 74-gunner, but the new *Temeraire* was a Second Rate three-decked 98-gunner. She was a little over 10 per cent longer, each broadside carried 258lb more gun power and her hull capacity was 425 tons greater.

The 74-gunners were the backbone of the fleet. Large enough to stand in the line of battle, but fast enough to cruise and even to chase frigates, they were the perfect compromise in ship design and they dominated the world's navies. The three-deckers, on the other hand, were the prestige ships. Larger in every dimension, their masts were taller, their yards longer, their sails bigger. The sails were exceptionally heavy when wet and more crew were needed aloft to handle them: it was not unusual for as many as eighty sailors to lie along the foreyard of the largest men of war. Because these ships were so much larger they were substantially more expensive both to build and to run. The 98-gun *Temeraire* cost a total of £73,241 to build and fit, whereas a 74-gunner cost somewhere around £50,000. A 98-gunner was therefore 50 per cent more expensive than a 74, but only mounted a third more guns. The gain in gun power was less than the extra cost might suggest, but the three decks gave a great deal more room, particularly for the officers' quarters. It was therefore more suitable as a flagship, in which an admiral might entertain his captains on a regular basis. The three decks also gave the ship a distinctive silhouette; they were easily recognized by both friend and enemy, which, in an age in which action defined leadership, was essential.

The make-up of the new ship's armament is also indicative of her strength in comparison to a 74-gunner. The two decks of the 74 were the equivalent of the lowest two decks of the 98-gunner: both ships carried their heaviest guns, 32-pounders, on the lowest deck and lighter guns, 24-pounders, or sometimes 18-pounders, on the deck above. That deck of lighter guns was then replicated aboard the three-deckers to make the upper deck. Therefore 74s did not represent the weaker two-thirds of the *Temeraire*'s armament, but the stronger. Still, with twelve more cannon on each side, together with eight 12-pounder long guns on her quarterdeck and two more on her forecastle, the firepower of the *Temeraire* could be devastating in battle, particularly against a smaller ship when the highest level of guns, still protected behind a wall of oak, would find themselves not faced with a similar wooden wall, but with open decks packed with humanity or a lattice of vulnerable rigging. That is why it was so essential in battle that the largest ships fought each other, and that there were sufficient ships of such a size to match those of the enemy. This, then, was the thinking behind the design and construction of the new *Temeraire*, which, when she was launched in 1798, entered a formidable fleet of eight First Rates of 100–120 guns, twenty Second Rates of 90–98 guns, a hundred and thirty Third Rates of 64–80 guns, twenty-five Fourth Rates of 50–60 guns, a hundred and thirty-five Fifth Rates of 32–44 guns, forty-nine Sixth Rates of 20–28 guns and two hundred and ninety-three other vessels. She was one of six hundred and sixty-one ships in the navy, but one of only twenty-eight of the most powerful.[11]

There were two more fundamental differences between the new *Temeraire* and the old, and they are most striking because the old *Téméraire* had spent the entirety of the previous war in the confined waters of Plymouth Sound. As a result she had not benefited from the two most significant developments in ship design of the 1780s and, arguably, of the entire century: by the 1790s, it was standard practice to fit warships with short and powerful guns known as carronades and to clad their hulls in copper.

The carronade was revolutionary because it was enormously powerful but extremely light, about a quarter of the weight of a long gun of the same calibre. It was short and fired a very large shot, and became known as the 'smasher' for its destructive capabilities. The key to this was its short barrel, which meant a low muzzle velocity. The large cannon ball, coming out at a relatively slow speed, caused the enemy hull to be crushed and splintered, rather than piercing it cleanly. It was light because it was short and because it was only used for short-range action, it only needed a smaller charge, which in turn meant that it could be cast from thinner metal. The result meant that the carronade could be mounted anywhere on a ship without endangering her stability and manned by only a handful of men. To arm a ship with carronades in addition to the armament for which it was originally designed was therefore a very effective way of increasing her firepower without compromising her stability. Crucially, the French gun foundries were simply unable to match these British guns, which were designed and cast at the Carron Iron Works in Scotland, and the French were forced to rely on the much weaker brass *orbusier*. The carronade was not only a leap forward in the armament of ships; it was a leap forward in the effectiveness of the Royal Navy at the expense of its rivals.

The impact of coppering ships' hulls was more subtle but no less significant. It had been known for some time that nailing copper sheeting onto the ships' hulls prevented infestation by the shipworm *Teredo navalis*, and also reduced fouling of the hull by weed and barnacles. Although the copper also became fouled, the length of time before the performance of the ship was significantly affected was longer than for a ship which was uncoppered. Coppering, therefore, greatly increased the service life of a ship and it vastly reduced the frequency of maintenance. This freed space and labour in the dockyards, whilst at sea the ships sailed faster than ever before. In a chase a coppered ship would now run down an uncoppered ship as surely as the tides rose and fell, while station-keeping in fleets became significantly easier as performance became more uniform. The cost of coppering the fleet was astounding – the fleet used around 949 tons of copper per year in the 1790s,[12] but it was a price that the Admiralty was prepared to bear. The benefits of coppering were also well known in France, but their ability to copper the fleet was gravely restricted by the ability of the French navy to source the copper nails which made the process possible: iron nails could not be used to fasten copper, as the resulting electrolysis rotted the fittings and, in the worst cases, the ships' bottoms simply fell out. One of the most significant aspects of the *Temeraire*'s construction, therefore, actually occurred in the days immediately after her launch, when she was hauled back out of the river and into dock no. 2, where she was coppered, the whole operation taking twelve days. A ship of her size would have required some 3,900 sheets of copper, each one measuring 4 feet by 1 foot 2 inches.[13]

Unfortunately no reliable record of the *Temeraire*'s decorations survive; they are not shown on her plans, and the only remaining model of her is made out of beef and mutton bone and built by one or more French prisoners of war, possibly interned in the 'Wool House' in Southampton (fig. 9). The model itself is a fine and particularly large example of a prisoner-of-war ship model, but it is unlikely to be accurate. Such models were built to be sold for food or better living and working conditions; the names of famous ships were attributed to them to increase their price but there is no guarantee that the prisoner had ever seen the ship he was modelling. Indeed, in many instances they acted as a blank canvas which allowed the modeller to demonstrate his skills at bone or wood carving with no reference to reality at all. Some of the finest prisoner-of-war models are so heavily carved that they are both a powerful expression of French artisanship and a troubling reminder of the time that they had on their hands. Undoubtedly some became an obsession, the only source of whiling away the hours. The *Temeraire* model is a particularly fine example not only for its size and quality of craftsmanship but for its obvious inaccuracies. Her hull is not quite right for a 98-gun Second Rate and is as fine as a Third Rate 74 in places, particularly the midship section. The rig is disproportionate, most noticeably in the dimensions of the bowsprit, jib boom and flying jib boom. Her stern, beautifully carved as it is, and the figurehead, a helmeted and armed Greek or Roman warrior, reproduced in a late nineteenth-century work on naval history and declared to be 'the head of the *Temeraire*', are both pure fantasy.[14]

The only painting that clearly shows the stern decorations of the *Temeraire* is that of her launch (fig. 7), by Philip Burgoyne, but it too is unreliable for a number of reasons. Buildings are depicted which did not exist at Chatham, and it is unlikely that she would have been painted in the stripes shown. That paint scheme, with the lids of the gunports painted black, was known as the 'Nelson Chequer' and, before 1805, was favoured only by those ships which served under Nelson. The *Temeraire* had at this stage not even been commissioned, and she was to spend her early years in the Channel

Fleet, while Nelson was commanding the Downs Squadron. It is far more likely that the *Temeraire* was painted in the traditional style of British ships of that period, with bright yellow sides and thick black strakes at the waterline, perhaps with her upper works picked out in red or blue. The marine artist Geoff Hunt's modern depiction is far more likely to be accurate (fig. 11).

It is more than possible, therefore, that Burgoyne's painting of her launch is imaginary and the accuracy of the details of the stern decoration must not be taken for granted. Nevertheless, that the painting shows the general style of the period is far more certain. Although it may appear heavily decorated, and there remains sufficient ornamentation on her taffrail at the top of the stern to demonstrate the *Temeraire*'s prestige as a flagship, the decorative scheme is remarkably austere in comparison with earlier ships, and there is a notable lack of carving on the quarter pieces and no carved or painted friezes on the side of the hull. Before 1700 average expenditure on carved works was £896, after 1737 it was £323 7s, and after 1815 it was only £100.[15] The stern of the *Temeraire* as depicted by Burgoyne, therefore, is in fact a perfect example of shipbuilding in the late eighteenth century: it is prestige without the glamour; it is a ship built to be strong and built to fight, her austerity reflecting the increased financial demands of war. The number of ships, not the quality of their decoration, had become the principal requirement. Faced with the combined might of the French and Spanish navies, and with a French government pouring more money into shipbuilding, it was numbers alone that would defeat Napoleon. This conservatism in design was a relatively new development. As recently as 1796, three years into the construction of the *Temeraire*, the Admiralty had ordered shipwrights to 'explode carved works'.[16]

Surprisingly, the only solid evidence we have of the stern decorations of the *Temeraire* can be seen at Balmoral Castle and Sandringham. Two great figures of Atlas, son of a sea nymph who herself was a daughter of Oceanus, were carved at either side of the ship's stern, their shoulders supporting the weight of the quarter gallery, just as in Greek mythology he bore the weight of the world. Replicas of these figures were built into two large gong-stands made from timber taken from the *Temeraire*, and presented to the Duke of York, the future King George V, on his marriage in July 1893, and another to Queen Victoria (figs 8, 30). It remains of some significance that the figures of Atlas were supporting a stern gallery at all, for the *Temeraire* was built at a time when the stern gallery – in effect a balcony – was falling out of fashion.

Much more research is needed to establish how and why this change came about, but it is certain that the *Temeraire* was a transitional ship. If one visits HMS *Victory* today, one can appreciate her 'closed' stern, the product of her 1800–1803 refit. The stern of the *Temeraire*, however, was 'closed' on the quarterdeck, but not on the upper deck, where she had a normal stern gallery which can just be made out from the shadows of a watercolour made on her return from the Battle of Trafalgar in 1805 (fig. 19).

The *Temeraire*'s other significant piece of decoration, the figurehead, is also something of a mystery. No images survive on her plans, but it is certain that the Admiralty's order of 1796 to 'explode carved works' was as applicable to figureheads as it was to stern carvings. Figureheads were now no longer full length, but half-length, or even busts or simple scrolls. There is some sketchy evidence that the *Temeraire* did not have a figurehead at all but a 'fiddle-head', a carved scroll like the curved volute at the head of a violin. These changes, however, were intensely unpopular in the navy. Ships needed eyes to find their way; they needed a personality with which the sailors could identify; they needed a figure in which to trust, as they lived their lives trapped between enemy, sea and sky. As a result the proposed fiddle-heads did not last long, but it has been suggested that the *Temeraire* was still fitted with one at the Battle of Trafalgar in 1805.[17] If the ship's crew were sufficiently well-off they could club together to pay for a new figurehead and it is possible that something like this happened after Trafalgar aboard the *Temeraire*. Her crew would have enjoyed some prize money and there is evidence that at some point she was fitted with a carved bust of a crowned head. In both Edward Cooke's painting of her at Sheerness in 1833 and J. J. William's sketch of her at Rotherhithe in 1838, a small bust of a crowned head, painted white, can clearly be seen (figs 31 and 33).

Even with a reduction in the detail of her carved and painted ornament, the *Temeraire* took a little over five years and two months to build, an average time for a three-decker. Some ships took a great deal longer. The *Royal George*, also a Second Rate but built a decade before the *Temeraire*, took eleven years and one month to build, one of the longest on record. She was laid down before the War of American Independence, and it is likely that her lengthy build-time was the result of financial restrictions imposed on the yard by that war, and a shortage of shipbuilding timber, some of which, prior to the outbreak of that war, would have come from New England. The

Temeraire, however, was built at a time when neither of these factors was significant. The government wholeheartedly supported the shipbuilding effort of the late 1780s and 1790s, a period when the administration of the navy itself underwent significant and successful reform.

Certainly there was some difficulty in finding the appropriate timber to construct the ships; the requirements of the navy were so specific that such difficulty was inevitable. The importance of the shape of the timbers has already been discussed, but it was also essential that each tree had reached full maturity, without being too old, so that the timbers were large enough but not rotten at the heart. An appropriate tree, therefore, would be somewhere between eighty and a hundred and twenty years old and between fifteen and eighteen inches in diameter. The timber for the all-important stern post, from which hung the rudder, had to be at least forty feet long and for the biggest ships twenty-eight inches thick. In every instance, the tree itself had to be within forty miles of a river, if the cost of moving the great logs was not to become prohibitive. Government purveyors would select a tree and mark it with a broad arrow, the traditional symbol of Crown property, and then tree-fellers would work in pairs, swinging their axes rhythmically and alternately into the thick oak. Usually the timbers were carted to the river and then loaded on barges or floated downstream to larger depots where they could be loaded. The difference between shipbuilding in the 1790s and in the 1770s, however, was that for the first time a conscious and systematic effort had been made to address the timber problem. Seasoning sheds were constructed in the major yards where the cut oak could dry out, and it was determined to build up and maintain a permanent stock of three years' supply of timber. By the time the *Temeraire* was built, therefore, the navy had both the money and the materials to construct her without interruption, and the shipwrights did so, working long hours. The normal working day was from 6 a.m. to 6 p.m. but frequently overtime was required and paid for fairly: just five hours' work at night warranted another entire day's pay.[18]

When the time came for her launch, the slip was greased with four firkins of soap, bought specially for the occasion, and she slipped into the Medway without drama. On 11 September 1798, the clerk to the commissioner of Chatham dockyard wrote briefly to the Admiralty, 'His majesty's Ship *Temeraire* was safely launched this day'.[19] Once the shipwrights had completed her coppering, she lay in the Medway for a full six months before she was commissioned and, on 21 March 1799, Captain Peter Puget came aboard and began to fit her out for active service. Puget was another man of some repute who had served as a lieutenant in George Vancouver's 1791 exploration of the Pacific north-west coast of America, where his name survives today in the vast expanse of inland sea known as Puget Sound.

Puget's first job, as it was for every captain in the Royal Navy, was to surround himself with those he had sailed with before. By 5 April he had petitioned the Admiralty for a master at arms, a midshipman, a coxswain, a master's mate and a number of seamen, all of whom were requested by name for transfer from other ships. These men at least were fit, but others Puget was provided with were in no state to sail on his magnificent new ship. In particular, the gunner appointed to the *Temeraire* suffered from an appalling cocktail of afflictions: rheumatic gout, asthmatic cough, and 'swimming in the head' which made him fall over suddenly and unexpectedly. Another was declared unfit simply due to old age, while Thomas Hitchcock had suffered that most common of sailor's ailments, an internal rupture – a hernia. William Phillips had broken his hand; Christopher Carrouche was wheezy; John Stubbs had bruised loins; and poor old John Davids was incontinent.[20]

Exact figures for the fitting out of the *Temeraire* do not survive but we can say with confidence that she would have been rigged with approximately seven hundred and fifty blocks, twenty-five miles of rigging, thirty-seven sails giving a total of 6,510 square yards of canvas, and her mainmast, when stepped, would have been around 205 feet high. She would have had seven anchors of varying size, the largest of which weighed nearly five tons. Such anchors were the largest objects of iron forged in the eighteenth century and, of course, they were made at Chatham. One visitor who witnessed the Chatham forge at work marvelled at the skill of the blacksmiths:

> We had the pleasure of being in the smith's shop at the instant the
> several workmen were turning the anchor of a man of war of four ton
> weight then in the fire; all our attentions were engrossed as it was a
> surprising thing, and we were filled with horror at the glowing heat
> of the several workmen, who with great dexterity managed the affair;
> anchors are made by hammering piece upon piece.[21]

In another special workshop at Chatham, the ship's boats would have been built and fitted. These boats were crucial to the operation of all sailing warships, which were so large and cumbersome that they very rarely came alongside wharves or jetties; *everything* therefore had to be transported to them by boat. The boats were specifically designed to carry both men and stores, particularly casks, and the largest boat of a ship as large as the *Temeraire* would have been designed to store as many as fourteen water-butts snugly on their back, and still allow room for extra passengers and for the men to row her if she was not to be sailed. The boats were also crucial for communication within the fleet and particularly so for the *Temeraire* which, as a three-decked second rate, was designed to be used as a flagship, the command centre of the fleet or squadron. Every ship in that squadron would look to the flagship for inspiration in uncertain times, her movements to be copied by all others. Even the distance between the flagship and her next astern was to be used as a template for the station-keeping of the entire fleet. While the fleet commander would signal to his squadron using flags, lights and guns, depending on the weather, the signalling system was still cumbersome in 1799 when the *Temeraire* was launched and it was still extremely difficult for a commander to explain exactly what he meant, particularly if a certain manoeuvre had not been prearranged. It was on the boats of his flagship that a commander would rely to reprimand, encourage, instruct and explain, usually in that order.

The ships' boats were also essential for navigation and anchor work. In unknown shoal water they would be sent ahead to sound a safe passage, and if fast aground or becalmed, the largest boat, the launch, would take the sheet anchor a distance away from the bow and drop it. The ship would then be hauled towards the anchor before it was raised, and the whole exhausting operation repeated, dragging the great bulk of the ship forward. In light winds the boats would even tow her if the need was great enough. Towing was appallingly hard work, but once she had gained momentum, a ship as large as the *Temeraire* could be towed at a steady, if slow, speed. Even the smallest headway was crucial, for at just one knot a ship could still retain some steerage and could manoeuvre. In a chase that could make all the difference as she would be able to protect her vulnerable stern and aim her broadside at will.

It is all too easy to consider the warship only as a gun-platform, but the boats themselves were also a very important part of her role as a weapon of war. They extended the warship's reach and influence far beyond her immediate locality or effective gun-range. In 'cutting-out' operations, a significant part of naval warfare throughout the eighteenth century, a ship's boats would be sent, usually under the cover of night, into an enemy anchorage where they would board an enemy ship, subdue the crew and sail her out as a prize. As the first *Temeraire* demonstrated at Belle Isle and Havana, boats were also critical in amphibious operations transporting troops and sailors ashore and keeping them well supplied once there. Although the concept of 'lifeboats' had not become firmly established by 1799, the ship's boats were also, of course, used to rescue anyone unfortunate enough to fall overboard and lucky enough for his fall to have been witnessed.

The ship's boats, therefore, were more than an addition to the *Temeraire*; they were a crucial component in her ability to sail and to fight, and all warships of her size were equipped with as many as six boats of varying design and size. Those that were to serve as flagships were always given an extra barge, the most prestigious and highly decorated of the ship's boats, to transport the admiral. That is what the Admiralty had in mind for the *Temeraire* for, in March 1799, fresh orders came through to Chatham, for the *Temeraire* be fitted 'in all respects proper for the reception of a flag officer'.[22] At this early stage the fitting out was supported at the Crown's expense and the ship remained remarkably stark inside. Little more than tables and chairs would have been stowed, although the admiral's living quarters would have been lined with deal panelling, and decorated with paintings or carvings. Once an admiral had been appointed, however, he would bring with him whatever furniture he wished. Most flag-officers made certain that their living quarters were carpeted, but this was often the first of many luxuries, and some admirals' quarters were notably lavish. When Admiral Rodney was appointed to his flagship in 1779 he brought with him five beds, a large and small mahogany bedstead, a field bedstead and two cots. He even brought aboard two sofas.[23]

The hold, meanwhile, was gradually filled with the necessary stores, and foremost of those was candles. At night they were the only source of light, and even in daytime the ship was incredibly dark. Decks below the waterline relied entirely on borrowed light through hatchways and companionway ladders, and were in pitch darkness for most of the time. Sailors could let light into the gundecks by opening small hatches set into the gunports, known as scuttles, but this was not always possible or advisable in heavy weather, particularly on the lowest decks where water could easily come in as the ship rolled with the swell or heeled with the wind. Only in the admiral's and captain's great cabins and the officers' wardroom at the stern were the men able to get access to light but still be sheltered from the elements by the great glass windows. On the largest ships such as *Temeraire*, the glazing was continued a little way around the side of the hull, so that those officers with cabins looking out to the side also had access to a window. Nevertheless, at night they all had to resort to candle light, and deep in the hold of the *Temeraire* a significant portion of her stowage was given over to candles. When she finally left for her first service in June 1799 she took with her over three tons of candles.[24]

None of this would be possible, of course, if the seven hundred and thirty-eight men in her crew could not be fed, and one of the most important pieces of equipment on board any sailing man of war was the stove. Iron stoves had been common for over forty years by the time the *Temeraire* was fitted out, and she would have been equipped with a stove a little over nine and a half feet long and eight and a half feet high. It is also likely that she was issued with as many as seven smaller stoves, for stewing. Pigsties, sheep pens and hen coops provided the accommodation for the livestock that would add to the sailors' basic diet. On her short maiden voyage with only a minimal crew she took with her seventy-seven tierces of beef and a hundred and twelve of pork (a tierce was a cask for salt provision, of a size between a hogshead and a barrel), a hundred and twenty-six butts of beer, a hundred and twenty leaguers and three hundred and fifteen butts of water (weighing two hundred and sixty-nine tons),* thirty-six tons of bread, six tons of oatmeal, nine tons of pease, and so crucial to the sailors' well-being, four tons of tobacco. Her guns were loaded aboard from a specialist gun-hoy on the last day of May 1799, and five days later the *Temeraire* fired those guns for the first time, in celebration of the King's birthday. Shortly thereafter, her magazines were filled with four hundred and sixty barrels of powder, and her sails bent.[25]

---

* A leaguer was the largest water cask, containing 159 Imperial gallons.

Thus provisioned and equipped, and with three hundred and fifteen tons of iron ballast to give her stability, the *Temeraire* left for her inaugural service in June 1799, her draught both fore and aft a respectable twenty-two feet eleven inches, and her foremost gunports on her lowest deck six feet six inches above the waterline, the sternmost, five and a half feet, and her midship ports an acceptable, but to our eyes surprising, four feet and nine inches above the waterline. On 26 June, for the first time in her life, the *Temeraire* spread her wings. Every stitch of canvas was set, right up to the royals, the highest. Even her studding sails were set, these being rigged as auxiliary sails at the very edges of the main yards and protruding clear of the ship's sides, hanging suspended over the water like kites. Reports on her sailing qualities made later in her life reveal the characteristics of the ship that would have been felt for the first time during those days. Her best sailing trim was twenty-three feet six inches at the bow and a little over twenty-four feet at the stern; to achieve those measurements she needed to carry three hundred tons of iron ballast, seventy tons of shingle and three hundred and twenty-three tons of water. She rode easily at anchor; stood well under her sails and rolled easily. As was typical of her class she was rather leewardly compared to other ships, but with all sail set and with the wind on the beam she could still make eleven knots – remarkable for a ship so large. She certainly seems to have stood out from other ships of her class: the *Duke* was neither 'weatherly nor fore-reaches with other men of war', the *London* 'does not stand under her canvas particularly well' and the *Prince* 'sailed worse than other ships'. Not so for the *Temeraire*, however, and she would have been a magnificent sight with her sails set, testing the waters around Beachy Head that June weekend, but it was not long before the realities of life under sail made themselves felt. On 30 June, just four days into her first cruise, Seaman William Pinder fell overboard and drowned despite the efforts of the crew who launched the jolly boat.[26]

She was ordered to the Channel Fleet, to serve as the flagship of Rear-Admiral Sir John Borlase Warren. Warren had served in the previous war as the first lieutenant aboard HMS *Victory*, and in the first few years of the war with France had established a reputation as an outstanding commander of a frigate squadron. In 1796 alone, his squadron destroyed or captured two hundred and twenty enemy vessels. Few knew the waters of the Channel better than Warren, but he had now been promoted, and his days of dashing around in frigates were over. He was ordered to command a squadron of ships of the line in the Channel Fleet, the real muscle over the sinew of the frigates, and the *Temeraire* was his designated flagship. It was to be a baptism of fire.

5.

The Blockading *Temeraire*

JULY 1799 – OCTOBER 1801

By 1799 the war at sea had reached a critical point. The French navy had been savaged at the Battle of the Glorious First of June in 1794 and again at the Battle of the Nile in 1798: indeed, by the end of 1798, France had lost sixty per cent of the fighting force that she had enjoyed at the start of the war, and there were over thirty thousand French prisoners of war in British prisons. The Spanish and the Dutch, both French allies and both equipped with formidable navies, had also been beaten soundly, at the Battle of St Vincent in 1797 and Camperdown in 1798 respectively. Royal naval success in all of these battles had been complete, but considerable numbers of enemy ships still survived. In particular, the Spanish and the French navies had potent squadrons which, if united, could challenge the British for command of the sea and make possible a French invasion of England. In many respects, therefore, the strategic situation in 1799 was very similar to that in 1759 when the first *Téméraire* was captured: the French planned to invade, but to do so they first needed to achieve a naval concentration that could challenge the Royal Navy in the Western Approaches or the Channel.

The British response was to blockade Brest with the Channel Fleet. In fact the 'Channel' Fleet is something of a misnomer when discussing its role between 1799 and 1801, for the fleet as a whole rarely ventured further east than Torbay. A separate squadron anchored in the Downs took responsibility for the safety of the British coast from the Thames to Beachy Head and was particularly concerned with the French invasion force massing at Boulogne. The Channel Fleet occupied itself with its main enemy, the French at Brest. To blockade Brest was far easier said than done, however. The navigational hazards of northern Brittany have already been discussed, but it is also important to consider the local topography of Brest. Anyone who has travelled to Brest by sea cannot fail to appreciate the dangers of the approach, even if the safest route is taken. Brest lies up a winding passage known as the Goulet, only two thousand yards wide. Before that is reached, however, one must first approach Brest by one of three routes. To the north the Passage du Four runs between savage rocks with a tide that could propel a sailing warship at four knots with no sail set, but gives quick access to the English Channel. Directly to the west lies the Iroise, a much broader channel, twenty miles at its widest, which leads straight out into Biscay. Finally, to the south lies the Raz de Sein, similar to the northerly passage, but longer, scattered with more rocks, bounded by large islands, and with tides that course through at even greater speeds.

Watching Brest closely, therefore, could not be achieved by a single squadron, unless it was so far inshore that it patrolled the entrance to the Goulet itself. But to do so with a force large enough to face the threat of the full French fleet if it decided to sail was impossible, as the waters are too narrow and the Breton coast is a deadly lee shore. Sailing warships were enormously cumbersome and while some of the finest could make ground to windward, that is to say in the direction from which the wind was blowing, the largest could do little more than hold their own against the wind. They could tack by putting their bows through the wind, but it was a lengthy process that would take as much as fifteen minutes, and was not guaranteed to succeed. The only other way to change tack in an attempt to make ground to windward was to wear ship, turning the stern through the eye of the wind. This was more reliable, but required acres of sea room for each ship. The problems of manoeuvring more than one ship together were truly formidable, and would only be attempted against a lee shore in the direst of situations.

The practical problems of watching Brest were not new in 1799; indeed, they had first come to light when the French navy became a threat in the second half of the seventeenth century. Warships of that period were so poor at making ground to windward that one admiral insisted that a warship should always maintain forty-eight hours of sea room to leeward, and squadrons rarely went to sea between September and May.[1] Warship design had changed a great deal since then, but the ships were still propelled by square sails, and were therefore restricted by the basic mechanics of their rig: they were simply unable to sail any closer than seven points or $67.5°$ to the wind. There were two possible solutions to this combined problem of the need to blockade Brest and the difficulty of doing so: the first was the 'loose' or 'distant' blockade, the second the 'close' blockade.

The loose blockade worked on the principle that the British main Channel Fleet was held in readiness at Torbay, a large and safe anchorage protected from the prevailing south-westerly winds and close enough to Plymouth for those in need of repairs to make the most of the facilities of the naval dockyard. It was also sufficiently close for victuals and supplies to be sent to the fleet, and a reservoir had even been built in Brixham with special pipes running to the shore to aid ships in watering. The process of watching Brest was carried out by smaller squadrons or even individual ships, much more suited to sustained cruising on a hostile shore than cumbersome ships of the line. The enemy fleet's preparations to sail were always apparent from the visible bustle of activity in the port, and the inshore squadron regularly intercepted fishermen, or even risked an occasional dart inshore in a fast rowing boat to see the detail for itself. It was also obvious when the fleet could sail, as it needed a northerly or easterly wind to sail out of Brest. Furthermore, because of the navigational hazards of the approach, no fleet could make its way out on a single tide, but would be forced to wait in one of the large anchorages of Bertheaume or Camaret, just beyond the mouth of the Goulet, before running through the Passage du Four, the Iroise, or the Raz de Sein. If any movement of the French fleet was reported, a relay of messages could be swiftly sent back to the main fleet at Torbay. Thus, although Torbay is a hundred and twenty miles or approximately three days' sail distant, the British fleet could lie there confident that it could reach Brest in time to intercept the French fleet.

The second option, of close blockade, involved smaller inshore squadrons watching the entrances and exits of Brest, while the main fleet cruised out to westward, off Biscay. The choice between the two strategies rather depended on the immediacy of the enemy threat and the personality of the Channel Fleet's Commander-in-Chief. In 1799 the man in charge was the elderly Lord Howe, a strong supporter of the loose blockade. He had, in fact, spent so long in Torbay that he became known by many of the locals as the Earl of Torbay.

To impose either type of blockade was never easy, however, and the French occasionally managed to evade their British jailers. One such

instance occurred in April 1799, just three months before the *Temeraire*
joined the Channel Fleet. A powerful squadron under the command of
Eustache Bruix emerged from the Goulet and anchored in Camaret Bay
with a formidable force of twenty-five ships of the line and eight frigates.
On the night of the 26th they sailed, and were seen leaving by the British
frigate *Nymphe*, who signalled that the French were at sea. Lord Bridport,
now in command of the Channel Fleet, prepared his ships for battle, but the
fog suddenly descended and the *Nymphe* lost sight of the French. Her captain, Percy Fraser, chose to respond by annulling his previous signal, as,
strictly speaking, the French were no longer in sight. It was a mistake that
was to cost him his naval career, and he was never promoted again. Unaware
that the French were actually at sea and already running south, Bridport
stood his fleet down.

When the *Temeraire* arrived in Torbay in July 1799, therefore, there was,
paradoxically, greater uncertainty and potential danger than ever before in
the Channel Fleet, for they had no enemy to guard against. It was possible
that they would meet a huge combined force of French and Spanish ships
determined to force their way up the Channel to cover an invasion from
Boulogne, but they did not know when, or if, such a threat would appear. All
they could do was to prepare to defend themselves and their country. Their
worst fears were soon realized when, on 8 August, Bruix re-entered Brest,
unopposed, and with a fleet almost twice the size of that with which he had
left. During his cruise Bruix had enjoyed little success in the Mediterranean
but, crucially, he had united his squadron with Spanish fleets from both
Cartagena and Cadiz. The combined French and Spanish fleet, now only a
hundred and twenty miles away from British shores, amounted to fifty-nine
sail and included forty-five ships of the line. Once Bruix had returned,
therefore, the stakes had very much risen: the combined fleet had to be
detained in Brest at all costs.

It was fortunate that the time was also ripe for a change in the command
of the Channel Fleet. The elderly and lacklustre Lord Bridport was due for
retirement, to the general relief of everyone. Captain Edward Pellew wrote
of the retirement of his superior:

You will have heard that we are to have a new commander-in-chief,
heaven be praised. The old one is scarcely worth drowning, a more

contemptible or more miserable animal does not exist. I believe there never was a man so universally despised by the whole Service. A mixture of ignorance, avarice and spleen.[2]

By the end of his career Bridport had also lost many of his admirers at the Admiralty, not least by his failure to prevent the escape – and then the return – of Bruix into the very port he was supposed to be blockading, and now the Admiralty had their eye on the man they wanted to replace him, the energetic John Jervis, Earl of St Vincent, who was recovering from an unpleasant cocktail of rheumatism and dropsy at his home in Bath.

St Vincent was clearly the man for the job. He had fought resolutely at the Battle of Cape St Vincent in 1797, for which he received his title, and had gone on to command the Mediterranean Fleet for three more years. During that time ships of his fleet were repeatedly infected with mutiny, particularly because a number of ships which had been present at the great mutinies at Spithead and the Nore earlier in the year were sent on to the Mediterranean. St Vincent crushed every hint of sedition with unmatched severity, and in one instance forced the crew of the *St George* to hang one of their shipmates for masterminding mutiny, when such punishment was usually carried out by boats' crews from other ships. He found this so effective that he repeated the procedure on nine more occasions between June 1797 and August 1798. St Vincent later himself admitted that he was acquiring a reputation as the hangman of the fleet. At the same time, he kept the men ceaselessly busy and focused on their French and Spanish enemies, while improving the dockyard facilities. When in 1798 the ships from Nelson's fleet came to Gibraltar damaged after the Battle of the Nile, St Vincent was so vigorous in his care of those battle-honoured ships that, once repaired, they were considered to be in better shape than if they had been repaired at home. To ease the pressure on the dockyards he also urged the ships of his squadron to be self-sufficient in the majority of their repair and upkeep; in the spring and summer of 1796, his *entire* Mediterranean squadron was caulked at sea, an astonishing feat of seamanship.

This was exactly what the Channel Fleet needed and Lord Spencer, First Lord of the Admiralty, visited St Vincent personally in Bath to ask him to take command of the fleet in this hour of need. It was in St Vincent's exquisite house, in one of the most beautiful streets in one of the most beautiful cities in Britain, that St Vincent committed himself back to a life of cold, wind, salt air and seasickness, sleep deprivation and the dangers of the enemy in the ultimate discomfort of close blockade in Biscay.

Anywhere in the world the rigours of close blockade jaded sailors more than anything else; the relentless manoeuvring to maintain position battered the ships as surely as the ceaseless vigilance and infrequent action sapped the men's morale. But nowhere in the world were the trials so severe as they were off the coast of Brest. This may seem surprising but anyone who has experienced Biscay in one of its moods will testify to its potential for misery. Great Atlantic depressions form in the Caribbean and unleash their fury as they spin diagonally northwards and eastwards. As they do so, they push huge swells ahead of them for hundreds of miles, so that by the time the winds hit any ship in the track of the storm, it will have been spun, rocked and dipped by the swell in unpredictable patterns for hours on end. The station just off the Black Rocks that guarded the Passage du Four was known by the sailors as New Siberia.

Even more surprising, perhaps, is that, of all the locations in which British warships could serve during 1799, no fleet was more susceptible to scurvy than the Channel Fleet, although it was usually no more than three days from friendly shores. This is because ships sent on long voyages would break their journey regularly to take on more supplies or maintain their ships in good condition. Moreover, the majority of warships sailed on well-established and well-known routes, where local suppliers made the most of the navy's custom. Vast quantities of fresh fruit, meat and vegetables were usually in easy supply and provided the sailors with the foods necessary to keep the scurvy at bay. Furthermore, when it was finally accepted that fruit and vegetables were an effective cure for scurvy, ships bound for foreign stations were issued with a good supply of lime juice, lemon juice and sauerkraut. Ships as close to home as the Channel Fleet, however, did not enjoy such luxuries, but were forced to cruise for extended periods. Cruises of fourteen weeks with no access to fresh victuals were not uncommon and it was accepted that scurvy would start to become a problem after only nine. As a result, ships of the Channel Fleet were particularly susceptible to the illness. Indeed, the surgeon of the *St George* claimed that the losses to scurvy in the Western Approaches to the Channel were 'greater than what we suffer in any other part of the world, even in the West Indies, at the worst of times, not excepted.'[3] The evidence seems to bear him out: in 1780 Admiral Geary had returned to Portsmouth after a ten-week cruise in Biscay with 2,400 sick with scurvy, and by 1800 the problems were still severe. Dr Thomas Trotter, Physician to the Navy, recorded in his diary how on 30 June 1800 the *Temeraire* arrived in Cawsand Bay 'overrun with scurvy'. He recommended a fortnight's allowance of fresh beef and vegetables to 'eradicate the disease'. It is worth noting that Trotter did not prescribe any lemon juice: although he knew it to be a useful cure for scurvy, he was also conscious that 'it weakens the digestive powers, consumes the fat, and lessens muscular vigour. By these means that strength of body is impaired, that can alone contend against the tempestuous weather to which the home seas are liable for eight months out of the twelve.'[4]

Scurvy was not the only ailment to afflict the crew of the *Temeraire* in these months. The physician of the fleet recorded in the summer of 1799 that 'the malignant ulcer' made its appearance aboard the *Temeraire* with all the characteristic symptoms and virulence which had marked it in other ships of the Channel Squadron. Every 'wound, abrasion of the cuticle, blistered part, scald or burn passed rapidly through the various stages of inflammation, gangrene and sphacelus, in a few days leaving the bones almost bare from the separation of immense sloughs.' The cause was unknown, as was the cure. Trotter suspected it was caused by excessive drinking, somehow linked with the recent return from foreign stations. He explained: 'the seaman in the channel station when in port and for a few weeks after going to sea is allowed a very wholesome beer; but when ever it can be obtained, he swallows, with extraordinary greediness, enormous quantities of spirit.' The fact that the *Temeraire* had been crewed by many men who had only recently returned from the West Indies confirmed his suspicions that it was also somehow linked with a change of climate. Attempts were made by the surgeon of the *Temeraire*, Mr Lloyd, to eradicate the ulcer by fumigation, from the belief that bad air caused the spread of disease, but Trotter was unremitting in his professional condemnation of such practice, describing it as a 'mock-heroic placebo' that only encouraged indolence and, in particular, that led sailors and surgeons to ignore what he believed to be of far more importance to the eradication of disease: the regular cleaning of bed linen and wound dressings. He was proved to be right when the *Temeraire*'s surgeon was replaced by Mr Burd, under whose 'attentive and scientific' treatment the men recovered.[5]

Service in the Western Approaches was undeniably grim, therefore, but it is entirely characteristic of St Vincent that he embraced the challenge, and left the luxury of his Bath townhouse with something of a bee in his bonnet. He wrote to his private physician explaining why he had to go: 'The King and Government require it, and the discipline of the British Navy demands it. It is of no consequence to me whether I die afloat or ashore: the die is cast.'[6] St Vincent's appointment was not well-received in the Channel Squadron; a matter of weeks before, a toast had been drunk at Lord Bridport's table that 'the discipline of the Mediterranean Squadron would never be seen in the Channel Fleet', and we know for certain that St Vincent had a very low opinion indeed of his predecessor's conduct. He also believed that the officers in the navy in general were 'with very few exceptions . . . so licentious, malingering and abominable that their conduct must bring about another mutiny.'[7]

St Vincent's plan as the new commander-in-chief was to reimpose the close blockade as Hawke had in 1759. Not only was the French fleet to be prevented from leaving Brest, but other ships were to be prevented from getting in. Brest was distinguished from the other French dockyards by having appalling communications on its landward side across Brittany and on to Paris. The guns, powder, food, timber, sails – *everything* that was needed to keep a fleet at sea or to prepare it for an expedition had to be imported. By imposing a close blockade St Vincent planned not only to stop the French from getting to the Atlantic, but to stop them from getting to sea at all. To this end he adopted a three-tiered system of blockade. Close inshore, at the mouth of the Goulet was stationed a frigate squadron, with another at the entrance to the Raz de Sein. The main British fleet patrolled just off the island of Ushant, where they had the sea-room to run into the Channel and to the safety of Torbay when faced by a westerly gale, but were close enough to pounce on the French should they try to leave Brest. Between the main fleet and the inshore squadron was another layer of defence, a smaller squadron of ships of the line. The *Temeraire*, being a cumbersome three-decker, remained with the main fleet off Ushant, although her logs occasionally record her being closer inshore.

There, under the close eye of St Vincent, the British fleet manoeuvred continuously by night and day. 'My maxim is to keep the fleet in constant movement', he wrote, 'we never bring to'.[8] When they manoeuvred at night, St Vincent required the captain and every officer to be on deck. If a ship was lucky enough to be sent ashore to re-victual or repair, or the main fleet was forced back to Torbay by poor weather, no ship's boat was allowed ashore after sunset, no officer was to be further than three miles from shore, and none was to sleep ashore. St Vincent believed that allowing the men ashore was not a cure for the 'profligate and abandoned life the crews of the Channel fleet have been and still are in the habit of leading when in port, their only gratification being in getting beastly drunk with ardent spirits in the lowest brothels'.⁹ In some cases he was certainly right, but the officers' wives were far from impressed by this enforced separation from their husbands. St Vincent reciprocated their distaste. 'All the married ones have their wives there', he wrote, 'which plays the devil with them.'¹⁰

Everything was done to minimize the time it took to repair or re-victual the ships. Food and water were demanded the moment they reached shore and only the most necessary repairs were carried out, usually the shifting of masts, resetting of the rigging and repairs to guns, magazines and rudders, and all of this while the ships were being re-stored and re-victualled, courts martial held, wages paid and rats destroyed. To reduce the time it took, everything was pre-prepared and in some cases dockyard workers worked seventeen-hour days. In 1800 the *Indefatigable* had her anchors, cables and some sails replaced in only forty-eight hours. Those ships that came back to shelter from the ferocity of the Atlantic were ordered back to their station the moment the wind changed. St Vincent expected his ships to be under way and well out of the bay within an hour and a half of the unmooring signal being raised. Senior officers would be left behind if they had not rejoined, and tradesmen too slow in disembarking would be taken to sea. Between May and September 1800, the *Temeraire* was only in port for fourteen days out of a hundred and twelve. Of two hundred and twenty days in 1801, there were only thirty-three when she was not at sea, and there were cruises that lasted seventy-three days and seventy-nine days at a stretch. And these were not only fair-weather summer cruises: from January 1801 she was at sea for nine weeks. That summer she took her station once again, and did not return for nineteen weeks.¹¹ St Vincent was particularly livid when he discovered that Dr Trotter's orders to provide the *Temeraire* with two weeks' worth of fresh provisions as a cure for scurvy had delayed her departure. His response was classic St Vincent: he immediately wrote a powerful and poisonous letter to the good doctor.

Sir,
I very much disapprove your officious interference to prevent His
Majesty's ships under my command from putting to sea, the moment
their beer, water, and provisions are completed, which is ordered to
be done with the utmost dispatch; and I desire you will discontinue
this practice.
    St Vincent. [12]

Trotter, a sensitive man imbued with a deep sympathy for the plight of
British sailors, was hurt deeply by St Vincent's letter and particularly
resented being reproached for carrying out his duty as he saw it. Severe as he
was, St Vincent was determined to set an example of endurance for all officers in the fleet and had committed himself to remain afloat for the rest of
the war. While some took to the enforcement of such routines well, others
did not. Collingwood bemoaned not having a night of rest for two months,
and declared that 'this incessant cruising seems to me beyond the power of
human endurance'.[13] Even St Vincent himself was forced ashore in the
winter of 1800 with a persistent cough, his constitution broken by his own
routine.

Breaks in that routine were few and far between, but on 22 July 1801 the
Investigator was spied through the mist carrying Matthew Flinders to
Australia, where he had been sent to map the unknown southern coast, and
in doing so, circumnavigate the continent. Flinders had already established a
reputation as the finest cartographer of his generation and his charts of
Australia formed the basis of Admiralty charts for most of the nineteenth
century.

With few such distractions, however, the incessant tedium and the physical and mental stress of blockade ensured that discipline remained a
problem in the Channel Fleet. Mutiny still simmered after the terrible out-
breaks of 1797 and St Vincent kept his fleet together with both the threat
and enforcement of particularly violent and severe punishment. As a rule,
twenty-four lashes were inflicted for insolence or drunkenness, thirty-six for
attempting to strike an officer, three hundred for desertion and five hundred
for other more serious non-capital offences, although aboard the *Temeraire*
punishment seems to have been relaxed, albeit only a little, with sentences of
twelve lashes for drunkenness and twenty-four for disobedience being

issued.[14] Such harsh discipline, however, provoked mutiny on some ships as surely as it quelled it in others. Most notoriously of all, when the frigate *Danae* mutinied in March 1800, her crew sailed her into Brest and handed her over to the French.

The sea-change in the Channel Fleet's operations was matched behind the scenes, where St Vincent was equally vigorous. Everything from the airing of beds to the employment of convalescent men came under his beady eye, and he intervened personally in instances of drunkenness among the officer corps. His principal philosophy, which he urged on anyone who would listen, was 'to rub out *can't* and put in *try*'.[15] Everyone was to do their best to improve the service, no matter how daunting the challenges. Nowhere is this philosophy more clear than in May 1800 when he received an extraordinary letter from the captain of the *Temeraire*. Captain Marsh explained to St Vincent how he had

> a Prussian styling himself a natural son of the King of Prussia ...
> serving as a landsman on board ... He has already represented his
> case to Baron de Jacobi, the Prussian Minister, and notwithstanding
> the Baron believes him to be an impostor, yet as the man is a for-
> eigner that cannot speak English, has never done any duty and is so
> far from being useful that he is a nuisance in the ship ... (he is) an
> object not worth keeping in the service.[16]

The true identity of this Prussian and how he came to be on board the *Temeraire* make a remarkable story. Marsh clearly thought that he was either an impostor or a fantasist. In an earlier letter to the Admiralty, to which he apparently received no reply, he had already complained of the man, claiming that 'his address does not warrant his assertion.' At the same time he enclosed a pleading letter, written by the Prussian to Captain Marsh, which deserves to be quoted in full:

> I was born at the court of Berlin, my mother the Countess of
> Lightno was privately married to the late King of Prussia; they had
> eleven children of whom I am one, my name is Hemmerick Louis
> Count of Lightno. In the year 1798 I left the Court of Berlin in com-
> pany with the young Prince of Orange; we went in disguise to

Holland merely for our own pleasure; we arrived in the town of Taxel, where we did stay some time – we then took a view of the country and came back to the Taxel; twas at this time that the French took it; in the confusion in which we were, we went on board of a Russian man of war; 'twas late when we arrived on board – I thought the Prince was safe with me but I was very surprised when in the morning I could not find him. We came to England and I was put on shore at Cows. I left the Isle of Wight in order to go to London, arriving in Portsmouth, I met with people who took me to an house and there I was made to understand that I was to be sent on board of the *Royal William* – I was surprised and made myself known, but to no purpose, nothing I did say could prevail. On board the *Royal William* I could not meet with anybody that I could speak to, but being sent here (the *Temeraire*) by the means of Sergeant Wart, I have wrote to the Duchess of York, and to our Ambassador, I have had no answer yet. I wish, sir, you would be pleased to write to the Duchess of York for to certify that I am here, hoping sir you will comply with my request I remain your obliged servant,

Hemmerick Louis Count of Lightno[17]

The King of Prussia to whom he refers – Frederick William II – did indeed have a mistress, Wilhelmine Enke, who had been created the Countess of Lichtenau (Lightno). The Duchess of York, who is referred to in the letter, was a legitimate daughter of Frederick William II. If his claims were true, therefore, the Duchess of York would have been the Prussian's half-sister. Notwithstanding these claims and appeals, St Vincent dryly forwarded the Admiralty's reply to Captain Marsh that he was to 'make him as useful as possible',[18] the unwritten addendum and rebuke being that Marsh had clearly not tried hard enough: whoever he was, and whoever he claimed to be, a Prussian was still a man with muscle, and men with muscle made the navy tick. This inflexible approach to manning the navy in these years also possibly explains the presence of seven Venetians aboard the *Temeraire* in September 1802, none of whom could speak English.[19]

St Vincent's concern over the labour efficiency of his fleet was matched by his concern over its health, and as soon as he took command he ordered that lemon juice be given to all sailors as a preventative to scurvy. Hitherto it had only been given as a cure, which was standard practice, and only then to those ships that specifically requested a supply. St Vincent was convinced of the value of vitamin C, and he would not let anyone stand in his way. Thomas Trotter, the incumbent physician to the Channel Fleet when St Vincent took command, was quickly replaced when St Vincent learned that he was one of the few who still did not wholly believe in the power of vitamin C as both preventative and cure. This put a new and great strain on the victuallers, but they responded well. In 1800 the Channel Fleet was provided with 42,894 gallons of lemon juice.[20]

To be part of the Channel Fleet in 1800, therefore, was to witness first hand a turning point in maritime history. Ever since man first took to the sea he had been limited in how long he could stay at sea by this curious disease that made gums bleed, teeth fall out, and men so weak they could not stand. Now, with regular doses of lemon or lime juice, taken neat or mixed with the sailors' grog, the Royal Navy's limitations were imposed only by seamanship and endurance.

St Vincent was also careful to ensure that the regular supply of lemon juice was augmented by continual supplies of fresh fruit, meat and vegetables, and if the introduction of lemon juice was a triumph of innovation and free thinking over institutional tradition, then the victualling of the Channel Fleet was a triumph of logistics. The challenge of feeding thousands of men off the Devon coast at unpredictable times of the year and at short notice was more than a century old when St Vincent took command. In 1692, when Admiral Russell brought sixty-four ships of the line and twenty-four fire-ships into Torbay, his entire force totalled over twenty-four thousand men, making his fleet easily the largest 'town' in the whole of Devon. The next largest was Exeter with only fourteen thousand, and there were only three towns in the whole of England larger than Russell's fleet. A little over a century later, when St Vincent commanded the Channel Fleet, only Plymouth had a larger population, and there were still only sixteen bigger towns in the whole of England. The only town that could possibly cope with absorbing so many extra mouths at short notice was London with its population of sixty thousand in 1700 and nine hundred thousand in 1800.

The numbers alone are enough to astound, but it is also important to consider that the fleet did not have to be victualled for one meal, one day, or even one week, but for months at a time. The whole purpose of the Western

Squadron was to stop the French from escaping, but if they did escape, then they would be followed, immediately, wherever they went, *anywhere* in the world, and for an unknown period of time. St Vincent's predecessor, Lord Bridport, received the following sobering instructions from the Admiralty, to cover the possibility of a French escape: 'Your lordship will direct the officer commanding the squadron to detach to follow the enemy to any part of the world to which it may go as long as he is able to obtain information on which he may certainly depend of the route it has taken.' But even if the commanding officer did not know for certain where the French had gone, he still had to make a decision based on the balance of probability and then act. With British interests all over the world, and the Caribbean economy in particular so crucial to the entire war effort, the French had to be stopped. To allow for such uncertainties, St Vincent required that his fleet was victualled for five months' service.

From the quantities of supplies required alone, it is not surprising that Devon was sporadically drained of food, particularly in years like 1800 when the previous grain harvest had been very poor and there had even been food riots up the Tamar valley. It was, however, the unpredictable nature of the demand that caused the most trouble. In 1759 one Exeter butcher had a contract with the navy to supply 'good, well-fed ox beef', but that summer Hawke came into Torbay and demanded 46,926 pounds of it, equivalent to about seventy oxen, and all to be delivered within forty-eight hours. And yet even this seems to have been exceptionally lenient: only twelve hours' notice was standard for greengrocers. In 1804, 4,880 oxen passed into naval pens at Plymouth, and in only three months between May and July 1805, 4½ tons of cabbages, 12½ tons of potatoes, nearly 1 ton of turnips and 3½ tons of onions were supplied to the fleet.[21]

All of this was delivered in small amounts, over numerous trips to the yard or meetings with storeships, so that in practice the ships were kept regularly topped up. In November 1799 the *Temeraire* had become the flagship of Rear-Admiral James Whitshed, and we know from Admiralty records that for the first month in charge his squadron was sent the following supplies:[22]

	Quantity	Days (which will serve 10,000 men)
Biscuit	2,761 cwt	30
Beer	215 tuns	5
Wine	23,251 galls	18
Spirits	3,655 galls	5
Beef	5,966 eight lb pieces	19
Pork	11,437 four lb pieces	16
Flour	45,651 lbs (included in the beef)	
Suet	7,665 lbs (included in the beef)	
Raisins	600 lbs	
Pease	976 bushels	21
Oatmeal	281 bushels	4
Molasses	22,800 lbs	7
Butter	13,646 lbs	4
Cheese	28,673 lbs	19
Sugar	4,038 lbs (included in butter and cheese)	
Rice	8,077 lbs (included in butter and cheese)	
Vinegar	1,243 lbs	13
Tobacco	2,000 lbs	

The quantities even for such a minor top-up are impressive, but so much more so are the quantities required for a squadron of eight thousand men, equipped for four months' service.

Bread	8,000 cwt
Spirits	56,000 gallons
Beef	32,000 double pieces
Pork	64,000 double pieces
Flour	192,000lbs
Suet	16,000lbs
Raisins	32,000 lbs
Pease	4,000 bushels
Oatmeal	24,000 gallons
Molasses	13,800 lbs
Butter	48,000 lbs
Cheeses	96,000 lbs
Vinegar	8,000 gallons
Lemon juice	56,000 lbs
Sugar	56,000 lbs[23]

Just one ship like the *Temeraire* would take on board twenty-five to thirty tons of beef and pork, forty-five tons of biscuit, two tons of butter, between nine and ten tons of flour, fourteen to fifteen tons of peas, fifty tons of beer and thirty tons of water. The navy paid well for its stores, however, and the Admiralty was careful to nurture the infrastructure around Plymouth and Torbay. Signals were sent from Plymouth to Torbay as soon as the ships were sighted, the stores were made ready and vessels from Brixham commissioned to help. The pipes from the reservoir at Brixham were enlarged in 1801 to make watering ship more efficient. Slaughterers gathered on the beach at Torbay to begin butchering the oxen, driven overland from Plymouth.[24] Ships that came into Torbay or Plymouth were quickly and efficiently supplied, and convoys of victuallers escorted by fast sloops of war reached the inshore squadron off the Black Rocks once a month.

St Vincent's efforts concerning the sailors' food had been matched by his concern for their surroundings and their general health. He had witnessed the ravages of the typhus epidemic in Halifax during the Seven Years War, and he had also served in the Western Squadron under Hawke which had first demonstrated how it was possible to keep a blockading fleet healthy. Hog sties were removed from the upper decks and replaced by sick bays; to prevent damp the lowest decks were scrubbed with hot sand, and not washed with water as was traditional; the men's bedding was aired and their hammocks regularly scrubbed. Vaccination against smallpox was offered to all who desired it; new methods of ventilating the ships were devised; flannel was advised to be worn against the skin to prevent rheumatism and the surgeons and surgeons' mates were all instructed to carry their pocket instruments with them at all times, afloat or ashore.[25]

The effects of all these changes were quickly felt. By August 1801 some of the Channel Fleet had been at sea continually for five months, and Edward Pellew for six, but the health of the sailors remained good. When the entire fleet returned in November 1800, there was concern that the hospital at Plymouth would be overwhelmed, and extra lodgings were rented throughout the city, but there were only sixteen hospital cases out of twenty-three thousand men. For men who did become ill, a new naval hospital was built at Paignton and was ready to receive its first patients in March 1801. As long as they were supplied regularly, it was now clear that entire squadrons could stay at sea indefinitely. Control of the sea could be exercised with greater efficiency. Put quite simply, British seapower became more powerful, and the *Temeraire* was at the very heart of that change.

The blockade was highly effective. The ships of the Channel Fleet provided defensive cover for operations in the Mediterranean, Baltic and West Indies, protected British merchant shipping and prevented an invasion. In two weeks in 1800, the inshore squadron sent back to Plymouth as prizes six chasse-marées laden with salt fish, cord, wood and other stores, two brigs laden with wheat, one with resin and pitch and a sloop with flour.[26] So effective had the blockade been that the French had been forced to build a canal from Brest to Nantes, parts of which were completed by 1801, but which was not opened until 1806. In the meantime the situation in the port was dire. '*Il manque de tout*' ('it lacks everything') wrote the newly appointed Prefect of Brest in 1800.[27] The Spanish sailors, incarcerated with their French allies after the return of Bruix, suffered particularly badly. Hundreds were lost to sickness, but because no more ships could enter the port, they could neither be replaced, nor be paid their wages, nor receive new clothes or victuals from the Spanish navy. Their physical state as well as their morale plummeted.

The real indication of St Vincent's success, however, lies in the fact that in the early 1800s Napoleon began a wholesale reorganization of his maritime policy. Brest ceased to be the focus of French naval power, which shifted further south into Biscay, to the ports of Rochefort and L'Orient, and even further afield to the naval bases of Spain. The increased distances involved in watching these bases would stretch the British resources too far, and a close blockade would become impossible. Of even more significance, Napoleon's focus began to shift to the north-east, and he dreamed of a powerful naval base in the Channel at Cherbourg or in the North Sea at Antwerp which could be used to threaten Britain from the east as well as from the west.

Although the blockade was particularly effective under St Vincent, it was still never complete. In spite of St Vincent's best efforts, and with one of the healthiest and most disciplined fleets ever seen in the British navy at his disposal, another powerful French squadron escaped on 23 January 1801, this time commanded by Vice-Admiral Honoré, comte de Ganteaume. The ships of the main blockading force, under the command of Rear-Admiral

Henry Harvey, had been blown back into Torbay and were unable to resume their station for almost a week. Pellew, in command of the inshore squadron, had likewise been driven off station, but only as far as the Iroise. Nevertheless his absence provided enough time and space for Ganteaume to get through the Goulet and make good his escape and the weather was so bad that he was not sighted until he was off Cape Finisterre. Ganteaume's force was not as large as that of Bruix's eighteen months earlier, but he was carrying five thousand troops. They were destined for Egypt, where the British were planning an ambitious attack to evict the French army, now well established after its victory over the Turks at the Second Battle of Aboukir in August 1799. Ganteaume was never intercepted, reaching Toulon before continuing to Egypt, where Napoleon was forced to urge him to act. However, when in sight of the Egyptian coast, he saw the distant sails of a British squadron and skulked back to Toulon having achieved nothing. Nevertheless, with regular reports of Ganteaume's activities filtering back to the Admiralty, it was clear that he was still at liberty and his force was still significant. Other reports of a Spanish squadron from Ferrol at large in the spring of 1801 further raised the tension on the British coast and the blockade of Brest could not be eased.

Shortly after Gantaume escaped, St Vincent was promoted to First Lord of the Admiralty, and handed his command over to Admiral Sir William Cornwallis. Cornwallis continued the blockade with as much energy as St Vincent, although some of St Vincent's most despised orders were quietly removed, and maintained effectively until the war had reached a lull. The Second Coalition against Napoleon had collapsed, and Britain was increasingly isolated against France. With his opposition weakening Napoleon seized his chance and in October 1801 proposed a peace that was greatly in his favour, in exchange for assurance of his good will. The British could do little but agree and returned all of their overseas conquests with the exception of Trinidad and Ceylon.

These three years of blockade duty had taken their toll on the *Temeraire* and her crew. The fleet that she had joined in 1799 had been the most likely to meet a large force of the enemy; the most likely to suffer from scurvy; and it offered the most unforgiving and tedious service. By 1801 its health, at least, could be relied upon, but the discipline imposed under St Vincent was the hardest of any fleet in the world. Those with the strongest wills responded well, and for them the Channel Fleet became the fire where the iron of British seamanship was forged. But such exacting requirements could be too much even for the fittest and most determined of men. For some the relentlessness of their duty began to eat away at them, their desire for duty corroding from within, and by 1801 they were broken and dispirited. The preliminaries of peace were agreed in October 1801 and the pressure that had accumulated over three hard years began to release: this was less a collective sigh of relief than an eruption of joy born from the bitterness of lengthy servitude. With peace now a real possibility, the *Temeraire* was likely to be paid off. With cash in hand the crew would be able to see their families; sign up for better-paid merchantmen if they wished; but, most important of all, celebrate their survival.

While the sailors of the *Temeraire* relaxed at the prospect, if not the immediate reality, of a peaceful routine, their superiors were still faced with a number of problems, not least how to secure British interests in the West Indies. Dutch, Danish and French forces were all preparing to sail to oversee the complex exchange of territory that was laid out in the peace proposals. There was also growing political pressure on the government to assist the French in quashing the negro republic established on St Domingue (modern Haiti) by the former slave Toussaint L'Ouverture, half a million strong. That pressure increased as news filtered back to Europe of terrible massacres of peaceful whites and mulattos of all nations. The French were determined to take action, and detailed plans were made to unite the Brest, L'Orient and Rochefort squadrons and send to the West Indies a combined force of forty-one sail and twelve thousand troops. Among that number were Napoleon's brother Jérôme Bonaparte, and his brother-in-law General Leclerc, who, until recently, had commanded the French army in Portugal. The French force was also to be reinforced by a strong Spanish squadron.

This build-up of troops, led by those so close to Napoleon, was far too much to ignore, and powerful voices in the British government were extremely concerned about the true value of Napoleon's word that he would maintain the peace. The result was that, although this was officially a time of peace, the British government had no choice but to reinforce the West Indies squadron. And so quite unknown to the crew of the *Temeraire* and her sister ships in the Channel Fleet, now resting snugly in Plymouth with their topmasts struck for the winter, plans were being made to post a strong force to the Caribbean, with no prospect of leave for at least another year. A detachment was sent immediately to Bantry Bay in Ireland to await further orders. Rumour flooded irresistibly through the crews so that before long they knew what they had not been told: they were going to be sent to the West Indies. None of the sailors took the news well, but the crew of the *Temeraire* reacted worst of all.

6.

The Mutinous *Temeraire*

DECEMBER 1801 – FEBRUARY 1802

The *Temeraire*'s captain was now Thomas Eyles, who knew the ship and the crew well from an earlier brief stint in command in the summer of 1799. We do not know if he had been summoned on deck on the morning of Thursday 3 December 1801, as the *Temeraire* lay in Bantry Bay off the south-west coast of Ireland, or if he had merely chosen to take the air, perhaps sensing that something was amiss. But once on deck it was clear that the calm and predictable daily routine of the ship had been disturbed. There was a gathering of men on the forecastle, apparently remonstrating with the first lieutenant, the highest-ranking officer below the captain. Captain Eyles left the quarterdeck, the territory of authority and command, and moved towards the forecastle. There at the very front of the ship, as far from the officers as it was possible to be without climbing onto the bowsprit, the men had gathered. This was their space. Pinched and cramped, with the great damp cables straining as the *Temeraire* pulled at her bow anchor, the forecastle deck was adjacent to the ship's heads, where the men relieved themselves, and it was cluttered with the rigging of the bowsprit and jibs; further forward and below, the dark spaces under the bowsprit itself afforded sailors a measure of privacy, far from the prying eyes of their officers. On that day secrecy was no longer in the minds of the sailors, however; this was no furtive gathering interrupted, but an open display of force and unanimity. On their own ground they grew in confidence and argued loudly with the ship's officers, an offence which itself could be labelled as mutiny, and punished accordingly with a severe flogging or, if found guilty at court martial, with death.

On the approach of their captain the men fell silent. It is unlikely that he would have ventured so far forward on a regular basis, and many captains of the largest ships remained resolutely aft; they slept in their cabin, they worked in their office, and they commanded from the quarterdeck while their power and influence was carried throughout the ship by the lieutenants and midshipmen. These officers formed a sort of cartilage between the captain and his crew. On the largest ships it was through them that the men were commanded and that the captain could gauge the tenor of the ship. Such a direct confrontation was rare indeed; the captain would only address the entire crew on occasions that required a formal presentation of officers and crew, such as witnessing the punishment of a sailor, reading the articles of war or performing the Sunday service. In every instance such meetings were summoned by the captain and conducted on the captain's terms. To demonstrate his authority over his men they were always conducted by the captain from his quarterdeck where, physically raised above his men, he could gaze down on those that he commanded. Now, however, he stood face to face with his men, on the forecastle of his ship. Everything about this meeting ran against the grain, therefore, and against routine that had been refined over three years of continuous service. Routine was the oil that made the ship work, kept the men busy and the ship in good condition and maintained order and discipline. Everyone aboard could sense when the rhythms of life had been broken. For those at the very centre of that fracture the impact was profound. With the arrival of the captain, the novelty of the situation struck the sailors dumb and the silence dripped with tension.

However lawless such a situation was, it is important to add that it was not necessarily unexpected, nor was there a complete absence of rules regarding how to act on either side. Mutiny had been endemic in the navy since 1797. There had been sporadic mutinies before then, of course, but 1797 heralded a major outbreak. The first occurrence was at Spithead, where the entire fleet refused to sail. All the mutineers had complained about their pay, which had not been changed since 1652, while in a number of instances particularly detested officers had been sent ashore. Of crucial importance to the years that followed was the fact that the Spithead mutineers were successful. Their cause had been justified, their actions moderate, and they had acted with honour and dignity. They had maintained throughout that they would set sail if the French broke out from Brest and they had even refused permission for frigates and other smaller ships to join the mutiny, so that they might continue to protect British trade. Once the mutiny had been openly declared, routines aboard every warship were maintained as usual, with men being flogged for drunkenness. Delegates were fairly elected from each ship to negotiate with the Admiralty, and most importantly of all, there was no violence. The Admiralty had conceded to most of the mutineers' demands, and the negotiations had closed formally with a ceremony and a banquet for the delegates. The sailors had been calmed as much by the respect with which they were dealt as by the concessions.

News of the mutiny at Spithead, and most importantly of its result, rapidly spread throughout the fleet. For those who wanted to see it, the Spithead mutiny proved to the sailors what they were capable of, if united in their action. Pockets of mutiny erupted throughout the fleet. The next major mutiny, and a far more extreme one, broke out at the Nore, with a number of ships joining from the North Sea Fleet. Once again the core complaint was over pay, but as this mutiny developed, the sailors became more extreme in their demands and actions, and the mutineers themselves became divided. A number of loyal ships managed to escape from the increasingly hostile mutineers, and eventually loyal seamen rose up on those ships still in mutineers' hands, and took them back by hand-to-hand fighting. The Admiralty reacted with no mercy and twenty-nine men were hanged.

If the power of the Admiralty was demonstrated so clearly at the Nore, equally, the lessons learned at Spithead were never forgotten by the sailors. Sailors knew their own value, and they lived their lives by an unwritten code. They accepted many of the conditions of their life that we today find so alarming: none of the mutineers at Spithead or the Nore, for example, complained about overcrowding or flogging. What they cared most about was fairness and the respect of those in authority for their skill and commitment. Only in very rare circumstances did they rise up against a captain that they considered too harsh; rather it was because their sense of what was acceptable or fair had been broken. Harshness in itself was acceptable so long as the lines were clearly drawn. The mutiny aboard the *Hermione* in 1797 is perhaps the most notable example of this. Captain Hugh Pigot, 'a shouter, a bully and a flogger',[1] despairing at the perceived incompetence of his crew, declared that he would beat the last man down from aloft. Inevitably these were the youngest of the crew, the most agile, and certainly the most valued for their skill and agility. In the race that followed to get to the decks, two men fell and were killed. Pigot dismissively ordered the 'lubbers' to be tossed overboard. This was wanton brutality; it was unfair and unjust. These were the actions of a man who had no respect for his crew, cared not for their lives, and by declaring them 'landlubbers' did not appreciate their phenomenal skill. It was, in short, a perfect recipe for enraging the British seaman. That night the captain and eight of his officers were murdered by the crew, their bodies thrown overboard and the ship handed over to the Spanish.

The *Hermione* mutiny, however, was very rare and must rank alongside the mutiny of the *Bounty* as one of the most extreme in naval history, if paradoxically one of the most well known. It thus inevitably skews our understanding of mutiny in the navy and how it actually worked. In practice the ship's captain was usually open to hearing the grievances of the crew, and in many instances mutinies were quickly and quietly settled by the officers. If the officers themselves were the problem, then the career of a captain with a violent reputation was far less valuable to the navy than the safety of one of its ships, and more often than not the dangerous officers would be quietly removed and appointed elsewhere. By 1801, therefore, there was a well-established history of mutiny, both failed and successful, and there had been sufficient rumblings in the Channel Fleet for the commander-in-chief, Admiral Cornwallis, to circulate a confidential letter to every captain, instructing them to be alert to the signs of mutiny.

If mutiny did break out, in almost every instance where the captain was confident that it was not his own behaviour that was the issue he was anxious to hear the grievances of his men: no man wished to command an unhappy ship. At the same time, the mutineers were well aware of the fine line that they trod. They risked death by refusing to act, but refusing to act was their only weapon to force the officers to take their complaints seriously if consistently ignored. They also knew that even when a captain gave his word that they would not be punished, the Admiralty might feel differently and hang the ringleaders, regardless of any promises made. No man wished to identify himself as a ringleader, therefore, and if a complaint was to be made by letter a 'round robin' could be prepared to demonstrate solidarity, with all the signatures in a circle, so the man who signed first could not be identified. If the grievance was to be spoken aloud, however, respected members of the crew were usually given the task, willingly, cajoled or threatened.

So when Captain Eyles surveyed the men before him, his overriding concern was not to order them back down below and out of sight, but to find out what had driven them to such extreme measures. Eyles did not order them to disperse nor even to speak up. He merely asked them what was wrong: this was no place for orders, but for negotiation. There was a certain degree of silent jostling amongst the men gathered there, but eventually three stood before him, the men chosen for the daunting task of airing the ship's grievance. As a man, they said that they wanted to know where the *Temeraire* was going, and that they would not raise anchor unless it was to sail to England. Eyles said that he did not know where they were going. Admiral Campbell himself then came to the forecastle, having been informed of the stand-off that was occurring. We do not know if Captain Eyles had experienced mutiny before, but Admiral Campbell certainly had; in fact he had been captain of the *Terrible* at Spithead and was one of the officers who had been forced ashore. There had also been a serious mutiny aboard his ship in 1795 over bad bread, which he had only been able to quell with force. A number of mutineers were wounded as the officers and marines confronted them, and eventually five were hanged for mutiny.

Campbell's first tactic was to remind the sailors of the usual routines of shipboard life, asking them: 'Have you ever been told before where you were going?' The inevitable reply, 'No,' soon followed but the sailors were not content with that: 'But now it is peace!' they cried. Campbell would not be moved. He explained that no peace had, as yet, actually been signed, and repeated Eyle's claim that the officers did not know where they were going. Campbell then ordered the men below, and there it might have rested, a minor insurrection quelled by the force of personality of the ship's officers and an incident lost to history. In this instance, however, the combined authority of Eyles and Campbell was insufficient to douse the fires of mutiny, stoked as they were by the promise of liberty. The men did as they were told, and quietly went below decks, but they did so with black hearts.

Once below the ringleaders gathered to plot their next move. The next morning, as Seaman John Ansey recalled, a group of nineteen or twenty men gathered together, drinking grog or wine – he was not sure which. This was the heart of the mutiny and they encouraged each other for the effort ahead. 'Drink to us like British heroes,' they said, 'there is no fear, we will go through the business, shake hands like brothers, stick to each other, there is no fear if there are no informers.'[2] If reported accurately, and there is no reason to doubt Ansey's testimony, the language of the mutineers was bold and persuasive. They were being led by a man or a group of men with a gift for words, exactly the type of man that was needed to convince his shipmates that mutiny was their only choice. It soon became clear, however, that the eloquence of the mutineers was backed up by muscle and thuggery, and it was that which sealed their fate.

If they were to act decisively it was critical that the crew act as one, for the officers would quickly sense if the crew were not united. The mutiny would soon fail and the ringleaders would be identified. To avoid this out-come while ever in fear of informers involved three separate tasks. The first and most important was to win over the sailors; the ringleaders would not act until they had asked the crew if they were willing to act together – 'to go aft and tell their officers now that the war was over, that they did not wish to go out of the land.' 'Come speak to your officers like men', they urged, 'now is the time.'[3] This open and peaceful negotiation was backed up by explicit threats targeted at known waverers. The ship's butcher threatened to smother the master's mate in his bed, and another sailor, suspected of being an informer, was to be put in a bread-bag and heaved overboard.

The second significant task was to sound out the feelings of the rest of the ships in the squadron. To mutiny in a fleet was particularly dangerous as ships loyal to their officers could be turned against a mutinous ship, which was exactly how the mutiny on the *Defiance* in 1795 was ended. To be ordered against another British ship was particularly distasteful for both crews, but the threat of a battle against their brother sailors was enough to weaken the mutineers' resolve. The mutiny on the *Defiance* ended shortly after the *Edgar*, anchored nearby, was ordered alongside 'to engage her, if necessary, to bring her to order.'[4] Before they took decisive action, therefore, the *Temeraire* mutineers were careful to canvass the opinion of the other ships of the squadron. It is unclear exactly how this was done, but boats would have passed frequently between ships in a squadron, and it was possible to hold a conversation with a boat through an open lower-deck gunport, out of sight and out of earshot of any officers. Before the *Temeraire*'s mutineers acted, they had been assured that the crews of the *Formidable*, *Vengeance* and *Majestic* were of the same mind. They were assured explicitly that the crews of those ships would not man their guns against the *Temeraire* and that if the men of the *Temeraire* were forced to barricade themselves below decks, they would receive supplies and reinforcements from the other ships of the squadron. It had even been arranged that if the mutineers found themselves in trouble, they would fire a rocket to show they were in need of assistance. The crews of those ships that pledged allegiance to the *Temeraire* also confronted their officers and refused to sail to England, but there was no violence and their captains later refused to try the mutineers.[5]

The final challenge for the ringleaders was to secure the loyalty of the marines, which was no easy task. The marines formed a distinct body of men aboard ship. They had a separate commanding officer, their own rules and their own discipline. They usually ate and slept in a different part of the ship from the sailors. To mark their separateness from the crew, marines on duty wore the uniform of the British army. The marine private wore white breeches with a short-waisted and bright red coat, while the officers were even more striking, their coats a brighter scarlet and cut as full-length frock-coats and made of much better quality material. The marines also had distinctive headgear, privates wearing the standard light infantry hat. In battle they lined the ship's sides, to protect against enemy boarding attempts and to sweep the enemy decks with volleys of musket fire. The most talented were allowed aloft to act as marksmen. The majority of their daily routine, however, was taken up by sentry duty. They guarded the captain's and admiral's cabins, the ship's magazine, and important store rooms. When boats were sent ashore, one or two marines were usually sent with them to guard the sailors and prevent them from deserting, and they stood guard whenever the captain ordered a man to be punished.

In a mutiny it was to the marines that the officers would turn to re-establish discipline, and their role in this regard had recently been strengthened by St Vincent. In his suppression of mutiny in the Mediterranean Fleet in 1797–8, he had clarified to the marines, and also to the ships' captains, that the marines were responsible for the safeguarding of discipline aboard ship. He issued instructions that whenever the ships were at anchor, the most common time for mutiny to break out as the sailors were not absorbed by the continual demands of sailing, the marines were to be constantly at drill 'and are not to be diverted therefrom by any of the ordinary duties of the ship'. They were to 'walk brisk on their posts, backwards and forwards, never to sit down, read or sing, whistle, smoke, eat or drink, but be continually alert and attentive to the execution of their orders, nor ever to quit their arms on any pretence whatsoever'. An inspector of marines was appointed to ensure that this role was carried out. From these duties alone, it is clear that the marines were not the sailors' natural allies; indeed, one contemporary explained that the use of the marines to impose order on a ship by force was 'completely overturning the natural order of things.' He continued: 'one consequence of this measure is certain; the seamen will be disgusted in a very high degree and much animosity may be expected to arise between the seamen and the landmen in every ship where violence is necessary. This state of hostility is not doubtful; it is an effect which will follow the cause as certainly as that seamen are essential to navigate ships.'[6] This animosity had developed through the complex social barriers between the sailors and the marines. They need to be understood because they had a significant bearing on what was to follow aboard the *Temeraire*.

The sailors loathed the marines, not only for their role as the ships' guards, but specifically because they were so clearly associated with the army and more generally because they were landsmen. In 1801 the reputation of the army was at its lowest ebb while that of the navy had reached unprecedented heights. The navy had won spectacular and repeated victories since 1794, most recently at the Battle of Copenhagen in April 1801, where Nelson had forced the Danes to capitulate, and the following July off Algeciras, where Sir James Saumarez, badly outnumbered, had boldly attacked a combined French and Spanish fleet, and had caused the destruction of two Spanish three-deckers and captured a French 74. The most recent exploit of the army, by contrast, was to land a force, graciously carried there by the navy, to attack Ferrol in Spain. They had marched inland, and got close enough to look at the defences of Ferrol before deciding that it looked a bit much and retreating back to the ships without a shot being fired. 'The sailor of our wars with France', wrote Captain Glascock, 'had so much *esprit de corps* for his own branch of the national service that he genuinely and heartily – not to say unreasonably – despised all that pertained to soldiering and pipeclay.'[7]

More specifically, the sailors had no respect for the marines' role on board ship. While they were not restrained from learning seamen's skills when they were off duty, most marines helped with the daily work of the ship, but only the daily work of the unskilled: they scrubbed the decks, hauled on the ropes and carried stores. None of their work involved the artistry or skill of the able seamen. Seamen knew every single line of the ship's entire rigging intimately, and they spoke the language of the sailing ship fluently. Perhaps as many as three hundred words or phrases were used to describe particular aspects of the ship's rig or activities that were impenetrable to the uninitiated: they knew the difference between a box-haul and a club-haul; between a futtock and a knee. They could tie at least thirty knots in the darkest of nights, frequently with only one hand – and with either hand. They had mastered the art of helming, which has variously been described as similar to riding a bike or playing a violin, skills impossible to the uninitiated. They were also adept at sewing, so that they could repair canvas as easily as they could repair rope and make it watertight through the curious skills of worming, parcelling and serving. Most importantly of all, they could climb aloft with dazzling surety, and stay there braced in the rigging for hours at a time in the most alarming weather. It was even essential that the sailors could remain safely aloft without actually holding on: they had to brace themselves with their chests and legs to leave their hands free to mend the rigging, or furl or reef the sails. To reflect their status, the marines were rated the same as landsmen, just one rank above the ship's boys, and they were paid even less.

The marines differed from the sailors in one more significant way: from 1755 they were permanently employed. In times of peace the sailors would be paid off and would be free to take their leave as they wished, to see friends and family or to work in the well-paid merchant ships. The marines, however, left their ships but were immediately employed as dockyard guards, a task taken over by militias in wartime. This in turn had two significant effects on them. First, they were under constant training and drill, with no respite. One contemporary claimed that when both parties are placed on board a ship, 'and the general discipline maintained in its fullest operation, the influence of regular order and exact subordination is at least twice as great over the marines as it can ever be over the sailors.'[8] In short, marines were more likely to do what they were told. Furthermore, the many and complex differences between their service and the sailors ensured that the marines did not necessarily share the same grievances as the sailors, particularly when it came to the question of peacetime and leave that was so vexing the crew of the *Temeraire*. For the marines, it was of little consequence whether they were at peace or at war; they would still be employed and would be required to do their duty as they always had.

To win the marines over to the sailors' side was crucial to the success of any mutiny. There were as many as a hundred and fifty marines on a ship as large as the *Temeraire*, although from October 1801 she was slightly short of complement with only a hundred and thirty-two.[9] While the crew might overwhelm the marines in a direct confrontation, it would not be without a great deal of bloodshed, and it would not happen at all if the majority of the crew were not prepared to risk their lives for the mutiny. Such dedication could not be relied upon from so many men. The marines would have to be turned. Aboard the *Temeraire* it was a seaman named John Allen who took the decisive step and he approached a private in the marines called James McEvoy. McEvoy told him that there were between twenty and twenty-four marines who would openly declare for the sailors' cause, and that the rest would fire over the sailors' heads if ordered to fire upon the mutineers. He was certain that they would then join the sailors 'perhaps with their arms if it was possible to get them, if not the bayonet would do'.[10] It was enough of a commitment for Allen; everything was set. The mutineers bided their time. They waited until the day after a regular despatch had left carrying the Admiralty correspondence from the fleet. Unless extraordinary measures were taken to inform the Admiralty of the forthcoming mutiny, this would buy them significantly more time to negotiate.[11]

The signal that the mutiny had begun was the lowering of the *Temeraire*'s gunports. It was common in mutinies for the men to barricade themselves below decks and sealing the gunports was the first stage in that process. At a later stage every companionway ladder giving access to the weather deck and hence to the senior officers' quarters could be unshipped if necessary, leaving the mutineers in control of the ship's stores, magazine and powder room. It was a position of formidable strength and the officers were anxious to prevent it from happening. As he saw the ports lowered, Lieutenant Forsar, standing on the fore grating, immediately ordered some midshipmen to open the ports again. Taylor, one of the ringleaders, stood beside him and ordered the ports lowered again. Forsar pushed him, and Taylor went to grab the lieutenant's sword, before jumping down and escaping below decks. It was his order and not Lieutenant Forsar's that was followed, and the ports were lowered, but still access remained to and from the weather deck so that the men could negotiate with the officers, or even attack them if it came to it. It had been decided that the mutineers would not draw their arms first, but if the officers did, then no mercy would be shown. Lowering the gunports was also an explicit signal to the rest of the fleet that the mutiny on the *Temeraire* had begun. Even those who did not know it was planned would guess that something was amiss. It was yet another break from the norm, as every warship at anchor kept her ports open to allow fresh air and daylight into the gloom of the gun decks. Such self-imposed incarceration would only happen under the most extreme provocation.

Once the gunports were lowered, the men cheered. Again, this was in part symbolic. The men cheered in unison regularly in battle, a demonstration of their united desire and will. Now that cheer showed their unanimity in defiance of their officers. It shattered the peaceful routine of the ship and was the surest way to summon one of the officers. Although more research needs to be done, we know that the mutiny at Spithead was begun by a cheer and it is more than possible that it was an accepted tactic to demonstrate that the crew was roused both in bark and bite.[12] Sure enough, it brought the ship's first lieutenant, Lieutenant Douglas, to the main hatch to demand what the noise was for. He did not venture below decks, however, but talked from the top of the main ladder, asking them to come on deck once again 'and let the admiral know what they wanted and he would grant it if he could.' But Douglas was met by a wall of jeering, and demands for the admiral himself to come below decks. At the same time two of the sailors tried to unship the ladder on which he stood amid cries of 'Break his neck and kill him!' Douglas fell but was helped up by one of the sailors, who advised him to go on deck for his own safety. Douglas escaped but when he returned later with the rest of the officers to present a united front, they were met again with cries of 'Shoot, shoot!' Although there was no violence and the officers remained unhurt, the mutiny had taken a nasty turn.

Finally the men came on deck, and the confrontation passed off much as before, with the men demanding to know where they were going and refusing to sail for anywhere but England. This time, however, Admiral Campbell made a direct reference to mutiny. He ordered the men back below decks, and reminded them that the *Temeraire* had an excellent reputation, and that 'he should be very sorry to report mutiny in the ship.'[13] The men went below once again. The ringleaders urged them all to carry on their routines as much as possible, and it was made clear that anyone found

drunk would be beaten. It was also declared that any man taking his ham-
mock on deck, the usual morning routine, would be knocked back down the
hatchway. More seriously, any man found lying out on a yard – the implica-
tion being that they were helping to set sail – would also be beaten by the
crew. In assuming responsibility for the discipline of the ship and issuing
their own orders, the mutineers had finally taken control of the crew and, in
doing so, they had taken control of the ship. There was, however, one more
particularly important rule: anyone who was found to be treacherous to the
mutineers would immediately be killed. The mutineers knew that they had
taken the final step and their fate was now in limbo. This was no longer a
question of peace and leave, but of life and death. Mutineers kept a close
watch out of the hawseholes to see if the officers had called for help.

Down below, the men secured the ammunition in case there was a fight,
while the ringleaders, perhaps twelve in all, composed a letter in the shadows
beneath the bowsprit. While they wrote they organized a series of code
words and phrases to warn of the presence of an officer. 'Catch the rat', a
plausible occupation for that part of the ship, would warn of an officer
approaching. Other codes were 'give me a chew of tobacco' and 'I want a
drink of water.'[14] The letter was sealed with a key from a chest and thrust
through the lattice of the admiral's steward's pantry. This is what it said.

Sir,
We beg leave to supplicate your Honour to accept these few lines,
which is to inform you of the Sentiments of our Minds. One and
all, that it is not our Inclinations to hurt any Person in the Ship, nor
to use any Violence whatever although we are under the disagreeable
Necessity at the Time of objecting to those Orders you might have
received from the Board of Admiralty. Our reasons are, Sir, We
know it was a peace prior to our leaving England, and Hostilities
ceased with all Nations, which has since been confirmed by many
incontrovertible Proofs, and we here beg to call to your Memory the
Words you desired to be circulated round the Ship on the third Day
of October last by your Coxswain.[15] We hope, Sir, You will take this
Case into Consideration, knowing that we have most of us served
our King and Country with the greatest Alacrity from Seven to
Nine Years. It has pleased God to bless our Country with a Peace.

We therefore expect the Indulgence of free born Britons of enjoying the Blessings arising from the same. We therefore both Seamen and Marines conclude with a final determination not to weigh Anchor except for England, and

> We are, Sir,
> His Majesty's Faithful and loyal Subjects,
> The Temeraires

P.S. We wait in with the greatest Impatience for your final Answer.
> H.M. Ship, *Temeraire*, Dec 7th 1801.[16]

Next day Campbell took the letter to Vice-Admiral Sir Andrew Mitchell. Mitchell immediately wrote to the Admiralty, expressing 'the most heartfelt mortification and pain' in acquainting them with the mutiny, or at least with his crew's resolution 'not to lift their anchors from this haven until they are acquainted where they are going, and no where will they move, but to England.'[17] We do not know what passed between Campbell and Mitchell, but we do know that both were extremely worried about the loyalty of the marines. They knew that the outcome of the mutiny would turn on the marines' decision, and Mitchell's first letter to the Admiralty contains a hastily written postscript after his signature. 'I have this instant received a letter from Rear-Admiral Campbell in which he states he has every reason to believe the marines will <u>act</u> and be guided by the conduct of the seamen.' Campbell's letter had indeed been specific, that he had 'more reason than ever before to doubt the marines of HMS *Temeraire* and I am sorry to say it is my opinion no dependence can be placed in them.'[18] Their concern is palpable, and one can sense from the clutter of letters exchanged that events had spiralled out of their control. All they could do was describe and record.

Campbell returned immediately to the *Temeraire* and once again summoned the men onto the weather deck. He read out the mutineers' letter, well aware that only a handful of men could have written it and that the exact detail of its contents would be unknown to the majority. He made it clear that both he and Vice-Admiral Mitchell believed the men had been very premature in their actions, even explaining what premature meant, and then cautioned them to be 'very wise and circumspect' and to do their duty. He then closed the meeting with a clever piece of manipulation, speaking directly to the marines and asking them if they were aware that they were specifically named in the letter as conspirators in the mutiny. Apparently he received no immediate reply, but he had sewn a seed of doubt in their minds and had offered them a way out by raising the possibility that they had been included in the mutiny unwittingly.

The assembly disbanded once more and the men went back down below, unsure how events would unfold. The young marine who had sworn to the mutineers that he could vouch for twenty or so of his fellows was told to go back to them with an order from the mutineers that 'all the marines are to be of one mind on the seamen's side if such a thing happens again'. At roughly the same time, order seems to have broken down as the men began to fight amongst themselves over issues which, while unrelated to the mutiny, had no doubt been enflamed by the tension which pervaded the ship. The boatswain's mate was found drunk and was struck eighteen times by one of the ringleaders and then one sailor, Patrick Canaan, accused another, George Dixon, of being a thief. He was unable to prove his charge and was about to be beaten for causing a disturbance when Dixon drew his knife and Canaan struck him in the face. The noise brought the officers down once more, to demand what was going on, and this time it was Lieutenant Pogsen who stood on the ladder and tried to restore order. He was told that a man was to be beaten for causing a disturbance. Pogsen, however, insisted they should punish no one themselves, but that in accordance with custom, the culprit should be sent aft to the officers for punishment. His attempt to restore the natural order of things was met with cries of derision, and he was hustled by the crowd and then struck.

Meanwhile, the young marine, McEvoy, instead of delivering his message to the marines had found a secret supply of liquor, for the next we hear of him, he is on deck and on duty, and blind drunk. Confronted by one of the ship's officers, McEvoy reacted badly. Buoyed by the fervour of revolution that had spread through the ship and encouraged by alcohol, the unwise McEvoy was insolent and rude. The officers knew that the fate of the mutiny hung on the actions of the marines, and they reacted immediately and vigorously, putting McEvoy in irons. The incident was witnessed by George Dixon, the troublemaker who only moments before had drawn a knife on one of his shipmates and been part of the crowd that had jostled and struck Lieutenant Pogsen. Dixon, already aflame with energy and violence, ran below. He knew the sight of one of their number in irons would be the final straw that would rouse the crew to the violent mutiny that he desired.

'Bear a hand,' he cried down the hatchway, 'here is a man in irons.' The crew rushed on deck, with Seaman Allen's voice ringing in their ears: 'Now my boys, don't be afraid'.[19] They headed aft to secure the arms, disarm the sentries and attack the officers, cheering all the way. Once on deck, however, they were confronted by an unwelcome sight: the marines were standing together with the officers, in rank, and armed. The frantic rush halted, and the stout Lieutenant Pogsen grabbed two of his attackers and began to drag them towards the officers. They were wrestled free by the mutineers and Pogsen, dishevelled and bruised, joined the officers and marines. Captain Eyles now stepped forward and walked towards the mutineers. Once again, he demanded to know what they wanted, and this time there was no mention of the West Indies, as poor McEvoy had become the focus of the mutiny. 'There is a man in irons,' they cried. 'Yes,' replied Eyles, 'and there he shall remain.'

Eyles then grabbed one of the mutineers, a seaman named William Waddy, and headed back towards the officers. The mutineers surged around him, blocking him off, but still Eyles kept walking and forced a passage right through. No one, it seemed, would dare touch the captain. Suddenly one man, John Collins, broke from the crowd, barred the captain's path and roughly shoved him back towards the forecastle, away from the officers and marines. This was too much for the boatswain. A warrant officer, and traditionally a link between officers and crew, he would not tolerate the men striking the captain. 'You damned rascal,' he shouted at Collins, 'who are you shoving? You'll pay for this.' It was enough to distract Collins, and Eyles made it back to the quarterdeck.

Admiral Campbell was now aware that although the sailors seemed united in their grievance, only a few were prepared for violence and there was a clear sense of irresolution. With the loyalty of the marines apparently secure, Campbell calmly called out the names of those he saw as ringleaders and ordered the marines to seize them. Nothing happened immediately: this was to be the mutineers' last stand, and they responded with threats of their own directed to the marines. George Dixon was once again in the thick of things, and he shouted that he would take knives and stab the marines while they were asleep in their hammocks. Together with George Comayne, one of the mutineers, they then shouted that if they could not destroy the marines, they would kill the officers out of revenge, and if that was not possible they would blow up the ship and kill everyone. Another man said he was sorry he had not already killed the officers at one of their earlier confrontations, when he was armed with a crowbar. He said he would sharpen and grind his knife for revenge. More cries of 'Stand your ground!' were directed to the marines by mutineers, but by now it was clear that McEvoy had badly misjudged the marines' loyalty. The captain ordered the gratings to be secured fore and aft to prevent the men from escaping into the ship, and the order was given for the marines to advance. Slowly and steadily they moved forwards, herding the men towards the bows. Some jumped overboard, others managed to escape through gunports and through the doors to the heads. For the majority, however, there was no escape, and one by one the ringleaders were identified and arrested. Shortly afterwards, a tour was made of the ship to see if there were any more pockets of resistance, but there were none, and the crew were summoned on deck to witness McEvoy's punishment. He was flogged thirty-six times for drunkenness and insolence, then Campbell said, '*Temeraire*s, if you will promise me to be quiet, orderly and attentive, I will allow you to go to your hammocks; if not, you shall remain up till daylight and to daylight again.' With cries of 'We will,' the men marched below. Order had been restored, but the threat of mutiny remained. Their discontent was so palpable that the marines were ordered to stay below with the sailors, not to take off their brightly distinguishing uniforms, and to patrol unceasingly.[20]

Two days later, a delegation of the ship's company, led by the captain of the forecastle and the captain of the foretop, once more asked to address the captain, but this time to apologize. They said they were sorry for what had happened; that many of them did not know the cause of the original disturbance; that they hoped the admiral would place confidence in them; and that they would bring any man making a disturbance aft. Heartfelt, maybe, since none of the men in this delegation were ringleaders of the mutiny, but the admiral replied that he could not place confidence in them so quickly after what had happened, and that such confidence could only be gained by time and their future good conduct. Nevertheless, the delegation reiterated their promises before going below.[21]

It was an important show of solidarity from the crew, but for the mutineers the wheels were already turning. News of the mutiny had arrived in
London that morning and immediately the decision was taken to bring the
squadron back to English shores, as it was clear that the resentment at being
sent to the West Indies was not specific to the *Temeraire*. In that, at least, the
mutiny had been successful, but there was to be a terrible reckoning. The
Admiralty had something of a varied history in its response to mutiny, but in
those few instances where leniency had been shown, it had been after a
mutiny caused by shipboard concerns. But the *Temeraire* mutineers had not
mutinied over pay or excessive punishment but over their destination, and in
so doing they had unwisely meddled in the affairs of state. They were not
being sent to the West Indies on a whim, but to secure British possessions
from a large and threatening French force. However much sympathy there
might have been with the concerns of the mutineers, to concede to their
demands with leniency was out of the question. There was also the question
of violence. Although no one had been murdered, numerous death threats
had been made, and the mutineers had armed themselves. In the court martial that followed it even became clear that they had made preparations to
point two cannon aft to 'cool the officers' tempers'.[22]

The Admiralty and the government wanted to make their point quickly.
St Vincent firmly believed in the power of immediate action, and was
renowned for having ordered the execution of mutineers in the
Mediterranean Fleet immediately after their trial. In one instance the executions went ahead on a Sunday contrary to all tradition. 'Prompt execution for
mutiny', wrote St Vincent, '(is) in my judgement of greater effect than the
punishment itself.'[23] The Prime Minister, Henry Addington, rushed in
person to St Vincent's country house, where he was recovering from another
bout of illness, to discuss their response. It was decided to take special
powers under the Great Seal to try the mutineers, and the Secretary of the
Admiralty hurried to the Royal Courts of Justice to summon the Lord
Chancellor. His case was interrupted so that he could affix the Great Seal to
the Commission for trying the mutineers, which gave Vice-Admiral
Mitchell extraordinary powers regarding the death sentence.[24] Four days
later the first report appeared in the *Times*. Mutiny was always front-page
news.

Meanwhile the troubled *Temeraire* was making her way home. Even when they set out for Spithead, however, some of the men had believed it was a trap to get them to sea and, in the words of Captain Eyles, they had been 'very much on the look-out and were rather wild and unquiet in their appearance.' Worryingly, he had observed 'that those who have been thought the best men I much fear are the most dangerous'. Admiral Campbell was equally unsettled on the return trip and claimed that there were as many 'bad-disposed men on board her as any ship I ever sailed in.' To counter any new threat Campbell had requested more marines from the Admiralty and their complement had been increased for the return trip by an extra fifteen men, half of the number requested, bringing their total complement to a hundred and forty-seven.[25] It was with some relief, therefore, that they anchored in Spithead just over a week later, but still there was concern over the crew: the officers were forbidden to sleep ashore and the *Temeraire* was refused communication with the shore or with any other ship.[26]

The mutineers were tried by court martial in two batches on 6 and 14 January. The severity of their offences stands out from the contemporary court-martial records. A few weeks earlier the master of the *Daphne* was court-martialled for 'ungentlemanlike behaviour', as he had repeatedly harangued a lieutenant of the marines, and on one occasion had burst into his cabin and threatened to 'kick his arse'. Days later a seaman was tried for hitting a fellow sailor over the head with a boathook, which 'penetrated his cheek' and knocked out two teeth; two seamen from the *Belliqueux* were tried for attempting to blow up the ship, one acquitted as being unaware of the 'diabolical designs' of the other, who was committed as insane; and the boatswain of the *Vestal* was found guilty of trying to make a few bob by selling his crew's hammocks.[27] Trials for such isolated and peculiar events were very much the norm in the navy throughout the eighteenth century: the trials of the *Temeraire* mutineers were not. They were all tried for the following three charges, all prosecuted by Captain Eyles:

> First – Making or endeavouring to make mutinous assemblies.
> Second – Uttering seditious expressions: and for concealing traitor-
> ous and seditious words spoken, and tending to the hindrance of his
> Majesty's service, and not revealing the same to their Commanding
> Officer.
> Third – being present at such mutiny and sedition and not using

their utmost endeavours to suppress the same, between the 1st and
11th days of December 1801.

What is perhaps most surprising about the trials that followed is that
those high-ranking officers who witnessed them, or indeed who were part of
the court, were deeply troubled by the proceedings. The mutineers were
young, many under the age of twenty, and they had all served valiantly on
the *Temeraire* during the blockade of Brest, a service recognized as one of the
hardest duties in the navy. Others had served for the entire war, for as many
as eight or nine years, and had fought with distinction at well-known bloody
battles: at Cape St Vincent, Cadiz, Fort Matilda and Convention Hill.
Convention Hill in Corsica and Fort Matilda in Guadeloupe were particularly remarkable for the courage and resourcefulness of British seamen. The
redoubt on Convention Hill mounted twenty-one heavy guns and was considered the key to San Fiorenzo. The seamen from the squadron, through
extraordinary exertions, dragged a number of eighteen-pounder cannon into
a commanding position which had been considered by the French to be
inaccessible. The redoubt was then stormed after a two-day bombardment.
In the summer of that year, the British and French fought over Guadeloupe
and the British were forced out until only one fort, Fort Matilda, remained.
That garrison bravely held out for a further two months before being taken
away by sleight of hand. At least one of the mutineers had been so well
behaved that he had never been flogged. Collingwood sat at the trial, and,
keenly aware of the fleet's recent escapades, wrote to his sister, 'there are
none more desirous than I am that they might return to their families.' The
trials gave St Vincent 'more pain than I can express'.[28]
To a man, the defendants behaved and appeared impeccably throughout.
They all admitted the charges, and were avowedly repentant. One witness
declared they were

The noblest fellows, with the most undaunted and prepossessing
mien, I ever beheld – the beau idol of British sailors; tall and athletic,
well-dressed, in blue jackets, red waistcoats and trowsers white as
driven snow. Their hair like the tail of the lion, hung in a cue down
their back.[29]

It is possible that their performances were genuine, but it is also likely that they appeared as polite and repentant as possible to gain public support. We know for certain that a reporter from one of the main London newspapers was openly taking notes, a very unusual proceeding for a court martial. It is certainly hard to reconcile their pleas for mercy with their graphic threats of murder in Bantry Bay, but most striking of all are their statements, made to the court after the sentences had been passed. Twelve of the fourteen were sentenced to hang, the remaining two to receive two hundred lashes each, a sentence which would bring them close to death, would certainly leave them scarred for life and possibly maimed.

John Collins, the man who roughly shoved Captain Eyles and was berated by the boatswain, acknowledged the justice of his sentence, admitting he had violated the laws of the country and the discipline of the navy. He concluded 'May God protect the British Isles and Government! And may God receive my Soul!' There was a resounding Amen from all of the prisoners. Edward Taylor only requested that he was given time to make his peace with God and George Dixon, perhaps the most violent of all the mutineers, wept as he handed his will to Admiral Campbell, asking that it be passed to his wife and child. Chesterman merely asked for a friend of his to bury his body.[30] In the short period after the sentences were passed and before the executions were carried out, the condemned men wrote a letter to the chaplain of the *Temeraire*.

Dear Sir,
We take the liberty of thus humbly begging you, in the name of
the lord our God, to attend us, and administer upon us poor and
miserable sinners the word of our blessed redeemer as the state we
are now in is of the most serious nature, our bodies not only being in
danger, but our unprepared souls; therefore we humbly implore your
assistance on this unfortunate occasion. Do pray not delay as our
time is now exceedingly precious, we, therefore conclude, humbly
begging your compliance Yours with humility,
    Unhappy Temeraries[31]

The men were hanged throughout the squadron on the ships that had shown signs of mutiny. Each ship erected a special platform at the bows.

After the first trial four were hanged on the *Temeraire*, one on the *Majestic* and one on the *Formidable*. After the next trial, five more were hanged, this time divided between the *Achille* and the *Centaur*. At both hangings, boats from each ship of the squadron were required to attend the execution. Every report agrees that the men died well. One of their number had prepared a statement which was handed over and later published. It is a thoughtful and articulate letter, and is the clearest possible reminder that mutinies rarely happened unless there was at least one man who was a natural orator and could spin his words around uncertain minds. He wrote in part:

> How could we so foolishly suffer our impatience to get the better of us, as, for the sake of a few months longer service, to sacrifice all the bless- ings of Peace we had been toiling for these nine long years. Oh! that we had made these reflections sooner ourselves! But our lot is cast – our course in this world is finished. Make good use of what remains of yours – It cannot be long before we must meet again before the judge- ment seat of that God, whom we have offended; but who, we trust, has seen and accepted our unfeigned repentance, and will forgive us, as we do truly and freely forgive all those who have any wise offended or injured us. Prepare yourselves also dear countrymen, for his forgive- ness, and when we meet in the world to come, we may not meet in everlasting misery. – Pray for us – we heartily pray for you. Amen.[32]

After a short period of prayer, a gun was fired as the fatal signal and, in the words of every contemporary report, 'the wretched men were launched into eternity'. Their bodies were left to swing for a full hour before they were cut down and taken to the naval hospital at Haslar for burial. 'It is a melan- choly thing', wrote Collingwood, 'but there is no possibility of governing ships, so as to make them useful to the state, but by making examples of those who resist the execution of their orders, and I hope this will have such an effect upon the whole fleet that we shall have no more commotions amongst them.'[33] They certainly did not forget it. For some it was 'an unkind and ungrateful return to the brave fellows who, during a war of unexampled success and glory, had faithfully served their country',[34] and when the men of the *Temeraire* were paid off they wore crêpe bands around their straw hats to show that the mutiny at Bantry Bay was not forgotten.

Nevertheless, the impact of the executions was profound. It was the final marker in that period of great mutiny and there was not another mutiny on that scale in the navy for almost a century. That internal peace had been bought at a great cost, however. The sailors aboard the ships that were sent to the West Indies in place of the *Temeraire* were sullen and lifeless, doing their duty from fear rather than love. Even when they crossed the equator, always an excuse for raucousness and frivolity, the men were subdued. 'In short', wrote one witness, 'we had the efficacies of the seamen, but their animation was fled.'[35] In the long term, the relationship between the men and their officers had been severely damaged.

The Admiralty's favoured tactic for managing mutinous ships was to keep them at sea, and this seems to have been what happened to the *Temeraire*. On the day after the executions she was sent to the Isle of Wight to prepare for foreign service and then she sailed to Barbados, arriving on 24 February, where she remained until late summer. But it would take much more than continuous service to reunite the fleet. What the fleet needed was a leader; a man whom the sailors loved as one of their own; a man who understood them; and a man who believed in them. The fleet needed Nelson.

7.

The Trafalgar *Temeraire*

MAY 1803 – DECEMBER 1805

Cape Spartel S.32.00 W. 34 Miles

By 1805 Rear-Admiral Horatio Nelson was renowned for his bravery as much as for his empathy with British sailors, two characteristics that won their hearts more than any other. He had been in action with the enemy more than a hundred and twenty times, most notably at the Battles of Cape St Vincent (1797), the Nile (1798) and Copenhagen (1801); he had damaged an eye and lost an arm, and he wore his scars and mutilations like medals. The personal contact he enjoyed with his crews generated loyalty that could not be surpassed, and there is perhaps no better example than his handling of the mutiny on the frigate *Blanche* in 1797. The *Blanche*'s crew had suffered under their captain, Charles Sawyer, for a number of months: Sawyer was a homosexual, and he had become increasingly incapable of suppressing his desires. He had taken to calling young men to his cot at night before taking hold of them 'about the privates'. Unwilling to discipline those he had lured there, Sawyer did not react when his coxswain and a young midshipman, both of whom had been victims of his attentions, were publicly insubordinate to him. Sawyer had entirely lost the respect of his crew and complete control of his vessel. Eventually his first lieutenant, Archibald Cowan, made a formal complaint to George Cockburn, senior captain of the fleet, having had numerous letters of complaint ignored by Sawyer, who reacted by pressing his own charges against Cowan. Cockburn dealt with the sensitive situation with commendable skill and Sawyer was quickly replaced as captain of the *Blanche* by Captain D'Arcy Preston.

There matters rested, and Preston was well-liked by his crew, but still the sailors felt bruised and shamed; their captain had been publicly court-martialled and found guilty of 'indecent familiarities' and was 'dismissed the service and rendered incapable of serving his Majesty, his heirs or successors in any military capacity whatever',[1] and their reputation had been tarnished by association. It was at this stage in the troubled history of the *Blanche* that Nelson first came into contact with her crew, when she, together with the *Minerve*, was forced to escape from a hostile Spanish fleet. They fled together and, once they had reached safety, Nelson came on board and shook the hand of every member of her crew, congratulating them on their performance in the action. Nelson knew that news of this personal approbation would spread around the fleet. By shaking their hands he was personally extending his sympathy for their recent history, while at the same time honouring their skill and bravery in action. The wounded pride of the *Blanche*'s crew began to heal.

Shortly after this action, the crew of the *Blanche* heard that their new captain was to be replaced by the newly arrived Henry Hotham. Hotham had joined the fleet on a small frigate, the *Dido*, and tradition decreed that as he was the more senior of the two they should swap places. But the crew of the *Blanche* would not have it. They had suffered under Sawyer for some time, they were happy with their new captain, and Hotham bore his reputation before him. He was, in the words of the *Blanche*'s crew, a 'dam'd tarter', and the crew mutinied violently. They were only persuaded to accept their new captain when Nelson, once more, personally visited the *Blanche*. He reminded them of their newly-acquired reputation as one of the finest frigate crews in the Mediterranean squadron, and promised that if Hotham treated them badly, they were to write a letter to him, and he would support them in their appeal to the Admiralty. Nelson's word was enough. They believed in him and they trusted him. Hotham was accepted, albeit temporarily, and the mutiny was quelled. Soon after, Nelson's reputation was so powerful among the fleet that when the *Theseus*, one of the ships that had mutinied at the Nore, was sent out to the Mediterranean Fleet in great disorder and placed under Nelson's command, a letter from the ship's company appeared on the quarterdeck a few days later. It read: 'Success attend Admiral Nelson, God Bless Captain Miller we thank them for the officers they have placed over us. We are happy and comfortable and will shed every drop of blood to support them, and the name of the *Theseus* shall be immortalised as high as *Captain*'s ship's company.'[2]

There was much rejoicing in the Mediterranean Fleet, therefore, when Nelson was appointed in sole command on 16 May 1803. The Peace of

Amiens had been revealed as a fraud, with Napoleon steadily building up troops in northern France to invade the British Isles, and two days after Nelson's appointment, Britain declared war on France once again. The men had a focus once more, and they had a leader that they respected and loved because he respected and loved them. In the coming months Nelson was to provide the balm that would heal many of the navy's wounds, so dramatically brought to the fore by the mutiny on board the *Temeraire*. For the crew of the *Temeraire*, however, that balm would have to wait because, when war broke out again, she was in no fit state to serve anywhere. The resolution of her crew was not the only casualty of her first years of war: the ship itself was in a very bad state of repair having suffered the continual punishment of blockade duty, and she was sent to Plymouth for a major refit. On 22 May, two days after war broke out, the *Temeraire* was in dry dock having her copper repaired. Immediately afterwards shipwrights swarmed over her in a refit which lasted nearly eighteen months and cost a staggering £16,898, only a little under a quarter of the cost of her original construction and fitting, when she had only been afloat for a fraction over four and half years. To make matters worse, the harbour at Plymouth in those years was unprotected from the rage of Atlantic storms by the great breakwater that was built in 1812 and now dominates the Sound. Ships at anchor were vulnerable and a terrible storm in January 1804 badly damaged the *Temeraire* and a number of other ships, delaying her departure and increasing the cost of the repairs.

Many other ships in the navy underwent significant structural alterations in this period, their hulls massively strengthened by adding additional timber, diagonal bracing and iron knees. Such a vast programme of repair was necessary to rectify the legacy of neglect from St Vincent's tenure as First Lord of the Admiralty. By attempting to cut costs and root out what he perceived as corruption or, in his word, 'mutiny', the dockyards had become demoralized to a point of paralysis. Stores were limited and many private contractors, so crucial to the efficient running of the navy, were unwilling to take on naval work. Indeed, the fate of the *Temeraire* in the spring of 1803 is highly indicative of the state of the entire navy at the start of this war. Visibly shattered, she had been paid off in October 1803, but no attempt had been made to repair her in the following eight months as she lay at Plymouth. At the same time, no effort was made to man the fleet for the war that was, for those who were willing to see it, inevitable: by March 1803 the rapid build-up of French troops on the north coast of France had become alarming. When war broke out again the navy was forced to take desperate measures. Seven hundred men were impressed in Portsmouth, Portsea and Gosport, and at Plymouth the press was the hottest in living memory. Men were also moved from the Downs Squadron to the Channel Fleet, and the great fleet gathered in Torbay. 'We made use of the peace, not to recruit our Navy, but to be the cause of its ruin,' wrote Nelson.[3]

When the *Temeraire* finally left Plymouth in February 1804, the strategic situation was much as it had been in the first years of the earlier war. Napoleon was still determined on an invasion of Britain, possibly via Ireland, and he needed to unite his fleets to make this possible. Once again, therefore, the blockades of Toulon and Brest became the focus of British maritime strategy, and the *Temeraire* was sent back to her well-known hunting grounds off Brest. Cornwallis, still in command of the Channel Fleet, had in fact sailed to reimpose the blockade the day that war was declared. As before, the blockades were effective, but not comprehensively so. Nevertheless, the blockade on Brest forced the French to cease their ship-building programme there, and by February 1805 coastal traffic there had almost eased. The *Temeraire* played another central role in the blockade, and took her turn to carry live bullocks and bread to the blockading squadron after a stint at Torbay. Within a year, however, the *Temeraire* was back in dock for yet another repair that took only a month but cost another £9,143. Her repairs between 1803 and 1805 now amounted to well over a third of her original construction cost.[4]

By the time she was back at sea, however, the strategic situation had altered dramatically. In December 1804, Spain had allied with France and declared war on Britain. Spanish ships were, as ever, magnificent, and their officer corps considerably more resolute than many of their French counterparts. Napoleon, who had recently crowned himself Emperor, a title to match his imperial ambition, now had access to a navy that could realize it: with the French and Spanish navies united, he controlled no fewer than a hundred and two ships of the line while the British had only eighty-three.

A month later, the French Mediterranean Fleet escaped from Toulon with orders to unite in the West Indies with the Rochefort Squadron before returning to the Channel to cover the invasion. They never made it to the

West Indies, however, as the French admiral, the comte de Villeneuve, was horrified at the rustiness of his men. He even begged Napoleon to be relieved of his duties, but was refused. In March he escaped again with slightly different, but deeply unrealistic, instructions. This time he was to sail to Cadiz and fight off the British blockading squadron. The Toulon fleet and the Cadiz fleet would then sail to the West Indies, where they would unite with the Brest fleet and the Franco-Spanish fleet at Ferrol. This enormous combined fleet would then head to pick up the French army at Boulogne, having beaten off the numerous British squadrons off Cadiz, Ferrol, Rochefort and Brest, and eluded the Mediterranean Fleet under Nelson. Only then would the invasion begin. However, the few practice attempts had demonstrated the many inadequacies of Boulogne as a port from which to launch an invasion force of over a hundred thousand men.

The first and most significant problem at Boulogne was that the harbour dried out completely at low water, which meant that men could only be embarked during a few short hours either side of high tide. The men would then have to wait, exposed in their boats and clear of the harbour, for almost twelve hours before the rest of the force could be embarked. If that was not enough, there was no safe anchorage where a large flotilla of boats could wait for the next tide. Wind and waves were only half of their concern, for even if the combined Franco-Spanish fleet avoided the British Channel Fleet, there was another British squadron based at the Downs, just east of London, which could enter the Channel if the wind and weather were favourable, which they would have to be to launch an invasion from Boulogne. Villeneuve's task, therefore, was all but impossible, but Napoleon refused to listen to his advisers who understood both British strategy and the limitations of maritime capability, and he insisted that the invasion plan should go ahead. Napoleon himself travelled to Boulogne to await his navy. While he was waiting he ordered coins to be minted and statues raised to celebrate the forthcoming invasion of England.

Villeneuve, meanwhile, had completed the first part of Napoleon's plan by successfully uniting with the Spanish at Cadiz, and was heading across the Atlantic with Nelson in pursuit. Having reached Caribbean waters, he captured a British convoy of merchantmen and the Diamond Rock, a small fortified island off Martinique. It was from the merchantmen that Villeneuve learned that Nelson had also arrived in the West Indies. Under strict instructions to avoid battle at all costs, Villeneuve headed back to Europe. The fleets at Brest and Ferrol had been unable to escape, and Villeneuve now headed to northern Spain to unite with the Ferrol fleet and then travel up to Brest. Nelson made his way back to his station at Gibraltar, unsure where the French were headed. With no detailed intelligence of their destination he declared that there were 'as many opinions as there are persons' and considered Havana, Cadiz, Toulon and Egypt all likely. Nothing would surprise anyone in the navy. Collingwood had admitted that they knew 'Bonaparte has as many tricks as a monkey.'[5]

The *Temeraire*, meanwhile, was at her station off Brest under the temporary command of George Fawke, who had been chosen to cover for her appointed captain, Eliab Harvey. Fawke was, in fact, the second captain to replace Harvey who, although he had been nominally in charge of the *Temeraire* from 1 January 1804, had been replaced by William Kelly for six months from August 1804 and then again by Fawke in April 1805. Indeed, by July 1805, Harvey, who was Member of Parliament for Essex, had had very little indeed to do with the *Temeraire* for almost a year.

Harvey had joined the navy at the age of only thirteen and had risen to captain by the age of twenty-five. Not a great deal of information survives about his professional life, but one incident shines out and illustrates the character of this extraordinarily determined man. In 1794, the Royal Navy attacked the Caribbean island of Martinique, the very island that the first *Temeraire* had played such an important role in capturing during the Seven Years War. This time, however, it was the young Eliab Harvey who had been faced with the daunting task of taking the mountainous and heavily defended island. He was put in charge of three hundred seamen and a small company of marines with orders to capture the heights of Sourrière, five miles away across some of the most difficult terrain imaginable. Harvey and his men had cut a road nearly a mile long through thick wood, crossed a river by filling it with rocks and limbs from trees, levelled the banks of another, climbed a slope that was too steep for a loaded mule and within four days had established themselves on the top of Sourrière. And they did all of this while dragging behind them a 24-pounder gun and two mortars.[6]

Harvey was a very wealthy man, having inherited his family estate and a large fortune at the age of only twenty-one. We also know that he was a compulsive gambler who once lost £10,000 in one night at hazard, an early form of craps. It could in fact have been much worse. Harvey actually lost £100,000 and offered his substantial estate to pay the debt, but his opponent, an Irish gamester named O'Byrne, felt sorry for him. 'No,' said O'Byrne, 'I will win £10,000; you shall throw for the odd ninety.' He did, and Harvey won.[7] Harvey was, in short, exactly the type of man that Nelson respected, as he was a shadow of the great man himself: compulsive, brave, and with an unshakeable belief in the value of personal honour and the glory of Britain. He represented his countrymen both at the ballot and on the gun deck, and he did so for the love of his country and his hatred of the French.

It was men like Harvey who stood between Villeneuve and the French troops at Boulogne, but Villeneuve would not meet their like for at least three months. On 7 July news arrived in Portsmouth from the *Curieux*, a frigate released from Nelson's fleet, that the French were returning from the West Indies. Once ashore, Captain Bettesworth rushed to London and delivered the news that the French were returning from the West Indies. Charles Middleton (Lord Barham), First Lord of the Admiralty, acted with insight. He decided to leave the squadron off Brest as it was, to act as a second line of defence, and sent the smaller Rochefort squadron to cruise off Ferrol where Admiral Sir Robert Calder was already patrolling with a considerable force. There, he hoped that they would intercept the French before they entered Ferrol. This was not his original plan, however, and his papers reveal that his first intention had been to order the Brest squadron, of which the *Temeraire* was part, to join Calder.[8] Thus, on 9 July 1805, the fate of the *Temeraire* lay in the hands of Lord Barham. She remained at Brest while the Rochefort squadron headed for Ferrol, with the combined French and Spanish fleets descending on them rapidly.

The action that followed took place at night and in a fog. Inevitably it was scrappy, but Calder captured two Spanish ships. He did not, however, prevent the allied fleet from making the safety of Ferrol. He was criticized then, and has been by historians ever since, for failing to renew the action when it was in his power to do so. Indeed, the official Spanish report of the battle claimed that Calder had specifically manoeuvred to avoid a second encounter.[9] Although he was palpably pleased with himself in his report to the Admiralty, he had casually passed up the very opportunity for which Nelson had so desperately been searching. With Villeneuve's ships largely undamaged and now united with the Ferrol squadron, the invasion threat

remained very real. Nevertheless, the combined fleets were temporarily bottled up in Ferrol and incapacitated by sick and wounded sailors and by a lack
of victuals after their long cruise. When Nelson found out where they were,
he came back to the Channel and was immediately sent home to recover by
Admiral Cornwallis. It was the first time that he had been ashore for
twenty-seven months.

In the few weeks that Nelson was at home, Napoleon was forced to
abandon his invasion plans. He believed, once again, that he had been let
down by the incompetent and traitorous navy, and blamed everyone but
himself for the failure of his grand schemes. There had been seven invasion
plans in all, and not one of them had been grounded in the realities which
dictated what was possible at sea. And so now, in a move that has been interpreted as a punishment of the French navy, Villeneuve was ordered to the
Mediterranean to cover troop movements in southern Italy, a minor element
of Napoleon's campaign against Austria. The first part of that move was to
travel from Ferrol to Cadiz. He succeeded in doing so by evading the
blockading squadron off Ferrol, but was spotted by Collingwood's small
patrolling force off Cadiz. Barham immediately summoned Nelson and
ordered him to Cadiz with as many ships as he wanted. It is reported that
Barham specifically asked Nelson which officers he wished to accompany
him, flourishing a Navy List and telling him to take his pick. Nelson is said
to have replied, 'Choose yourself, my lord, the same spirit actuates the whole
profession; you cannot choose wrong.' That seems to have been only a gesture, however, for Nelson then sat down and carefully selected the ships that
he most wanted to take with him, dictating them to Barham's secretary. One
of them, personally selected by Nelson, was the *Temeraire*.

Nelson arrived to assume command on 28 September, and on 9 October
he issued a tactical memorandum which outlined his ideas for an attack on
the combined fleet. One can see from this memorandum why Nelson was so
anxious to bring the *Temeraire* with him to Cadiz, for he outlined an attack
by two divisions, together with an 'advance squadron' of fast-sailing ships
which could be ordered to join either line as necessary. The two main divisions would attack the enemy at right angles, cutting through their line, in
effect severing the foremost ships of the enemy fleet, which would then be
unable to support their middle and rear. To make this easier to achieve,
Nelson placed the largest and most powerful ships, the three-deckers, at the

very head of each line. They would absorb the first broadsides of the enemy, and were the best suited to attack the largest enemy ships, the flagships, which was where Nelson was determined to make the break. A day after he issued his tactical memorandum Nelson issued his first Order of Sailing, which was also to be the Order of Battle. He knew that time was of the essence and once the enemy had been sighted there would not be sufficient time to rearrange the fleet, manoeuvres which could take hours. The very first ship on that list, the ship designated to lead Nelson's own division, the ship commanded by the senior captain of the fleet, was the *Temeraire* (fig 15).

Thus in early October, Nelson had taken the main body of his fleet clear of Cadiz, leaving only a squadron of frigates to keep watch on the movements of the combined fleet. The weather was pleasant, which allowed the crews of the Channel Fleet, which had come to join Nelson, to paint their ships in the distinctive 'Nelson Chequer', the style favoured by the Mediterranean Fleet because it appealed to Nelson. The sides were painted in yellow, or possibly white, and black stripes, and the lids of the gunports picked out in black, to create the 'chequered' appearance. It is quite possible that this was more than a decorative whim: a ship with broad yellow sides and yellow gunports that had her guns run out appeared 'chequered', as the darkness of the guns themselves and the gun decks beyond appeared black at any distance. To paint the exterior of the gunports black, therefore, was to make the ship appear at a distance to have her guns run out, even if she had them all sealed shut: it reflected an aggressive mindset. While the ships were painting their sides, a number also painted the hoops of their masts yellow to distinguish them from the Franco-Spanish fleet which all had black mast-hoops. Frequently in battle the smoke of the guns rendered the hulls of the enemy completely invisible, and gunners could only direct their fire by aiming at the masts protruding clear of the smoke. It was vital, therefore, that one's masts were distinguishable by nationality.

The fine weather also allowed ships' boats to pass easily among the fleet. Nelson placed no restriction on such visits; the men were relaxed and he took advantage of the calm conditions to hold regular meetings aboard the *Victory*. Harvey was invited across on 3 October, but was required to come before noon. Nelson had never met him before and he declared in his invitation to Harvey that he desired 'an opportunity of cultivating your acquaintance'.[10] It was in meetings such as this that Nelson outlined his plans for battle. He described it himself as the 'Nelson touch'; it was 'new, it was singular, it was simple.'[11] Historians have debated ever since exactly how original Nelson's tactics were, but perhaps the most important point is that Villeneuve knew, in the broadest of terms, exactly what was coming. Before leaving Cadiz, his final instructions to the combined fleet included the paragraph:

> The enemy will not confine himself to forming on a line of battle
> with our own and engaging us in an artillery duel . . . he will endeav-
> our to envelop our rear, to break through our line and to direct his
> ships in groups upon such of ours as he shall have cut off, so as to
> surround them and defeat them.[12]

Nelson's intention of attacking in two divisions and at right angles to the enemy has already been discussed, but there were a number of other important aspects to his plan. He was determined to attack under full sail, contrary to any established tradition of fleet action. Chase actions such as the Battles of Lagos and Quiberon Bay were fought under full sail, but formal fleet actions, in which the enemy fleet calmly awaited attack, were always fought under topsails only to reduce the likelihood of damage to the rigging, relieve the pressure of manpower on deck for sail handling, and ease station-keeping. But Nelson's new head-on attack required speed. The bows of warships were particularly vulnerable as the bowsprit provided the security for the entire rig. If a ship lost her bowsprit, she would be unable to support any canvas on any of her three masts. Moreover, the construction at the bows was very weak, and shot that broke through the bows, as it was likely to do as the ship drew closer to the enemy, would travel unimpeded down the entire length of the ship, maiming or killing all in its path, dismounting guns, damaging the masts below decks and disabling important equipment which ran vertically through the ship such as the pumps and companionway ladders.

Nelson also required that, in the British tradition, his ships should withhold their fire until very close to the enemy. In an enigmatic statement that has been interpreted as both a statement and in instruction, Nelson declared that 'No captain can do very wrong if he places his ship alongside that of an enemy.' However it is interpreted, the key word in that order is *alongside*:

Nelson required his men to fight close. By doing so, every shot would be made to count, and the superiority of the British gunners, particularly in their ability to maintain a high rate of fire, would eventually wear down the enemy gun crews.

By midnight the British fleet was equidistant between Cape Trafalgar and Cape Spartel, the very stretch of coast where the French *Téméraire* had been chased and captured by Boscawen forty-six years previously. Now it was Eliab Harvey who was determined to burn the name of the *Temeraire* deep into the fabric of British naval history, and it was with the doctrine of close action foremost in his mind that Harvey ordered all sail to be set on the morning of 21 October 1805. The enemy had been sighted and Nelson feared that they would make a dash for the Mediterranean through the Straits of Gibraltar. In the light and variable airs of an Indian summer, it was perfectly possible for the combined fleet to escape under a steady breeze while Nelson lay becalmed. Gradually a light breeze filled the British sails and they headed for Cadiz at four knots. The masts of the vast combined fleet now appeared, in the words of one British sailor, like 'a great wood on our lee bow.'[13]

Seventeen thousand British sailors prepared twenty-seven ships of the line for battle, running out 2,148 guns. No specific details of the *Temeraire*'s preparations survive, except the bald statement 'cleared ship for action and made all sail' entered into her log.[14] She would, however, have taken the same precautions as every other ship. Important parts of the rigging would have been doubled-up or supported by chain; buckets of water would have been placed at handy places around the deck and even in the tops in case of fire; the ship's boats would have been launched and towed astern or even cut adrift to avoid damage and to ease communication in battle; the wood and canvas screens that formed the officers' cabins would have been unshipped and stowed in the hold to allow the guns room to be worked where the officers had slept only hours before; and the officers' furniture would have been carefully stowed or even hoisted into the rigging out of danger.

What we do know, however, is exactly who the men were that were doing these duties, and they were an eclectic bunch. The last muster before the battle reveals that the *Temeraire* was slightly undermanned, with only seven hundred and twenty men. Nearly half of them were English, and a full third of those came from Devon. Almost a third of her crew were Irish and there were smaller percentages of men from Scotland, Ireland, Wales, America, the West Indies, Germany, Sweden, Norway, Portugal, Holland, Austria and South Africa, and there were even three Frenchmen, a Spaniard and a hundred and fifty-four men whose nationality is not stated in the muster.[15] Such a diverse crew was entirely normal. It is also quite interesting to consider who was *not* there. The muster book records that a young midshipman named Frederick Parker had not returned from leave on 3 August, and he was marked as 'R', meaning 'Run' or deserted. There is no further information about why he had not returned, but by January 1806 he was back in the navy, this time serving as first lieutenant in the sloop *Nightingale*, in which he went on to fight courageously in the Baltic campaign, and eventually reached the rank of commander.

Once these men had made their preparations, they waited: more than five hours elapsed between Nelson making his last manoeuvring signal and the first shot being fired. To alleviate the boredom at least, a charming exchange occurred between the *Temeraire* and the *Victory*, the two ships at the head of the weather column. The *Victory* was now leading the *Temeraire*, contrary to Nelson's original Order of Sailing. Nelson had been careful to keep a number of his frigate captains on his flagship so that they could be sent around the fleet with specific instructions as they occurred to him. One of those captains was his good friend Henry Blackwood. Blackwood was horrified at the prospect of Nelson leading the British line into the enemy fleet. They were all aware of the situation in which they placed themselves: Nelson's plan placed his ships at their weakest point on a slow approach to a waiting and fully prepared enemy. Brilliant though the plan to divide the enemy fleet was, it could not be implemented without considerable cost and Blackwood, both as a friend and a naval officer who appreciated the importance of Nelson as a talisman for the rest of the fleet, urged him to reconsider his position. His first suggestion, that Nelson direct the battle from a frigate safe from the enemy's fire, was given short shrift by Nelson. He knew the value of leading from the front, and had done so all his life. Blackwood's next suggestion was that the *Victory* should simply change places with the *Temeraire*. Nelson would thus be protected from the first and inevitably the most violent onslaught of the enemy, while the *Temeraire*'s reassuming her place at the head of the line would conform to the original Order of Sailing, distributed to the captains on 10 October.

I. Mayfield.   J. Ward.   J. Chesterman.   I. Fitzgerald.

J. Rowland.   T. Jones.   T. Cross.   W. Cook.

C. White.   J. Collins.   J. Locker.   I. Cummins.

W. Hillier.   I. Dayley.

PORTRAITS of the MUTINEERS

12. Portraits of the *Temeraire* mutineers, from sketches taken at their trial.

13. Admiral Sir Eliab Harvey by L. F. Abbott, *c*.1806.

14. A contemporary print showing Eliab Harvey 'clearing the deck of the French and Spaniards' at Trafalgar.

Proceedings of the Fleet under the Command of the Admiral
Lord Viscount Nelson K. B – Duke of Bronte – Off Cadiz –

Order of Battle –

1	Temeraire	1	Prince
2	Superb	2	Mars
3	Victory	3	Royal Sovereign
4	Neptune	4	Tonnant
5	Tigre	5	Bellisle
6	Canopus	6	Bellerophon
7	Conqueror	7	Colossus
8	Agamemnon	8	Achille
9	Leviathan	9	Polyphemus
10	Ajax	10	Revenge
11	Orion	11	Britannia
12	Minotaur	12	Swiftsure
13	Queen	13	Africa
14	Donegal	14	Defence
15	Spencer	15	Kent
16	Spartiate	16	Zealous
17		17	Thunderer
18		18	Defiance
19		19	Dreadnought
20		20	

Memorandum.   Victory Off Cadiz the 10th Day of Octr 1805

Thinking it almost impossible to bring a Fleet of
Forty Sail of the Line into a Line of Battle in variable Winds
thick Weather, and other circumstances which must occur –
without such a loss of time that the opportunity would probably be
lost of bringing the Enemy to Battle in such a Manner as
to make the business Decisive – –

I have therefore made up my Mind to keep
the Fleet in that position of Sailing – with the exception of
the First and Second in Command – that the Order of Sailing
is to be the Order of Battle – placing the Fleet in two Lines
of Sixteen Ships each – with an Advanced Squadron of eight
[...] [the] Management of [...]

15. Order of Battle issued by Nelson, 10 October 1805.

16. *The Battle of Trafalgar* by Clarkson Stanfield, 1836.

17. A drawing of the first stage of the Battle of Trafalgar, a copy of the original made aboard HMS *Neptune* at the battle.

18. Eliab Harvey's
coat of arms.

19. Sketch of the *Temeraire* by
John Livesay, made as she lay at
Portsmouth on her return from
the Battle of Trafalgar,
December 1805.

20. Gunboat attack on HMS *Melpomene*, 23 May 1809.

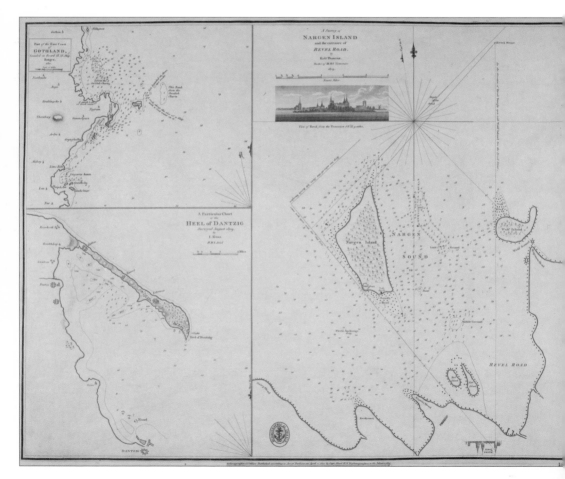

21. A survey of Nargen Island, drawn from the decks of HMS *Temeraire*, 1810.

Grudgingly, Nelson acknowledged the wisdom of Blackwood's proposal, and made the appropriate signal. The *Temeraire*, which had been pressing hard on the *Victory*, surged forward. This is interesting in itself as Second Rates had a reputation as terrible sailers. In fact so poorly did the *Temeraire's* sister ships *Britannia*, *Prince* and *Dreadnought* sail that Nelson specifically ordered them to approach the combined fleet at an angle, to allow more of their sails to draw and ensure that they would not impede the rest of the fleet. Their cumbersome approach was so distinctive that the French thought they had been formed into a distinct *escadre d'observation*. And yet here we have the Second Rate *Temeraire*, surging past the *Victory*, a First Rate with an exceptional sailing reputation. The *Temeraire* had, of course, recently been coppered and so had no weed or barnacles on her hull to slow her down, but speed was also very much linked to the individual skill of the captain and her crew. This brief exchange between the *Victory* and the *Temeraire* is remarkable in itself, but no historian has previously acknowledged that it is strong evidence of the skill of the *Temeraire's* crew. In their eagerness to get at the French they eked every knot of speed from their ship; the trim of her hull was perfect and the sails set in exactly the right number and at exactly the right angle to maximize their effectiveness. This was not a matter of simply setting as many sails as possible. The *Temeraire* may well have noted in her log that she 'made all sail', but in practice when it came to setting the studding sails, those extra sails attached to the very edges of the ship's principal sails, she only set her lower topmast and topgallant studding sails, and only on the larboard side.[16] In spite of their size, sailing warships were exceptionally sensitive, their performance the result of a highly complex equation negotiated by her crew. This episode, therefore, is proof that the *Temeraire's* crew was very good indeed.

When Nelson saw the *Temeraire* begin to surge past him, he changed his mind. He felt that he could not change his position unless Admiral Collingwood in the *Royal Sovereign*, who was leading the other British line, also assumed a position behind the leading ship of his division. If Nelson was the only one to change position, then it would appear that he had shirked the challenge of leading his line into battle. Shortly after signalling to the *Temeraire* to lead the line, therefore, he attempted to get Collingwood to allow another ship to lead his squadron. Every signal that Nelson sent, however, was simply ignored by Collingwood, who pressed on under full sail towards the enemy. Nelson therefore had no choice but to lead his own line, and one account says that he hailed the disappointed Eliab Harvey, who had been swelled with pride at the opportunity to lead the fleet, and told him to resume his position: 'I'll thank you, Captain Harvey, to keep in your proper station, which is *astern* of the *Victory*.' It is unclear if this verbal exchange actually took place, but it is certain from the log of the *Conqueror* that at 12.15, only minutes before the engagement began, the *Victory* signalled to the *Temeraire* with the explicit instruction to take her position astern of the *Victory*.[17] In any event, in the aftermath of the battle it was one of a few occurrences that really caught the public's imagination, and was immortalized by the poet Henry Newbolt:

> The Victory led
> To her flag it was due
> Tho' the *Temeraires* thought themselves admirals too
> But Lord Nelson he hailed them
> With masterful grace
> Cap'n Harvey, I'll thank you to keep in your place.[18]

And so they sailed into battle, the *Victory* leading the *Temeraire*, with the rest of the weather column following. Harvey clearly resented having to give up his place at the head of the line, as he stayed exceptionally close to the *Victory*, within a ship's length or 185 feet. This was far closer than naval convention prescribed, and it nearly ended in disaster. Just as the two ships met the French line, Harvey was forced to sheer away dramatically to avoid colliding with the *Victory*, which had broken through across the bows of Villeneuve's flagship, *Bucentaur*. Moments later, the *Temeraire* cut away her studding sails, an action that has been misinterpreted as being made to avoid collision with the *Victory* but was in fact exactly what had been stipulated for all ships made in Nelson's tactical memorandum of 9 October.

Although there are many first-hand accounts of the Battle of Trafalgar, there are surprisingly few from the ordinary sailors of the *Temeraire*. Almost everything we know of the action from the *Temeraire*'s perspective comes from the pens of Captain Eliab Harvey and the master, Thomas Price. We are, however, particularly fortunate that of all the captains there, Eliab

Harvey was one of the most systematic and detailed in his description of the battle, and the captain's log reflects that rigour: it provides one of the finest accounts of the battle of any of the twenty-seven British ships. Harvey also wrote a lengthy letter to his wife only two days after the battle which provides a great deal more information. The log of Thomas Price is equally comprehensive and we are further blessed that officers of the two ships which the *Temeraire* fought closely, the *Redoutable* and the *Fougueux*, were equally diligent and, moreover, lucky enough to survive her attack. Combined, these sources provide a description which rates as highly as any other account of a sea battle in the entire age of sail.

It is entirely characteristic of Harvey that his first decision was to steer away from the *Victory* and to head towards *La Santísima Trinidad*. Harvey was a man who fought his own battles, and he feared no one, not least the *Santísima Trinidad*, flagship of Rear Admiral Baltazar Hidalgo de Cisneros, and by some distance the largest ship in the world. She mounted a hundred and thirty guns and was the only ship afloat in the world to have four complete gun decks. There could be no finer prize and no surer way of demonstrating his courage and zeal than by attacking this Spanish monster. British sailors enjoyed identifying enemy ships from their silhouettes and, with such a high freeboard, that of the *Santísima Trinidad* was unmistakable. It is particularly interesting that both the *Temeraire*'s log and Harvey's letter to his wife record that he engaged the *Santísima Trinidad* and some 'other ships'[19] for twenty minutes. Harvey neither knew nor cared who else he was engaging: he only had eyes for the giant Spaniard.

For twenty minutes the *Temeraire* poured fire into the great hull of the *Santísima Trinidad* and any other ship that was within range and sight, but so great was the smoke caused by the guns that Harvey was suddenly concerned that he was firing into the *Victory* herself. Such incidents of friendly fire were common, but as soon as the smoke cleared, Harvey saw the *Victory* to the south, grappling with a French 74-gunner. This was *La Redoutable*, one of the finest ships in the French fleet. Her captain, Jean-Jacques Lucas, had drilled his crew as well as the best of the British fleet, and she had been positioned just astern of the French flagship where the fighting would be hottest. Soon after the *Victory* had opened fire on Villeneuve's flagship she drifted into the path of *La Redoutable* and was now experiencing the full force of the French onslaught.

Lucas's men rained shot and hand grenades onto the deck with such ferocity that they drove every sailor below, and in the process, a shot struck Nelson in the left shoulder, burrowed through his upper body and shattered his spine. Nelson was carried below, and the irrepressible Lucas decided to board the *Victory*. This was an extraordinary decision and reveals a man very much of the same ilk as Harvey or Nelson himself. In comparison to the *Victory*, the *Redoutable* was tiny. She had twenty-six fewer guns, and only two gun decks to *Victory*'s three. The British flagship towered over her and yet Lucas was still determined to board her and sensed that the moment was right. Two attempts were made to board, but the French found it impossible to get sufficient men onto the decks of the larger ship: every man somehow had to climb the *Victory*'s hull or leap across from the rigging of the *Redoutable*. Two French sailors did clamber onto *Victory*'s decks by way of her anchor but it proved impossible to get a large body of men across from the one to the other and all at once.

It was at this moment that the *Temeraire* appeared out of the smoke, and Harvey saw the massed Frenchmen preparing to board the deserted weather deck of *Victory*, their grappling irons clinging to her hull and rigging. As Able Seaman John Brown of the *Victory* recorded: 'We engaged five ships at one time but they would have sunk us only for the *Timmera* (*Temeraire*) took the firy edge off us.'[20] Seeing the *Victory* so hard pressed, Harvey took immediate and decisive action. He took his ship across the stern of the *Redoutable* and raked her through the unprotected stern galleries. Lucas later wrote:

> It would be difficult to describe the horrible carnage caused by the murderous broadside of this ship; More than 200 of our brave lads were killed or wounded, I was wounded at the same time, but not so seriously as to prevent me from remaining at my post.[21]

The *Temeraire* then rammed the *Redoutable* with such force that many of the French guns were dismounted in the collision. Once alongside, the British crew tied the ships together and only stopped firing briefly to put out a fire that had started on the *Temeraire*.

The French returned fire with those guns that were still serviceable, but the destruction caused by the *Temeraire* continued. 'In less than half an hour', wrote Lucas, 'our vessel was so riddled that she seemed to be no more than a mass of wreckage'. Their fire must have stopped, for Harvey called to Lucas, demanding his surrender. But still Lucas was not beaten and ordered 'some soldiers who were near me to reply to answer this summons with musket-shots, which was performed with the greatest of zeal.'[22] In fact, Lucas did not surrender *La Redoutable* until he was certain that without British help she would sink, drowning the many hundreds of living wounded scattered about her decks. Lucas knew that his only alternative was to burn the *Redoutable*, which would inevitably destroy both the *Victory* and the *Temeraire*. It would have been a terrible blow to the British at this early stage in the battle, but Lucas could not bring himself to sacrifice his wounded men.

It was not until all of the *Redoutable*'s guns were broken or dismounted that Lucas called for quarter from the *Temeraire*. Two guns had exploded, killing their crews; all of the gunports were cut to pieces; four out of the ship's six pumps were broken, as were all of the ship's ladders, making the transmission of orders throughout the ship almost impossible; great piles of debris and dead covered the decks; 522 of the original crew of 643 were unable to fight and of those 300, including almost all of the officers, were dead. They had few men, no leadership and no cannon. Harvey sent his second lieutenant, John Wallace, to take command of the ship. Only moments before, the *Redoutable*'s mainmast had come crashing down onto the poop deck of the *Temeraire*, causing terrible damage, but providing a useful bridge to board the enemy ship. It also caused three beautiful French carronades to fall onto the *Temeraire*'s decks.* Harvey immediately marked them down as souvenirs 'with which . . . to commemorate the event every year in May by firing them off from the mound at Chigwell.'[23]

As the boarding party stepped across to the *Redoutable*, one French sailor, wounded with a bullet in his leg, picked up a musket and stabbed a British sailor through the hip with such force that he was driven overboard and fell between the two ships. The British were outraged at this breach of faith and prepared to leave to renew the onslaught, and it took all of Lucas's considerable charm to entreat them to stay. He handed over his sword, and

---

* Although the source is explicit in its use of the term carronade, it is likely that this was one of the French brass *orbusiers*.

the *Temeraire* took *La Redoutable* as her prize. Meanwhile, on board *Victory*, Nelson had been taken to the cockpit in the darkness of the orlop deck where *Victory*'s surgeon, William Beatty, was treating the wounded. He knew that Nelson was dying, and he told him so. The British had lost their admiral but, thanks to Harvey and the *Temeraire*, they had not lost their flagship. Though shattered, she still floated, and still flew the British ensign, giving encouragement to every British sailor that could see her through the fog of war.

To engage in this manner with one ship, albeit a smaller vessel, was a feat of the highest order, but Harvey and his crew had more on their minds than just *La Redoutable*. As the *Temeraire* fought the *Redoutable* to a standstill, another Spanish flagship, the *Santa Ana*, continued to pour broadside after broadside into the *Temeraire*'s stern while another French ship, the *Fougueux*, bore down to the assistance of the *Redoutable*. It appeared to the captain of the *Fougueux* that she had taken the *Temeraire* by surprise because it was normal for an entire ship's crew to fight the guns on the one side of the ship that was engaged, leaving the guns on the side facing the *Fougueux* silent. In reality, however, Harvey was well aware of the situation and his starboard guns had not yet been fired at all. They were loaded and aimed, and their crews were fresh. He had not been surprised but, in a perfect example of British gunnery doctrine, he was simply waiting to make his first broadside as destructive as possible. When it came, the broadside was augmented by a fusillade of small-arms fire which swept the decks of the *Fougueux* and drove the French below. The *Fougueux* was so badly cut up in her rigging that she could not be steered and crashed into the *Temeraire*, now sandwiched between *La Redoutable* and the *Fougueux*. The crew of the *Temeraire* were swift to not let her get away and lashed her securely to their ship. 'Perhaps never was a ship so circumstanced as mine', wrote Harvey to his wife, 'to have for more than three hours two of the enemy's line of battle ships lashed to her.'[24]

It was a precarious position indeed, and the French soon came swarming back on deck armed with sabres and axes to defend their ship. As the crew of the *Redoutable* had found, however, they could not compete with the greater height of the British ships, and marksmen on the *Temeraire*'s weather deck continued to rain fire down onto the crew of the *Fougueux*. When the British boarded her, they did so in a rush, through the main deck ports and from the chains, led by the *Temeraire*'s first lieutenant, Thomas Kennedy. The first few 'paid dearly for their temerity', but almost immediately the French captain was shot in the heart, dying instantly. The French crews defended their decks, port by port, but could not compete with the greater numbers of British sailors. The second in command, Commander Bezin, recorded the shocking state of the French ship after the death of her captain:

> As I had received several wounds at the beginning of the action,
> I called for the 1st lieutenant to assist me in this grievous situation;
> I was informed that he was no longer alive; (of) the two next in sen-
> iority one was nearly dead and the other, M. Peltier, had a ball in the
> leg; I summoned the 4th Lieutenant, who informed me that his bat-
> tery was nearly silenced; Enseigne de vaisseau Drudésit sent me word
> that he had only fifteen men left and all his guns dismounted; all the
> people that I had on deck or in the tops were killed or wounded.[25]

Bazin ran to the captain's cabin, found the lead box full of confidential papers, threw them overboard and then surrendered his ship to the crew of the *Temeraire*.

By this stage in the battle, the *Temeraire* had followed the *Victory* as she smashed through the enemy's line, engaged the largest ship in the world, saved the *Victory* from capture and taken two prizes, one of them the best-trained ship in the entire French navy. In doing so forty-seven of her crew had been killed and seventy-six more wounded, and the ship was in a terrible state. Every sail and yard had been destroyed, only the lower masts were left standing and they were shot through in many places. The rudder head had also been shot off, together with the starboard cat-head, from which the starboard anchor would have been suspended. Eight feet of her hull on the starboard side below the mainmast was stove in and the quarter galleries on both sides of the ship had been completely destroyed when the ships had collided with each other. It could have been even worse. At one stage a grenade thrown from the rigging of the *Redoutable* had found its way into the powder-screen on the *Temeraire*'s quarterdeck and caused an explosion. It took the quick thinking of John Toohig, the *Temeraire*'s master at arms, to prevent the fire from spreading to the after magazine. The resulting explosion would have destroyed all three ships together.

With his ship entirely disabled and the action around him at a lull, Harvey believed that his battle was over and signalled for assistance from a frigate. The *Sirius* dutifully bore down to take the *Temeraire* in tow, when the whole tenor of the moment suddenly altered. Out of the haze appeared five ships of the French van, some of those ships that had been 'cut' from the main battle by Nelson's manoeuvre. They had managed to turn around and make their way back to the battle and were bearing down on the *Victory* and *Temeraire* in good order. Their crews were fresh and, if they joined the battle around the *Temeraire* and *Victory*, they could still make a difference. With Nelson now dead, this was a potential turning point.

Three-quarters of a mile distant, the French squadron, led by Rear-Admiral Dumanoir in the *Formidable*, opened fire on the *Temeraire*. Most shocking of all to those who witnessed it, they also opened fire on the French and Spanish ships that had struck – 'A bloody deed so worthy (of) the days of Robespierre, by which several hundred of the Spaniards were killed or wounded,'[26] wrote one French sailor. William Pitts, a young midshipman from the *Temeraire*, had just stepped aboard the *Redoutable* when he was struck by a shot from one of Dumanoir's squadron. It took off his leg and the boy needed immediate help. Horrified at their countrymen's action, seamen of the *Redoutable* took Pitts straight down to see their surgeon and insisted that he was attended to before their own wounded. The leg was amputated, but Pitts died that night. The *Temeraire* responded by opening fire with whatever guns could bear, and the master's log records that they cut away one of their prizes to fire at Dumanoir. The attack had no real bite, however, and Dumanoir's vessels soon escaped.

Dumanoir's attack was the last gasp of the combined fleet and Villeneuve surrendered. The French and Spanish lost twenty-one ships of the line, almost seventy thousand tons in all; it is not known exactly how many men died, but more than four thousand is likely. The British lost no ships and only 449 men dead and 1,242 wounded. The storm that followed the battle was by some accounts a hurricane, and it was devastating. It was so bad that Harvey was unable to write his journal for those days; for a man who enjoyed writing as much as he did, and who was used to writing at sea in all conditions, this is significant indeed. When he did take up his pen once more, he immediately noted 'the weather at present moderate, but ever since the battle it has been very bad, almost a constant gale of wind with constant rain; *shocking* for our poor wounded.'[27] Worse still, the prize crew of thirty of the finest sailors hand-picked from the *Temeraire* that had taken charge of the *Fougueux* all died when she sank. By now 546 of the *Fougueux*'s original crew of 680 had died. Aboard the *Redoutable* conditions were also horrendous. Her captain wrote: 'The few Frenchmen fit for service united with the English to pump, to fother some leaks, to patch up the ports, to shore up the vessel's stern which was ready to collapse – in fine, never was a night more laborious.' The poor British sailors even had to cope with the threat of mutiny from the French sailors, who were collecting arms on the orlop deck to 'rescue' the *Redoutable*. 'Never were so many deeds of courage, valour, and daring displayed on board the same ship', wrote Captain Lucas, 'and never has the history of the navy offered a similar example.'[28] It was all in vain, however. At noon the next day she lost her last remaining mast; at 5 p.m. the water began to gain on the pumps; and at seven her stern collapsed and she sank. Some men were taken off before she went down, and fifty more were recovered from her wreck. The British sailors were now in command of her, however. The wreck had become their responsibility, and only fifteen of the *Temeraire*'s prize crew were eventually rescued.

There is surprisingly little mention of the storm in the log of the *Temeraire*, but she was so battered already that little more damage could be done to her. Harvey wrote: 'The state of the *Temeraire* is so bad we have been in constant apprehension of our lives.'[29] The *Victory* lost her main yard at the height of the storm, and the *Royal Sovereign* lost her foremast, but before the storm even began the *Temeraire* had nothing but her lower masts standing and her rudder did not work. She was even a danger in the complete calm that followed the storm, colliding with the *Defiance* which was supposed to be towing her. We know that she was one of five ships that Collingwood was particularly concerned about in the aftermath of the battle.[30]

In the days that followed, various ships towed the *Temeraire* which, as she was such a large ship, was used as a temporary prison for the many French and Spanish captives. At one stage she had 168 aboard. As the weather settled the ships crept back to Gibraltar, the *Temeraire* arriving on 2 November, a full eleven days after a battle which had taken place less than forty miles away. It was not until another day had passed that the wounded could be taken to the hospital onshore. The delay in returning was avoidable. Harvey was incensed when the *Africa*, which had been sent to assist him into port, sailed near him all day before informing him in the evening that she was there to assist the *Temeraire*. An angry Harvey later wrote: 'I desired him to stay by the ship, but the good Captain Digby thought proper to take care of himself and made off in the night.'[31] We now know this to be more than a little unfair. The *Africa* was, in fact, in no fit state to tow any ship as her bowsprit and all three lower masts had been badly damaged. She also had numerous holes in her hull and 62 men killed or wounded and was eventually towed into Gibraltar herself.

Nevertheless, Harvey's complaint about the *Africa* was not the only one made by sailors of the *Temeraire* about their countrymen. The master was very curt in his description of the behaviour of the *Sirius* as Dumanoir bore down on them. The *Sirius*, he reported, sailed away as Dumanoir approached, and only came back to help once the French squadron had ceased to be a danger.[32] Another of the *Temeraire*'s men claimed with righteous and rightful indignation that the *Neptune*, stationed immediately astern of the *Temeraire*, 'might as well (have) been laying in Cawsand Bay'. He later wrote that they had been sent up the Mediterranean 'as punishment'.[33] Modern research has shown that these were not isolated examples of British disaffection with their fellow countrymen, and that a number of British captains did not act as Nelson, and the best of his captains, would have expected. Nevertheless, the grumbles of the fleet were hushed up and, unusually, no courts marital followed the battle.

Fame immediately attached itself to the *Temeraire*. At Gibraltar she was named 'Pride of England and Terror of France'[34] and she was the only ship singled out for praise in Collingwood's report of the battle, published nationwide in newspapers and journals. 'After such a victory', wrote Collingwood,

it may appear unnecessary to enter into encomiums on the particular parts taken by the several Commanders; the conclusion says more on the subject than I have language to express; the spirit which animated all was the same: when all exert themselves zealously in their country's service, all deserve that their high merits would stand recorded; and never was high merit more conspicuous than in the battle I have described.

And yet he still felt that he had to mention the *Temeraire* by name:

> A circumstance occurred during the action which so strongly marks
> the invincible spirit of British seamen, when engaging the enemies of
> their country, that I cannot resist the pleasure I have in making it
> known to their Lordships; the *Temeraire* was boarded by accident; or
> design, by a French ship on one side, and a Spaniard on the other;
> the contest was vigorous, but, in the end the combined Ensigns were
> torn from the poop and the British hoisted in their places.[35]

'Nothing could be finer', wrote Collingwood in a more personal note to
Harvey, 'I have not words in which I can sufficiently express my admiration.'[36] Exactly why Collingwood chose to concentrate on the activities of
Harvey at the expense of other gallant captains remains open to debate, but
it must not be overlooked that Harvey was the only one who spoke to him in
person in the few hours before Collingwood wrote his despatch. In the
words of one contemporary, and astute, observer: 'of course he (Harvey) did
not hide his light under a bushel when he put it on Collingwood's table, and
as he saw no other Captain until his despatches were written *Temeraire*
shines the brightest star of the Trafalgar constellation.'[37]

In fact, Harvey's support for his superiors extended beyond the fighting
itself. During the voyage home, the crew of the *Temeraire* received a proposal
from Collingwood that two thousand pounds be deducted from the prize
money to establish a fund for erecting a monument to the memory of
Nelson. The proposal was unanimously approved by the captain and crew of
the *Temeraire*.[38]

The British united in celebration and grief as the news of the battle
reached London and weeks later the ships themselves started to arrive in
British ports. The *Temeraire* had carried out some preliminary repairs in
Cadiz and then Gibraltar, replacing eight panes of glass and loading aboard
twenty-two gallons of black paint to clean her battle-scarred sides.[39] She
soon sailed for England and eventually returned to Portsmouth on 1
December 1805. That very day, safely at home having survived one of the
fiercest battles of the entire age of sail, one of the fiercest storms in living
memory and a voyage across the treacherous Bay of Biscay in mid-winter in
a heavily damaged ship, a young seaman named James Allen ran out of luck.

At ten that morning, and within sight of Portsmouth, he fell overboard and was drowned. Three days later the *Temeraire* dipped her ensign as HMS *Victory* passed by with Nelson's body aboard.[40]

Word of the arrival of the battered ships quickly spread, and a lovely letter survives between two of Harvey's nine children, his daughter Emma, writing to her sister Louisa the day after the ships arrived: 'We have this instant heard that papa and the *Temeraire* are at Portsmouth, delightful.'[41] The ships and their contents soon proved to be tourist attractions in their own right. Flocks of the curious came to pay their respects and ogle the damage and the captured French captains, one of whom, in the words of Harvey's wife, 'is a great strapping man with emence (sic) earrings, the other a little man like a dancing master.'[42] Among the observers of the Trafalgar fleet were artists, drawn there to make their living by documenting events of national importance. One of the men who used the ships as source material for his work was Nicholas Pocock. He had begun his early working life as a sailor before becoming a full-time artist, and his paintings are imbued with a unique sense of dramatic realism. As a result his services were much in demand, particularly by naval officers who wanted their ships or battles recorded by an artist who understood ships and the sea. By 1805 he was wealthy and successful. Unsurprisingly, Pocock was lured by the promise of the Trafalgar ships, and he shared correspondence with the drawing master at the Royal Naval Academy in Portsmouth, John Livesay. Livesay sent a number of sketches of the Trafalgar ships to Pocock, who worked them up into even more detailed drawings as a basis for his two great works on the battle. It is from Livesay's hand that we have the only surviving image of the *Temeraire* as she looked on her return to England. It is indistinct and vague, and the *Temeraire*'s carpenters had been repairing her shot holes for almost six weeks, but still great dark patches, dents or holes, are clearly visible in the sketch (fig. 19).

Another artist drawn to the Trafalgar ships was the thirty-year-old Joseph Turner who, by now, had made quite a name for himself. He had exhibited regularly at the Royal Academy for fifteen years and it had been ten years since his work was first mentioned in the press. By 1803 he had enjoyed sufficient success to build a large gallery of his own, attached to his house in Harley Street. Although the range of his subject matter was already breathtaking, he had spent a great deal of his time focusing on his love of ships and the sea. Born in London, he would always have had access to ships and shipping, albeit in the heart of the largest city on earth and moored in a muddy river. It is unclear exactly when Turner first saw the sea itself, but it is certain that he travelled to Margate where he stayed with a relative around 1786 when he was eleven. There is no evidence that he ever visited the *Temeraire*, but he certainly visited the *Victory* when she finally returned to Sheerness on 22 December 1805. Her flag hung at half mast as she bore the body of Nelson, now embalmed and placed in a lead coffin filled with brandy, camphor and myrrh. This coffin had replaced the makeshift barrel of brandy in which the body had been pickled immediately after the battle, and the barrel of spirits of wine or pure alcohol in which it had made the journey home. The body was swiftly removed to the commissioner's yacht in the evening, and it is unclear whether Turner boarded the *Victory* while it was still aboard. Once he was on board, however, Turner filled two entire sketch-books with views of the ship, sketches of sailors and their uniforms and annotated interviews with the crew. Thus he wrote of the marines: 'Undress a red jacket; sometimes a red fancy shirt.' Of Captain Hardy he wrote:

C. Hardy wore B. gaiters, 4 sailors carried some officers down about the time L.N. fell, on his left arm. Some one forwarded to help him. A marine to every gun stands aft 8 others. C. Hardy looks rather tall, dreadful (?), fair, about 36 years. Marshall, young, long tail, round face, proud lips.[43]

These sketches and notes would form the main source material for Turner's two magnificent paintings of Trafalgar and would plant a seed in his mind that would germinate thirty years later.

The final piece of the puzzle of how the *Temeraire*'s fame became cemented into British history was the fate of Eliab Harvey. Much honoured on his return, he was one of the 'supporters of the pall' at Nelson's funeral, was promoted to Rear-Admiral of the Red and received a gold medal and a sword of honour. The House of Commons, in which he still sat, added his name (and only his name) to those of Nelson and Collingwood in its vote of thanks to the heroes of Trafalgar. Never a man for modesty in victory, Harvey's bragging irritated his fellow captains. The thoughtful and wise Captain Codrington of the *Orion* wrote to his wife: 'There will always be some whose vanity leads them to paint their conduct in too warm a tint, and to sound their own trumpets without regard to concord or harmony, but above all I have ever heard of is Harvey . . . he is become the greatest bore I ever met with',[44] and Captain Thomas Fremantle of the *Neptune* wrote to his wife Betsey that 'he thinks every ship was subdued by him, and he wears us all to death with his incessant jargon.'[45]

The honours lauded on him were still not enough, however, and Harvey demanded respect from his peers. In 1809 he was so outraged that he was overlooked to command a fireship attack on the French fleet at Basque Roads that he vehemently and publicly insulted his superior, Admiral Gambier, and was court-martialled and dismissed the service. With his reputation now in tatters, Harvey was determined that the world should never forget the role of the *Temeraire*, and by definition *his* role, in the success at Trafalgar. When he was made Knight Grand Cross of the Order of the Bath some twenty years after the battle, he asked the College of Heralds for special permission to carry the name '*Temeraire*' as a motto above his family crest, in the position usually associated with battle-cries. He also included the names of his prizes '*Redoutable* et *Fougueux*' as another motto, and still further he decorated the White Horse of Hanover to the right of the arms with a gold naval crown, whose rim was lettered 'Trafalgar' and from it hung a gold Trafalgar medal. As an example of brash conceit displayed through arms it has few rivals, and it can be still viewed today in its full audacity at the little church of St Andrew in Hempstead near Saffron Walden in Essex, where Harvey is buried in his family tomb.

Perhaps here also lies the explanation for Harvey's brazen self-promotion: he came from a large and successful family and one of his distant relatives, William Harvey, had for more than three generations enjoyed his position as the Harveys' most famous son. An experimental physician famous for his discovery of the circulation of the blood, he had been the personal physician to Charles I and had been present with him at the Battle of Edgehill in 1642. Research in the Harvey family papers has also revealed that he was responsible for the only known scientific examination of a witch's familiar. Personally ordered by Charles I to examine a lady suspected of witchcraft who lived on the outskirts of Newmarket, the dubious Harvey visited her in the guise of a wizard. He succeeded in capturing and dissecting her pet toad. The animal, Harvey concluded dryly, was a toad.[46]

Even with such a distinguished relative, Eliab Harvey need not have worried over his new-found fame, however. The impact of the Battle of Trafalgar and the death of Nelson on British history was already more profound than he could have believed possible. In the coming years it would only grow as historians, poets and artists encouraged and exploited an unprecedented level of public interest in the story of the British fleet at Trafalgar, and of the *Temeraire* in particular.

8.

The Baltic and Iberian *Temeraire*

MAY 1809 – AUGUST 1811

At Single Anchor off Carteronas

It is only very recently that historians have begun to develop a sophisticated perception of the impact of Trafalgar on British history. For many years it was believed that Trafalgar was the turning point of the war. It was, after all, one of the most decisive battles in history: the allied fleet lost twenty-one ships of the line while the British lost none. It was certainly devastating for the Spanish navy, which had been declining steadily since the 1790s, and the loss of so many fine men and fine ships weakened it still further. The French navy, on the other hand, was a formidable force. It had lost thirteen ships, but still had more than seventy ships of the line.* Napoleon, moreover, although disgusted by its inability to effect an invasion of England, had not turned his back fully on the navy. He still poured money into shipbuilding, and aimed for a target of a hundred and fifty ships of the line. He also focused his resources on the construction of two great shipbuilding centres to the south and east of Britain: at Cherbourg and Antwerp. With direct access to the Channel and North Sea, they would make an invasion of England far easier as the navy would be forced to divide its resources between the western and eastern entrances to the Channel. There is no more powerful testament to continuing British concern over Napoleonic invasion in the years immediately after Trafalgar than the magnificent Martello towers that guard the British south coast to this day. Between 1804 and 1812 a hundred and five of these small, circular defensive forts were built around the British coastline. Thirty feet high, with solid walls nine feet thick and with bomb-proof roofs, they were designed to withstand a small siege and

---

* French losses were eight in the battle, one in the hurricane immediately after it and four in Strachan's action of 4 November.

hold up an invading army long enough for the main defensive forces to arrive. And while these post-Trafalgar precautions were made in home waters against potential French aggression, on the far side of the world, meanwhile, the reality of continued French aggression was felt in the Indian Ocean where French frigate squadrons based on the island of Mauritius continued their highly successful war against British trade, preying on the valuable shipping routes of the East India Company.

After Trafalgar, therefore, French maritime strategy remained a major threat to British interests in both the long and short term, in both home waters and abroad, and direct action was taken against the French with blockades maintained at all of their major ports. Moreover, while Napoleon rebuilt his fleet he adopted a new strategy designed to cripple Britain economically. He called it the 'Continental System', and he ordered all continental powers to exclude Britain absolutely from the economy of Europe. That this was at all conceivable says a great deal about the immediate impact of the Battle of Trafalgar on the European land campaigns. Shortly after the battle, Napoleon's land forces reached a new apogee of success and inflicted heavy defeats on the Austrians and the Russians at Ulm, Austerlitz and Friedland, and all the while they celebrated the death of Nelson. With the Spanish still in alliance with Napoleon and Portugal invaded, the French controlled the entire European coastline with the exception of Denmark and Sweden, which was ruled by the unstable Gustavus Adolphus IV. Gustavus was famously irrational and prone to bouts of insanity. These bouts did not manifest themselves in confusion but in a focused loathing of Napoleon, whom he believed to be the Beast of the Apocalypse. In Sweden, therefore, Britain had her only European ally. Sweden thus became not only a source of friendship, but the focus of Napoleon's Continental System. He knew that Britain's ability to wage war rested on the masts, hemp, flax, iron and tar that came from the Baltic, and particularly from Russia, Denmark and Sweden.

The final piece of the jigsaw that drew British maritime focus to the Baltic as well as to the traditional strongholds of Napoleonic maritime power were the navies of the Baltic states themselves. The Russian navy was already hostile to Britain, Tsar Alexander I having pledged his support to Napoleon at a meeting on a decorated raft on the River Niemen in July 1807, shortly after the Russian defeat at Friedland. This was a significant development. The Russian navy existed in some strength and, after the collapse of Spanish seapower in the wake of the Battle of Trafalgar, gradually replaced Spain as Europe's third most important naval power. Indeed, the two decades from 1787 to 1807 have been described as the most successful in Russian naval history.[1] The Baltic was also home to both the Swedish and Danish navies. The Swedish navy was weaker than the Danish, and had suffered in the naval wars with Russia between 1788 and 1790. Nevertheless it retained a significant force of around a dozen battleships and a large flotilla of smaller oared gunboats. Originally intended to meet the threat posed by the Swedes, the Danish navy maintained a larger force of around twenty battleships, and in the early years of the nineteenth century Denmark began to build a far larger navy to defend against Napoleonic aggression. This significant Danish force became the focus of a power struggle between Britain and France. Napoleon's armies were starting to spread into the Baltic and the British believed that it would not be long before they took control of Copenhagen itself and its great naval dockyard. Combined, the Russian and Danish navies would amount to thirty-six ships of the line, a formidable naval presence. If that force came under Napoleonic control, British resistance to an invasion from the east would become even more difficult. There was even the specific concern, albeit possibly unfounded, that the French were planning to use the combined Russian, Danish and Swedish fleets to land men in Ireland.

For all of these reasons, therefore, British success at Trafalgar did not provide an immediate cure to British concerns and, to combat Napoleonic aggression, the British government still needed every single ship that it could lay its hands on. Although Britain lost no ships at Trafalgar, those that had been most heavily engaged were in a terrible state, and none more so than the *Temeraire*. She went straight into dry dock in Portsmouth, and stayed there for a full sixteen months. The total cost of her repair was £25,352, no less than £20,352 over the forecast budget, and more than a third of the cost of her original construction and fitting. *Victory* by contrast was repaired for £9,936, less than half of the cost, and her repairs only took two months.[2]

With the Trafalgar ships refitting and some already repaired, the British response to the Baltic question was to seize the initiative, which they did brilliantly. At the end of July 1807, a powerful British squadron was sent to the Baltic under the command of Admiral James Gambier to neutralize the Danish fleet. His success was absolute. The Danish army was in Jutland, preparing to defend Denmark against the French, and the British besieged Copenhagen with a heavy and particularly brutal bombardment for three days before it capitulated. The entire Danish navy was seized and returned to Britain. Over two thousand men, women and children died, fifteen ships of the line and fifteen frigates were captured along with twenty thousand tons of naval stores. Although only four Danish ships were deemed of suffi-cient quality to enter into the Royal Navy, they had been denied to Napoleon along with the numerous others which could easily have been converted into troop transports, the very type of ship that Napoleon needed to launch an invasion of England. The elimination of the Danish navy in 1807 counts as the second most important change in the European balance of power in this period, after the collapse of Spanish naval power following the Battle of Trafalgar. Britain had a hand in both, and her grip was starting to tighten on her control of the world's oceans.

While the capture of the Danish fleet solved one immediate problem, it created another that was far less easy to solve: the Danes were enraged. Their fleet was their pride, protection and hope, and the entire nation was gripped by indignation and grief at its destruction and at British cruelty towards Danish civilians. The British were simply referred to as 'the robbers' in the local press.[3] British violence at the attack on Copenhagen and the theft of their entire fleet united the Danes with Russia and France in their hatred of the British, and it did more to threaten British shipbuilding supplies than Napoleon's Continental System ever could. This is because there are only two principal entrances to the Baltic: the Sound and the Great Belt. Both are extremely narrow, and both are controlled by Denmark. Any ship wish-ing to pass into or out of the Baltic first had to negotiate more than three hundred miles of hostile, narrow Danish waters. The Danes no longer had a navy, but they did have thousands of highly skilled, resourceful and coura-geous seamen and every Danish man was required to serve six years if called upon. Needless to say, the Danes also had an endless supply of shipbuilding material. It would take too long to rebuild a navy of ships of the line but it was far easier to build small, handy, fast and powerful gunboats that could terrorize the larger British warships in the shallow waters and frequent calms of the Baltic, and that is exactly what they did.

They raised the money by public subscription and by many towns selling their silver. It is also now believed that Napoleon gave a great deal of financial assistance. The sound of shipbuilding echoed all over Denmark and Norway as they built a vast fleet of gunboats to guard the entrances to the Baltic. They lurked in the fjords and inlets that lined the main shipping channels, invisible until the last moment. When a large merchantman or warship was unlucky enough to ground, as they so frequently did in the shoal water of the Baltic, or was becalmed on a mirror-glass sea, the gunboats descended in swarms of twenty or more. With powerful guns and numerous, violent crews, they were a terrifying and formidable opponent. Like a pack of dogs they could bring any opponent, of any size, to its knees. Moreover, the calms, shallows and gunboats were not the only problems of policing the Baltic: there were currents in the narrow waterways that were so strong that even in a fresh breeze a large warship could make no headway. It was to these unfamiliar waters, infested with an unfamiliar foe, that the *Temeraire* now sailed into what would become, in the words of one historian, one of 'Britain's strangest and least known naval wars.'[4]

Second Rates such as the *Temeraire* were particularly favoured by the Admiralty for Baltic service: they carried all the trappings of the prestigious First Rates but had a significantly shallower draught. By now the First Rate ships of the line were over sixteen feet longer and had a draught greater by almost two feet. Indeed, when the Baltic expedition was first mooted, it was proposed that all the flagships should be Second Rates. The Second Rate *Prince of Wales* was the flagship for Gambier's 1807 attack on Copenhagen and Saumarez hoisted his flag in the *Victory* (now classed as a Second Rate) between 1808 and 1812. At various stages his fleet included the Second Rates *Formidable, Dreadnought, Temeraire* and *St George*. Almost since their inception, Second Rates had enjoyed a tainted reputation, but in the Baltic in the early nineteenth century, they found their natural home.

By the time the *Temeraire* sailed to the Baltic, as the flagship of Rear-Admiral Sir Manley Dixon, third in command of the entire expedition, the strategic situation had changed once again, and ostensibly for the worse. Russian forces had made dramatic inroads into the Baltic, and Finland had fallen into Russian hands. With mounting pressure on her borders, the mad

Gustavus was forced from the Swedish throne by a dramatic palace coup, and his uncle, Charles XIII, took his place. Charles was swift to accept French influence. Finland was ceded to Russia, and alliances were made with both Denmark and France. Shortly after, he even named one of Napoleon's marshals, Jean-Baptiste Bernadotte, as his hereditary heir. Bernadotte became Charles XIV John, and the dynasty of that Napoleonic general still rules Sweden today. When the *Temeraire* made sail for the Baltic in the spring of 1809, therefore, Sweden, Denmark and Russia were all bound by treaty against Britain. The British, meanwhile, needed access to Baltic shipbuilding stores more than ever before.

We are particularly fortunate for our knowledge of this period of the *Temeraire*'s life that a young marine named Thomas Rees decided to join the Royal Navy to see the world and to fight the French. For two years he had been apprenticed to a tailor in Carmarthen, Wales, but had found the work dull. When, in 1808, his father died, Rees took his opportunity and volunteered for the Carmarthen fusiliers. From there he joined the county militia and thence moved to Plymouth, where he joined the marines. At Plymouth lay the *Temeraire*, and he came aboard her in April 1808, aged eighteen. He served aboard the *Temeraire* until December 1811 and throughout his time on board he kept a journal. In old age he enjoyed arranging and rewriting his journal, and eventually a publisher recognized its value and it was published in 1822.

The *Temeraire*'s first experience of the Baltic was alarming. She arrived in May 1809, and met up with Saumarez's force at Wingo Sound in the Kattegat, fourteen miles offshore from the nearest Swedish town of Gothenburg. Wingo Sound was the centre of the convoy system. It was dreary beyond belief and protected by large clusters of rocks and small islands. In the Baltic calms these could be approached closely and with confidence, even by the largest ships, but they still made their crews deeply nervous. The *Temeraire* was then sent to Carlscrona, the principal Swedish naval base and the equivalent of Portsmouth, to replace Richard Keats in the *Superb*, who had been watching the harbour all winter. The crew, once again, found the unfamiliar landscape alarming, particularly the narrowness and shallowness of the Sound through which they passed. It was in these unsettling surroundings that they witnessed one of the most vicious gunboat attacks of the whole Danish war.

She had been cruising in company with the 64-gun *Ardent* and the frigate *Melpomene*, and had anchored near the small island of Anholt. Like many tiny islands in the Baltic, a barren appearance concealed sources of fresh water and even patches of ground that could be cultivated to provide vegetables. As a result Anholt was considered sufficiently important to the safety and well-being of the blockading squadron to be held by a permanent detachment of marines and sailors. Anholt, however, was in the Kattegat – some distance from Danish troops – but now the *Temeraire*, *Melpomene* and *Ardent* were ordered to Carlscrona via the tortuous and narrow Great Belt, within sight of Danish naval forces. The journey took them close to the fertile island of Romsø and, having so recently experienced the tranquillity and bounty of Anholt, it was too good an opportunity to overlook. The island was even more attractive as it had been abandoned by the cautious, or perhaps calculating, Danes. The *Ardent* landed a large number of her crew, the shore party a mixture of both women and men, with the women detailed to washing duty and the men to cutting timber. It was usual for such parties to spend the night onshore, and it was under the cover of darkness that the Danes attacked. It is unclear if they had been hiding on the island, or if they launched an amphibious assault from a gunboat fleet, possibly from Nyborg. Taken completely by surprise, and convincingly overwhelmed, eighty-six British sailors surrendered with only a minimal struggle. One sailor was killed and a woman was shot on the beach as she tried to launch one of the boats. Numerous others were injured, including Alex Pringle, who had a musket ball lodged in his head, William Wilson, who had one in his knee, and Lieutenant Andrew Morris, whose left leg was broken by the recoil of the launch's carronade while covering the British retreat to the boats.[5]

When the extent of the British loss became clear the next morning, Rear-Admiral Dixon aboard the *Temeraire* ordered the *Melpomene* to Nyborg under a flag of truce to negotiate the release of the prisoners. We do not know the result of those negotiations, but it is characteristic of Danish tactics that on the *Melpomene*'s return to her squadron, with her flag of truce now expired, she was shadowed by a fleet of thirty gunboats, waiting for an opportunity to attack. Perhaps they knew what was coming from their local knowledge of weather conditions in the Great Belt, for they were certainly ready when the wind died and the *Melpomene* was forced to anchor. With no wind she had no steerage way, and with no steerage way she was unable to bring her broadside to bear on any would-be attacker. She had anchored, and if she had run a spring to her anchor it would have been possible to move the ship one way or another, but it would have been a cumbersome and slow process, and the small, manoeuvrable craft of the Danes would have remained at her bows or stern as she turned, where they could not be targeted. A few hours after night fell, the Danes attacked, crowding at her vulnerable stern and bow. At times, only six of the *Melpomene*'s guns could be brought to bear on her attackers, while for a little over two hours, the Danes fired relentlessly with long 18- and 24-pounder cannon. When a breeze finally sprang up, the *Melpomene* was too damaged to chase but she could at least bring her broadside to bear. Her report reveals the shocking extent of her damage. Her sails and rigging were badly cut up; two studding-sail booms were lost overboard; her bowsprit was so damaged that it had to be fished by binding spare timber to it in a splint, and her hull was shattered both above and below the waterline. Over a hundred grapeshot were embedded in her topsides; all the windows in the captain's cabin were shattered; the spare topmast was unusable; the boats' davits were shot away; two guns and two gun carriages were unusable; and the rudder head was shot through. Five of her crew lay dead and twenty-nine were wounded including poor old Thomas Proctor who had severely wounded buttocks.[6]

At the onset of the attack she had burned blue lights – the signal for emergency assistance – and the *Temeraire* had woken her sleeping crew and launched her boats, armed with carronades in the bows. They engaged the Danish gunboats but these soon fled for shore, too quickly to be pursued by the more cumbersome British craft. Thomas Rees, who had manned one of the *Temeraire*'s boats, was among the first aboard the *Melpomene*. 'I shall never forget the dreadful sight which met our eyes', he wrote. Many of the *Melpomene*'s crew wore only their shirts, which suggests that they had been taken completely by surprise while asleep. Rees was particularly concerned over the fate of one of his fellow marines, who, standing sentry on the gangway, had been cut in half by a shot, and now lay in a bloody heap with his musket and pouch by his side. The *Melpomene*'s captain, Frederick Warren, wept as he surveyed the carnage. His ship was so battered that she was unable to play any active role in the forthcoming cruise. Sailors and carpenters were immediately sent aboard her from the *Temeraire*, and they were still there five days later. Two months later she was finally forced to return home for substantial repair.[7] Rear-Admiral Dixon witnessed everything from the quarterdeck of the *Temeraire* and immediately wrote to his commanding officer, James Saumarez, attesting to the bravery of the *Melpomene*'s crew.[8]

Having witnessed the carnage on the *Melpomene* and resumed their course to Carlscrona, the concerns of the *Temeraire*'s crew were further raised as they passed Richard Keats in the *Superb*, heading in the opposite direction and to the safety of uncontested waters. As the ships passed they exchanged news, and the *Temeraire* heard, with no small degree of horror, that the *Superb* had been iced in over the winter, and that a number of her crew had died on the ice.

The attack on the *Melpomene* was one of a handful of vicious attacks on British shipping, all of which received a great deal of attention at home. In June 1808, the gunbrig *Turbulent*, part of the escort for a seventy-strong convoy, was attacked by a swarm of twenty-five Danish gunboats which took twenty-five of the convoy into Copenhagen. In the same month the *Tickler* was attacked, much as the *Melpomene* was a year later, becalmed in the Great Belt. Of her crew of fifty, twenty-two died and another twenty-two were wounded, and the ship was taken. More British losses followed, and in those instances where British ships were not captured, a number were forced to retreat in defeat. The Danes proved themselves time and again to be talented seamen and resourceful fighters but, if a broad perspective is taken of the war, British success is unmistakeable.

The Danish gunboat attacks made headline news but in comparison with the sheer quantity of British shipping in the Baltic in those years, Danish successes were rare. By heavily protecting few but large convoys, and routing them through the Great Belt, thus avoiding the nests of gunboats in the Sound near Copenhagen, vast numbers of merchant ships regularly broke out of the Baltic. Between June and December 1809 alone, the first seven months of the *Temeraire*'s Baltic tour, 2,210 merchant ships were escorted through the straits with no losses recorded at all. The following summer, 884 vessels cleared the Belts to the Baltic in June and July and 791 came the other way. The architect of this success was Admiral James Saumarez. Saumarez was a man of exceptional political awareness, and his role in the Baltic was as much diplomatic as it was martial. He was keenly aware that the Swedish, Danish and Russian merchants, although bound by treaty with Napoleon against Britain, resented Napoleon's orders not to trade with the British. In time of war there was no better client than the British government, and for many merchants no trade with Britain meant no trade at all. The Baltic market forces were simply too powerful for Napoleon to control. Even when Marshal Bernadotte was crowned King of Sweden, he found those market forces as irresistible as had his predecessors and eventually rebelled against Napoleon himself. At the same time, it was, in part, Napoleon's frustration with the Russians at not imposing a blanket trade blockade against the British that led to his declaration of war in 1812. The Baltic campaign, therefore, was a curious one of public hostility, particularly with the Danes, and both formal and informal private amicable agreement with Sweden and Russia. The result was that, in direct contravention of Napoleon's avowed intentions, exported British goods flooded Europe and Britain had almost unrestricted access to Baltic shipbuilding supplies.

Guaranteeing the safety of merchant ships trading in shipbuilding supplies was only part of the Royal Navy's role in the Baltic in these years, however, for the presence of the British fleet itself represented a useful source of manpower and shipping to gather and then transport stores to and from the Baltic. Reliable and successful supplements to the merchant convoys, large ships like the *Temeraire* with access to the formidable manpower of their crews played an important part in this direct acquisition of stores for the navy, and the crew of the *Temeraire*, so alarmed by their first experience in the Baltic, soon found themselves caught up in a Scandinavian idyll.

On 22 June 1809 the *Temeraire* intercepted a Prussian ship which told them that the Russian fleet was out of port and cruising in the Gulf of Finland, and the *Temeraire* and *St George* were immediately dispatched to keep an eye on Russian movements. There had only been one abortive action with the Russian fleet in the Baltic campaign, in August 1808, and it had been deeply unsatisfactory. Only one Russian ship, the *Sevolod*, had been destroyed, and the Russians had escaped to the security of the heavily defended harbour at Ragersvik. The British were forced to withdraw as winter fell and the Russians escaped to Kronstadt. Now, therefore, there seemed the possibility of another confrontation, and Saumarez was anxious to make the most of any chance, however small.

As soon as the *Temeraire* arrived off the city of Revel (modern Tallinn), it was immediately clear that the Russian fleet was back in port. Nevertheless, Revel is situated only a few miles from the mouth of the Gulf of Finland and nearby is the island of Nargen, opposite modern Helsinki. There, the British squadron could keep a close watch on Revel itself, and also guard the entrance to the Baltic should more Russian ships leave the shelter of Kronstadt, at the very far end of the Gulf. While they were there, the crews of the British squadron would be able to strip the heavily wooded Nargen Island of its valuable shipbuilding timber. And so, in the summer of 1809, the crew of the *Temeraire* settled into a remarkably quiet life, with the ship at anchor. The Russians never ventured out again and the British assumed a routine that lasted for three full months, cavorting around on the island while teams of sailors cut down the beautiful Russian timber. It was during this brief stay that the *Temeraire*'s master, now Robert Duncan, surveyed the island from her decks, clearly and carefully including sailing directions for approaching the safe anchorage to the south-east of the island. He even provided a nice sketch of the island of Revel from the anchorage, nine miles away. To view this is to see through the eyes of a sailor aboard the *Temeraire*; it is the only surviving image drawn from her decks. The chart survives today in the British Library (fig. 21).

We can see from the chart that Nargen Island is a little over three miles wide and six miles long, and we know from Rees's journal that there were sixteen farmhouses built on it. There was a largely symbolic display of resistance as armed British crews first descended on the beaches, but as soon as they landed the firing stopped, the locals disappeared into the woods and the governor formally presented his sword. Rees's first impression was not at all favourable. He declared that all of the inhabitants were 'dirty and full of vermin', the weather was excessively hot and the island was infested with mosquitoes – so much so that one of the *Temeraire*'s officers who had seen service in the swamps of the southern United States declared Nargen Island was even worse. Soon enough, however, the locals and the British sailors softened towards each other, and Rees later admitted that they were remarkably good-tempered and harmless. In a rather cryptic passage in his diary, Rees, in the roundabout way of a curate's son, even admits to striking up a relationship with a local young lady. He was frequently employed ashore as an officer's servant or as an aid to the washing parties, and he gave his silk neck-scarf to the young lady who had been admiring it, and presumably him, for some time. Rees assures the reader that this attention was purely due to the scarcity of silk on the island, but as soon as he had presented her with his scarf, the young Rees was, in his words, 'ever after welcome to every thing her house afforded.'

Such refreshing company was augmented by delicious local berries washed down by a powerful local liquor called 'snops', probably what we now know as schnapps. A number of thoughtless officers seem to have created temporary disharmony between the islanders and the sailors by shooting their chickens, and in one instance an officer rode one of the islander's horses so hard that the poor beast died. In every case, however, the damage was paid for and harmony restored. When winter fell and the British squadron finally left, the islanders promised to tend the graves of the few British sailors who had died and been buried in the islanders' cemetery, their names and the names of their ships carved deeply into the oak planks that served as headstones.

On her return across the Baltic to the main British force off Gothenburg, the *Temeraire* had yet another close run-in with Danish forces at Romsø. Once again, a shore party had landed for wood and water, but as night fell an onshore wind and strong current made it impossible for the last fifteen men to get clear of the shore. Those men knew that the very same wind and current could swiftly bring Danish gunboats across from the mainland, only three miles away and clearly visible, and they split up, lighting fires all over the island to give the impression of a much larger force encamped there. Anxious for their stranded shipmates, a boat from the *Temeraire* eventually made it ashore and, a few hours later, brought every man back to the ship.

That was the final drama of the *Temeraire*'s Baltic service, and by November 1809 she was back in Plymouth. She had not taken part in any-thing more than a scrap with gunboats but, through her Baltic service, had still managed to augment her reputation as one of the finest ships in the fleet. Her flag-officer, Rear-Admiral Dixon, was much loved by his men, who appear to have been a remarkably young and fit crew, and he drilled them to a degree of excellence that was unmatched in the entire Baltic Fleet. There was at this stage a great deal of intra-service rivalry, and during the Baltic tour, the crew of the *Victory* challenged the *Temeraire* to a competition in seamanship. Each ship had to furl sails, get all her boats in and out, reef topsails, and hoist and strike topgallant and royal masts and yards. Dixon, who was quite a character, immediately accepted the challenge and deliberately ordered his crew to run the drill poorly and to come last, for by now the entire squadron was taking part. He did this in the utter confidence that the crew of the *Temeraire* was unmatchable, and shortly after they had, as planned, come last of all, Dixon sent aboard a fresh challenge to the *Victory*. It was accepted, but this time the *Temeraire* crew gave it their all, and soundly beat the *Victory*. Again and again the competition was re-run, and each time the *Temeraire* won.

There were few better reasons for a ship to be proud in the age of sail than to excel in seamanship. That pride throbs like a pulse through Rees's journal and colours another highly distinctive episode in the *Temeraire*'s life. Shortly after her return from Baltic service, she was at Plymouth in November 1809 when a terrible storm struck. There was then still no breakwater and the Sound was vulnerable to southerly gales and rough weather in storms. The *Temeraire*, the largest ship seeking shelter there, and square-rigged, was anchored much further out than any other vessel so that she could easily run out to sea if the wind turned on-shore. In such deep water the *Temeraire* was ceaselessly battered by mighty waves that flooded in through the hawseholes and bow ports. At one stage there was three feet of water on the lower deck and two in the middle. Then, above the shrieking of the wind, the crew heard the unmistakeable cries of a child and, through the spray, made out the outline of a tiny boat, its mast and sails torn from its hull. It was clear that it had been blown clear of shore, and had already passed by three other vessels, none of which had attempted to save the boy.

The *Temeraire*'s captain, Edward Clay, gave his men leave to volunteer to try and save the child, and a boat was swiftly filled with eight of the *Temeraire*'s finest men. They made it to the craft and transferred the young boy to their boat moments before his stricken craft capsized, and then hauled themselves back to the pitching hulk of the *Temeraire* from a buoy cast over the stern. It is a mark of the pride with which they measured their seamanship that the crew of the *Temeraire* believed it their responsibility to tow the boy's little boat to safety, which they had been unable to do; once he was safely aboard, they agreed amongst themselves to replace it out of their own wages and as soon as they were paid off, the sailors raised between them

£8 5s 6d and bought him a new boat. They christened it the *Temeraire Johnson* after the boy's surname.

A fortnight after that terrible storm in Plymouth, the *Temeraire* was summoned once more, and for the final time, for active duty against Napoleon. In 1807 the only country apart from Sweden that had not signed up to Napoleon's Continental System was Portugal, and just as Napoleon had made military and political inroads into the Baltic, so too had he made great advances in Portugal. By 28 November 1807, a bedraggled French army had finally completed a shattering march across the centre of Spain and had reached the gates of Lisbon, where they met no resistance: the preceding day the Portuguese royal family had sailed to Brazil to set up court in the New World. At first all seemed well; Portuguese ports were immediately closed to British trade and, in theory at least, so was every port in Europe. However, to maintain a French force in Portugal required regular supplies and reinforcements to be sent from France across the full breadth of Spain. It did not take the Spaniards long to grow resentful and highly suspicious of the now permanent presence of French troops on Spanish soil. And they were right to be suspicious as, little by little, French troops began to occupy major Spanish cities and significant fortresses by a mixture of outrageous deception and brutality. By the beginning of March, Pamplona, San Sebastian, Barcelona and Figueras were all in French hands. It was not long before Napoleon revealed his true colours, and summoned the Spanish royal family to Bayonne to 'discuss' the Spanish throne. There he informed King Carlos IV and Queen Maria Luisa that the royal family was to be dissolved and replaced by a French prince, who was, in classic Napoleonic fashion, his elder brother, Joseph.

Unlike in Sweden, however, where overt friendship with Napoleon masked hidden antipathies, the reaction in Spain was immediate, public and powerful, and the entire Iberian peninsula dissolved into a series of bitter and prolonged campaigns to drive out the French. The British government immediately offered its services to Spain. Sir Arthur Wellesley, the future Duke of Wellington, arrived on 1 August 1807 and within just sixteen days was in action with the French. By 1809 the British had been beaten back by an enormous army of ninety thousand troops led by Napoleon himself, and in January 1810 the French pushed into Andalusia. Seville, the seat of the Spanish government, fell at the beginning of February 1810 and the government retreated to the island citadel of Cadiz. The French swiftly descended on the city and summoned it to surrender, but were met with defiance. The siege had begun.

It was to Cadiz that the *Temeraire* now headed, as flagship of Rear-Admiral Francis Pickmore, and part of a squadron of eleven sail of the line, two frigates and four bomb vessels, which arrived in March 1810. The British government knew that it was a crucial point in the war. Cadiz was the only stronghold in the whole of southern Spain which had not fallen to the French, and it was tying down thousands of French troops. Moreover, it had to be retained as a major base of Spanish naval power: nothing was more important for British security than keeping the naval bases of the French and Spanish divided. It was also essential that the Spanish government be easily evacuated to the New World if it became clear that the French would take the city.

In both cases, sea power was going to be crucial to the outcome of the siege, and the Spanish navy, broken by Trafalgar, could not provide that support. No strategy to replace the ships lost at the battle was ever implemented, and the financial difficulties created by the Peninsular War further starved the Spanish navy of funds. As a result the magnificent Spanish navy, which in 1790 had totalled almost a quarter of a million tons of shipping, would be reduced to only sixty thousand tons by 1815, and all the ships that were still afloat were in a poor state of repair. The fate of Cadiz, therefore, rested with the Royal Navy. This is because Cadiz is unlike the majority of European cities. It is built at the very tip of an island, the Isla de León, and to access it from the mainland one must first cross the Sancti Petri River. In 1810 this was only possible across a large causeway, the Puenta de Suazo, which had been destroyed as soon as it was clear that the city would be besieged. The Sancti Petri runs through a wide salt marsh, and the island was heavily defended with batteries and redoubts along its entire length. The city itself was a separate and defended entity at the far tip of the island, only accessible across the island's narrowest point. The city, which juts out proudly into the outer harbour and has some four-fifths of its circumference protected by water, is completely enclosed by massive walls.

When the French army arrived it immediately became clear that no assault could be made from the landward side. Not only were the salt marshes and the Sancti Petri formidable natural barriers, but the Spanish navy had succeeded in finding sufficient men and craft to form a permanent gunboat flotilla in the river. Napoleon was unwilling to risk any of his precious warships in the siege, which was therefore maintained from the tip of the Trocadero peninsula, on the opposite side of the harbour to the city itself. At this point the harbour is only three-quarters of a mile wide, close enough to allow the French to bombard the city at will. Three strong forts were built facing the city, the closest on the tidal mudflats that reached into the estuary. This was known as Fort Matagorda and it was to become the focus of the battle for Cadiz. In February, a detachment of British marines had succeeded in destroying Matagorda, and had driven the French back so far that their shot was unable to reach the city. A British force of a hundred and fifty men, a mixture of marines, soldiers and sailors, was then posted to hold the fort but with the sea at their backs, and the almost unlimited resources of the French army at their front, it was a dreadful task. It was to this battle that the *Temeraire* now sailed.

When she arrived, the weather was as awful as it had been in Plymouth that winter. The bay was filled with ships which were driven together and ashore by the unremitting ferocity of a hurricane. The *Santa Ana*, a large Spanish three-decker which had fired on the *Temeraire* at Trafalgar, but which now was working in harmony with the Royal Navy to transport British and Portuguese troops to Cadiz, arrived at the same time as the *Temeraire*, with two troop transports in convoy. All three ships were driven ashore within hours of arrival. The crews were captured by the French and the ships burned on the beaches. A number of ships at anchor in the bay were prison hulks, some of them large French warships. The *Temeraire* anchored alongside one of these, *La Neptune*, again a ship which she had fought against at Trafalgar. However, the weather was so poor that she could not do so without colliding with her, damaging both ships.

As soon as the storm died down, the *Temeraire* became involved in the battle for Fort Matagorda, and sent boats manned with almost a hundred and seventy sailors and marines.[9] The fort was about a hundred yards square and had been largely destroyed on its seaward side where it had been battered by artillery from Cadiz when the French had occupied it. To the landward side was a small village which had been used as cover for the

French when they were building their batteries and preparing for an assault to re-take the fort and resume their barrage. When all was ready the French destroyed the houses that hid them from the prying eyes of the British in the fort. As the dust settled, the British were horrified to see that where harmless houses had once been, a formidable array of batteries could now target the fort from numerous directions. Their first salvo was a small burst of grapeshot that 'ploughed the earth on every side of us'[10] but the most telling blow was yet to come.

The fort was also protected by a flotilla of gunboats and by the formidable broadside of a Spanish 74 anchored behind the fort and manned by British sailors. The crew of the *Temeraire* manned two of the gunboats, with thirty men in each. Only at high tide could they be really effective, but one of the bomb vessels nevertheless fired 558 mortar shells in ten days as the battle reached its height. At the same time, they were targeted by a constant rain of shot from the French positions, and they suffered from the inevitable weaknesses of a seaborne attack against a land position as the ships had to struggle continually against the motions of tide and swell, which made their aim difficult, while the French were able to target the wooden vessels with red-hot shot and with relative ease. Shortly after the gunboats crewed by the *Temeraire* joined the battle, one was struck by a red-hot shot, which entered the little vessel's magazine, destroying it completely. Only seven survived from a crew of thirty.[11] The British-manned Spanish 74 also suffered badly from the French red-hot shot and was set alight in several places. The flotilla of gunboats was forced to scatter and the 74 to slip her cable: the fort was now on its own.

A week later, a party from the *Temeraire* was ordered to man the guns of the fort itself. Eighty men manned nine guns, taking it in shifts with half the men working for two hours at a time. A young soldier named Joseph Donaldson from the 94th Foot fought those guns alongside men from the *Temeraire*, and described the scene:

Death now began to stalk about in the most dreadful form . . . The largest shot were certain messengers when they struck. The first man killed was a sailor who belonged to the *Temeraire*. The whole of his face was carried away. It was a horrid looking wound. He was at the same gun with me. 'Ah! what will we do with him' said I to a seaman next me. 'Let him lie there' was the reply 'we have no time to look after dead men now' at that time I thought it a hardened expression; but this was my first engagement. Not so with the tar. He had been well used to them.

The unfortunate soul from the *Temeraire* was not the last to die that day. Donaldson continues:

The French soon acquired a fatal precision with their shot, sending them in through our embrasures, killing and wounding men every volley. I was on the left of the gun at the front wheel we were running her up after loading. I had stooped to take a fresh purchase, a cannon ball whistled through the embrasure, carried the forage cap off my head, and struck the man behind me in the breast, and he fell to rise no more. The carnage now became dreadful; the ramparts were strewed with the dead and wounded; and blood, brains and mangled limbs lay scattered in every direction: but our men's spirits and enthusiasm seemed to rise with the danger.

Against such an attack, the fort could not be held indefinitely, and the garrison was forced to abandon it, spiking the guns and breaking the carriages as they left. They also did their best to bury their dead in a temporary cist of mud. Donaldson was deeply affected. 'Hurried and rude was their burial, and a heartfelt sigh all their requiem, but it was more valuable than the ostentatious trappings of affected woe.'[12]

The loss of Fort Matagorda was not the last of the *Temeraire*'s grisly experiences of Cadiz, however, as the prison hulk that she was moored alongside was as much a morgue as a hulk. The men inside were the remnants of General Pierre Dupont's 17,563-strong army which had surrendered to the Spanish at the Battle of Bailén in July. Some of the prisoners were condemned to starvation on the remote Balearic island of Cabrera, while a great many were confined to hulks in Cadiz harbour where they met a similar fate. The prison ship was scattered with great piles of dead, with heaps of bodies lying in the main and fore chains. Some of the dead were taken ashore and buried in the sand by their Spanish guards, but the graves were so shallow that the vigorous Atlantic quickly opened them and the currents dragged the corpses out to sea to be eaten by birds and fish. The crew of the *Temeraire* did all they could; reburying those that could be hauled into a boat and firing into the most rotten to make them sink. It is a particularly unpleasant story, difficult to believe, but the state of the Spanish prison hulk is confirmed by another witness, a soldier at Fort Matagorda, who added that the dead from the prison ship were always kept until sunset before being tossed overboard. Time and again, he and his fellow soldiers buried corpses on the beach, but the scattered bodies were totally unheeded by the Spanish 'unless when they practised some barbarity on them – such as dashing large stones on their heads, or cutting and mutilating them in such a way that the very soul would sicken at the idea.'[13]

Meanwhile, the siege reached a temporary lull as the French refortified the Trocadero peninsula and started to build boats in preparation for an amphibious assault from Fort Matagorda. New mortars were cast in Seville especially for the task of bombarding the city from across the harbour. The British, meanwhile, maintained their role of patrolling the outer harbour while the Spanish patrolled the Sancti Petri River and the inner harbour. The British also played their most important role of keeping Cadiz supplied with troops, food and crucially water, as there are no natural springs on the island. This they did with great success. One British sailor wrote to his father celebrating the beautiful food they enjoyed: melons, oranges, figs, raisins, pomegranates and chestnuts, all of which could be bought very cheap, while there was also almost unrestricted access to fresh fish.[14]

The next few weeks proved uneventful until one of the British cutters that patrolled the outer harbour – the 'Black Cutter', so named because it was manned entirely by black sailors – mutinied when under command of one of the *Temeraire*'s midshipmen and a coxswain. The *Temeraire*'s officers were badly beaten and the mutinous crew turned themselves over to the French. A few weeks later two Irishmen from the *Temeraire* also mutinied, again in one of the ship's boats, and turned themselves over to the enemy. Some months later, while serving on a French privateer, they captured a British transport bound for Britain and among the troops heading home found the very officer of the *Temeraire* who had commanded the boat that they had taken in their mutiny. He was treated cruelly by the mutineers until the transport was recaptured by a British frigate and the mutineers themselves arrested. These examples of British sailors deserting to the French were not isolated and four more were court-martialled aboard the *Temeraire* and sentenced to be hanged.[15] Nor was it a one-way process: there were also examples of French deserters joining the British.

In July the *Temeraire* received orders to sail to the Mediterranean, and the crew were delighted to leave. 'Right glad we were to get away from that slaughter-house', wrote Rees. They left 'blessing the day when we had lost sight of it'.[16] The squadron's flag officer, Rear-Admiral Francis Pickmore, was not so keen to leave. This was an opportunity to excel and in the months that he had been there he had made no mistakes. The Admiralty was careful to explain that it was not dissatisfied with his conduct, but there was no disguising the fact that his new station as Port Admiral at Mahón in Minorca was no promotion. He took the *Temeraire* with him as his flagship to the Mediterranean, where she divided her time between Port Mahón and her blockading station off Toulon. There the British kept a close eye on the French Mediterranean Fleet, under the command of Vice-Admiral Emerieu. He had a formidable force of sixteen of the line, including three new huge three-deckers, while more giants were being built. His crews were insufficient and inexperienced, though, and Emerieu restricted them to brief voyages and avoided contact with the British blockading force at all costs. They were also ready to strike at a vessel in distress, however, and in August 1811 the *Temeraire* had a narrow escape from a sniping French attack. Ordered from Toulon to Minorca, she tried to tack out of Hyères Bay outside Toulon harbour, a notoriously difficult anchorage to leave. She quickly got into trouble as the wind died, and the currents started to take her ashore, directly under the guns of the French battery on the Pointe des Mèdes, which opened fire. The first shot missed completely, but the French gunners soon found their range. The second went through the maintop and the third took off the master's leg, dismounted a gun and knocked a bayonet out of Rees's hand as he was standing guard at the entrance to the admiral's cabin. The ship's boats were frantically manned in an attempt to tow her clear of the guns, and the *Temeraire* returned fire. Eventually boats from every ship in the squadron came to her aid, as none could bear to see this prestigious ship taken into the enemy's hands in such an undignified manner. As shot rained down on her, the fleet of boats pulled the *Temeraire* to safety.

9.

The Retired *Temeraire*

DECEMBER 1811 – AUGUST 1838

The *Temeraire* did not remain in the Mediterranean for long. Only weeks after her narrow escape from the Pointe des Mèdes fortress she was sent home. Those last few weeks of service, moreover, were remarkable not for their maritime glory, but for the drudgery of their day-to-day existence and the evil breath of sickness that seeped through the *Temeraire*'s gunports and down her companion ladders. The yellow fever spread from Cartagena and struck the entire Mediterranean Fleet. Prevailing medical theory taught that infections were spread by foul air – 'fogs, vapours, humidity and poisonous exhalations'[1] – and the way to destroy the disease was to clean the men and the ship. The *Temeraire*, therefore, was scrubbed with vinegar and gunpowder and the lower deck whitewashed.

Despite these precautions over a hundred died on the *Temeraire* alone and only nine of her entire crew of more than seven hundred escaped the disease.[2] When she was finally sent back to England, many of her faithful crew remained in the naval hospital at Port Mahón. This landlocked incarceration was particularly melancholy for those left behind: never again would they feel the *Temeraire*'s hull heave with the swell of the deep ocean, for this was to be her last significant voyage. The *Temeraire* had reached the end of her useful service life, and on Christmas Day 1811 she left Mahón and headed home for retirement. As soon as she returned to England the process of dismantlement began: her guns were hoisted out, her ballast removed, her shot unloaded, her topmast rigging lowered and her masts removed. The immediate future of the *Temeraire* now certain, her captain was freed from the habitual constraints on space for his log entries, and her final log for this period in her life is characterized by increasingly large handwriting in flowing, expressive script. The last entry of all takes up almost an entire page, whereas in the peak of her service life two weeks' worth of log entries would fit in the same space. His words tumble onto the page in wonky abandon. They read: 'Discharged the ship's company in to the *Union*. At sunset put the *Temeraire* out of commission.'[3]

She had seen a great deal in her time, but in comparison with other ships she was not old: she had been in service for only fourteen years, whereas the *Victory*, for example, was by then forty-seven years old. The considerations which led to the retirement of the *Temeraire* were specific to the ship itself, rather than to broader British naval strategy. In February 1812, Wellington's campaign in Spain was gaining real momentum and his army had to be kept supplied by the Royal Navy, while French convoys had to be attacked, and the French navy blockaded to allow British naval support to continue unmolested. Moreover, relations between Britain and the United States, particularly regarding British impressment of American sailors, had reached a level that was no longer acceptable to the United States, which eyed the vast landscapes of British-controlled Canada with envy. President Madison's beleaguered and divided Republican Party saw war as an opportunity to unite the country and drive for another term in office, and in June 1812 America declared war on Britain. The Americans had no significant navy, but the ships they had in commission were powerful. Six frigates, larger than any in the Royal Navy, were the spearhead and they had demonstrated their power in the 1798 Quasi-War with France and again in 1804 when they waged war against the unremitting piracy of the Barbary States by attacking Tripoli. Since then the American government had ordered three 74-gun ships and two more 44-gun frigates, and although these were still on the stocks at the outbreak of the war, the threats posed by American privateers against English merchantmen, and by the large and powerful American army against British possessions in Canada, ensured that the Royal Navy would be required to fight a naval war with America: British trade would need to be protected, and British troops transported and maintained on the far side of the Atlantic.

So British demand for powerful ships was not in decline from 1812, rather the *Temeraire* herself now belonged to a bygone era. The French had long specialized in two-decked ships of 80 guns, and although they tended to be structurally unsound, the principle of using two-decked ships larger than the standard 74-gunner as the core of the battle fleet was widely admired in England. At the same time, three-deckers were now significantly larger and more powerful than they had been in the late 1790s when the *Temeraire* was built. The *Caledonia*, launched in June 1808, was the first British ship to mount 120 guns, and at 205ft was 20ft longer than the *Temeraire*. She was not a one-off either, but set the future direction of large ship construction. The *Nelson* class, of a similar size to the *Caledonia*, followed soon after. The ability to build such large ships was the result of dramatic changes in hull construction, introduced by Sir Robert Seppings. By adding diagonal bracing to the traditional rectangular frames, Seppings' ships drew their strength from a jigsaw of triangles. These hulls were further strengthened by the first use of iron straps and a new design for knee-pieces. As the ships became stronger, so they could be built longer. One result was that the much admired French 80-gun two-deckers could now be built in the British style and to exacting British standards. New 80-gun ships began to replace the 74s as the backbone of the fleet. They were soon reclassed as 84-gunners and this process of steady enlargement eventually led to the design of the *Rodney* of 1827, the first 90-gun two-decker. At the same time, Seppings introduced alterations to the bows and sterns of the ships, traditionally their weakest parts. His 'round' bow reflected the new emphasis on aggressive British naval tactics, born from Nelson's head-on attack at Trafalgar. The *Temeraire*, therefore, once the largest ship of her class, now seemed short and weak in comparison with the latest generation of battleships, and her latest service in the Baltic, Atlantic and Mediterranean had further worn her out. Her fate was not unusual: in the years immediately after 1815, a total of ten three-deckers of an older generation were retired from active duty, and the Admiralty ordered seven of the finest new three-deckers to replace them.

While the Royal Navy no longer wanted ships like the *Temeraire* for active duty, however, with the British still committed to fighting both the French and the Americans, there was an unrelenting demand for prisoner accommodation. Between 1803 and 1814, 122,440 French prisoners were brought to Britain, an astonishing figure in itself, but one that makes no allowance for the Italians, Swiss, Poles, Saxons, Spaniards, Dutchmen and, of course, Americans who were also held as prisoners of war in Britain. In fact it has been estimated that, during the war of 1812, fourteen per cent of all American naval and private seamen were held as prisoners of war in Britain, perhaps ten thousand in all.[4] The accommodation problem was therefore acute. Officers were allowed on parole if they signed a document promising not to escape, and there were five thousand such paroled men in 1813. Some of them lived in style. Admiral Linois, captured in March 1806, spent the rest of the war in Cheltenham and Bath enjoying the social scene, and was even joined by his wife and daughter.

The thousands of ordinary sailors and soldiers were far harder to accommodate. Even the largest purpose-built prisons, those at Norman Cross in Peterborough and at Perth, were designed to hold only seven thousand men, and the new prison at Dartmoor only six thousand. Dartmoor was one of a handful of purpose-built prisons, but they were augmented by borough gaols, county prisons, adapted farms and barracks. Even the magnificent gateway of the monastery at St Albans that can still be seen today was used to hold prisoners. One obvious solution to this crisis was to use hulks: a single medium-sized ship such as a 74-gunner could hold as many as seven hundred and fifty men. Aboard the *Brunswick* at Chatham in 1813, four hundred and sixty men slept on one deck alone. That deck, the orlop, was 125ft long, 40ft wide and, being the lowest deck on the ship and traditionally used for storage, was a little less than 5ft high. Despite all the inconveniences of access for provisioning and maintenance, it even proved much cheaper to keep prisoners on hulks than on land, and sixty were in service by the end of the Napoleonic Wars. In particular, in autumn 1813, more hulks were needed at Plymouth. In October, the superintendent of the hulks there had complained that his prison ships were all being rapidly filled owing to the success of the war in Spain and Admiral Sir Robert Calder's requirement that between three and four hundred places were to be kept available at a moment's notice.[5] In December 1813, therefore, the *Temeraire* was fitted as a prison ship to serve in Plymouth.

Beyond that basic fact we know nothing about how much it cost to transform her into a prison ship, or, indeed, exactly what work was carried out to alter her both internally and externally. Nevertheless, there is some limited evidence concerning prison ships in general from the Napoleonic Wars that suggests the likely changes. All of those sources are written: no wooden ships of the line that served as prison ships survived long after their transformation, a fact which is indicative of the radical changes that were usually made to transform these elegant men of war into sinister beasts.

Once the wars had ended and the demand for prisoner-of-war accommodation eased, few of the ships that had been so absolutely transformed were wanted and they were swiftly broken up. Where prisons on land were built, there is at least some evidence that prisoners of war were there, even if the prisons themselves have gone. At Norman Cross, on the A1 near Peterborough, although the prefabricated wooden prison itself has gone, the stone barrack master's house and the superintendent's and the agent's houses all survive and opposite the prison cemetery is a towering memorial topped with a large bronze eagle. Another memorial to French prisoners of war stands near the old naval barracks in Chatham. The situation in Dartmoor is even more impressive. The prisoners built the granite prison buildings themselves, and although the surrounding landscape appears as unspoilt or natural as any in the British Isles, it was in fact constructed by prisoners of war. They became so much a part of Dartmoor life that the landscape as we perceive it now is testament to their presence. They cut and laid the original roads on which the modern ones now lie; they built walls that still stand in the village and in the surrounding fields; they drained bogs; they cut down forests; and they built beautiful slab bridges over the surrounding streams.

For those who know where to look, therefore, there are signs of French prisoners of war all over the British landscape, but if one searches for evidence of the hulks, where the vast majority of the prisoners were housed, there is none: they have simply been lost to history. Modern archaeology would be able to analyse the scarring and alterations to a ship's skeleton to rebuild her past with astonishing accuracy, but with no physical remains to work from, our knowledge of prison hulks rests heavily on a handful of accounts, all of them written by prisoners, most of whom were French, although some valuable accounts by Danish and American prisoners also survive. They all agree over the basic facts.

The ship's ornamentation and decorative carving would be removed, and her painted sides covered in a thick coat of black paint and tar to protect them from the weather. The smooth lines of their hulls were mutated by growths, as wooden shacks were constructed on forecastle and poop, and the graceful masts were amputated. The ship would never be required to sail again, and since the great masts were stepped right down through the ship, their removal freed up even more room for the prisoners. Soldiers appear to have been housed forward, in, or on, the forecastle, while the ship's commanding officer and his assistants – and occasionally his family – lived in the officers' quarters aft, behind an immensely thick oak partition, studded with iron. Spy holes were let into this bulkhead at regular intervals through which the prisoners could be observed and muskets fired from complete safety. The centre of the ship was gutted, and a single, narrow bench built around the circumference with a number of benches running athwartships in the centre of each deck. All the guns were removed, to make space for the prisoners and to raise the ship high enough out of the water to make the lowest deck, the orlop, inhabitable by cutting small scuttles into the hull just above the waterline. This allowed fresh air and light into this darkest recess of the ship, a platform only feet above the ship's bilge. These new scuttles and the ship's gunports were then all fitted with cast-iron bars, two inches square. In some instances it appears that a type of walkway or platform was constructed around the hull itself, just above the waterline. With access to the interior of the ship so difficult and dangerous to any but a strong and coordinated force of soldiers, this was the only way to monitor the gunports themselves. A group of guards would augment their observation by patrolling the ship daily with iron rods with which they tapped the grilles to test their strength and probed the hull to confirm its security.

There is nothing surprising in these alterations or precautions. The identities of these ships as instruments of policy, weapons of war and magnificent symbols of empire were stripped to create purely functional objects for the retention of foreigners: a symbol of empire in their own right but of an altogether different type from the gilded and beautifully carved ships that they had been at their launch. Indeed, for all the stunning images of British success in sea battles that were produced in these years, none is a more potent symbol of British success than the paintings of Louis Garneray, a French convict and artist who spent nine years in the hulks in Portsmouth. His images of the black prison hulks (fig. 23) emit an aura of crushing victory free from the rich embellishment of more famous paintings of 'glorious' British success in naval battle. It is that simplicity that makes them so powerful. These captured and retired ships, too battered to serve at sea, teem with unseen prisoners and pulse with hidden menace. Ships and men were the currency of the war, and here they were both kept in security and put on display by their conquerors. Their appearance made a particularly powerful impression on all who saw them. One of the earliest historians of the hulks commented that 'Sunshine, which can give a touch of picturesqueness, if not of beauty, to so much that is bare and featureless, only brought out into greater prominence the dirt, the shabbiness, the patchiness of the thing. In fog it was weird. In moonlight it was spectral.'[6] The French prisoner Garneray, when he first came alongside the hulk that was to be his prison, described her as an 'immense sarcophagus'.[7] Another captive similarly described them as tombs in which the prisoners were buried alive.[8] But it is Charles Dickens who captures their nature most poetically. In the first few pages of *Great Expectations*, the young Pip encounters an escaped convict on the marshes of Kent, and through the mist he glimpses the hulk whence he came, 'like a wicked Noah's Ark. Cribbed and barred and moored by massive rusty chains, the prison ship seemed in my young eyes to be ironed like the prisoners.'[9]

No images of the *Temeraire* as a prison ship survive, however, and so we will never know for certain how she appeared during those years. Turner himself painted a view of hulks on the Tamar (fig. 22), but it is most likely that it was painted during Turner's first trip to Devon in the winter of 1811–12, more than a year before the *Temeraire* arrived. The ship on the right of the image, moreover, is an uncertain guide to the appearance of the Tamar hulks. After a recent inspection prior to an exhibition at the Tate Gallery in St Ives in 2006, it was clear that the original image had been significantly altered when it was restored in 1931. In particular, the conservator added his own rigging, line-ruled, perhaps in the mistaken belief that the masts had been removed in a previous restoration. We know that Turner drew his rigging freehand and it has been concluded that the original image of that ship carried no rigging. It is most likely that when the *Temeraire* was a hulk on the Tamar she, too, would have struck her masts.

In fact, no image of the *Temeraire* during these years survives at all until she was painted in 1833 by the celebrated British marine artist Edward Cooke (fig. 31). By then she had assumed her new role as a victualling depot and her appearance is altogether respectable for a retired warship. Indeed, from her appearance in the Cooke painting, one would never guess that she had ever served as a prison ship: she is not painted black, nor are there any ramshackle additions to her deck or visible scars where ports might have been cut into her hull to allow light and air into her orlop deck. Although it is possible, therefore, that her appearance was only altered very slightly when

she served as a prison ship, her progress books suggest that she may well
have been altered quite substantially. When she underwent her transformation from prison ship to receiving ship, the staggering sum of £27,733 was
spent on those alterations – that is nearly £2,500 *more* than her repair costs
after Trafalgar, and the alterations took a full nine months, from September
1819 to June 1820.[10] A large part of that cost was in fresh copper sheeting
applied to her hull, but it is still a remarkable amount and it can only be
assumed that if her external appearance had been significantly altered in her
years as a prison ship, it was reversed before she became a receiving ship and
was painted by Cooke.

Regardless of her actual appearance, however, it was the knowledge that
a hulk was a prison ship that made one's perception of her all the more
dreadful, for she artfully concealed the troubles within, and that conceal-
ment bred a deep and sinister fascination. The dishevelled and emaciated
prisoners were viewed frequently, much as the lunatics at the Bethlem
Hospital for the mentally ill (Bedlam) became a popular visitor attraction in
the nineteenth century. In 1814 alone there were ninety-six thousand visits to
Bedlam. On the hulks, visitors came to look down from the safe and lofty
heights of the quarterdeck, as the prisoners exercised on the main deck. It
was particularly striking to some (male) contemporaries that many of those
visitors were women.[11] Nevertheless, the lives actually lived by the convicts
remained very much a closed book for many years. In 1812, John Wilson
Croker, Secretary to the Admiralty, declared to Parliament that the prisoners
at Portsmouth were 'comfortable and happy and well provided with amuse-
ment'.[12] But gradually a more accurate picture emerged as convicts
repatriated after the wars published their memoirs and historians sifted
through the evidence and records of the Transport Board – the government
department responsible for convict transportation, and after 1795, for the
administration of all of the prison hulks. The conclusions are stark.

There is some disagreement over the death rate of the prisoners, but it
seems certain that by 1814, 12,845 French prisoners had died. 1,770 men alone
died at the Norman Cross prison near Peterborough.[13] More hotly disputed
is the health of the remainder. French sources claimed that ten per cent of
the prisoners were so ill that they died shortly after they returned, and that
fifty-seven per cent were so brutalized by their time in British prisons that
their health was permanently impaired.[14] A contemporary London report

concluded that six years was enough to wreck even the strongest and healthiest.[15] Most striking of all, however, are the words spoken to Garneray by a convict as he arrived on board his appointed hulk: 'Remember this well . . . on board the hulks a prudent man never lets himself be carried away by generosity, nor by any other feeling whatsoever. You must get used to shutting your heart, your eyes and your ears to all pity.'[16]

In theory the prisoners received one and a half pounds of coarse bread per day and half a pound of beef, mutton or other meat (including the bone), substituted on two days by one pound of salt cod, red herrings or other fish with potatoes, a quantity of barley and one or two turnips. This was not desperately insufficient. Modern historical research has suggested that the prisoners were entitled to receive 2,410 calories per day, when the modern recommended intake is 2,800. They were entitled to 126 grams of protein per day – nearly twice the modern recommended allowance – and, if measured by weight, 64 per cent of the food was carbohydrate, more than the modern recommendation of 58 per cent.[17] In practice, however, prisoners' diaries record that the bread was often too hard to eat and the meat and fish were of very poor quality. In one instance, a British officer was foolish enough to take his large pet dog aboard and it was too tempting for the prisoners. As he rowed away from the ship he saw its skin nailed to her side.[18] Corrupt contractors exacerbated the problem. One ploy was for the contractors to buy back their stock from the prisoners, and then reissue the victuals a week later. In 1798 the Plymouth contractor was imprisoned for six months and fined £300 for failing to provide the prisoners with good provisions of full weight. Similar corruption seems to have occurred with the prisoners' uniforms. In summer 1807 twelve hundred suits were ordered for Plymouth for the forthcoming winter. By the spring only three hundred had been received, but all had been paid for.[19]

It is tempting to use these examples to describe the weakness of the system, but it must be emphasized that this corrupt contractor was caught, found guilty and imprisoned; the prisoners were not entirely unsupported nor were they unprotected. Indeed, each depot or prison ship was supervised by an agent of the Transport Office, who was an officer of the Royal Navy. They were guided in the running of their prison and in the treatment of the prisoners by an extremely detailed set of printed instructions established by an Order in Council in 1808. The instructions were strict, but relatively humane. A committee of prisoners was required to inspect the food provided by the contractors, who were held to exacting standards, and the instructions even provided for barbers from among the prisoners to be paid. They also provided for a daily market in which the prisoners could buy food and clothing and sell goods that they had made. Flogging was forbidden, and replaced with enforced isolation and a reduction in rations. In the case of an attempted or even a successful escape, every prisoner on that deck suffered a reduction in rations. Modern research suggests that the regulations were followed and the prisoners treated fairly and with forbearance, but as with all regulations, they are an uncertain guide to the reality of the situation. Gambling, for example, was rife, even though it was explicitly forbidden.[20]

That there was terrible dirt and malnutrition, disease and despondency caused by the poor conditions in which the prisoners were held is certain, however. The 'enforced isolation' of the instructions actually was confinement in a *cachot* – a wooden box six feet square at the bottom of the hold to which the only air came through tiny holes. There was no light at all. Almost without exception, those who saw the prisoners were sickened. 'Imagine a generation of the dead coming forth from their graves, their eyes sunken, their faces haggard and wan, their backs bent, their beards wild, their bodies terrifyingly thin and scarcely covered by tattered yellow rags, and still you have no more than a feeble and incomplete idea of how my companions in misfortune appeared', wrote Garneray.[21] Frostbite was just one of the problems suffered by the prisoners (there was no heating), and there are reports of fingers, toes and even feet being lost. Typhus was particularly rampant in the closed quarters of the ships; the prisoners were only allowed into the fresh air for thirty minutes at a time, per day. Those who suffered worst were a sort of sub-class of prisoner, known as the *rafalés*, from the French *rafaler*, a verb used by sailors to describe being caught in a squall. These were men who were so addicted to gambling that they wagered their rations far in advance of receiving them, and even gambled away their clothes.

Historians initially baulked at the possibility of large numbers of men living naked aboard these ships, but gradually more and more evidence has come to light to corroborate the more famous sources that describe them. Perhaps most significantly, the *rafalés* were also known as 'Romains' (Romans) as they frequently wore blankets, in the style of a Roman toga, to protect themselves from the cold. Another name born from their appearance was 'Les Peuple Souverain' as their 'togas' resembled, in shape at least, the robes of royalty. Others knew them, like their more famous city-dwelling cousins, as 'Les Misérables'. They survived together by scavenging for food. The weakest were taken to the hospital ships to recover, but their cycle of self-destruction quickly began again on their return, for this was a two-way economy: as surely as drug addicts need their dealers, the *rafalés* needed the *rafaleurs* who bought and sold everything the *rafalés* had to offer. The medical reports for those who died are the most striking confirmation that these men existed. A few examples read: 'Debility from the effect of selling provisions and clothes' or 'from the effect of cold having repeatedly sold their clothes and hammocks' or 'from the effect of want of due sustenance having gambled away his rations for fourteen days.'[22]

There was no organized work or exercise for the prisoners, but it would be a mistake to assume that the result was an atmosphere of indifferent idleness, for this only seems to have been the case for the most despondent. The food was barely sufficient to survive, and the discomforts were extreme. For any prisoner intent on improving his lot even by the smallest of margins it was necessary to find something with which to occupy himself and turn a profit. Many who worked as tailors, cobblers or cooks have left no trace; it is particularly ironic, therefore, that the only substantial body of material to have survived from the hideous prison hulks is some of the most exquisite works of art, the finest of which are comparable to, and in some cases far exceed, the quality of those created by artists in the most favourable of conditions. Garneray's paintings have already been mentioned, but the term 'works of art' is used here in its broadest sense to include the ingenious straw marquetry, the wood and bone carving, the clever mechanical toys and the magnificent ship models at which the prisoners excelled. In most instances the toys and models are carved from animal bone scavenged from the kitchens, or from the meals themselves. The bones were augmented by materials bartered from land, including luxuries such as boxwood, ivory, glass, bronze and tortoiseshell in small amounts. Prisoners used their own hair for the smallest models, but horse hair, smuggled into the ship, was used for the largest models or the longest rigging. Home-made tools were augmented by professional tools acquired from land, and in some instances the intricacy of their skill is astounding, none more so than in the beautiful model of the *Ocean*, now kept in the London Science Museum (fig. 24). Some have sails made out of single pieces of bone so thin that they are almost transparent and seem like sheets of pearl. Restricted by available material, the majority of these models are small, the quality being in the detail, but some are vast. The largest, on display in the Watermen's Hall in London, is almost three feet long, and that of the *Temeraire*, already mentioned, is only slightly smaller, measuring thirty-three inches from figurehead to taffrail, and, like a handful of others, contains an internal mechanism by which the guns can all be run out. These objects were sold through intermediaries ashore: Garneray's was a Jewish picture dealer from Portsmouth named Abraham Curtis.

In the prisoner-of-war jails ashore, regular markets were held to sell the prisoners' goods: this production of material was fully approved by the authorities. It was an important addition to the local economy and the economies of the prisons themselves. Some rose to the very top. On board the *Vengeance* at Portsmouth one prisoner became exceptionally wealthy by running a type of restaurant after his attempts to sell ratatouille to the prisoners had proved successful. On board another ship, the *Crown*, it is possible, although the source is prone to episodes of exaggeration and fiction, that a man named Duvert ran a business forging banknotes, and he ruled that ship almost as a Hollywood Mafia godfather, in luxurious dressing gown and fur-lined slippers. Even if Duvert is a caricature, it is historically certain that one of the primary products of the prison hulks was forged currency, and that some prisoners made a great deal of (real) money. For those with sufficient energy and motivation there also appears to have been every opportunity for non-profit self-improvement in the hulks, as those with knowledge of mathematics, history, poetry, fencing, boxing and countless other skills taught those who were prepared to listen. Others put on theatricals, and at least one ship staged a Molière farce to enlighten their gloom.

Unfortunately most of the sources are from prisoners incarcerated in Portsmouth or Chatham, and we know very little from prisoners' hands about the situation in Plymouth, where the *Temeraire* was stationed. Some very detailed papers belonging to the Superintendent of the Prison Hulks at Plymouth from 1804 to 1813 survive, however, and from them we know that the *Temeraire* was in exalted company. In these years the hulk stations were a visible family tree of British naval history populated not by anonymous ships but by giants. In Plymouth alone the *Temeraire*, one of the most prestigious ships of the navy, was moored in the Hamoaze alongside the *Vanguard*, Nelson's flagship at the Battle of the Nile in 1798 at which he annihilated a French fleet for the first time; the *Genereux*, one of only two French ships of the line to have escaped from that battle, but later captured, appropriately, by Nelson; the *Brave*, previously the *Formidable*, flagship of Rear-Admiral Dumanoir at the Battle of Trafalgar; the Spanish *El Firme*, captured by Sir Robert Calder in 1805; the Spanish *San Ysidro* and *San Nicholas*, both captured at the Battle of Cape St Vincent in 1797, the *San Nicholas* having been taken by a boarding party led in person by Nelson himself, the first time a British flag officer had led a boarding party in person since Sir Edward Howard in 1513.[23] There were even remnants of earlier wars: *Le Caton* was captured in a skirmish with Hood a week after Rodney's famous victory at the Battle of the Saints in April 1782 fought during the American War of Independence; even older was the *Bienfaisant*, in her prime a beautiful French 64-gunner, cut out in a daring boat-attack at the siege of Louisbourg in 1758 during the Seven Years War. She went on to excellent service in the Royal Navy and fought at the Battle of Ushant in 1778. At the other depots for prison hulks, at Chatham, Portsmouth, Plymouth, Deptford, Woolwich and Sheerness, Gibraltar, Bermuda, Antigua, Halifax, Newfoundland, Quebec and the Cape of Good Hope, the ships were equally famous. The *Vryheid* at Chatham was Admiral de Wynter's flagship at Camperdown in 1797, while the *Sandwich*, *Nassau* and *Belliqueux* had all been prominent ships in the mutiny at the Nore in 1797; indeed it was aboard the *Sandwich* that the leader of the Nore Mutiny, Richard Parker, had been arrested, court-martialled and shot.

Some registers for the *Temeraire* during her time as a prison ship survive. Each prisoner has his own entry explaining where and when he was taken prisoner, and from where he came to the *Temeraire*. There is a column marked for their fate: the options being discharged, died or escaped. Of more than a thousand entries, none was marked as escaped: the *Temeraire* did her job well, which is more than can be said for other ships at Plymouth. In January 1813 two prisoners were caught climbing through a hole almost three feet square that had been cut in the hull of the *San Ysidro*. There was a similar attempt at a breakout aboard the *Genereux* three years earlier, but that was successful, and twelve prisoners escaped.[24] Failed escape attempts were met by the British authorities with as much severity as was allowed within the confines of the regulations and in most cases the would-be escapers were sent to the *cachot* for an extended period. If an escape was foiled by betrayal, however, the prisoners themselves might exact their own punishment. In one instance in Plymouth an informer was tied to a ringbolt and given sixty lashes with a rope to the end of which was attached an iron thimble as thick as a man's wrist. When he fell where he was cut down his neck was broken and his body dismembered before being posted through a waste-pipe into the sea. Five men were eventually hanged in Exeter for his murder.[25]

Another section in the register records the name, age and appearance of the prisoner with another space for distinguishing features, marks or wounds, useful for identifying anyone who did manage to escape. These give us a rare glimpse of the men aboard. We know from these registers that the *Temeraire* at one point housed seventy-six Danish prisoners, including William Thoresen, a short man at only five feet and four inches tall, with an oval visage, swarthy complexion, grey eyes and a face marked with the small-pox. Incarcerated alongside him was the one-grey-eyed Ole Olesen, a seventeen year-old captured in the English Channel in 1807 who had a scar that ran from his damaged eye socket right down to his nose. These Danes were but a fraction of her complement, however, the bulk of which was made up of Frenchmen, soldiers and sailors both. There were even sixteen women and a twenty-two-month-old baby boy, born 'at the army in Spain' and taken at Pamplona in November 1813. He was released six months later and sent back to France.[26]

The only other certain fact about the prisoners held aboard the hulks at Plymouth is not reassuring for the *Temeraire's* possible fate in these years. In April 1813 American prisoners were taken from the hulks at Plymouth and forced to march the eighteen miles to Dartmoor Prison. The distance in itself was nothing compared with the hundred and thirty-four miles others were forced to march to Bristol, but Dartmoor Prison is built in one of the most isolated spots in the entire British Isles, amidst three hundred and sixty square miles of wilderness and a full fifteen hundred feet above sea level. When the prisoners arrived it was snowing. The Americans were not met kindly by the French prisoners already there, and shortly after their arrival, a tribe of Romans – that is to say the *rafalés* or Misérables already described – isolated a group of Americans from the prison guards and viciously attacked them with home-made weapons. When the fight was finally broken up, forty Americans were taken to hospital with terrible wounds inflicted by sharp granite stones, clubs and knives. On 16 October 1813 the troublemakers were forcibly scrubbed, clothed and marched back to Plymouth where they were put on the hulks. A matter of weeks later the *Temeraire*, freshly converted and empty, arrived at Plymouth. And this was not the first time that prisoners had been sent back from Dartmoor 'for the purpose of being confined together aboard a ship' on account of their having been guilty of 'selling their clothing and other bad practices'.[27] We know for certain that the *Temeraire* was not used for housing American prisoners[28] and so it is quite possible that she was used to house this tribe of dangerous *rafalés*.

Her dismal routine was only broken in July 1815 when the most famous prisoner of them all, Napoleon Bonaparte, arrived in Plymouth aboard the *Bellerophon*. He had surrendered to the *Bellerophon*'s Captain Maitland in July, and was kept at Plymouth until his fate was decided. While he was there, scores of inquisitive visitors came as close as they could to the *Bellerophon* to catch a glimpse of the deposed Emperor, but the *Bellerophon* was only there for eight days before sailing to Start Point and thence to Torbay where she exchanged her prisoner with the *Northumberland*, which then took him all the way to the remote island of St Helena, Napoleon's personal island prison. Shortly before, at the Treaty of Ghent signed on Christmas Eve 1814, Britain had also concluded her unsatisfactory war with America, but it took some time to repatriate all of the prisoners accumulated from both the French and American wars. In 1814, 70,041 Frenchmen still awaited return and it was not until 1819 that the *Temeraire* was no longer required as a prison hulk. She was refitted and moved to Sheerness where she began a new life as a receiving ship, a ship where new recruits were gathered before being posted: even after the conclusion of wars with both America and France, there was still a very high demand for sailors to man the Royal Navy.

The success of the Royal Navy in the Revolutionary and Napoleonic Wars had been extraordinary. Between 1793 and 1815 the British had lost in action just five line of battle ships and sixteen frigates, while her enemies had lost ninety-two and a hundred and seventy-two respectively. In the same period, the Royal Navy lost through combat alone a hundred and sixty-six warships of all types while her enemies lost a thousand and twenty-one. In spite of this overwhelming success, one of the most remarkable combat records in history, the peace did not bring with it complacency about British maritime power, even though there was no one left to fight. The government was clear that the navy must be retained in some formidable strength to protect Britain from invasion, to protect British interests abroad and to expand British trade and the Empire itself. The defeated French were bitter, while to the east the Russian navy had developed into a formidable presence with powerful fleets in both the Baltic and the Black Sea. Although the Russian navy was only ever designed for minor operations against Turkey and Sweden, the closest rivals with navies of their own, the British could not overlook her potential challenge to Royal Naval superiority, particularly if it was united with the French. The immediate threat of attack from a Napoleonic pan-European fleet of extraordinary strength had vanished, however, and so it was possible and economically necessary to reduce the British fleet by as much as half, while at the same time maintaining a navy that was more powerful than the next two largest navies combined. The fleet that was proposed to fulfil this role would contain no fewer than a hundred ships of the line and a hundred and sixty-two frigates.[29] The majority of the fleet would lie in Ordinary, but under pressure of war could be manned by a hundred thousand sailors within two years. Acting as a receiving ship in Sheerness, therefore, the *Temeraire* was as much a symbol of the formidable naval infrastructure that was prepared for war in the years immediately after 1815 as it was of active British maritime power. Indeed it was the combination of Britain's preparedness for war and her patrolling of the world's oceans that won her the grudging acknowledgement of every other nation as the world's dominant maritime power after 1815.

In 1829 the *Temeraire*'s role changed from receiving ship to victualling depot. The fleet's victuals were delivered to her and then distributed amongst the ships by tenders that plied their way to and from the *Temeraire*. By now all those ships that had fought in the British fleet at Trafalgar and had survived had assumed similar, unglamorous support roles. The *Victory* had even suffered the indignity of having a roof built over her deck, although she retained a measure of decorum by serving as the flagship of the Port Admiral at Portsmouth until 1830. Others were not so lucky. *Neptune*, *Defiance*, *Leviathan*, *Bellerophon* and *Euryalus* all served their time as prison ships. *Polyphemus* became a powder magazine, *Naiad* a coal depot and, worst

of all, poor old *Leviathan* became a target ship. While the veteran partici-
pants of Trafalgar were suffering the ignominy of obsolescence, however, the
myth of the battle itself was undergoing a glorious renaissance.

A number of tributes to Nelson had appeared shortly after his death and
can still be seen today from Birmingham to Barbados but now, with the
coronation of a young queen in an era of unprecedented British imperial
power and cultural and technological change, the British had a growing need
to feel the foundations of British history securely beneath their feet.
Acknowledging the past made it possible to confront a present and future
dominated by new technology and new ideals. The story of Nelson, moreover, fitted neatly with the Romantic sensibilities of the age. Passionate and
brave and dying for his cause, he was in every sense the romantic hero.
Nelson and Trafalgar had never been forgotten in the Royal Navy. At San
Domingo in 1806 Richard Keats hung a portrait of Nelson on the mizzen
stay as he entered battle and in 1811 Captain Hoste, leading a squadron of
frigates into battle in the Adriatic, signalled 'Remember Nelson' as the ships
closed. To the public, however, the importance of Trafalgar had faded as the
war dragged on; it was a full ten years between the death of Nelson and the
final downfall of Napoleon. As the last few men who had fought in the
battle began to die, however, so historians, artists and poets began to respond
to the fear of lost memory. By the end of the 1820s, evocations and representations of Trafalgar and the death of Nelson had become major features of
Britain's cultural landscape.

By 1835 the newly cleared space at the north end of Whitehall had been
named Trafalgar Square, and shortly afterwards, a committee sat for the first
time to discuss an appropriate memorial to commemorate Nelson. This was
a debate played out not in the confines of a musty Whitehall committee
room, but in the national newspapers. Design proposals from artists, archi-
tects and naval officers were discussed, criticized and applauded, all in the
public eye, and while there was general agreement that a suitable memorial
was required, there was almost total disagreement about what form it should
take. Statues, cathedrals, obelisks and pyramids were each considered, all in
their own way designed to celebrate British maritime success, heroism and
sacrifice through Nelson, the embodiment of those ideals. Ever since
Nelson's Column, the design finally agreed upon in 1827 and finished in 1844
– a towering edifice influenced by Trajan's column in Rome – has symbol-

ized Britain's imperial domination through the worship of its God of war. It is no surprise that Hitler intended to take it back to Berlin if he ever occupied London.

The popularity of Trafalgar in the late 1820s and early 1830s was certainly helped by the enthusiasm of King George IV. He had met Nelson once and been deeply impressed by him. Now, as king, he pursued a hobby of collecting memorabilia of the downfall of Napoleon. In particular, he wanted a picture celebrating the Battle of Trafalgar to hang as a pendant piece alongside the dramatic rendition of the Battle of the Glorious First of June, 1794, painted by Loutherbourg, which was already in position in the state rooms at St James's Palace. He turned to the rising star of British art: Joseph Turner. This was Turner's first, and only, royal commission. By now, Turner had established himself as an artist of extraordinary scope, and his philosophy of art had matured. Artists, he believed, 'should not be content with depiction of the immediately visible, but should combine experiences to produce works of art'.[30] He had already explored these ideas in previous works, most famously and dramatically in *The Decline of the Carthaginian Empire* (1817) (fig. 25). Turner produced two canvasses depicting the fate of Carthage, and both were designed to offer moral and civic lessons to Imperial Britain in her struggle against France, illustrated by Turner through the prism of classical history. Turner therefore painted his royally-commissioned image of Trafalgar with his creativity driven by this philosophy, rather than by the factual accuracy desired by the naval community for which a generation of maritime artists had so carefully striven. Turner was not painting for the naval community but for Britain as a whole, and he was determined to produce a work of national significance. It was to be a commentary on the state of Britain at the moment of the painting's creation as on the Battle of Trafalgar itself and, as such, a commentary on sacrifice, martyrdom, heroism and victory.

The result, *The Battle of Trafalgar, 21 October 1805* (fig. 26), was very poorly received, not least by the King himself, and hung only briefly in Carlton House before being removed from the blinkered royal gaze to the Naval Hospital at Greenwich. Historians and naval officers scathingly criticized the picture, almost to the point of ridicule. The painting, they crowed, showed Nelson's signal being raised at 11.40 a.m., but it also showed the *Victory*'s mizzen-mast falling, which did not happen for another hour and a half. The *Achille*, burning in the background, did not explode until 5.45, and the *Victory*'s foremast was shown falling when it never fell at all. The British were simply not ready for Turner's new interpretation of maritime art, but in those same years there were changes afoot which would shake the maritime world to its very core, and in so doing, cause a seismic shift in what the general public expected from maritime art. Steam had arrived.

That arrival was not sudden but a slow and creeping infection that by the mid-1830s had become irresistible. In fact, the first vessel ordered by the navy that used steam in any form was an anonymous dredger, built as early as 1802. By 1815 the Royal Navy had 210,000hp of steam-engine capacity, but it was all in converted sailing vessels. The first purpose-built steam-ship, the tug *Comet*, was ordered in 1819. Hitherto, however, all of these steam vessels were small, auxiliary ships and the first steam-ship designed to carry armament was not ordered for another eight years, and not launched until 1832. Four years later, when the steam tug *Lightning* and the *Firebrand*, a paddle gunvessel, chugged their way past the *Temeraire*, the event was deemed so significant that it is entered into her log.[31] With this new technology came excitement, uncertainty and resentment. Only the most narrow-minded could not see or refused to admit that steam would revolutionize naval warfare, but no one understood exactly how. Would steam tugs be used to help manoeuvre traditional but cumbersome ships of the line, or would the steam ships themselves be able to fight? If so, how could their vulnerable paddles and engines be protected? How would the tactics of fighting and of global strategy change, now that ships were no longer so dependent upon the wind? Only the most far-sighted dreamt of a day when engines would become so powerful and reliable that ships would be able to progress entirely independent of the wind. The technology that would solve many of these problems, the screw propeller, was still in its infancy, and was not even fitted to a Royal Navy ship until the *Rattler* was launched in 1843, her engines and screw having been designed by Isambard Kingdom Brunel.

Not only did the introduction of steam power transform naval warfare, but it subtly altered British expectations of maritime art, and this slight shift was central to the legacy of the *Temeraire*. Simply put, while the Royal Navy was increasingly made up of steam-ships, there was no history, illuminated by art, to inform naval officers of how to wield their new naval power. Hitherto, the purpose of maritime art had been to provide a transparent interpretation of 'facts', the images themselves forming a historical narrative, and the artist bearing the responsibility of the historian to inform the public of his chosen subject with accuracy. The image was thus expected to become a source of knowledge, a building block in the history of the nation to be used to teach future generations. The introduction of steam threatened the foundations of this logic, and in response the 'purpose' of maritime art shifted from the informative to the discursive, from the factual to the poetic. Maritime art could now explore themes and narratives and entertain in ways that it had never done in the eighteenth century. The world was now ready for the genius of Turner, an artist already dedicated to this new style of painting.[32]

With the cultural and technological world changing around her faster than ever before, the *Temeraire* was promoted to a new and final role, as 'Guardship of the Ordinary and Captain-Superintendent's ship of the Fleet Reserve in the Medway'. The *Temeraire*, therefore, had come full circle. She was now flagship of the Medway Reserve, where forty years before she had been launched as the newest, largest and most exciting of the navy's new generation of Second Rates. This was not her only comfort, moreover. As guardship she was freshly painted and re-armed, and so in her last moments began to reclaim some of the dignity lost in her years as a prison hulk, receiving ship and victualling depot. Her guns were exercised twice a week; her masts and yards were used regularly to train destitute boys saved by the Marine Society; and her crew were occupied in the maintenance of other ships less fortunate than her. On 25 June 1838, sailors from the *Temeraire* were assigned to paint the *Coromandel*, a convict ship bound with her sorry crew for the forgotten world of Van Diemen's Land, the modern Tasmania, where they were to be transported for life.[33]

It was during these years that Edward Cooke painted the *Temeraire* (fig. 31). From a very early age Cooke had been unrelenting in his drive to record both the natural and the man-made environment, and it has been argued that his obsessive recording, particularly in the 1830s, when he painted the *Temeraire*, was fuelled by an awareness of profound cultural change. Viewed together, his prolific works have the air of an archaeological record, the paintings capturing the appearance of hundreds of objects and landscapes before they were lost to history. His work is all minutely observed, no doubt a trait encouraged in the years during which he worked as an assistant to the celebrated marine artist Clarkson Stanfield, who employed him specifically to record nautical details. We can be fairly certain, therefore, that Cooke's rendering of the *Temeraire* as a guardship is indeed faithful to her appearance at that time.

She is shown with her port broadside to the observer, towering above another ship alongside her. This is the *Ocean*, a Second Rate of similar design to the *Temeraire*, although fractionally longer. With no particularly impressive reputation to safeguard her, however, the *Ocean* had been cut down to a Third Rate two-decker in 1819. The admiral is being rowed ashore in the launch in the foreground. The *Temeraire* herself has had her topmasts lowered, but not removed, and her topsides between the forecastle and quarterdeck have been filled in, giving the impression of a ship with four complete decks. Otherwise her condition is impressive. Her stern galleries are intact, her lower masts are gleaming with fresh paint, and her hull is a noticeably lighter shade than the tired-looking *Ocean* behind her; a flotilla of small craft fusses around her, each awaiting its turn to land or retrieve visitors.

The man who oversaw the *Temeraire's* activities in these years provided another fitting comfort for her. In the summer of 1836, Captain T. F. Kennedy was piped aboard. He was no stranger to the ship. Indeed, he was the man who had helped establish her reputation as one of the fiercest fighters in the Royal Navy. As first lieutenant of the *Temeraire* at Trafalgar, Kennedy had led the boarding party that captured the *Fougueux* as the *Temeraire* lay between her and the *Redoutable*, a French ship lashed to each side. It is particularly fitting that it was to Kennedy that the responsibility fell to organize her sale, on 29 June 1838, having been ordered by the Admiralty to 'state the value of the *Temeraire*'. Only the day before, she had fired her guns in celebration of the coronation of Queen Victoria. She would never fire them again. Shortly afterwards, with her sailors dispersed by the Admiralty, the commander of the *Ocean* was ordered to prepare the *Temeraire* for sale. The progress of her dismantlement was swift, and by the end of July she was nothing but a hollow carcass, stripped back to the bare simplicity of her frames and planks. As she had once stood, so full of promise on the slip at Chatham, so she now rested, her potential fulfilled with glory, and her work done.

She was sold by Dutch auction on 16 August 1838, along with twelve other ships. However, as the largest ship that had ever been sold out of the Royal Navy, the *Temeraire* stood out as the star lot of the auction. She was bought for £5,530 by a Rotherhithe ship-breaker named John Beatson who was then faced with the formidable challenge of getting all 2,121 tons of her fifty-five miles up the Thames from Sheerness to Rotherhithe. No vessel that large had ever been taken so far upriver. Beatson commissioned two steam tugs, the *Sampson* and the *Newcastle*, and employed a Rotherhithe pilot named William Scott and a crew of twenty-five men to tow her back to his yard.[34] It was a journey full of significance. She was being led not out to sea, but inland, away from her natural environment. She was heading back to the heart of London, itself the heart of the country that had built her and had used her to fight in its defence. It was a trip back to the womb. The scene was set for one of the greatest paintings ever produced by an Englishman, and one of the finest in the world.

10.

The Fighting *Temeraire*

AUGUST 1838 – AUGUST 2009

Sheerness Harbor 1838

A modern X-ray of Turner's *Fighting Temeraire* reveals a large sail in the centre-left of the canvas, painted in lead-white with traces of red and yellow ochre. This ghostly sail lies in exactly the spot occupied by the steam-tug in the finished painting, and it has been argued that a small sailing vessel dominating the picture is hard to reconcile with Turner's finished image. The obvious conclusion, therefore, is that Turner used a discarded canvas to paint *The Fighting Temeraire*.[1] It is important to note, however, that the subject he chose, the final voyage of the *Temeraire*, was not similarly plucked from obscurity.

We are familiar now with that particular incident in the *Temeraire's* life because of Turner's painting, but at the time Turner was riding a wave of popular interest in the fate of the ship. Her purchase out of the navy and her voyage to the ship-breaker's yard at Rotherhithe were headline news and reported in every major newspaper or periodical of the day: *The Times*, the *Morning Post*, the *Morning Advertiser*, the *Shipping and Mercantile Gazette*, *Bell's Life in London* and the *Gentleman's Magazine*. That public interest was based on the fame of the ship herself, raised further by the powerful resurgence of public interest in Nelson and, through him, of the Battle of Trafalgar. Nelson's most famous contemporary biography, by Robert Southey, was a bestseller; by 1837 it had already been reprinted eight times. Crucially, Southey's narrative of the Battle of Trafalgar, and of Nelson's death in particular, makes specific reference to the role of the *Temeraire* in both the approach to battle and the battle itself. He even claimed, not unreasonably, that the *Victory's* gunners were forced to depress the angle of their fire when firing into the *Redoutable*, to avoid damaging the *Temeraire* lashed to the starboard side of the Frenchman.[2]

The Nelson memorial committee had been founded in 1838 and had launched the competition for the design of a memorial to be built in Trafalgar Square. The world of fine art was also responding to the re-found interest in Nelson and Trafalgar and, inevitably, the *Temeraire* played a significant part in those images as her fate was so entwined with that of the *Victory* during the battle. It was also in these years that three of the finest paintings of the battle were produced. In Clarkson Stanfield's *Trafalgar* (1836) (fig. 16), the *Temeraire*, the leftmost of the three ships in the centre, is lashed on her port side to the *Redoutable*, whose mizzen-mast lies across her decks, and is simultaneously opening fire from her starboard broadside on the approaching *Fougueux*. Images by John Christian Schetky and Charles Henry Seaforth both focused on the death of Nelson and implicitly or explicitly depicted the role of the *Temeraire* in the battle. Seaforth's image was even exhibited with a citation from James' recently published *Naval History* that specifically mentioned the role of the *Temeraire*.[3]

Not only was the world of fine art awakening once more to the potential of Nelson and Trafalgar as subject matter, but the very heart of British art, the Royal Academy of Arts, had moved from Somerset House to new premises in Trafalgar Square itself, where it shared building space with the National Gallery. The final link in this remarkable chain of events was that Turner had been appointed for the first time to the hanging committee. As such he was part of a team that was to decide which pictures were appropriate to be hung in the new premises for the forthcoming summer exhibition. It must also be remembered that the poor reception of his *Trafalgar* would have inspired him to respond to his critics by creating a painting worthy to grace the new halls of the Royal Academy in Trafalgar Square. It is no coincidence that when he left *The Fighting Temeraire* along with all of his other paintings to the nation in his will, he insisted that they be housed in a building added to the National Gallery – in Trafalgar Square. Of even more direct significance, an anonymous poem of the time entitled 'The Wooden Walls of Old England' appeared in *Fraser's Magazine* – one of the leading journals of the time and likely to have been read by the intellectually inquisitive and restless Turner – shortly after the *Temeraire* had arrived at Beatson's yard. The poet, lamenting how the once glorious sailing battleships rotted on England's shores, includes the lines 'Fame's spectral sons leap forth and point to England's sailless tide / a wan and faded lustre shines, our sun is in eclipse / woe to the memory of the past; what's glory but a shroud'.[4] The *Temeraire* had even been the subject of a poem by the talented amateur poet James Duff when she served as a prison ship between 1813 and 1819. Although it is unclear whether Turner had read the poem, the penultimate verse reads:

> Our friends depart, and are forgot,
> As time rolls fleetly by;
> In after years none, none are left,
> For them to heave a sigh:
> But hist'ry's page will ever mark
> The glories she did share,
> And gild the sunset of her fate,
> The brave old Temeraire.[5]

In the autumn of 1838, therefore, both the British public and Turner himself were primed to appreciate both the spectacle and the symbolic significance of the final voyage of the *Temeraire*. The public response was inquisitiveness: hundreds, possibly thousands, saw her make that final journey, and even more came to see her when she was safely berthed at Beatson's yard. *The Times* for 12 October claimed that some of the visitors included several naval officers and seamen who had fought on board her at Trafalgar.

Certainly this was the famous ship that had saved the *Victory* at Trafalgar, but she was much more than that as a visitor attraction. Not only was she the largest ship that had ever come so far up the Thames, but the biggest ships of the line spent most of their time at a great distance from land, even when at anchor, for fear of being driven onto a lee shore. Only when in dry dock were they ever really close to land, and one need only stand in front of the great gates at Chatham Dockyard to realize that it was not possible for anyone simply to walk in and look around. Those with access to a boat could get a close view of a warship in her element, but for the majority of the population these magnificent ships were simply figments of their imagination. Now, for the very first time, one of them was accessible by foot in the heart of London and she was visible to everyone who wished to see her.

Even for those familiar with warships, her appearance at Beatson's wharf offered something new, as all her stores had been removed to navigate her so far up the Thames. When the tide went out her entire hull could be seen clearly. This was not just an opportunity to see a warship, therefore, but an opportunity to see the parts of a warship that were usually hidden below the surface. Even when only her topsides were visible she was a formidable sight, but now, resting in the mud at Rotherhithe, she could be appreciated in all her considerable and extraordinary glory. It is not insignificant that in one of the two images made of her as she lay at Beatson's wharf, a passer-by is gesticulating towards the ship with a gesture that is traditionally interpreted as admiring size (fig. 32). *The Times* of 13 September 1838 noted that every other ship 'appeared like a pygmy' alongside her.

Her size was also significant in another way. This was not just any warship, but one of the largest, and therefore one of those ships that defined the Royal Navy in comparison with its rivals. Other navies had large ships of course and, in 1805, the Spanish navy had the largest in the world in the four-decked *Santísima Trinidad*, but no other navy had large ships in the same quantity as the Royal Navy. British naval policy centred on these prestigious ships that, while admittedly slow, were awesome in battle. They could inflict and, perhaps more crucially they could absorb, more damage than any other and, at its most basic level, it was that ability that won Britain so many naval battles throughout the eighteenth century. These large ships were also built to endure the worst Atlantic weather so that they could impose blockades on Britain's enemies, and it had been the effectiveness of those blockades as surely as the decisive naval battles that she had won that had made Britain the imperial power she was by the 1830s. The very existence of the *Temeraire* was therefore a symbol of that endurance and a testament to the quality of British shipbuilding and seamanship that had helped secure maritime supremacy. The hulk of the *Temeraire* was as symbolic of British naval mastery as was the ship herself.

Her name enhanced the power of that symbolism still further. *Temeraire* is clearly a French word; it means nothing in English. The only possible explanation for the use of her name in the Royal Navy, therefore, was that a ship named *Temeraire* had, at one time, been captured by the Royal Navy. Indeed, so powerful does this association seem to have been that, when Turner's painting was first exhibited, she was mistakenly identified as the first *Temeraire*, originally *La Téméraire*, captured in 1759. The ship, therefore, is not just generally symbolic of British maritime power, but of the British superiority over the French that reached its apogee in the wars against

Napoleon. '*Down, down* with the French villains,' wrote Nelson, 'excuse my warmth but my blood boils at the name of a Frenchman . . . you may safely rely that I never trust a Frenchman . . . I hate the French most damnably.' [6] The popularity of the painting is therefore a reflection of that part of British national identity that celebrates our island nation as being separate from the Continent: it reflects a Britain that is proud of its independence from Europe and from the rest of the world, a characteristic that as many modern Britons find troubling as find it reassuring. The fact that Turner was British, and, like Shakespeare, was born on St George's Day further reinforces this link between *The Fighting Temeraire* and British national identity.

While the immediate public response was fascination with the great ship as she lay in the mud of Rotherhithe and was slowly picked clean of her timbers by Beatson's ship-breaking vultures, Turner's response was to create a masterpiece. In 1838 he finished his canvas which he carefully entitled: *The Fighting Temeraire Tugged To Her Last Berth To Be Broken Up, 1838*. This was the first time that the word 'fighting' had been associated with the *Temeraire*. She was in fact known by many British sailors as the 'saucy' *Temeraire*.* Purely aesthetically, the painting is stunning, and its deceptively simple subject matter has been the subject of countless descriptions. Even the most talented wordsmiths have struggled to do the image justice, but perhaps the finest description comes from the pen of William Thackeray, one of the most talented and influential authors and critics of his time.

> The Old *Temeraire* is dragged to her last home by a little, spiteful, diabolical steamer. A mighty red sun, amidst a host of flaring clouds, sinks to rest on one side of the picture, and illumines a river that seems interminable, and a countless navy that fades away into such a wonderful distance as never was painted before. The little demon of a steamer is belching out a volume (why do I say a volume? Not a hundred volumes could express it) of foul, lurid, red-hot, malignant smoke, paddling furiously and lashing up the water round about it; while behind it (a cold grey moon looking down on it), slow, sad and majestic, follows the brave old ship, with death, as it were written on her . . . [7]

---

*The reason for her nickname is lost. The problem is that we don't know what eighteenth-century sailors understood by 'saucy'; if it's similar to how we understand it, it may have had very important subtle variations.

In that description alone there is incentive to revisit the painting time and again to appreciate the little details to which a cursory gaze does not do justice, but one must also appreciate that such dazzling colour had never previously been created by the hand of any artist. This was the period before Turner's work became increasingly abstract and colour became almost an end in itself. His work, hitherto, had included testimony to his potential to use colours in innovative ways, but that potential had not been fully realized until *The Fighting Temeraire*. In that image and thereafter Turner used colour 'as the musician uses his tones, chords, and melody, as a living thing and delightful for its own sake, and as a means of awakening, sustaining and controlling emotion.'[8] In that alone he was an innovator, and in *The Fighting Temeraire* in particular he even used colours that had only recently been created: notice particularly the lemon yellow in the sky above the sunset and the scarlet just above the sun itself – a colour that had been newly invented by a chemist and was notoriously unstable. A review in the *Literary Gazette* is particularly indicative of the impact this had: 'The sun of the glorious vessel is setting in a flood of light, such as we do not remember ever to have seen represented before, and such as, we think, no one but Mr Turner could paint.'[9]

Certainly, reproductions of the painting do it little justice, and one must visit it in person to appreciate its full majesty. In particular, one is drawn by the extraordinary contrast between the ship and its reflection, and the transition from the gorgeous dark turquoise and deep aquamarine of the water where the steamer's paddles churn, to the eerily calm waters that lie ahead, colours that are at once crimson with sunset and silvery still. The colours around the steamer are particularly complex and are all but lost by modern photography. There is a swirl of crimson dotted with purple on her decks, and the steamer is even given a sheen of the lightest green, like a coating of engine oil, on the iron of her hull. The gloomy visage of London to the right of the image is also powerful and yet so often overlooked; it is indistinct and yet an unmistakeable, brooding presence. And finally, there is the moon at the top left. A bold single stroke of a brush laden with paint, the moon now stands proud of the canvas, its texture unlike its smooth surroundings, both a physical presence and one that is powerful through the pureness of its colour. In reproductions of the painting it is barely visible; in front of the actual canvas it is one of the first things that is noticed. It provides a high focal point to the left-to-right diagonal structure of the image that ends at the bottom right with the sunset: as soon as one sees the moon, one is caught in Turner's web.

These aesthetic qualities, however, represent only a part of the painting's appeal, for it was not painted simply to record an event but was designed as a sophisticated commentary on past, present and future. 'Turner makes you see and think of a great deal more than the objects before you', wrote one contemporary critic.[10] Today, art historians are still arguing over its intended 'meaning' and there are a number of alternative narratives that can be read into the painting. Of one thing, however, everyone is certain: Turner had been fascinated with the ships of Trafalgar ever since their return from that battle; he had visited the *Victory* itself and made numerous sketches and full paintings of warships in full sail and as hulks, and had even made particular studies of parts of ships such as their rigging and stern galleries. He was also familiar with the stretch of water up which the *Temeraire* made her last voyage, and while the latest research suggests that he did not actually witness the voyage himself as generations of historians and biographers have led us to believe,[11] the detail and number of reports in contemporary newspapers would have provided him with a great deal of information regarding the passage. Despite this, however, Turner carefully and quite deliberately painted the event inaccurately and it is those inaccuracies which suggest that the painting has its own story to tell.

We know for certain that the ship was towed by two tugs and not by a single tug as depicted in the painting, although it is likely that one would have led the *Temeraire*, as depicted, while another followed her and could perhaps have been invisible. The inaccuracy that caused the most contemporary discussion, however, was the position of the funnel on the steam tug. It is painted by Turner clearly towards the bows of the vessel, in front of the mast, but 1830s steam tugs were rigged with the mast at the front of the vessel and the funnel amidships. A minor detail, one might think, but it is actually central to the design of the painting. When the painting came to be engraved by J. T. Willmore in 1845 (fig. 29), he corrected the 'mistake', and swapped the position of the mast and the funnel. Turner was enraged, dissolving into a 'paroxysm of wrath'.[12] It was essential for the construction of his painting that the funnel was located towards the bows of the tug without appearing so close that the rig of the *Temeraire* must be set on fire by the flames and smoke pouring from the funnel. The smoke from Turner's tug drifts naturally over the bowsprit of the *Temeraire*, obscuring the flagstaff where her ensign would have been hung before she was sold. At the same time, locating the funnel in the bows naturally draws the eye from the height of the *Temeraire*'s masts on a smooth diagonal trajectory towards the sunset at the right of the picture, the sunset itself thus being given equal weight in the painting to the great ship. These easy lines are disrupted in the engraving by the vertical and short burst of steam from Willmore's tug. Finally, and most significantly of all, the black funnel placed in the bows makes Turner's point particularly clear: steam was now at the front in all naval matters.[13]

The discussion of the steam tug thus leads to another inaccuracy in the painting which is also central to its design: the sunset. Based upon knowledge of the piloting hazards of a voyage from Sheerness to Rotherhithe and on contemporary tide-tables, the final journey of the *Temeraire* has been recreated by historians. The steam tugs were powerful enough to work against the tide, but with such a mighty weight to tow, it is most likely that they worked with it. The *Temeraire*'s final journey, therefore, probably began at 7.30 a.m. on 5 September just before slack water on a spring tide. By 1.30 p.m. she would have anchored off Greenhithe or Purfleet while the tide ebbed. The following day her journey would have resumed an hour later at 8.30 a.m., and she would have passed Greenwich Hospital about noon. By 2.00 p.m., just before the tide turned once more, she would have been alongside Beatson's wharf at Rotherhithe.[14] Although this interpretation is not certain but is simply the most likely turn of events, what *is* certain is that the voyages on both days were conducted in daylight, and both finished long before the sun set.

The final and most obvious inaccuracy of Turner's image concerns the masts of the *Temeraire* herself. She is shown with her masts raised. Each of the three masts – the foremast, mainmast and mizzen-mast – also has its topmast and topgallant mast stepped. She carries sails furled on the main yards of her foremast and mainmast, and also on her foretopmast. The yards of her mizzen-mast remain bare. There is nothing particularly surprising about how these masts are depicted. Turner's freehand technique is particularly suited to the flexibility of the rigging, and the foreyard, the lowest on the foremast, is even painted at a convincing and slightly jaunty angle. The rigging is certainly bare, with only the most essential lines being visible, but that is to be expected for a ship that will not sail in the immediate future or, as in the case of the *Temeraire*, ever again. The issue is not to do with the appearance of the rigging, therefore, but with its depiction at all, for we now know that the *Temeraire* was entirely unrigged when she was towed to Beatson's yard. She was a hulk in its purest definition; all that remained of her was her hull. Every single mast and yard had already been removed before the auction when she was being prepared for sale. A far more realistic depiction of her appearance, therefore, can be seen in the two lithographs made of her shortly after she arrived (figs 32 and 33). And yet Turner chose to depict her with sails, to compare her more strongly with the steam tug at her bows. He shows her as she would have appeared in her days of glory, and not as the ugly, undignified and helpless hulk that she was, in reality, on her final journey. Turner's rigging of the *Temeraire* was as symbolic as the sunset which illuminates it.

These, therefore, are the main points that contemporary and modern historical research have proved to be inaccurate and which are central to Turner's intention: the misplaced funnel obscures the flagstaff and leads the eye to the sunset, while the rays of an imagined setting sun illuminate the ship, rigged with masts and sail rather than the helpless hulk that she was. To these 'mistakes' can be added a handful of other observations that are all of significance. The moon rises to the top left of the painting, and in its glow the ivory *Temeraire* has a remarkably skeletal and deathly appearance while the loopy appearance of the timber at her bows is reminiscent of cobwebs.[15] In stark comparison, the black steamer stands in front of her bold and brazen, her hull aglow with scarlet and gold as it reflects the rays of the setting sun. The buoy to the right of the picture is the final berth referred to in the title and it broods like a full stop. Exactly what we are to make of these observations is uncertain, and our interpretations are as open to the influences of time and culture as Turner and his audience were in 1838. Correspondingly, our reading of the painting has altered over time.

Crucially, when compared with the criticism that was levelled at Turner's *Battle of Trafalgar*, painted a decade earlier, his allegorical treatment of events in *The Fighting Temeraire* was not derided, but admired and celebrated. It was 'the most wonderful of all the works of the great master of the age . . . a nobly composed poem, one to which the pen of genius can add nothing in the way of illustration'; it was compared to a 'magnificent national ode or piece of music . . . as grand a painting as ever figured on the walls of any academy, or came from the easel of any painter'. Quite simply, the critic in *Blackwood's* magazine wrote, 'here is genius'.[16]

One of the earliest reactions to the image suggested that it was a lament to the lost days of sail, with the sun setting on the career of the *Temeraire*, and on the glorious days of the wooden walls that had made Britain the great imperial power that she was in the 1830s. Now steam had come to the front in all naval matters. More recent readings have suggested that Turner's thoughts were more nuanced and that it is not sufficient to observe the painting purely as an allegorical study of changing times. What, we must ask ourselves, was Turner's reaction to those changes?

In the 1820s resistance to steam had been vocal and active. It was deliberately discouraged by the Royal Navy, and the US Secretary of the Navy of 1838–41 declared that he would 'never consent to let our old ships perish, and transform our navy into a fleet of sea monsters'.[17] But Turner, it can be argued, did not share this view; his reaction was not uncertain or bitter. The little steamer, although described by Thackeray as 'diabolical', and by another reviewer as having an expression 'of such malignant alacrity as might befit an executioner',[18] is actually beautifully painted in comparison to Turner's other, avowedly sinister depictions of steam boats (fig. 28). The steamboat in Turner's *Peace – Burial at Sea* was described at the time as 'an object resembling a burnt and blackened fish-kettle', and yet his depiction of the little tug in the *Temeraire* is remarkably soft, with the last rays of the dying sun reflecting on her hull.[19] She is made beautiful in her own way and in her own right; she is appreciated, valued and respected. She displays Turner's respect for British engineers leading the way in the technological revolution that was taking over the world. The behemoth of the *Temeraire* herself and the little steam tug are both reasons to celebrate, therefore. One made Britain what she was, and the other was boldly navigating the unknown waters into the future. Together, they are representative of British success, and their depiction, and the modern appreciation of their depiction, is a national pat on the back – a celebration of achievement. Moreover, through his careful inclusion of the rising moon to the left of the painting, an important level of continuity is provided that follows on from the setting of the sun so that together they frame the ships. The change which he depicts, Turner suggests, is inevitable; as inevitable as the setting of the sun and the rising of the moon. The *Temeraire* is part of that natural cycle.

Significantly, she is not going to be destroyed, but dismantled; her timbers are to be sold on, to be re-used in ships, houses, even furniture: we are witnessing just one stage in the *Temeraire*'s circle of life.

The painting, therefore, can be viewed as an image of acceptance rather than resistance. There is no terror in the painting, just a calmness and serenity. If, indeed, there is any conflict in the image at all, then it is perhaps that the little tug is literally dragging the deadweight of institutionalized tradition into a new era; this is change being forced upon an unwilling victim. And yet the Victorian society to which Turner belonged was very much a mixture of acceptance and resistance, with some embracing the new technology while others defied it, and our ability to see both aspects of that reaction to change is a mark of Turner's merit as an artist. The passage of time, the 'death' of an era, is here presented, but is not seen as distressing. When Gabriel Fauré wrote his 'Requiem' in 1888, widely accepted as one of the most serene ever composed, he responded to criticism that it did not express the 'terror of death' by explaining that he viewed death as 'a joyful deliverance, an aspiration towards a happiness beyond the grave, rather than as a painful experience'.[20] His work was consequently dubbed by one critic as 'death's lullaby', a phrase that is certainly applicable to Turner's *Fighting Temeraire* and an observation which takes on even more significance if one considers Turner's age when he painted it. He was sixty-three and although he was still to produce some of his finest work, he was no longer the rising star of his generation. On the contrary, like the *Temeraire*, he was cruising serenely towards retirement and his own death. His father, to whom he was particularly close, had recently died, and a friend commented that he was never the same afterwards. To compound matters still further, a number of his close friends had also recently died and we know that he had begun to question how he would be remembered at his death. After he was a pallbearer at the elaborate state funeral of a friend he lamented: 'who will do the like for me, or when, God only knows'.[21] Nor was he the only respected member of the wider artistic fraternity contemplating death or decline in these years. Wordsworth's inspirational *Essay on Epitaphs* had been published in 1810, and by 1830 Tennyson was struggling with the words of his unfinished poem *In Memoriam*.[22]

Even if one takes a step back from the event of death itself, the picture certainly depicts the *Temeraire* as an object no longer at home in a new era; a dinosaur of an earlier age. It is an observation which is reflected in striking parallels in Turner's own life. He had suffered years of criticism that had grown vicious and personal. He was a man born of the Romantic age, whose values had long since given way to the more pragmatic and utilitarian mindset of early Victorian society. His painting *Juliet and her Nurse* had been publicly criticized as a composition 'thrown higgledy-piggledy together, streaked blue and pink, and thrown into a flour tub.' A year later another of his works was described as 'White brimstone and stone-blue . . . daubed about in a dreadful and dreamy disorder.'[23] The deaths of his father and friends had left him isolated personally, and he was increasingly isolated professionally. Commissions for prints, the staple of his existence for many years, dried up. The fate of the *Temeraire* in 1838 can, therefore, be closely paralleled with the fate of Turner himself as an artist, an observation that can also be applied to other paintings from this period. While Turner in his pomp painted HMS *Victory* at her moment of triumph, now in his increasing maturity he painted HMS *Temeraire* in decline. In the same way he had shown Napoleon at the victorious Battle of Marengo when he was younger, but now preferred to depict Napoleon in his declining years as a captive of the British on St Helena. It is not insignificant that after he finished the painting, Turner uncharacteristically relaxed into a long period of inactivity and it has been suggested that he saw the *Temeraire* as his swan song.[24]

Also of importance to the painting is the tug's smoke that obscures the *Temeraire's* flagstaff, set alongside the flag of the tug itself, which flies high as it busily and eagerly goes about its duty. Now sold out of the navy, the *Temeraire* was no longer entitled to fly the naval ensign, a fact to which Turner specifically drew the public's attention. When the painting was first exhibited, he carefully included some text, borrowed from a famous contemporary poem by Thomas Campbell and entitled 'Ye Mariners of England'. Turner altered it slightly for his own purposes, and underneath the title of the painting, wrote:

> *The flag which braved the battle and the breeze,*
> *No longer owns her.*

It is the question of ownership here that particularly exercised Turner, and he was not alone. Naval policy in those years was to reduce the battle fleet from its bloated extremes of 1815 to a more manageable, although still powerful, force, and the *Temeraire* was one of a number of large ships sold out of the navy after 1815. Understandably, this was met by some public concern. The old wooden walls were there to be marvelled at for their role in the decisive battles that helped bring Napoleon to his knees, but their destruction was as disconcerting as their appearance was fascinating. By the 1830s they were not being replaced by like-for-like ships, or, indeed, by ships which British sailors knew how to sail and how to fight: they were being replaced by steam-frigates. Much less powerful and propelled by a technology that was in its infancy, this first generation of steam-ships was no stranger to explosions, fires and disasters with scalding water. Even more disturbing, by the late 1830s it was the French who had begun to edge ahead in the new technologies of steam and shellfire. Turner's observation that 'The flag no longer owns her' can therefore be seen as reflecting contemporary concern over naval policy, as it silently asks the question: to what is the safety of Britain now to be entrusted?

The painting also makes a statement about the government's approach to maritime heritage which resounds loudly throughout history to the present day. Turner's focus on the new ownership of the *Temeraire* is at the same time a reproach to the authorities who sold her; it is a commentary on a government policy that failed to appreciate the value of historical objects and the value of history itself. Indeed the very existence of the painting is proof of that: it is her only memorial. Thackeray picked up this theme in his appraisal of the painting and claimed:

> I think . . . we ought not in common gratitude, to sacrifice entirely these noble old champions of ours, but that we should have somewhere a museum of their skeletons, which our children might visit, and think of the brave deeds which were done in them. The bones of the *Agamemnon* and the *Captain*, the *Vanguard*, the *Culloden*, and the *Victory*, ought to be sacred relics, for Englishmen to worship . . .[25]

Ruskin agreed: 'surely, if ever anything without a soul deserved honour or affection, we owed them here.'[26] The contemporary relevance is important. In 1839 the last survivors of the Battle of Trafalgar and of the days of sail itself were rapidly thinning. Memory itself was at risk, a concern that we share today as the individual deaths of the few remaining survivors of the

Great War make headline news. And yet in 1838 no concept of maintaining the maritime heritage by the nation for the nation existed. It is possible that awareness of this informed Turner's attitude to the painting. He cherished it; he called it 'his darling'; he only lent it out once, vowed never to do so again, and refused to sell it 'for any consideration of money'. Moreover, in a revoked codicil to his will written about 1846, he offered each of his seven executors any painting in his studio *except* the *Fighting Temeraire*.[27] The painting was an important part of his development as an artist and as a man, as much as the *Temeraire* was an important part of Britain's development as a military power and as a nation. And Turner was not going to ignore the lessons of history; he would treasure his painting as surely as the nation had neglected its ship. In his lifetime he did exactly that, and he even cared for the painting after his death, as he did for all of his works, by bequeathing them to the nation. And so Turner's *Fighting Temeraire* hangs today in room thirty-four of the National Gallery, usually surrounded by visitors. It is not hidden from sight in the private rooms of an anonymous collector, and it has not suffered at the hand of unskilled or over-enthusiastic conservators. It is in magnificent condition, and still hangs on its original stretcher. It is considered to be the best preserved of Turner's later paintings; it has never been cleaned apart from the removal of surface dirt, and was not even lined until 1963. The quality of its preservation is particularly remarkable, as some of Turner's innovative painting techniques have led to significant conservation problems with many of his other works. So anxious were they to ensure that *The Fighting Temeraire* did not suffer material degradation or damage, the curators of the National Gallery displayed it behind glass until well into the twentieth century, and this precaution is generally considered to have assisted its preservation.[28]

The painting survives, therefore, as a sophisticated memorial to the memory of 1759, when the name *Temeraire* first entered the navy; to the Battle of Trafalgar in 1805; to the resurgence of interest in Nelson and Trafalgar in the 1820s and 1830s; to Turner's genius with a paintbrush; to Turner's laudable passion for history and heritage; to his death in 1851; and finally to Turner's enduring popularity in the twenty-first century. That popularity is testimony to the fact that the British like their art to tell stories. The complexity of the painting will ensure that its 'meaning' or 'meanings' remain elusive, but it is much more certain that, if taken together, both the painting itself and

Turner's care for it are a powerful lesson in the value of history and the esteem which it should be granted. It is certainly one of the reasons for its continued popularity today. To declare that one appreciates *The Fighting Temeraire* is a statement that transcends our views of art and artists and makes a more profound comment about our approach to life. Consequently, that *The Fighting Temeraire* won the competition for the nation's favourite painting in 2005 is deeply reassuring. It demonstrates that the desire to remember burns in Britain like the sunset in the painting itself. The painting is a memorial, and deserves the respect offered to all memorials. It is a reminder of a sense of duty; a reminder of sacrifice past. In that respect, therefore, we have no choice *but* to prefer the painting to others with less significant themes. To ignore *The Fighting Temeraire* is to be ungrateful – even ungracious – to the memories of those who have lived and died for us today. Ironically therefore, by acknowledging the importance of the painting we acknowledge that there are far more important things in the world than art.

While we may all admire Turner's painting on a whole host of different levels, however, it is quite possible that Turner is turning in his grave. We may demonstrate a general desire to appreciate the nation's historic ships through admiration of his painting and, more specifically, through the volume of public distress that met the near-destruction of the *Cutty Sark* in May 2007, but of far more concern is the lack of national infrastructure in place to safeguard our historic vessels. The National Historic Ships Committee was formed in 1992 to monitor the state of Britain's historic ships. One of its most impressive achievements is the creation of the National Register of Historic Vessels. The creation of this database has done much to increase public awareness of the plight of our historic vessels in general, and provides a detailed background of specific endangered ships, or those that are likely to become endangered in the near future.

Nevertheless, the financial realities of historic ship preservation are stark. Ship conservation is immensely complex and requires innovative, sophisticated solutions. Waterlogged wood, once removed from the anaerobic conditions which preserved it, can be costly to preserve and maintain indefinitely. Iron has similar problems. Vessels kept in dry docks such as the SS *Great Britain* or the *Cutty Sark* face very different conditions from those for which they were designed. To prevent hogging and sagging, the SS *Great Britain* has an iron 'girdle', and the *Cutty Sark* will be suspended in a Kevlar web to take the weight off her hull. One can only hope, therefore, that the most significant contemporary legacy for Turner's painting is to serve as a warning to present and future generations of what can happen if active steps are not taken to safeguard our historic ships.

At the time of writing, there are sixty-one vessels considered by the National Historic Ships Committee to be of exceptional historical value, and the survival of all of them is uncertain. The more famous are household names: the SS *Great Britain*, the world's first propeller-driven iron-built passenger ship and the forerunner of all modern liners; Henry VIII's magnificent carrack *Mary Rose*; and HMS *Warrior*, the first British iron warship. But there are many more that do not share a similar profile but are of great significance. The RRS *Discovery* was the first purpose-built research ship and the ship which took Captain Robert Falcon Scott to Antarctica on his first expedition, an expedition that launched the careers of both Scott and Shackleton. The *Zetland* is the world's oldest existing lifeboat and the *Bertha* is the oldest working steamboat in existence, while the *Landfall* is the only surviving landing craft from the Second World War. There are only a handful of 'little ships' remaining that took part in the Dunkirk evacuation, and many of them do not receive the care they deserve. It is unrealistic to assume that all of these can be saved, and yet the most significant ships, ships with histories equivalent to the *Temeraire*, must surely be saved for future generations to enjoy.

In the case of HMS *Temeraire*, we are particularly fortunate that Turner chose to paint her and that he did so to such popular acclaim. Not only does the painting survive as a memorial to her, but its popularity created a surge of interest in her history. A number of songs and poems were composed in her honour, and were warmly received by the public. Sir Henry Newbolt's poem 'The Fighting Temeraire' was still being memorized and recited in British schoolrooms in the 1960s.[29] Others were produced by Richard Monkton Milnes, Gerald Massey, and undoubtedly the finest of them all by one of the most talented authors of the age, Herman Melville. His final lines are worth quoting in full:

> O, Titan Temeraire,
> Your stern-lights fade away;
> Your bulwarks to the years must yield

And heart-of-oak decay.
A pigmy steam-tug tows you,
Gigantic, to the shore –
Dismantled of your guns and spars
And sweeping wings of war.
The rivets clinch the iron-clades
Men learn a deadlier lore;
But Fame has nailed your battle-flags –
Your ghost it sails before:
O, the navies old and oaken,
O, Temeraire no more!

Many of these poems are well known, but few appreciate that they were all inspired as much by Turner's painting as they were by the final voyage of the *Temeraire* itself.

The *Temeraire* thus survives in art and literature, but her physical remains are few indeed. All copper sheathing plates, nails and fastenings were sold back to the Admiralty, and the timber sold to a variety of tradesmen, to house-builders and church-builders, shipyards and furniture-makers. Wood from the *Temeraire* survives today deep in a vault in Balmoral Castle, in the form of a gong stand presented to the Duke of York, the future King George V, on his marriage in July 1893 to Princess Mary of Teck (fig. 30). The Latin inscription, 'Nemo me impune lacessit', translates as 'No one provokes me with impunity'. In storage in the National Maritime Museum in Greenwich, London, is a beautiful barometer made from oak taken from the *Temeraire*'s sternpost, together with a gavel and a number of 'miscellaneous timbers'. The Royal Naval Museum in Portsmouth has a chair made from her timbers and another is owned by Lloyd's Register of Shipping in London. There is even a chair made from her oak in the Whanganui Regional Museum in New Zealand, as the museum's founder Samuel Drew married Beatson's daughter, Catherine.[30] Other chairs built from oak from the *Temeraire* occasionally appear at auction. There is also a stand for the prisoner-of-war ship model in the Watermen's Hall in London that is built from oak from the *Temeraire*, and fittingly, it is the largest such model known to exist.

A beautiful tea caddy made from *Temeraire* oak, given to James Eaton, the *Temeraire*'s signal midshipman at Trafalgar, was sold at Christie's in London in 2000, and in New York in 2007 an oil painting of a Newfoundland dog named Neptune by Sir Edwin Landseer, the pre-eminent animal painter of the nineteenth century, was sold for $824,000 (fig. 34). It was commissioned by a certain W. Ellis Gosling in 1824 and shows the Newfoundland, a breed famed for its lifesaving ability at sea, on the verge of leaping into action. His name, Neptune – the Roman god of the sea – was particularly appropriate therefore. After the dog's death, Gosling further commemorated his faithful maritime hound by framing the image in oak from the *Temeraire* and including a plaque that likened Neptune's sense of duty to that of Nelson's sailors.

For relics of the *Temeraire* that are immediately accessible to the public, one must visit the tiny church of St Mary's in Rotherhithe, which has numerous maritime connections. Christopher Jones, the captain of the *Mayflower*, whose passengers founded the Plymouth Colony in New England in 1620, is buried here, along with Prince Lee Boo, son of a canni-bal chief brought back from the Palau Islands by British sailors in 1783. Unable to survive the British winter, he died shortly afterwards. In the lady chapel is an altar, made from *Temeraire* oak, along with the altar rails and two extraordinary timber thrones. Countless other smaller artefacts have been lost to history, not least the wooden leg of one Trafalgar veteran who reportedly begged Mr Beatson for timber from the *Temeraire* to replace his 'larboard leg', a request that Beatson granted.[31] More recognizable would be the brass plaque affixed to the deck of the *Temeraire* that commemorated Nelson's famous signal at Trafalgar: 'England expects that every man will do his duty.' Beatson refused to sell it, but it has never been found.

These, therefore, are the handful of relics which we know about, but we also know for certain that all the timbers from the five thousand trees from which she was built were sold, and it is quite possible that the beam holding up the roof of a house in Rotherhithe or the timber of an ornament in an antique shop in Greenwich has a hidden past, a past that stirs the nation's blood with a passion that has endured as the physical past has decayed. The *Temeraire* has been absorbed back into the England whence she came; she was made of England and we are made of her; she has travelled full circle, from dust unto dust. The *Temeraire* may now be scattered but she lives on in our hearts and minds today as surely and as steadfastly as she once lived on the seas that surround us.

Postscript

The *Temeraire* had become so integral to the history of the Royal Navy that her name was used several times more, and in 1876 a beautiful and state of the art central-battery ironclad named HMS *Temeraire* was finished at Chatham and slipped into the waters of the Medway. She was equipped with twin screw propellers and a capacity to hold six hundred and twenty tons of coal. That fuel fired her two sets of two-cylinder vertical inverted compound expansion engines, which in turn augmented her vast rig – she was the largest brig-rigged vessel ever built, with 25,000 square feet of sail area. She too was to have a significant role in both British and global maritime history, as on 3 October 1890 her log records that at 11.35 in the morning she stopped engines and 'proceeded towards Suda Bay under sail'. Here in the Mediterranean, near the island of Crete, this *Temeraire* was the last British battleship ever to proceed under sail alone. A little over half a century after he had painted *The Fighting Temeraire*, Turner's vision of a world dominated by steam and iron had come to pass, and it was aboard the new HMS *Temeraire* that sailors made that final leap into the modern world. For a ship whose name was already carved deep into British naval history and also linked to a visionary artist, nothing could have been more appropriate.

Epilogue:
On Iconic Warships

HMS *Temeraire* is just one of a large number of historic warships that can be described as iconic. It is worthwhile taking a few moments to consider the phenomenon of the iconic warship, because these ships matter to modern society to a far greater extent than one might expect. They all deserve our attention and those that have survived need our support.

As this book has shown, the biographies of warships are multi-layered and complex. Most obviously, the story of the *Temeraire* matters to our society because it was immortalized by one of the greatest artists ever to have lived, but Turner immortalized that story because it mattered to his society. In 1839 the *Temeraire* had already become iconic, and therein lies one of the peculiar values of iconic warships. They are potent historical objects because they transcend eras, and the ability to illuminate both our own times and those more distant offers an immediate and unmistakable example of the value of history. Moreover, the story of the *Temeraire* can be used to illuminate a whole range of historical topics, from the very broadest perspective of self-perception on an international stage – the question of how the navy serves to carry a nation's message around the world – to the tightest possible focus on day-to-day life in a warship. The ship as a focus to this story further serves to broaden our horizons by highlighting the value of a maritime perspective on international history and demonstrating changing attitudes towards the maritime world.

One example of those changing attitudes will suffice. To us, perhaps the most extraordinary aspect of the *Temeraire* story is the outpouring of public emotion when she was scrapped. When the veterans of the allied American and British fleets that launched the Gulf War come to be scrapped, there will be high emotion among their crews, but it will not spill out into the streets as it did for the *Temeraire*. But now consider this: an unprecedented economic downturn cripples banks and governments and causes financial shockwaves that are felt sorely in the heritage industry. The great walls of thirteenth-century castles crack and tumble; gorse and bindweed cover Iron Age hill forts; the landscaped gardens of country houses are lost to forest while the houses themselves rot with damp. Our historic ships, always so vulnerable to the elements, lose the continual fight against salt water, salt air and coastal winds. Nelson's *Victory*, which broke the line at Trafalgar, or the American equivalent, the USS *Constitution*, one of the handful of powerful frigates that signalled the birth of the US Navy, are superfluous and destined for the breaker's yard. There is no private investor sufficiently interested in maritime history or aware of the significance of iconic warships to come to their aid. Just as the *Temeraire* was, they are sold at public auction, towed to a scrapyard in the heart of one of the world's largest cities, and taken to pieces. Like vultures feasting on an elephant carcass, or crabs on a dead whale, the shipbreakers' progress is too slow to see, but within weeks the ships are gone, their masts never gracing the skyline again.

A touch apocalyptic, maybe, but a useful exercise nevertheless. What, we must ask ourselves, would the public reaction be in that scenario? Fortunately we have some guidance. In 2008 there was public outrage that the fire that destroyed much of the iconic clipper ship *Cutty Sark* might have been started on purpose. The story was whipped around the press, countless expressions of sympathy flooded in, and the money required to restore her soon followed. Her future is now relatively secure. History tells us, however, and not least through the story of the *Temeraire*, that most other ships are not so fortunate, even in the face of public outcry. Consider the *Implacable*. Originally the *Duguay-Trouin*, captured from the French at the Battle of Trafalgar, she was soon the only surviving representative of the Franco-Spanish fleet. By 1904 she and the *Victory* were the only surviving combatants. But by 1949, the economic downturn after the Second World War left her at the mercy of private benefactors, including the Royal Family, who did their best to secure her future but ultimately failed. On 2 December 1949, flying both English and French ensigns and packed with explosives, she was towed nine miles off the south coast and destroyed. Her salvaged stern, which hangs in the entrance hall of the National Maritime Museum in Greenwich, is one of the most potent artefacts in its collection as it speaks not only of the splendour of eighteenth-century warships, but also of our failure to protect our significant maritime heritage in the mid-twentieth century. The World Ship Trust, founded in 1979 to oversee the welfare of historic ships, adopted the motto *'Implacable*, Never Again'.

Although the money was not found to save *Implacable*, the public outcry at her proposed and eventual destruction was real and forceful, and we can only suspect that in our imaginary scenario of *Victory* or *Constitution* being threatened, the response would be similar to that shown for *Implacable* or *Cutty Sark*. The point, of course, is that although we may not (yet) be so emotionally attached to our modern warships, those with iconic status will retain a very real presence in our modern society.

Warships of any era are extraordinary to those who are lucky enough to see them. Remember that their natural habitat is deep in the oceans, often on the far side of the world. Only very rarely do they come within sight of shore and usually they are quickly enfolded in the comforting embrace of a heavily defended dockyard. The rarity with which they can be seen adds to their mystique now as it did in the past, but their size and potential for destruction adds to that imposing air. Those decommissioned warships that survive, moored up in rivers of great cities, are uncomfortable splinters in an urban heart. Their very alien nature is what makes them so fascinating. Square-rigged ships, moreover, have their own power in attracting attention. Most now appreciate their web-like rigging and impossibly high masts as feats of architecture comparable to medieval cathedrals. Certainly in terms of their impact on the immediate landscape it is a useful analogy. For centuries before high-rise office blocks, cathedrals dominated the skyline and drew the eye as something extraordinary, just as the masts of square-rigged ships will draw the eye today in a modern port full of fishing boats and fibre-glass yachts.

To go aboard them is to get an immediate sense of the dark, cramped lives of their seamen, even if one acknowledges the necessary limitations of modern health and safety rules. But there is more to these surviving ships' value. One can see the masts are tall from a painting, but it is impossible to get the awful sense of dizziness unless one is standing at their foot, or lucky enough to climb aloft. To stand under the rig, moreover, is to become immediately aware of these ships' startling noise. They whistle, clang, slap, creak, groan, rattle and ping as the wind plays with their canvas, ropes and timber. For those still afloat like HMS *Warrior* the sea still objects to their presence and the horizon shifts ever so slightly with the swell. The smell of the tar and oil is but part of the daily stench of hundreds of men and animals who used to live aboard, and today there is no trace of the pervasive acrid smell of gunpowder. But even those initial smells, noises and motions quickly remind the visitor that warships assault all of the senses, if only with a fraction of the power they once exercised.

The ships that survive, but not in such a perfect state as *Constitution* or *Victory*, have a presence that is still formidable, and none more so than the *Mary Rose*. She is not the product of the great eighteenth- and early nineteenth-century wars fought for control of the world's seas, but is three hundred years older, built and sunk during the reign of Henry VIII. One cannot move around her decks or look up at her rigging, but the thousands of artefacts recovered from her wreck provide an immediate and potent insight into Tudor seafaring. The most remarkable survival of all historic warships, however, is the Swedish king Gustavus Adolphus' *Vasa*, which sank on her maiden voyage in 1628 and was recovered almost completely intact in the 1960s. Now preserved in a purpose-built museum in Stockholm, she provides visitors with an exceptional taste of Baltic sea warfare from the seventeenth century and is the most effective way of educating the world that a significant portion of the history of the fighting ship occurred in the seventeenth-century Baltic, a period too often, and quite wrongly, assumed to be dominated in northern waters by the Dutch, English and French navies.

All of the above examples of iconic ships survive, however, and although a major part of the lesson of the *Temeraire* is that we should care for such ships, the lesser part is that iconic status is fleeting. If the *Temeraire* had not been immortalized by Turner, we must ask ourselves, would we be aware that she had caused such an uproar in the 1830s? Perhaps: the poetry inspired by her break-up and her regular presence in contemporary newspapers may have alerted an historian to a story worth investigating, but it is unlikely. It is far more probable that her iconic status would have been lost as surely as the ship herself. There are a great number of iconic ships which have not survived, and because of that their iconic status is threatened or already lost. In short, we are in danger of losing the memory of iconic ships as well as the ships themselves.

The list of iconic ships that do not survive is long and it is impossible to name them all, but *Warspite, Hood, Bismarck* and *Tirpitz* from the twentieth century, *Gloire, Devastation* and *Inflexible* from the nineteenth, *Santísima Trinidad* and *Indefatigable* from the eighteenth, *Royal Sovereign* and *Soleil Royale* from the seventeenth, Henry VIII's *Henry Grace à Dieu* from the sixteenth and Henry V's mighty *Grace Dieu* from the early fifteenth century all appear on it. Anyone with an interest in warships will miss their favourite here and, moreover, this list includes only English, French and German warships. It does not include any American, Russian, Chilean, Peruvian, Mexican, Swedish, Danish, Dutch, Chinese, Japanese, Korean, Australian, Turkish, Italian, Venetian, Genoese, Austrian or Portuguese historic warships. Nor does it include any aircraft carriers or submarines. Ships are iconic to different people for different reasons. There are, in short, a large number of iconic ships out there that we know next to nothing about.

Finally, it is important to emphasize that the creation of iconic warships is a continual process. Perhaps now the *Bellerophon* can be attributed with iconic status after David Cordingly raised her public profile to reflect that which she enjoyed in the nineteenth century in his book *Billy Ruffian: The Bellerophon and the Downfall of Napoleon* (2003). Perhaps also the USS *Cole* will attain iconic status for being attacked by suicide bombers in October 2000. Although our modern ships inherit the names of their predecessors, however, their function now is increasingly anonymous and that anonymity will inevitably lead to a quest for tales of individual significance from the past. This is a pattern that is repeating itself, a fact emphasized by the *Temeraire* story. When Turner painted her in 1838 he tapped into a public enthusiasm for historic ships and historic tales of maritime glory fuelled in part by a contemporary change in the use of maritime power. In the late 1830s most naval activity was centred on peacetime activities: the 1830s, as now, was no era of widespread maritime war and fleet battle. It is unlikely, therefore, that our current interest in warships will shift to reflect the modern roles that dominate naval power today, the constant battle against piracy and smuggling and the frequent demand for maritime-borne aid in disaster zones. Rather, it will remain focused on individual examples of maritime glory. The popularity and corresponding importance of the iconic warship is not dead, therefore, but very much alive, and its historical value remains unquestionable. It is hoped that this work will inspire others to seek out the stories of iconic warships that have been lost, or are in danger of being lost, and that it will encourage everyone to appreciate a little more those ships that are lucky enough to survive. Go and visit them while you can.

Ship Diagrams

No detailed contemporary images of HMS *Temeraire* survive, but we do know that in most of her significant dimensions and layout she was almost identical to HMS *Victory*. These beautiful modern illustrations of HMS *Victory* by John McKay, therefore, give the best possible impression of the *Temeraire*'s layout and sail plan.

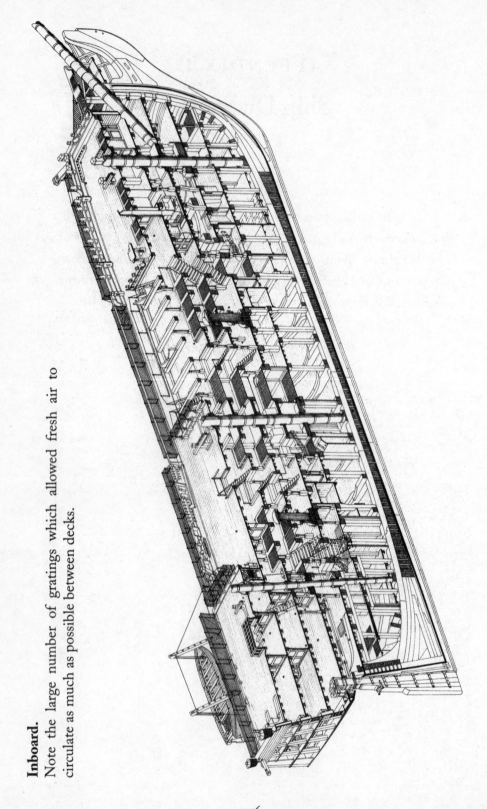

Inboard.
Note the large number of gratings which allowed fresh air to circulate as much as possible between decks.

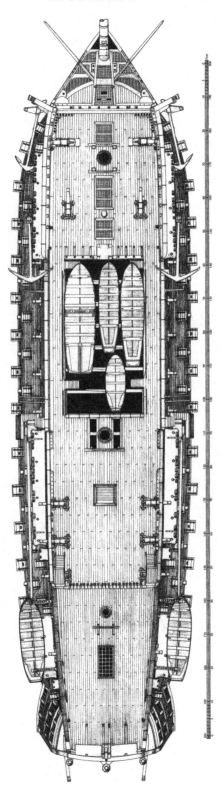

Poop, quarterdeck, waist and forecastle.
Note the storage of boats and anchors.

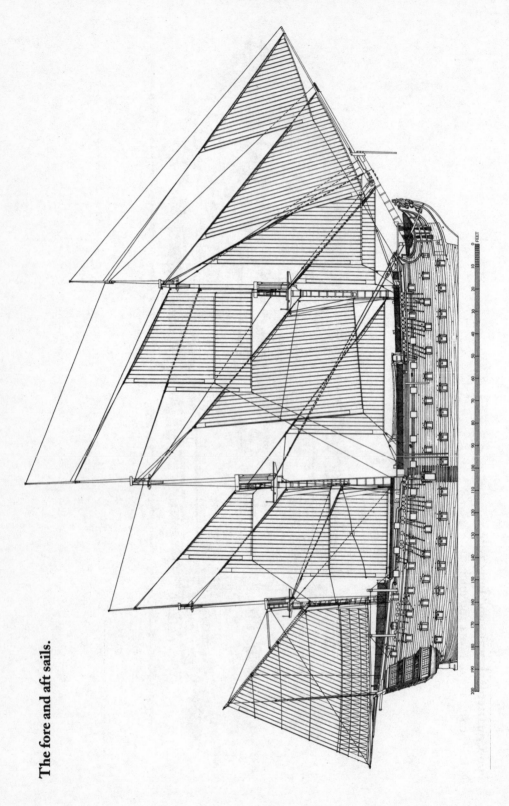

The fore and aft sails.

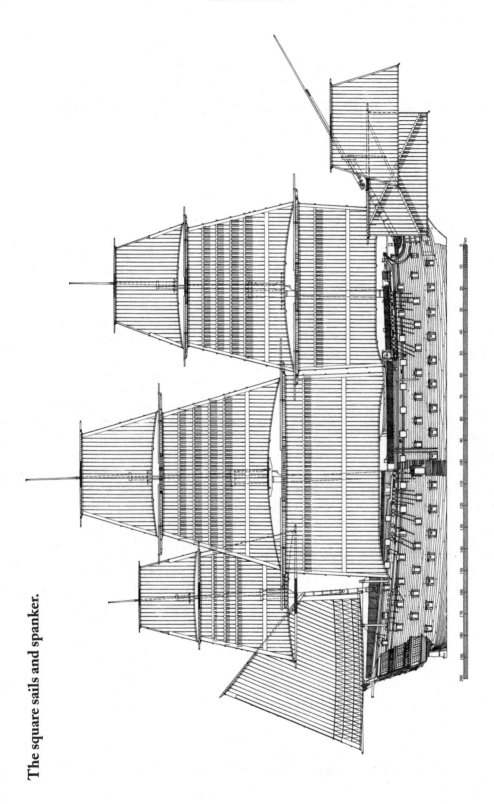

The square sails and spanker.

The crew of HMS *Temeraire* at the Battle of Trafalgar, 21 October 1805

John	Abraham	22	Cape of Good Hope, South Africa	Ordinary Seaman
Thomas	Abram	20	Carnarvon, Wales	Landsman
Edward	Aldgate			Private Marine
John	Alexander	24	Scotland	Able Seaman
James	Allen	25	Entrim	Able Seaman
John	Allen	23	Northumberland, England	Able Seaman
Robert	Allen	20	Addington, Scotland	Able Seaman
William E.	Allen	20	London, England	Midshipman
Archibald	Anderson	20	Greenock, Scotland	Landsman
Samuel	Andrews			Private Marine
James	Arscott	20	Tinmouth	Master's Mate
James	Ashman			Sergeant, Royal Marines
Oliver	Asplin	20	Manchester, Lancashire, England	Landsman
Thomas	Asplin	22	Lewisham, Kent, England	Able Seaman
William	Atkins	26	Bristol, Gloucestershire, England	Ordinary Seaman
James	Atkinson			Private Marine
James	Bailey	25	Cork, Ireland	Carpenter's Crew
John	Bailey			Private Marine
John	Baker	35	Bristol, Gloucestershire, England	Ordinary Seaman
William	Ballingall			Purser
Philip?	Barbary	26	Truro, Cornwall, England	Able Seaman
Thomas	Barber	20	Deptford	Ordinary Seaman
Henry	Bariham?	32	North Yarmouth, Norfolk, England	Caulker
John	Barker			Private Marine
Edward	Barlowe			Private Marine
Thomas	Barlowe			Private Marine
John	Barry	18	Dublin, Ireland	Ordinary Seaman
James	Bate			Private Marine
Robert S.	Bayly	18	Poole, Dorset, England	Midshipman
William	Beale	21	Gloucester, Gloucestershire, England	Able Seaman
James	Bellhouse			Private Marine
Thomas	Berry	18	Dublin, Ireland	Landsman
William	Bickell	40	Devon, England	Ordinary Seaman
John	Bilsborrow	20	Lancaster, Lancashire, England	Boy

22. A view of hulks on the Tamar, Plymouth, by Turner, 1812.

24. Stern detail of the prisoner-of-war model of HMS *Ocean*.

23. A view of the prison hulks at Portsmouth by the French convict Louis Garneray, 1810.

25. *The Decline of the Carthaginian Empire* by Turner, 1817.

26. *The Battle of Trafalga*r by Turner, 1822–4.

OVERLEAF: 27. *The Fighting Temeraire Tugged To Her Last Berth To Be Broken Up, 1838*, by Turner.

28. *Peace – Burial at Sea* by Turner, 1842.

29. J. T. Willmore's engraving *The Old Temeraire*, 1845.

30. Gong stand made of oak from the *Temeraire*.

31. The *Temeraire* shown in her role as guardship of the Medway
by Edward Cooke, 1833.

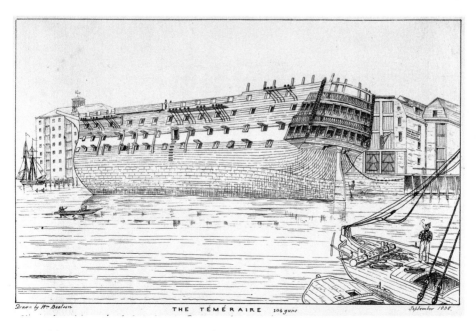

Drawn by Wm Beatson   THE TÉMÉRAIRE 104 guns   September 1838.

32. The *Temeraire* shown at John Beatson's yard in Rotherhithe by William
Beatson, his younger brother, September 1838.

33. The *Temeraire* at Beatson's yard, Rotherhithe, 1838–9.

34. *Neptune* by Sir Edwin Landseer, 1824.

Joseph	Birch			Private Marine
Thomas	Birch	21	Chester, Cheshire, England	Ordinary Seaman
James	Bird	27	Somerset, England	Able Seaman
Alexander	Black	25	Aberdeen, Scotland	Able Seaman
Robert	Blagg			Private Marine
John	Blake	40	Catdown, Devon, England	Yeoman of the Sheets
James J.	Blenkins	20	Essex, England	Midshipman
William	Blower			Private Marine
Abraham	Boddington	45	Isle of Wight, England	Quarter Gunner
Johannes?	Bolam	21	County Kildare, Ireland	Landsman
William	Bolton	21	Liverpool, Lancashire, England	Ordinary Seaman
John	Bond			Private Marine
John	Bond			Private Marine
Robert	Bond	20	North Yarmouth, Norfolk, England	Ordinary Seaman
Robert	Bonny	14	London, England	Boy
William	Booth	33	Manchester, Lancashire, England	Quartermaster's Mate
John	Bourne	24	Dublin, Ireland	Ordinary Seaman
Benjamin	Bowden	31	Falmouth, Cornwall, England	Boatswain's Mate
James	Bowman	26	Dunkirk, France	Able Seaman
Robert	Bowsey	26	Burminster	Ordinary Seaman
Thomas	Brannon	22	Queen's County, Ireland	Landsman
William	Braund	19	Plymouth, Devon, England	Ordinary Seaman
Alexander	Brenan	12	Dublin, Ireland	Midshipman
John	Brooks			Boatswain
Christopher	Brown	21	Castle Carbury, Ireland	Landsman
James	Brown	17	Dublin, Ireland	Boy
John	Brown	23	Waterford, Ireland	Able Seaman
John	Brown			Private Marine
Joseph	Brown			Private Marine
Michael	Brown	22	County Galway, Ireland	Landsman
Michael	Brown	22	Waterford, Ireland	Landsman
Robert	Brown	45	Linlithgow, Scotland	Carpenter's Crew
Dennis	Bryan	50	Tipperary, Ireland	Ordinary Seaman
Pat	Bryan	21	County Carlow, Ireland	Landsman
William	Buckland	21	Gloucester, Gloucestershire, England	Landsman
Michael	Buckley	15	Cork, Ireland	Boy
Terrance	Bulger		Dublin, Ireland	Landsman
Thomas	Bulger	21	Waterford, Ireland	Landsman
James	Burk	28	Wexford, Ireland	Landsman
John	Burk	31	Ireland	Landsman
John	Burke	30	Castle Barr, Scotland	Able Seaman
Thomas	Burnet	28	London, England	Able Seaman
Henry	Burns	17	Manchester, Lancashire, England	Boy
Thomas	Burrell	22	St Ives, Cornwall, England	Ordinary Seaman
Simon	Busigny			Captain, Royal Marines
Michael	Butler	40	County Carlow, Ireland	Ordinary Seaman

John	Butterworth	49	Lancashire, England	Landsman
John	Cahill	33	Cork, Ireland	Ordinary Seaman
Thomas	Caird			Surgeon
George	Calaghan	21	Dublin, Ireland	Landsman
James	Campbell	21	Greenock, Scotland	Ordinary Seaman
John	Campbell	21	America	Ordinary Seaman
John	Campbell	22	America	Able Seaman
William	Cannon			Private Marine
Thomas L.	Cardew	19	Plymouth, Devon, England	Midshipman
Samuel	Carew			Private Marine
Michael	Carey	28	Kinsale	Landsman
William	Carey			Private Marine
James	Carroll			Private Marine
Thomas	Carson	24	Newry, Ireland	Landsman
Edward	Carthy	21	County Wicklow, Ireland	Landsman
Richard	Carty	22	Dublin, Ireland	Landsman
John	Casey	38	County Dublin, Ireland	Landsman
William	Caslick	35	Hatherley, Devon, England	Landsman
Samuel	Cater	23	Dorlisk, Devon, England	Ordinary Seaman
George	Cavanagh	24	Dublin, Ireland	Landsman
John	Cawle	20	Isle of Man	Landsman
David	Chalk			Private Marine
Samuel	Chamberlain	42	Exminster, Devon, England	Ordinary Seaman
William	Chate?	21	Shannon, Barry, Ireland	Ordinary Seaman
Peter	Cherry	21	Calais, France	Ordinary Seaman
Joseph	Churchill	16	Norwich, Norfolk, England	Midshipman
John	Clarke	41	Aberdeen, Scotland	Quarter Gunner
Thomas	Clarke	20	Liverpool, Lancashire, England	Able Seaman
Henry	Claudge?	28	London, England	Landsman
William	Clinch			Boy, Marine
Thomas	Coakley	23	Providence, America	Lieutenant
John	Coffy	27	Dublin, Ireland	Ordinary Seaman
Thomas	Coish			Private Marine
John	Cole			Boy, Royal Marines
Thomas	Cole	23	Sunderland, Durham, England	Ordinary Seaman
Charles	Collier	20	Manchester, Lancashire, England	Landsman
John	Collier	23	North Yarmouth, Norfolk, England	Able Seaman
William	Collins	46	Cork, Ireland	Ordinary Seaman
Samuel	Conduit			Corporal, Royal Marines
Patrick	Connell	18	County Cork, Ireland	Boy
Matthew	Connelly	25	Liverpool, Lancashire, England	Ordinary Seaman
Peter	Conroan	20	Wexford, Ireland	Landsman
Charles	Cook			Private Marine
William	Cook			Carpenter
Joseph	Coombe	23	Modbury, Devon, England	Ordinary Seaman
Daniel	Coonan	40	Waterford, Ireland	Ordinary Seaman

John	Cooper	31	London, England	Ordinary Seaman
Samuel	Cordwell			Private Marine
James	Corney	39	America	Sailmaker
Thomas	Corsley	15	Tipperary, Ireland	Boy
James	Cossey	21	Devon, England	Landsman
Thomas	Cowley			Private Marine
H. C.	Coxen			Lieutenant
Robert	Crane			Private Marine
Richard	Crawley	38	Exeter, Devon, England	Able Seaman
Robert	Crawley	21	London, England	Able Seaman
Thomas	Crawley	22	London, England	Able Seaman
Francis	Crawson	24	Lancaster, Lancashire, England	Ordinary Seaman
John	Croaker	26	London, England	Able Seaman
George	Crokan	20	Ilfracombe, Devon, England	Ordinary Seaman
John	Crosby	25	North Yarmouth, Norfolk, England	Able Seaman
Matthew	Crotty	21	Waterford, Ireland	Landsman
William	Crow	20	County Clare, Ireland	Landsman
Edward	Cummins	21	Dublin, Ireland	Landsman
John	Cummins	28	Waterford, Ireland	Ordinary Seaman
John	Cummins	21	Crediton, Devon, England	Ordinary Seaman
Thomas	Cummins	22	County Tipperary, Ireland	Landsman
Daniel	Cunningham	23	Tipperary, Ireland	Landsman
Dennis	Cunningham	20	Dublin, Ireland	Landsman
John	Cunningham	21	County Down, Ireland	Able Seaman
John	Currier	28	Dartmouth, Kent, England	Quartermaster
Benjamin	Dacosta	23	London, England	Midshipman
John	Dailey	23	Dublin, Ireland	Landsman
John	Dalling			Private Marine
John	Daniels	20	Lancashire, England	Landsman
Thomas	Darnels			Private Marine
Alexander	Davidson			Lieutenant
John	Davis	21	America	Ordinary Seaman
Joseph	Davis	16	Brecknock, Scotland	Ordinary Seaman
Lewis	Davis	16	Pembroke	Midshipman
William	Davis	22	Anglesey, Wales	Able Seaman
William	Davis	38	Liverpool, Lancashire, England	Able Seaman
William	Davis	32	Falmouth, Cornwall, England	Able Seaman
John	Deal	36	Hornsey, London, England	Able Seaman
James	Delahoy	21	Dublin, Ireland	Landsman
John	Denbow	28	Hallenton, Devon, England	Ordinary Seaman
John	Dennis	42	Devon, England	Ordinary Seaman
John	Denohoe?	21	Dublin, Ireland	Ordinary Seaman
Henry	Dent	20	Dublin, Ireland	Landsman
Thomas	Desby	21	Kilkenny, Ireland	Landsman
John	Dike			Private Marine
Barnad	Ditts	35	Portugal	Ordinary Seaman

John	Dixon	30	London, England	Able Seaman
Michael	Dogerty	14	Liverpool, Lancashire, England	Boy
John	Dogherty	20	Dublin, Ireland	Landsman
Felan	Dolan	21	Dublin, Ireland	Landsman
Cornelius	Donegan	41	Cork, Ireland	Quarter Gunner
Morgan	Doris?	23	Tenby, Pembrokeshire, Wales	Able Seaman
David	Douglas	16	Glasgow, Scotland	Boy
Daniel	Dowlin	22	Farmanaugh, Ireland	Landsman
Matthew	Downie	33	Stockton, Durham, England	Able Seaman
John	Doyle	26	Kildare, Ireland	Landsman
William	Draper	40	Baltimore	Able Seaman
Charles	Dryborough	26	Leith, Edinburgh, Scotland	Able Seaman
John	Duckworth	21	Madeira, Portugal	Landsman
Pat	Duff	31	Dublin, Ireland	Landsman
Andrew	Duncan	29	Leith, Edinburgh, Scotland	Quartermaster's Mate
John	Duncan	50	South Shields, Durham, England	Able Seaman
John	Duncan	24	Greenock, Scotland	Able Seaman
Edward	Dunn	26	Dublin, Ireland	Ordinary Seaman
Patrick	Dunn	22	County Kildare, Ireland	Landsman
John	Dwyre	23	Wexford, Ireland	Landsman
William	Dwyre	38	Tipperary, Ireland	Ordinary Seaman
William	Dyer	27	Salisbury, Wiltshire, England	Landsman
John	Eastman	27	Plymouth, Devon, England	Midshipman
James	Eaton	22	London, England	Midshipman
John	Ellens	33	Plymouth, Devon, England	Quartermaster's Mate
Richard	Elliott	11	Dublin, Ireland	Volunteer 1st Class
William	Elliott	13	Falmouth, Cornwall, England	Boy
William	Ellis	25	Ross, Herefordshire, England	Ordinary Seaman
John	Elvert	23	Waterford, Ireland	Ordinary Seaman
John	Ennis	21	Dublin, Ireland	Landsman
John	Ephraim	20	Calabar Coast, Africa	Landsman
William	Essary	27	Barnstable, Devon, England	Ordinary Seaman
Robert	Essex	28	Philadelphia, America	Ordinary Seaman
Andrew	Essexon?	25	Sweden	Ordinary Seaman
Gregory	Evans	14	Paignton, Devon, England	Boy
William	Evans	23	Cardiff, Wales	Ordinary Seaman
John	Ewen	27	Scotland	Able Seaman
John	Fane	22	Queen's County, Ireland	Landsman
John	Farrell	36	Dublin, Ireland	Ordinary Seaman
Patrick	Feagan			Private Marine
John	Feakes			Private Marine
William	Featherstonehaugh			
		48	Sunderland, Durham, England	Ordinary Seaman
Samuel	Fiegan	22	Dublin, Ireland	Landsman
Edward	Finn	22	Wexford, Ireland	Landsman
George	Fisher	30	Boston, America	Landsman

Philip	Fisher			Private Marine
James	Fitzgerald	20	Dublin, Ireland	Landsman
Thomas	Fitzgerald	21	Ross, Ireland	Landsman
Michael	Flanigan	34	Westmeath, Ireland	Ordinary Seaman
Alexander	Fleming	37	Dublin, Ireland	Landsman
John	Fleming	33	Greenock, Scotland	Able Seaman
Abel?	Fletcher	21	Birmingham, Warwickshire, England	Landsman
Daniel	Flowers			Private Marine
James	Flynn	23	County Westmeath, Ireland	Landsman
John	Flynn	31	Dublin, Ireland	Landsman
Patrick	Flynn	21	Dublin, Ireland	Landsman
Thomas	Foran	21	Dublin, Ireland	Landsman
Richard	Ford			Private Marine
Peter	Francis	20	Chatham, Kent, England	Ordinary Seaman
Hugh	Frazier	23	Ireland	Landsman
Andrew	Freeman	25	Dublin, Ireland	Landsman
Thomas	Fullar	40	Wexford, Ireland	Able Seaman
Peter	Galkin	15	Guernsey, Channel Islands	Boy
James	Galton	28	Portsmouth, Hampshire, England	Carpenter's Mate
William	Galway	33	West Indies	Quarter Gunner
James	Gameson	18	London, England	Ordinary Seaman
Peter	Gardner	29	America	Ordinary Seaman
Robert	Garland	20	Dublin, Ireland	Landsman
Robert	Garland	20	Dublin, Ireland	Landsman
James	Gayner	28	Kildare, Ireland	Landsman
William	George	27	Wales	Ordinary Seaman
James	Gibson			Private Marine
Thomas	Gill	47	Callagtran, Ireland	Landsman
George	Gillard	28	Exeter, Devon, England	Ordinary Seaman
Hugh	Gillis	33	North Shields, Northumberland, England	Boatswain's Mate
Pat	Gilmore	41	County Down, Ireland	Gunner's Mate
Walter	Gilmore	20	Ireland	Landsman
Peter	Gilmour	21	Belfast, Ireland	Able Seaman
Thomas	Glandenning	50	Newcastle Upon Tyne, Northumberland, England	Yeoman of the Sheets
Caleb	Goldberry	27	Sweden	Able Seaman
Richard	Goldsworthy	26	Falmouth, Cornwall, England	Landsman
Henry C.	Gordon	12	Essex, England	Volunteer 1st Class
William	Gordon	36	Newcastle	Able Seaman
William	Gore	28	Scotland	Landsman
Richard	Gorston			Private Marine
John	Grace	21	Waterford, Ireland	Landsman
Francis	Graham	46	Belfast, Ireland	Ordinary Seaman
William	Grant	50	Scotland	Landsman
James	Gray			Private Marine

Edward	Green	37	Cockermouth, Cumberland, England	Able Seaman
Francis	Green	40	Jamaica, West Indies	Landsman
John	Green	40	Ireland	Ordinary Seaman
Thomas	Green			Private Marine
Thomas	Green			Private Marine
Thomas	Greenless			Private Marine
Benjamin	Greenup	24	Lancaster, Lancashire, England	Able Seaman
John	Gregory			Boy, Royal Marines
Thomas	Gregson			Private Marine
Grifith?	Griffiths	20	Wales	Ordinary Seaman
Gabriel	Grigg			Private Marine
Richard	Groves			Private Marine
John	Guinea	21	Ireland	Landsman
Michael	Hacket	21	Daindalk	Ordinary Seaman
George	Hagley	29	Exeter, Devon, England	Able Seaman
William	Hale	30	Neighton, Devon, England	Able Seaman
John	Hall			Sergeant, Royal Marines
James	Hallarum	23	Dublin, Ireland	Landsman
Christopher	Halpeny	23	Dublin, Ireland	Landsman
James	Hamilton	24	Scotland	Able Seaman
James	Hamilton	50	Port Glasgow, Scotland	Able Seaman
Isaas?	Hancock	21	St Bartholomews, West Indies	Landsman
Hans	Handerson	30	America	Quartermaster
George	Hanfield?	45	Dublin, Ireland	Ordinary Seaman
Thomas	Harding			Boy, Royal Marines
Thomas	Harding			Private Marine
James	Harper	17	Edinburgh, Scotland	Boy
Francis	Harris			Gunner
Francis	Harris	13	Chatham, Kent, England	Volunteer 1st Class
Edward	Harrison	25	Liverpool, Lancashire, England	Able Seaman
Robert	Harrison	26	Isle of Man	Ordinary Seaman
William	Harrison	22	Liverpool, Lancashire, England	Ordinary Seaman
Thomas	Harrison	24	Hull, Yorkshire, England	Able Seaman
Eliab	Harvey		Rolls Park near Chigwell, Essex, England	Captain
John	Harvey		Penzance, Cornwall, England	Ordinary Seaman
William	Harvey	28	Aberdeen, Scotland	Quarter Gunner
Edward	Hawkins	36	Worcester, Worcestershire, England	Able Seaman
Patrick	Hayes	20	Wexford, Ireland	Ordinary Seaman
John	Hearle	13	Plymouth, Devon, England	Volunteer 1st Class
Charles	Heaven			Private Marine
George	Hewit	26	Cheshire, England	Ordinary Seaman
Benjamin	Hewitson	23	Whitehaven, Cumberland, England	Quarter Gunner
John	Hiatt			Carpenter
James	Higgins	21	County Down, Ireland	Landsman
Benjamin	Hill	20	Derbyshire, England	Landsman

John	Hill	32	Dundee, Scotland	Able Seaman
John	Hill			Private Marine
William	Hitchcock			Private Marine
Edward	Hoare			Private Marine
Joseph	Hobkinson	23	Chardlow, Derbyshire, England	Ordinary Seaman
Henry	Holey	18	Stopford, Cheshire, England	Boy
Robert	Holgate	20	Essex, England	Midshipman
Robert	Holliday	31	Maryport, Cumberland, England	Able Seaman
John	Holmes	26	Sweden	Ordinary Seaman
George	Hooper	24	America	Quarter Gunner
Robert	Hope	28	Dover, Kent, England	Sailmaker's Crew
Timothy	Hopkins	37	London, England	Quarter Gunner
Joseph	Hoskins	46	Penzance, Cornwall, England	Ordinary Seaman
Samuel	Howell			Private Marine
William	Howell	21	Manilsford, Gloucester, Gloucestershire, England	Landsman
Richard	Hugh		Stockton on Tees, Durham, England	Landsman
William	Hughes	26	Swansea, Wales	Ordinary Seaman
John	Hunter	25	London, England	Landsman
Thomas	Hurle			Private Marine
David	Hurley	27	Tipperary, Ireland	Landsman
James	Hurst	27	Yorkshire, England	Quarter Gunner
George	Ives	21	Scotland	Able Seaman
Daniel	Jackson	21	County Mead, Ireland	Landsman
Thomas	Jackson	29	Sunderland, Durham, England	Quartermaster's Mate
William	Jackson	19	Chipstow, Monmouth, England	Ordinary Seaman
Richard	James	24	Wexford, Ireland	Ordinary Seaman
Stephen	James	27	Newcastle	Landsman
Thomas	James			Private Marine
William	James	33	Upton Warren, Worcester, Worcestershire, England	Landsman
Benjamin	Jeffry	20	Tavistock, Devon, England	Landsman
Edward	Jennings	21	Mayo, Ireland	Landsman
John	Jerry			Private Marine
William C.	Jervoise	18	London, England	Midshipman
Emanuel?	Joaquine	30	Vienna, Austria	Landsman
Nicholas	Johns	32	Cornwall, England	Landsman
Christopher	Johnson	19	Norway	Ordinary Seaman
James	Johnson	20	Portsmouth, Hampshire, England	Able Seaman
John	Johnson			Cook
John	Johnson	22	Wexford, Ireland	Landsman
John	Johnson	18	Plymouth, Devon, England	Purser's Steward
John	Johnson	28	Dublin, Ireland	Able Seaman
Thomas	Johnson	46	Sunderland, Durham, England	Quartermaster
David	Jones	19	Liverpool, Lancashire, England	Ordinary Seaman
John	Jones	20	Cardigan, Wales	Landsman

John	Jones			Private Marine
Owen	Jones	25	Anglesey, Wales	Landsman
Samuel	Jones			Private Marine
Thomas	Jones	30	Lancashire, England	Able Seaman
William	Jones	27	Carnarvon, Wales	Carpenter's Crew
William	Jones	14	Plymouth, Devon, England	Boy
John	Jordan			Private Marine
Manuel	Jose	30	Lisbon, Portugal	Landsman
Joseph	Kane	22	County Dublin, Ireland	Landsman
William	Kay			Private Marine
Michael	Keating	22	Dublin, Ireland	Landsman
Richard	Keating	25	Waterford, Ireland	Landsman
David	Keefe	58	Kilkenny, Ireland	Landsman
Thomas	Keevan?	21	Wexford, Ireland	Landsman
Daniel	Keirns	29	Dublin, Ireland	Ordinary Seaman
Francis	Kelly	32	Roscommon, Ireland	Landsman
James	Kelly	30	Ireland	Landsman
John	Kelly			Private Marine
John	Kelly			Private Marine
Patrick	Kelly	38	County Tipperary, Ireland	Landsman
T. F.	Kennedy			Lieutenant
Richard	King			Boy, Royal Marines
John	Kingston			Second Lieutenant, Royal Marines
Thomas	Kinston			Boy, Royal Marines
Robert	Kirkland	22	Scotland	Able Seaman
John	Knapman	18	Plymouth, Devon, England	Midshipman
George	Knowles	21	County Sligo, Ireland	Landsman
James	Lahey	24	Tipperary, Ireland	Landsman
James	Lambert			Private Marine
John	Langdon	15	Ilfracombe, Devon, England	Boy
Patrick? Or Philip	Langley			Supernumerary
James	Lashwood	21	Warrington, Lancashire, England	Landsman
William	Lawless	19	Manchester, Lancashire, England	Ordinary Seaman
Thomas	Lawrence	21	Dublin, Ireland	Landsman
James	Lawson	25	Monoughan, Ireland	Able Seaman
William	Le Compt	27	America	Able Seaman
Samuel	Le Grady	19	Jersey, Channel Islands	Landsman
Samuel	Leaker	16	Appledore	Boy
William	Leaky	26	Bath, Somerset, England	Ordinary Seaman
Thomas	Leavy	24	Dublin, Ireland	Landsman
John R.	Lee			Private Marine
Lawrence	Lehay	47	Waterford, Ireland	Quarter Gunner
John	Leidler	45	Edinburgh, Scotland	Quartermaster
Andrew	Leitch	18	Uxbridge, Devon, England	Ordinary Seaman

Michael	Leonard	62	Ireland	Ordinary Seaman
William	Lewis			Private Marine
Richard	Libertine	34	Chudleigh, Devon, England	Gunner's Mate
Daniel	Linnen	22	County Louth, Ireland	Landsman
John	Linshot	25	Sweden	Able Seaman
John	Long	44	London, England	Able Seaman
Andrew	Lorin?	35	Dartmouth, Devon, England	Able Seaman
Thomas	Loyd	28	Cork, Ireland	Ordinary Seaman
Neil	Lunbar	31	Sweden	Ordinary Seaman
Owen	Lynch	21	Dublin, Ireland	Landsman
John	Mackie	32	Stirlingshire, Scotland	Able Seaman
James	Mackin	25	Manchester, Lancashire, England	Able Seaman
Silvester	Madden			Private Marine
Edward	Mahol	23	Kildare, Ireland	Landsman
James	Mahon	50	Tipperary, Ireland	Ordinary Seaman
Thomas	Mahon	20	Dublin, Ireland	Landsman
Benjamin	Mainwaring	18	London, England	Able Seaman
Daniel	Malone	17	Dublin, Ireland	Landsman
Daniel	Maloney	35	Cork, Ireland	Ordinary Seaman
Edward	Maloney	38	Kildare, Ireland	Ship's Corporal
Nicholas	Mandeville	21	Dublin, Ireland	Landsman
Thomas	Mandeville	21	Kilkenny, Ireland	Ordinary Seaman
Robert	Manning			Boy, Royal Marines
Samuel	Manning	32	North Yarmouth, Norfolk, England	Able Seaman
Alexander	Mansell?			Private Marine
Joseph	Marshall			Boatswain
William	Marshall	26	Bristol, Gloucestershire, England	Ordinary Seaman
Bar?	Martin	20	Belfast, Ireland	Landsman
Charles	Martin	21	Cardigan, Wales	Ordinary Seaman
John A.	Mathison	24	London, England	Clerk
William	Matthew	29	Renfrewshire, Scotland	Able Seaman
Edward	Matthews	23	Cornwall, England	Landsman
John	Matthews	21	Valenciennes, France	Ordinary Seaman
Alexander	McArthur	50	Entrim	Able Seaman
John	McCann	26	Dublin, Ireland	Landsman
Cornelius	McClare	28	Londonderry, Ireland	Able Seaman
Peter	McCoy	20	Arundel, Sussex, England	Ordinary Seaman
Robert	McCoy	36	Dublin, Ireland	Landsman
William	McCray	20	Dublin, Ireland	Able Seaman
Daniel	McCullam	21	Newry, Ireland	Landsman
Thomas	McDonald	22	Waterford, Ireland	Able Seaman
Pierce?	McEvoy	23	County Carlow, Ireland	Landsman
Dennis	McFarlin	19	Londonderry, Ireland	Ordinary Seaman
Neil	McGown	24	Greenock, Scotland	Ordinary Seaman
John	McGuire	21	Dublin, Ireland	Landsman
Patrick	McGuire	20	Belfast, Ireland	Landsman

Daniel	McIntire	19	Greenock, Scotland	Landsman
John	McIntire	21	Greenock, Scotland	Landsman
James	McKeen	32	County Down, Ireland	Landsman
William	McKew			Private Marine
James	McKickney	25	Anglesey, Wales	Ordinary Seaman
Charles	McLaughlin	26	Ireland	Landsman
John	McManagale	12	Dublin, Ireland	Boy
Lawrence	McNamara	27	Limerick, Ireland	Landsman
Thomas	McReady	21	Glasgow, Scotland	Ordinary Seaman
John	Meadon			Private Marine
Peter	Mealey	30	Daindalk	Ordinary Seaman
Thomas	Membury			Private Marine
George	Mercer			Private Marine
John	Miller	40	Scotland	Quarter Gunner
John	Miller	19	Bristol, Gloucestershire, England	Ordinary Seaman
Richard	Millon?			Private Marine
William	Mitchell			Carpenter
John	Moffatt	24	Carrickfergus, Ireland	Able Seaman
James	Moore	20	Dublin, Ireland	Landsman
John	Moore	32	Ipswich, Suffolk, England	Yeoman of the Powder Room
James	Morris	24	Bristol, Gloucestershire, England	Ordinary Seaman
John	Morris	22	Armagh, Ireland	Ordinary Seaman
Stephen	Morris			Private Marine
Thomas	Morris			Corporal, Royal Marines
N.?	Morrison	23	County Clare, Ireland	Landsman
John	Morton	32	North Shields, Northumberland, England	Coxswain
Thomas	Morton			Private Marine
Benjamin	Mosely	27	America	Carpenter's Crew
James	Mould			Lieutenant
John	Mullard	27	Emden, Germany	Able Seaman
Michael	Mullholland			Private Marine
John	Mulvanie	21	Dublin, Ireland	Landsman
Daniel	Murphy	21	Kinsale, Ireland	Landsman
Patrick	Murphy	30	Wexford, Ireland	Able Seaman
Thomas	Murphy	21	Dublin, Ireland	Landsman
Timothy	Murphy	21	Wexford, Ireland	Ordinary Seaman
William	Napper	22	Rochester, Kent, England	Midshipman
Arthur	Neale	24	Ireland	Landsman
Robert	Neild	38	Liverpool, Lancashire, England	Able Seaman
Richard	Nelvin	22	Anglesey, Wales	Ordinary Seaman
John	Nicholas	23	Guernsey, Channel Islands	Landsman
John	Nicholson	20	Whitby, Yorkshire, England	Ordinary Seaman
John	Nicholson			Private Marine
John	Noel		Jersey, Channel Islands	Landsman

John	Norman	50	Barnstaple, Devon, England	Ordinary Seaman
Pat	Nowland	20	Dublin, Ireland	Landsman
John	Nulty	28	Dublin, Ireland	Landsman
Lewis	Oades	46		Carpenter
Alexander	Ogg	36	Scotland	Able Seaman
John	O'Hair	20	Newry, Ireland	Landsman
Henry	Oliver			Drummer, Royal Marines
Johannes?	Oliver	22	Port o Port	Able Seaman
Tully	O'Neil	36	Dublin, Ireland	Ordinary Seaman
Edward	Owens	26	Anglesey, Wales	Able Seaman
Thomas	Owens	20	Devon, England	Ordinary Seaman
Thomas	Page			Private Marine
Thomas	Painter	27	St Ives, Cornwall, England	Able Seaman
John	Parker			Private Marine
Edward	Pascoe	21	Penzance, Cornwall, England	Landsman
Thomas	Patterson	22	Newfoundland, Canada	Landsman
Amos	Paulson			Private Marine
Samuel John Payne				Second Lieutenant, Royal Marines
Jonas	Pearce			Boy, Royal Marines
Thomas	Pearce	14	Liverpool, Lancashire, England	Boy
Joseph?	Pendergast	20	Waterford, Ireland	Landsman
Anthony	Perks	43	Bristol, Gloucestershire, England	Ordinary Seaman
Edward	Perry	22	Flintshire, Wales	Ordinary Seaman
James	Perry	50	Falmouth, Cornwall, England	Boatswain's Mate
Joseph	Perry	25	Flintshire, Wales	Landsman
James	Peter	23	Holland	Ordinary Seaman
James	Peters	22	Brentford, Middlesex, England	Ordinary Seaman
Edward	Petherick	30	Bridgwater, Somerset, England	Able Seaman
James	Peverell	13	London, England	Boy
Thomas	Pheelan	22	Waterford, Ireland	Landsman
John	Philips	16	Sherbrooke, Canada	Boy
Caleb	Phillips	21	London, England	Ordinary Seaman
John	Pienlive?			Private Marine
Charles	Pinker			Private Marine
Joseph	Pinose?	21	Cadiz, Spain	Ordinary Seaman
William	Pitts	20	London, England	Midshipman
James	Pointon	26	Somerset, England	Ordinary Seaman
James	Pomeroy	20	Pool	Able Seaman
James	Pook	42	Paignton, Devon, England	Able Seaman
Robert	Porteus	13	Preston, Lancashire, England	Boy
Edward	Posher?	40	Weymouth, Dorset, England	Carpenter's Crew
William	Pound			Private Marine
Richard	Powell			Boy, Royal Marines
Thomas	Powell			Private Marine
William	Power	30	Waterford, Ireland	Landsman

Francis S.	Price	21	Bideford, Devon, England	Master's Mate
Thomas	Price			Master
Thomas	Prior	21	Bristol, Gloucestershire, England	Ordinary Seaman
John	Pullibank			Private Marine
Thomas	Pye	21	Preston, Lancashire, England	Landsman
Thomas	Quine	34	Dublin, Ireland	Landsman
David	Quinn	26	Ireland	Landsman
William	Rainsford			Supernumerary
Thomas	Randle	30	Shropshire, England	Able Seaman
William	Randle	26	Hardway, Hampshire, England	Yeoman of the Sheets
William	Rankin	22	Greenock, Scotland	Quarter Gunner
George	Rathburne	17	Manchester, Lancashire, England	Boy
Matthew	Reardon	20	Cork, Ireland	Ordinary Seaman
George	Reed	27	Edinburgh, Scotland	Able Seaman
Thomas	Reed	26	Knowle, Warwickshire, England	Landsman
Gilbert	Reekshaw?	19	Plymouth, Devon, England	Ordinary Seaman
Michael	Reynolds	21	Dublin, Ireland	Landsman
George	Rich			Private Marine
Richard	Richards	20	Forditch, Kent, England	Landsman
Nicholas	Richardson	22	Newcastle Upon Tyne, Northumberland, England	Landsman
Abraham	Rickets			Ordinary Seaman
Henry	Ricks			Private Marine
Bryan?	Rielly	42	Dublin, Ireland	Ordinary Seaman
William	Rielly	34	Dublin, Ireland	Landsman
James	Riley			Private Marine
John	Riley	22	Kildare, Ireland	Landsman
James	Roach	24	Dublin, Ireland	Landsman
Nicholas	Roach			Private Marine
William	Roach	21	Dublin, Ireland	Landsman
James	Robbins			Private Marine
John	Roberts	22	Pembroke, Pembrokeshire, Wales	Quarter Gunner
Thomas	Roberts	14	Denbigh, Wales	Boy
Thomas	Robertson	25	Waterford, Ireland	Able Seaman
James	Robinson	48	Lancashire, England	Ordinary Seaman
John	Robinson	24	America	Able Seaman
John	Robinson	31	Glasgow, Scotland	Able Seaman
Thomas	Robinson	28	Belfast, Ireland	Able Seaman
Ellis	Rochley	21	Liverpool, Lancashire, England	Ordinary Seaman
William N.	Roe			Second Lieutenant, Royal Marines
John	Rogan	50	Dublin, Ireland	Quarter Gunner
William	Rogers	21	Manchester, Lancashire, England	Landsman
William	Rogers	36	Greenock, Scotland	Quarter Gunner
John	Rosser	46	Swansea, Wales	Landsman
James	Rourke	21	Wexford, Ireland	Landsman

Thomas	Rowe	33	Saltash, Cornwall, England	Quarter Gunner
James	Rowland			Private Marine
John	Ryan	22	Wexford, Ireland	Able Seaman
William	Ryder	49	Middlesex, England	Ordinary Seaman
John	Sampson	22	Cornwall, England	Gunsmith
David	Samuel	22	Cardigan, Wales	Ordinary Seaman
Bryan?	Sandelim	21	County Sligo, Ireland	Landsman
Robert	Sands	17	St Margaret's, Rochester, Kent, England	Boy
John	Saunders	22	Croydon, Surrey, England	Landsman
William	Scollick			Private Marine
William	Scott			Assistant Surgeon
Joseph	Selby	14	Bradford, Wiltshire, England	Boy
John	Sharp	43	Kildare, Ireland	Ordinary Seaman
John	Shaw	34	Carlisle, Cumberland, England	Able Seaman
William	Shaw	36	America	Able Seaman
Edmund	Sheen	16	Cork, Ireland	Boy
William	Shepheard	11	London, England	Volunteer 1st Class
Joseph	Sherer?			Chaplain
Patrick	Sheridan	20	Dublin, Ireland	Landsman
James	Shipman			Private Marine
Charles	Sibley	30	Paington, Devon, England	Landsman
Richard	Silverthorn			Private Marine
Robert	Simms	28	Ilchester, Somerset, England	Yeoman of the Sheets
Samuel	Simpson			Boatswain
Daniel	Sinclair	25	Sheffield, Yorkshire, England	Quarter Gunner
James	Sinclair	24	Aberdeen, Scotland	Able Seaman
John	Sinnet	19	Dublin, Ireland	Landsman
John	Slater	36	Belfast, Ireland	Carpenter's Crew
John	Slater			Private Marine
Neil	Sloane	28	County Devon	Landsman
Anthony	Smith	29	Newry, Ireland	Ordinary Seaman
George	Smith			Private Marine
James	Smith	23	Dublin, Ireland	Able Seaman
James	Smith			Private Marine
John	Smith	33	Tiverton, Devon, England	Gunner's Mate
John	Smith	31	Yorkshire, England	Quarter Gunner
Thomas	Smith	25	Lancashire, England	Ordinary Seaman
William	Smith	44	London, England	Able Seaman
William	Smith	32	Whitby, Yorkshire, England	Quarter Gunner
William	Smith			Lieutenant
Thomas	Smith	27	County Carron, Ireland	Landsman
John	Snelgrove	28	London, England	Able Seaman
John	Snoles	25	Halifax	Ordinary Seaman
Phil?	Somers	26	Wexford, Ireland	Landsman
William	Spiller			Private Marine

Benjamin	Stanbury	25	South Dorton, Devon, England	Armourer
Samuel	Stephenson	29	London, England	Ship's Corporal
Thomas	Stone			Private Marine
Robert H.	Storck	19	London, England	Midshipman
William	Strathan	23	Perthshire, Scotland	Landsman
Jeremiah?	Sullivan	40	Cork, Ireland	Landsman
Morris	Sullivan	20	Youghal, Ireland	Landsman
Adm?	Summers	33	Sunderland, Durham, England	Ordinary Seaman
Joseph	Summers			Private Marine
James	Sweet	25	Taunton, Somerset, England	Armourer's Mate
William	Swift	27	County Mead, Ireland	Landsman
Patrick	Swiney	20	Waterford, Ireland	Landsman
William	Symonds	23	Bristol, Gloucestershire, England	Landsman
William	Symonds	33	Bristol, Gloucestershire, England	Landsman
John	Taggant	40	Isle of Man	Landsman
Jacob?	Taut	27	Plymouth, Devon, England	Ropemaker
James	Taylor	14	Boston, Lincolnshire, England	Boy
John	Taylor			Private Marine
George	Teel?	42	Sweden	Yeoman of the Powder Room
John	Tenpenny	17	Lancashire, England	Boy
William	Tex?	22	Norwich, Norfolk, England	Landsman
Alexander	Thompson	28	Queens Ferry, Scotland	Able Seaman
Daniel	Thompson	45	County Caton, Scotland	Quarter Gunner
William	Thompson	29	Belsreid, Scotland	Quarter Gunner
William	Thompson			Private Marine
William	Thorn			Boy, Royal Marines
William	Thurlow			Private Marine
William	Tibbs	22	Tinmouth	Carpenter's Crew
John	Tipper	18	Dublin, Ireland	Ordinary Seaman
Thomas	Tittle	24	Swansea, Wales	Yeoman of the Sheets
Edward	Tomkins	20	America	Ordinary Seaman
John	Toohig	34	Cork, Ireland	Master at Arms
Samuel	Tremble?	32	Belfast, Ireland	Landsman
William	Tribute			Boy, Royal Marines
Francis	Trounce	36	Castle Townsend, Ireland	Quarter Gunner
Thomas	Turner		Chatham, Kent, England	Boy
Peter	Valentine	36	Sclavonia, Austria	Able Seaman
Benjamin	Vallack			Lieutenant
Patrick	Victory	21	County Westmeath, Ireland	Landsman
Bartholomew	Voxen?	22	Hamburg, Germany	Able Seaman
Henry	Walker	15	New Malton, Yorkshire, England	Volunteer 1st Class
James	Walker	21	Glasgow, Scotland	Landsman
James	Wallace	24	New York, America	Able Seaman
John	Wallace			Lieutenant
Archibald	Wallis	25	Glasgow, Scotland	Able Seaman

Robert	Walter	28	Renfrewshire, Scotland	Carpenter's Crew
William	Warman	20	Stoke	Ordinary Seaman
Robert	Watman	32	Glasgow, Scotland	Quarter Gunner
James	Watsley	30	Cheshire, England	Able Seaman
David	Watson	18	Edinburgh, Scotland	Ordinary Seaman
Thomas	Watson	23	Swansea, Wales	Able Seaman
Charles	Webb	21	London, England	Ordinary Seaman
John	Webb			Corporal, Royal Marines
Richard	Webber	50	Ashburton, Devon, England	Quartermaster's Mate
John	Webster	26	Norwich, Norfolk, England	Boatswain's Mate
John	Wellington			Private Marine
Lawrence	Welsh	40	Kilkenny, Ireland	Landsman
Michael	Welsh	34	Kilkenny, Ireland	Landsman
Thomas	Welsh	22	Waterford, Ireland	Able Seaman
J.	West	26	Wordoth, Somerset, England	Able Seaman
Robert	West	38	Wisbech, Cambridgeshire, England	Able Seaman
Mark	Weston			Private Marine
Michael	Wheelan	24	Cork, Ireland	Landsman
John	Wheeling	33	Newfoundland, Canada	Carpenter's Mate
Patrick	Whelan	28	Dungarvon, Ireland	Quarter Gunner
Joseph	White	28	Inverness, Scotland	Gunner's Mate
Robert	White	40	America	Ordinary Seaman
Thomas	White			Private Marine
Oliver	Whitney	30	America	Landsman
Henry	Wickham	27	Bristol, Gloucestershire, England	Carpenter's Crew
William	Wilcox			Private Marine
William	Wild?			Private Marine
Edward	Williams			Private Marine
George	Williams			Private Marine
Hugh	Williams	22	Anglesey, Wales	Ordinary Seaman
Humphrey	Williams	27	Pembroke, Pembrokeshire, Wales	Ordinary Seaman
James	Williams	54	Cornwall, England	Landsman
John	Williams	24	Hamburg, Germany	Ordinary Seaman
John	Williams	23	Carmarthen, Wales	Able Seaman
John	Williams	23	America	Able Seaman
Ralph	Williams	21	Liverpool, Lancashire, England	Landsman
Robert	Williams	32	Wales	Able Seaman
Thomas	Williams			Boy, Royal Marines
William	Williams	24	Anglesey, Wales	Able Seaman
James	Williamson	22	Manchester, Lancashire, England	Landsman
William	Willis	21	Carmarthen, Wales	Landsman
James	Willson			Private Marine
Thomas	Willson	36	Broughton	Landsman
Thomas	Wilmot	42	Cornwall, England	Landsman
John	Wilson	24	Tipperary, Ireland	Ordinary Seaman
Michael	Wilson	36	Galway, Ireland	Able Seaman

Walter	Windeward			Private Marine
John	Winterburn	20	Liverpool, Lancashire, England	Ordinary Seaman
John	Witmarsh			Private Marine
Henry	Wodcock	19	London, England	Ordinary Seaman
Isaac	Wood	27	Somerset, England	Ordinary Seaman
James	Wood	26	Glasgow, Scotland	Landsman
Christopher	Wright	21	County Mead, Ireland	Landsman
James	Yenkinson?	18	Hull, Yorkshire, England	Ordinary Seaman
Alexander	Young	17	Liverpool, Lancashire, England	Boy
Robert	Young	22	Santa Cruz	Able Seaman
Thomas	Young	29	Liverpool, Lancashire, England	Sailmaker's Mate

APPENDIX III

Poems and Songs

THE FIGHTING TEMERAIRE
Henry Newbolt

It was eight bells ringing,
  For the morning watch was done,
And the gunner's lads were singing
  As they polished every gun.
It was eight bells ringing,
And the gunner's lads were singing,
For the ship she rode a-swinging,
  As they polished every gun.

  Oh! to see the linstock lighting,
    Temeraire! Temeraire!
  Oh! to hear the round shot biting,
    Temeraire! Temeraire!

  Oh! to see the linstock lighting,
    And to hear the round shot biting,
  For we're all in love with fighting
    On the fighting Temeraire.

It was noontide ringing,
  And the battle just begun,
When the ship her way was winging,
  As they loaded every gun.
It was noontide ringing,
When the ship her way was winging,
And the gunner's lads were singing
  As they loaded every gun.

There'll be many grim and gory,
  Temeraire! Temeraire!
There'll be few to tell the story,
  Temeraire! Temeraire!

There'll be many grim and gory,
  There'll be few to tell the story,
But we'll all be one in glory
  With the Fighting Temeraire.

There's a far bell ringing
  At the setting of the sun,
And a phantom voice is singing
  Of the great days done.
There's a far bell ringing,
And a phantom voice is singing
Of renown for ever clinging
  To the great days done.

  Now the sunset breezes shiver,
    Temeraire! Temeraire!
  And she's fading down the river,
    Temeraire! Temeraire!

  Now the sunset's breezes shiver,
    And she's fading down the river,
  But in England's song for ever
    She's the Fighting Temeraire.

THE TEMERAIRE
Herman Melville

The gloomy hulls, in armour grim,
　Like clouds o'er moors have met,
And prove that oak, and iron, and man
　Are tough in fibre yet.

But Splendours wane. The sea-fight yields
　No front of old display;
The garniture, emblazonment,
　And heraldry decay.

Towering afar in parting light,
　The fleets like Albion's forelands shine –
The full-sailed fleets, the shrouded show
　Of Ships-of-the-Line.

The fighting Temeraire,
　Built of a thousand trees,
Lunging out her lightnings,
　And beetling o'er the seas –
O Ship, how brave and fair,
　That fought so oft and well,
On open decks you manned the gun
　Armorial.
What cheerings did you share,
　Impulsive in the van,
When down upon leagued France
　and Spain
We English ran –
The freshet at your bowsprit
　Like the foam upon the can.
Bickering, your colours
　Licked up the Spanish air,
You flapped with flames of battle-flags –
　Your challenge, Temeraire!
The rear ones of our fleet

They yearned to share your place,
Still vying with the Victory
　Throughout that earnest race –
The Victory, whose Admiral,
　With orders nobly won,
Shone in the globe of the battle glow –
　The angel in that sun.
Parallel in story,
　Lo, the stately pair,
As late in grapple ranging,
　The foe between them there –
When four great hulls lay tiered,
　And the fiery tempest cleared,
And your prizes twain appeared,
　　Temeraire!

But Trafalgar is over now,
　The quarterdeck undone;
The carved and castled navies fire
　Their evening gun.
O, Titan Temeraire,
　Your stern-lights fade away;
Your bulwarks to the years must yield,
　And heart-of-oak decay.
A pigmy steam-tug tows you,
　Gigantic to the shore –
Dismantled of your guns and spars,
　And sweeping wings of war.
The rivets clinch the ironclads,
　Men learn a deadlier lore;
But Fame has nailed your battle-flags –
　Your ghost it sails before:
O, navies old and oaken,
　O, Temeraire no more!

THE FIGHTING TEMERAIRE TUGGED TO HER LAST BERTH
Gerald Massey

It is a glorious tale to tell
  When nights are long and mirk;
How well she fought our fight, how well
  She did our England's work;
    Our good Ship Temeraire!
    The fighting Temeraire!
She goeth to her last-long home,
    Our grand old Temeraire.

Bravely over the breezy blue
  They went to do or die;
And nobly on herself she drew
  The Battle's burning eye!
    Our good Ship Temeraire!
    The fighting Temeraire!
She goeth to her last-long home,
    Our grand old Temeraire.

Round her the Glory fell in flood,
  From Nelson's loving smile,
When, raked with fire, she ran with blood
  In England's hour of trial!
    Our good Ship Temeraire!
    The fighting Temeraire!
She goeth to her last-long home,
    Our grand old Temeraire.

And when our darling of the Sea
  Sank dying on his deck,
With her revenging thunders she
  Struck down his foe – a wreck.
    Our good Ship Temeraire!
    The fighting Temeraire!
She goeth to her last-long home,
    Our grand old Temeraire.

Her day now draweth to its close
  With solemn sunset crowned;
To death her crested beauty bows,
  The night is folding round.

Our good Ship Temeraire!
    The fighting Temeraire!
She goeth to her last-long home,
    Our grand old Temeraire.

No more the big heart in her breast
  Will heave from wave to wave.
Weary and war-worn, ripe for rest,
  She glideth to her grave.
    Our good Ship Temeraire!
    The fighting Temeraire!
She goeth to her last-long home,
    Our grand old Temeraire.

In her dumb pathos desolate
  As night among the dead!
Yet wearing an exceeding weight
  Of glory on her head.
    Our good Ship Temeraire!
    The fighting Temeraire!
She goeth to her last-long home,
    Our grand old Temeraire.

Good bye! good bye! Old Temeraire,
  A sad and proud good bye!
The stalwart spirit that did wear
  Your sternness, shall not die.
    Our good Ship Temeraire!
    The fighting Temeraire!
She goeth to her last-long home,
    Our grand Old Temeraire.

Thro' battle blast, and storm of shot,
  Your Banner we shall bear;
And fight for it like those who fought
    Our good Ship Temeraire.
    The fighting Temeraire!
    The conquering Temeraire!
She goeth to her last-long home,
    Our grand Old Temeraire.

THE BRAVE OLD TEMERAIRE
James Duff
Set to music by J. W. Hobbs, London, 1857

Behold! Behold! How chang'd is yonder ship,
The wreck of former pride;
Methinks I see her, as of old,
The glory, the glory of the tide
As when she came to Nelson's aid,
The battle's brunt to bear,
And Harvey sought to lead the van
With the brave old Temeraire

    The fighting Temeraire
    The fighting Temeraire
    That nobody sought to lead the van,
    With the fighting Temeraire

When sailors speak of Trafalgar,
So fam'd for Nelson's fight,
With pride they tell of her career,
Her onward course, her might.
How, when the victory was won,
She shone triumphant there,
With noble prize on either side.
The brave old Temeraire.

    The brave old Temeraire,
    The brave old Temeraire,
    With noble prize on either side,
    The brave old Temeraire.

Our friends depart, and are forgot,
As time rolls fleetly by;
In after years none, none are left,
For them to heave a sigh:
But hist'ry's page will ever mark
The glories she did share,
And gild the sunset of her fate,
The brave old Temeraire.

    The brave old Temeraire
    The brave old Temeraire,
    And gild the sunset of her fate,
    The brave old Temeraire.

ON TURNER'S PICTURE, OF THE TEMERAIRE
MAN-OF-WAR TOWED INTO PORT BY A STEAMER
FOR THE PURPOSE OF BEING BROKEN UP

Richard Monckton Milnes

Poetry for the People and Other Poems, London, 1840.

See how that small concentrate fiery force
Is grappling with the glory of the main,
That follows, like some grave heroic corse,
Dragged by a suttler from the heap of slain.
Thy solemn presence brings us more than pain –
Something which fancy moulds into remorse,
That We, who of thine honour hold the gain,
Should from its dignity thy form divorce.
Yet will we read in thy vaunting Name,
How Britain did what France could only *dare*,
And, while the sunset gilds the darke'ning air,
We will fill up thy shadowy lines with fame,
And tomb or temple, hail thee still the same,
Home of great thoughts, memorial Temeraire!

GLOSSARY

Admiral of the Red, White, Blue. The officer nominally commanding ships of the Red, White or Blue squadron, ranking in seniority in that (descending) order; the rank of Admiral of the Red was created after the Battle of Trafalgar, the post having been occupied by Admiral of the Fleet. In practice, by the end of the eighteenth century the Admiralty created as many admirals of each rank as it required.

Blue lights. Combustibles used for signalling at night. Also called **Bengal lights**.

Bomb ship. A warship fitted to fire heavy mortars for shore bombardment.

Chasse-marée. A lugger-rigged French coasting vessel.

Companion ladder. Ladders giving access throughout the ship, often with particular emphasis on the ladders by which the officers accessed the quarter-deck.

Cutter. 1. A small vessel fore-and-aft rigged on one mast with topmast and bowsprit. 2. A ship's boat designed for sailing, 25ft long in a ship-of-the-line.

False fire. Combustibles packed into a wooden tube and then lit for signalling at night. Similar to a flare. See also **Blue lights.**

Fish. To strengthen a damaged spar or mast by lashing spars to it in the manner of splints.

Fother. To stop a leak in a ship's hull by working a sail into a heavy matt using rough yarn, then using water pressure to force the fothered sail into the hole.

Flag-captain. The captain of a flagship.

Forecastle. A deck built over the forward end of the main deck.

Foretopsail. The topsail on the foremast.

Grapeshot. Anti-personnel shot consisting of small shot that scatters on firing.

Gundeck. The deck carrying the main battery.

Heave-to. To stop by backing some of the sails.

Hot press. The response to a particularly severe manning crisis, in which numbers of men were of greater concern than their quality. In a hot press, protections against impressment were not valid.

In irons. A punishment in which the offender's legs were confined by shackles attached to a long iron bar with a padlock at the end.

Jolly boat. A small ship's boat, usually no more than 18ft x 4ft, especially useful in harbour.

Landman/Landsman. An unskilled member of the ship's company.

League. Three miles.

Longboat. The largest of the ship's boats, designed for carrying heavy weights.

Lower deck. On a two- or three-decker, the lowest deck carrying the ship's main battery.

Maintopsail. The topsail on the mainmast.

Master. 1. On a warship, the warrant officer responsible for navigation. 2. The commanding officer of a merchant ship.

Master at arms. A petty officer responsible for ship's discipline.

Master's mate. A petty officer assisting the master.

Middle deck. On a three-decker, the deck between the lower deck and the upper deck.

Mizzen mast. The aftermost mast.

The Nore. An anchorage in the mouth of the Thames near the entrance to the River Medway, which led to Chatham naval dockyard.

Ordinary. Ships in reserve.

Orlop (deck). The lowest deck.

Poop. A short deck built over the after end of the quarterdeck.

Privateer. A merchant ship licensed by a letter of marque issued by the government to attack shipping of a named enemy nation (or nations).

Progress book. An administrative volume recording the date and cost of a ship's repairs.

Quarterdeck. A deck over the after part of the upper deck.

Quarter gallery. A balcony projecting from the stern and quarter of large ships, accessed via the admiral's or captain's cabin.

Quarter gunner. A rating under the direction of the gunner. One quarter gunner was allocated to every four guns.

Rear-admiral. A flag officer ranking below vice-admiral and admiral.

Receiving ship. A depot used to hold entered or impressed seamen before they were distributed to their ships.

Red-hot shot. Shot which has been heated in a furnace before firing.

Scuttle. A hole cut in the ship's deck or side, generally for ventilation.

Sheet. A rope controlling the clew (bottom corner) of a sail.

Ship of the line. A warship large enough to lie in the line of battle.

Slip (a cable). To cast off; especially to sail without weighing anchor, in which case the anchor cable is let slip and buoyed for later retrieval.

Spithead. An area of the Solent, off Portsmouth.

Step (a mast). To place a ship's mast.

Strike (a mast). To lower a mast.

Studdingsail. A light sail temporarily set outboard of a square sail in light airs.

Taffrail (of a mast). Bulwark at the after end of the poop or quarterdeck.

Top (of a mast). A platform built at the top of the lower mast.

Upper deck. On a three-decker, the deck above the middle deck.

Van division. The leading division of a fleet or squadron divided into van, centre and rear.

Vice-admiral. A flag officer ranking below admiral and above rear-admiral.

Volunteer 1st class. An officer cadet.

NOTES

Abbreviations:
B. Lib – British Library
MM – *Mariner's Mirror*
NMM – National Maritime Museum
SLSL – Southwark Local Studies Library
TNA – The National Archives
WDRO – West Devon Record Office
ERO – Essex Record Office

Preface

[1] There has only ever been one major work on the *Temeraire*, Judy Egerton's impressive book *Turner: The Fighting Temeraire: Making and Meaning* (London, The National Gallery, 1995), but it was written, designed and sold as an exhibition catalogue, and for all of its excellent qualities there remain significant gaps and inaccuracies in its telling of the ship's history and Egerton makes only passing reference to the first *Téméraire*. Grant Uden's *The Fighting Temeraire* (1961) briefly tells some of the story of the ship, but is based on only a handful of sources and includes no analysis of Turner's painting.
[2] Cook and Wedderburn, eds., *The Works of John Ruskin*, vol. 13 (1904), 171.
[3] Ibid., 173.

1. The Escaping *Téméraire*

[1] Dull, *The French Navy and the Seven Years' War*, 159.
[2] Admiralty to Boscawen, 7 March 1759, TNA: ADM 2/82.
[3] Aspinall-Oglander, ed., *Admiral's Wife*, 278.
[4] Jenkins, *A History of the French Navy*, 118, 130.
[5] French Narrative . . . , NMM AGC 1/25.
[6] Log of the *Gibraltar*, 17 August 1759, TNA: ADM 51/393.
[7] Boscawen to his wife, 20 June 1756, in Lloyd, ed., *The Naval Miscellany*, IV, 225.
[8] Quoted in Rodger, *The Command of the Ocean*, 253.
[9] Boscawen to his wife, 21 July 1756, in Lloyd, ed., *The Naval Miscellany*, IV, 238.
[10] Boscawen to his wife, 3 June 1756, in Lloyd, ed., *The Naval Miscellany*, IV, 219.
[11] Callender, *The Naval Side of British History*, 164.
[12] Journal of Captain Buckle, 17 August 1759, quoted in Colomb, *Naval Warfare*, I, 173; Log of the *Namur*, TNA: ADM 51/621.
[13] 'Extract of a narrative of the Defeat of de la Clue . . .' in Ekins, *Naval Battles*, 36.
[14] Beatson, *Memoirs* II, Appendix 148–9 n.143; Log of the *Edgar*, TNA: ADM 51/300.
[15] Log of the *Prince*, TNA: ADM 51/722; Log of the *America*, TNA: ADM 51/35;

Edwards, ed., *Equiano's Travels*, 41; 'Extract of a narrative' in Ekins, *Naval Battles*, 36.

[16] Boscawen to M. Cleveland, 20 August 1759, NMM AGC 1/25.

[17] Dull, *The French Navy and the Seven Years' War*, 137.

[18] 'Lorsque le Général éteindra ses feux de poupe, on redoublera d'attention dans tous les vaisseaux pour ne laisser voir aucun feu' in *Signaux de Nuit et de Brume qui Seront Observés par l'Escadre du Roi Commandée par M. de la Clue Chef d'Escadre des Armées Navales de sa Majesté* (Toulon, 1757), 3; Boscawen to the Secretary of the Admiralty, 20 August 1759, TNA: ADM 1/384; Dull, *The French Navy and the Seven Years' War*, 137; Colomb, *Naval Warfare*, 172 n.9.

[19] Journal of Captain Buckle, 17 August 1759, quoted in Colomb, *Naval Warfare*, 173.

[20] NMM AGC 1/25; Jenkins, *A History of the French Navy*, 130.

[21] Aspinall-Oglander, ed., *Admiral's Wife*, 188–9.

[22] Knox Laughton, ed., *From Howard to Nelson*, 270.

[23] Boscawen to his wife, 24 June 1756, in Lloyd, ed., *The Naval Miscellany*, IV, 229.

[24] Knox Laughton, ed., *From Howard to Nelson*, 271.

[25] Jenkins, *A History of the French Navy*, 67n, 106, 109.

[26] Edwards, ed., Equiano's Travels, 30.

2. The Captured *Téméraire*

[1] Lewis, ed., *A Narrative*, I, 156.

[2] Edwards, ed., *Equiano's Travels*, 42; Ekins, *Naval Battles*, 36.

[3] Ekins, *Naval Battles*, 36.

[4] Ekins, *Naval Battles*, 36.

[5] Hervey, *The Naval History of Great Britain*, V, 182n.

[6] Edwards, ed., *Equiano's Travels*, 43.

[7] French narrative, NMM AGC 1/25.

[8] Boscawen to the Secretary of the Admiralty, 20 August 1759, NMM AGC 1/25.

[9] Some accounts say they both went to Rochefort. See for example Jenkins, *History of the French Navy*, 131.

[10] Lacour-Gayet, *Marine Militaire*, 310–13.

[11] Ekins, *Naval Battles*, 36ff.

[12] Edwards, ed., *Equiano's Travels*, 42.

[13] Ekins, *Naval Battles*, 36.

[14] Log of the *Warspite*, TNA: ADM 51/4004; Log of the *Culloden*, TNA: ADM 51/219.

[15] Laughton and Pearsall, 'Thomas Brodrick (1704–1769)', 795.

[16] Newcastle to Hardwick, 31 August 1759, quoted in Corbett, *Seven Years War*, II, 41.

[17] Knox Laughton, ed., *From Howard to Nelson*, 266.

[18] See Brit. Lib: Add 20847 38–63; Jenkins, *A History of the French Navy*, 131; Knox Laughton, ed., *From Howard to Nelson*, 268.

[19] Quoted in Aspinall-Oglander, ed., *Admiral's Wife*, 283.

[20] *British Magazine*, February 1760: 'An Ode to the Ever-Memorable Year, 1759'.

[21] Pritchard, *Louis XV's Navy 1748–1762*, 134.

[22] Pritchard, *Louis XV's Navy 1748–1762*, 128–34; Winfield, *British Warships 1714–1792*, 70.

[23] Lavery, *Ship of the Line*, I, 85, 99.

[24] Pritchard, *Louis XV's Navy 1748–1762*, 127,132; Rodger, *The Command of the Ocean*, 413.

[25] Barton to the Secretary of the Admiralty, February 1761, TNA: ADM 1/1492.

[26] Lavery, *Arming and Fitting*, 68; Lavery, *The Ship of the Line*, II, 118–21; Oertling, *Bilge Pumps*, 58.

[27] Demerliac, *La Marine de Louis XIV*, 23; Villette-Mursay, *Campagnes*, 43–6.

[28] R. Winfield, *British Warships 1714–1792*, 70.

3. The Amphibious *Temeraire*

[1] Sailing Quality Reports of the *Temeraire* TNA: ADM 95/34; 95/32.

[2] George II quickly changed his mind, however, when he heard Admiral Hawke's reservations about the scheme, and it only became a feasible plan when George II died, and his son George III was crowned. Pitt managed to convince the new King of the worthiness of the plan. Corbett, *England in the Seven Years War*, II, 99; Middleton, *The Bells of Victory*, 167, 173.

[3] Hebbert, 'The Belle-Isle Expedition of 1761', 84.

[4] Corbett, *England in the Seven Years War*, II, 97.

[5] Wareham, *Frigate Commander*, 125.

[6] Keppel to Barrington, 26 March 1761, Bonner-Smith, ed., *Barrington Papers*, I, 296–7.

[7] Rodger, *Wooden World*, 260.

[8] Keppel fleet orders 26 March 1761, Bonner-Smith, ed., *Barrington Papers*, I, 298.

[9] TNA: ADM 36/6913.

[10] Log of the *Temeraire*, 29 March 1761, TNA: ADM 51/4366.

[11] Keppel to Barrington, 31 March 1761, Bonner-Smith, ed., *Barrington Papers*, I, 298.

[12] Hawke to Pitt, 15 December 1760, Mackay, ed., *Hawke Papers*, 374.

[13] Keppel, Fleet orders, 3 April 1761, Bonner-Smith, ed., *Barrington Papers*, I, 301.

[14] Keppel, *Life of Keppel*, I, 307.

[15] Keppel to Lieutenant Roch, 16 May 1761; Keppel Fleet orders 24 April 1761, Bonner-Smith, ed., *Barrington Papers*, I, 306, 308.

[16] Smith, *An Authentic Journal*, 26–9.

[17] Bonner-Smith, ed., *Barrington Papers*, I, 311–12.

[18] Keppel to the Secretary of the Admiralty, 8 October 1761, Bonner-Smith, ed., *Barrington Papers*, I, 319.

[19] Barton to Rodney, 20 February 1761, TNA: ADM 1/93; Norbury to Rodney, 18 February 1761, Syrett, ed., *Rodney Papers*, I, 412.

[20] Log of the *Temeraire*, 6 November 1761, TNA: ADM 51/4366; Spinney, *Rodney*, 179; Syrett, ed., *Rodney Papers*, I, 268.

[21] Log of the *Temeraire*, 8 January 1762, TNA: ADM 51/4366.

[22] Log of the *Temeraire*, 26 January 1762, TNA: ADM 51/4366.

[23] An officer of Colonel Scott's light infantry, quoted in Spinney, *Rodney*, 187.

[24] Spinney, *Rodney*, 187–8.

[25] Syrett, ed., *Siege and Capture of Havana*, xvii.

[26] Log of the *Temeraire*, TNA: ADM 51/4366.

[27] Keppel, *Life of Keppel*, I, 346.

[28] Marley, 'Havana Surprised', 300–303.

[29] Beatson, ed., *Naval and Military Memoirs*, III, 179.

[30] Keppel's Order Book 9 June, Syrett, ed., *Siege and Capture of Havana*, 175.

[31] Syrett, ed., *Siege and Capture of Havana*, 244; Log of the *Temeraire* 18–20 July 1762, TNA: ADM 51/4366; Pocock to Keppel 24 June 1762, Syrett, ed., *Siege and Capture of*

Havana, 202; Log of the *Temeraire* 26 June 1762, TNA: ADM 51/4366.

32 Syrett, ed., *Siege and Capture of Havana*, xxix.

33 Keppel, *Life of Keppel*, 357; also see Syrett, ed., *Siege and Capture of Havana*, 244.

34 Keppel, *Life of Keppel*, I, 358.

35 Quoted in Corbett, *England in the Seven Years War*, II, 273.

36 Log of the *Temeraire*, 31 July 1762, TNA: ADM 51/4366.

37 Corbett, *England in the Seven Years War*, II, 283; Syrett, ed., *Siege and Capture of Havana*, 305–13.

38 Keppel, *Life of Keppel*, I, 365; Syrett, ed., *Siege and Capture of Havana*, 305.

39 Charnock, *Biographia Navalis*, 27.

40 Anonymous Journal in Beatson, ed., *Naval and Military Memoirs*, III, 178.

4. The New *Temeraire*

1 Log of the *Temeraire* 27/28 October 1762 TNA: ADM 51/974.

2 Winfield, *British Warships 1714–1792*, 70.

3 Lavery, *Ship of the Line*, I, 119.

4 Jenkins, *History of the French Navy*, 199.

5 Morriss, *Royal Dockyards*, 15; Webb, 'The Rebuilding and Repair of the Fleet 1783–93', 206, 209.

6 NMM: ZAZ0325/J1630.

7 J. G. Coad, *Royal Dockyards*, 3; Morriss, *Royal Dockyards*, 45.

8 Defoe, *A Tour Through the Whole Island of Great Britain*, 125.

9 Albion, *Forests and Seapower*, 107; Goodwin, *Ships of Trafalgar*, 41; Lavery, *Building the Wooden Walls*, 56.

10 Albion, *Forests and Seapower*, 38, 103.

11 Morriss, *Royal Dockyards*, 12.

12 Morriss, *Royal Dockyards*, 73.

13 NMM: CHA/X/3; CHA/L/34; Lavery, *Ship of the Line*, II, 116; TNA: PRO/ADM 180/6 Entry 78.

14 Leslie, *Old Sea Wings*, 134; Pritchard, 'Prisoner-of-War Bone Model of H.M.S. *Temeraire*', 111–16.

15 Gardiner, ed., *Campaign of Trafalgar*, 142.

16 Lavery, *The Ship of the Line*, II, 68.

17 Carr Laughton, *Old Ship Figure-Heads*, 88.

18 Lavery, *Building the Wooden Walls*, 54.

19 NMM: CHA/X/3; CHA/T.

20 Puget to the Secretary of the Admiralty, 3 April and 5 July 1799, TNA: ADM 1/2318.

21 Quoted in Lavery, *Building the Wooden Walls*, 163.

22 Quoted in Uden, *Fighting Temeraire*, 4.

23 TNA: PRO 30/20/17; Lavery, *Arming and Fitting of English Ships of War*, p. 177.

24 TNA: ADM 95/71.

25 Log of the *Temeraire* 31 May and 4, 9 and 13 June 1799, TNA: ADM 51/1256; TNA: ADM 95/71.

26 TNA: ADM 95/38; TNA: ADM 95/46; Log of the *Temeraire* 9, 26 and 30 June 1799, TNA: ADM 51/1256.

5. The Blockading *Temeraire*

[1] Duffy, 'The Establishment of the Western Squadron', 64; Ryan, 'The Royal Navy and the Blockade of Brest', 179.

[2] Quoted in Rodger, *The Command of the Ocean*, 464.

[3] Quoted in Duffy, 'The Establishment of the Western Squadron', 69.

[4] Lloyd, *The Health of Seamen*, 244–6.

[5] Trotter, *Medicina Nautica*, II, 61–2; III, 467–9.

[6] Quoted in Crimmin, 'John Jervis', 341.

[7] Quoted in Rodger, *The Command of the Ocean*, 464.

[8] Quoted in Crimmin, 'John Jervis', 343.

[9] St Vincent to the Admiralty, 8 July 1800, Morriss, ed., *The Channel Fleet*, 531–2.

[10] Quoted in Steer, 'The Blockade of Brest', 199.

[11] Log of the *Temeraire*: TNA ADM 51/1349; ADM 51/1345.

[12] Lloyd, *The Health of Seamen*, 245.

[13] Quoted in Uden, *The Fighting Temeraire*, 12.

[14] Steer, 'The Blockade of Brest', 209; Log of the *Temeraire* 11/18 December 1800, TNA: ADM 51/1345.

[15] Quoted in Rodger, *The Command of the Ocean*, 465.

[16] E. Marsh to St Vincent, 23 May 1800, Morriss, ed., *The Channel Fleet*, 475.

[17] Puget to the Secretary of the Admiralty, 11 February 1800, TNA: ADM 1/2321.

[18] St Vincent to Marsh, 2 June 1800, Morriss, ed., *The Channel Fleet*, 478.

[19] Eyles to the Secretary of the Admiralty, 28 September 1802, TNA: ADM 1/1767.

[20] Steer, 'The Blockade of Brest', 227.

[21] Duffy, 'The Establishment of the Western Squadron' 66–7; Duffy, 'Devon and the Naval Strategy', 186–7.

[22] Victualling Board to the Secretary of the Admiralty, 27 December 1799, Morriss, ed., *The Channel Fleet*, 425–6.

[23] Steer, 'The Blockade of Brest', 264.

[24] Duffy, 'Devon and the Naval Strategy', 188.

[25] Log of the *Temeraire* 6 August 1800, TNA: ADM 51/1345; Crimmin, 'John Jervis', 342.

[26] Duffy, 'Devon and the Naval Strategy of the French Wars', 187.

[27] Roger, *The Command of the Ocean*, p. 530; Leyland, ed., *Dispatches and Letters Relating to the Blockade of Brest*, xi; Morriss, ed., *The Channel Fleet*, 622.

6. The Mutinous *Temeraire*

[1] Neale, *The Cutlass & The Lash*, 1.

[2] Anon., *Trial of the Mutineers, Late of His Majesty's Ship Temeraire held on board His Majesty's Ship Gladiator, Portsmouth Harbour* (London, 1802), 3.

[3] Anon., *Trial of the Mutineers, Late of His Majesty's Ship Temeraire held on board His Majesty's Ship Gladiator, Portsmouth Harbour*, 3.

[4] Nicol, *Life and Adventures*, 159.

[5] Anon, *The Trials of Fourteen Seamen*, 5; 'Trial of the Mutineers'; Owen, *Mutiny in the Royal Navy*, 92.

[6] Lavery, ed., *Shipboard Life and Organisation*, 151–2.

[7] Quoted in Lavery, *Nelson's Navy*, 152.

[8] Quoted in Lavery, *Nelson's Navy*, 152.

9 TNA: ADM 36/14368.

10 Anon, *The Trials of Fourteen Seamen*, 6.

11 Vice-Admiral Sir Andrew Mitchell to Admiralty, 7 December 1801, TNA: ADM 1/120.

12 See for example the court martial of Captain Kelly. ADM 1/5363. Many thanks to Nicholas Blake for providing this reference.

13 Anon., *Trial of the Mutineers, Late of His Majesty's Ship Temeraire held on board His Majesty's Ship Gladiator, Portsmouth Harbour*, 4.

14 Anon., *The Trials of Fourteen Seamen*, 5.

15 Two days before the preliminary articles of peace had been signed in London. It is likely that this refers to news of the peace being announced on the *Temeraire*.

16 TNA: ADM 1/120.

17 Mitchell to Admiralty, 7 December 1801, TNA: ADM 1/120.

18 Mitchell to Admiralty, 7 December 1801; Campbell to Mitchell, 7 and 9 December 1801, TNA: ADM 1/120.

19 Anon, 'Trial of the Mutineers', *The Times*, 18 January 1802.

20 Log of the *Temeraire*, 11 December 1801, TNA: ADM 51/1418.

21 Log of the *Temeraire*, 13 December 1801, TNA: ADM 51/1418.

22 Anon., 'Trial of the Mutineers', *Gentlemen's Magazine* (1802).

23 Quoted in Owen, *Mutiny in the Royal Navy*, 93.

24 D. Bonner-Smith, ed., *Letters of Earl St Vincent*, 264–5.

25 TNA: ADM 36/14368; Eyles to Admiralty, 24 December 1801, TNA: ADM 1/120.

26 Owen, *Mutiny in the Royal Navy*, 94.

27 TNA: ADM 1/5359.

28 Collingwood to his sister, 16 January 1802, Hughes, ed., *The Private Correspondence of Admiral Lord Collingwood*, 135. Brenton, *Life and Correspondence of the Earl St. Vincent*, II, 109.

29 Brenton, *Life and Correspondence of the Earl St. Vincent*, II, 102–3. At the time this hair style was the distinguishing mark of a thoroughbred seaman.

30 Anon., *Trial of the Mutineers, Late of His Majesty's Ship Temeraire held on board His Majesty's Ship Gladiator, Portsmouth Harbour*, 8.

31 *The Trials of Fourteen Seamen for mutiny . . . late of His Majesty's Ship Temeraire . . . before a court-martial held on board the Gladiator in Portsmouth Harbour January 6 1802* (London, 1802), 32.

32 Anon., *The Trials of Fourteen Seamen*, 32.

33 Collingwood to his sister, 16 January 1802, Hughes, ed., *Collingwood Correspondence*, 135.

34 Brenton, *Life and Correspondence of the Earl St. Vincent*, II, 101.

35 Brenton, *Life and Correspondence of the Earl St. Vincent*, II, 105.

7. The Trafalgar *Temeraire*

1 TNA: ADM 1/5337. Many thanks to Nicholas Blake for this reference.

2 Quoted in Rodger, 'Nelson and the British Navy', 13–14. The 74-gun *Captain* was Nelson's ship at the Battle of St Vincent in 1797 from which Nelson boarded and captured two Spanish ships of the line.

3 Quoted in Rodger, *The Command of the Ocean*, 531.

4 Leyland, ed., *Blockade of Brest*, 356; Albion, *Forests and Seapower*, 419.

5 Quoted in Lavery, *Nelson's Fleet*, 94.

6 James, *The Naval History of Britain*, I, 217.

7 Lewis et al. (eds), *Horace Walpole's Correspondence*, XXV, 12.

8 Laughton, ed., *Barham Papers*, III, 256–7.

9 Laughton, ed., *Barham Papers*, III, 262.

10 Nelson to Harvey, 3 October 1805, ERO: D/DGu/C8.

11 Nelson to Emma Hamilton, 1 October 1805, Nicholas, *Dispatches and Letters of Lord Nelson*, VII, 60.

12 Quoted in Tunstall, *Naval Warfare*, 251.

13 Quoted in Knight, *Pursuit*, 512.

14 Jackson, ed., *Logs*, II, 219.

15 TNA: ADM 36/15851; the muster book is reproduced on pp. 260–276.

16 Harvey to his wife, 23 October 1805, Jackson, ed., *Logs*, II.

17 Nicholas, ed., *Letters*, VII, 147 n.8, 148.

18 Newbolt, 'Quarter Gunner's Yarn', 7–11.

19 Jackson, ed., *Logs*, II, 220–2, 226.

20 Thursfield, ed., *Five Naval Journals*, 365.

21 Desbrière, *Trafalgar*, II, 217.

22 Desbrière, *Trafalgar*, II, 217.

23 L. Harvey to W. Lloyd, 6 December 1805, ERO: D/DGu/C8.

24 Harvey to his wife, 23 October 1805, Jackson, ed., *Logs* II, 226.

25 Desbrière, *Trafalgar* II, 232.

26 NMM LBK/38.

27 Jackson, ed., *Logs*, II, 228.

28 Desbrière, *Trafalgar*, 220.

29 Jackson, ed., *Logs*, II, 227.

30 Collingwood to Admiralty, 24 October 1805, TNA ADM 1/411.

31 Jackson, ed., *Logs*, II, 227.

32 Jackson, ed., *Logs*, II, 220–2.

33 Edward Harrison to his mother, 13 December 1805, NMM: AGC/30/4/6.

34 Louisa Harvey to Louisa Lloyd, 3 December 1805, ERO: D/DGu/Z2.

35 *The Times*, 7 November 1805. Both ships were actually French.

36 Collingwood to Harvey, 28 October 1805, TNA: ADM 1/5396.

37 H. Robinson, *Sea Drift*, 217.

38 Log of the *Temeraire*, 24 November 1805, TNA: ADM 51/1530.

39 Carpenter's expenses November 1805, NMM ADL/D/11.

40 Log of the *Temeraire*, 1 December 1805, TNA: ADM 51/1530.

41 E. Harvey to L. Lloyd, 2 December 1805, ERO: D/DGu/Z2.

42 L. Harvey to L. Lloyd, 3 December 1805, ERO: D/DGu/Z2.

43 Quoted in Lindsay, *J.M.W. Turner*, 91–2.

44 Bourchier, *Codrington*, I, 71–2.

45 Fremantle (ed.), *The Wynne Diaries 1798–1820*, III, 228–9.

46 ERO: T/Z/11/51.

8. The Baltic and Iberian *Temeraire*

1 Glete, *Navies and Nations*, II, 376, 390, 421.

2 TNA: ADM 180/10 Entry 32; Webb, 'Construction, Repair and Maintenance', 216; Winfield, *British Warships*, 2.

3 Quoted in Voelcker, 'Saumarez', 60.

4 Glover, *Britain at Bay*, 57.

5 Captain of the *Ardent* to Admiralty, 28 May 1809, TNA: ADM 1/8.

6 Warren to Saumarez, 24 May 1809, TNA: ADM 1/8; *Melpomene* damage report 18 May 1809, TNA: ADM 1/8.

7 Logs of the *Temeraire* and *Melpomene*, 23–28 May 1809, TNA: ADM 51/1980; 51/1987.

8 Dixon to Saumarez, 24 May 1809, TNA: ADM 1/8.

9 Log of the *Temeraire*, 16–17 March 1810, TNA: ADM 51/2068.

10 Donaldson, 'Recollections', 67.

11 Rees, *Journal*, 30.

12 Donaldson, 'Recollections', 71–8.

13 Donaldson, 'Recollections', 67.

14 Stafford ? to his father, 25 November 1810, in *Five Naval Journals*, 371.

15 Pickmore to Admiralty, 14 July 1810, TNA: ADM 1/417.

16 Rees, *Journal*, 36.

9. The Retired *Temeraire*

1 Lloyd, *The Health of Seamen*, 4.

2 Rees, *Journal*, 45–6.

3 Log of the *Temeraire*, 19 March 1812, TNA: ADM 51/2068.

4 Abell, *Prisoners of War*, 42–4; Dye, 'American Maritime Prisoners of War', 293, 298.

5 Hawkins to Secretary of the Transport Board, 10 and 13 October 1813, WDRO 413/1/14.

6 Abell, *Prisoners of War*, 37.

7 Garneray, *The Floating Prison*, xi.

8 Branch Johnson, *The English Prison Hulks*, 47.

9 Dickens, *Great Expectations*, p. 34.

10 TNA: ADM 180/6 Entry 78; ADM 180/10 Entry 32.

11 Branch Johnson, *The English Prison Hulks*, 57–8.

12 Branch Johnson, *The English Prison Hulks*, 46.

13 Freeston, *Prisoner of War Ship Models*, 7.

14 Garneray, *The Floating Prison*, 229.

15 Branch Johnson, *The English Prison Hulks*, 52.

16 Garneray, *The Floating Prison*, 15.

17 Dye, 'American Maritime Prisoners of War', 314.

18 Abell, *Prisoners of War*, 71.

19 Duffy, 'Devon and the Naval Strategy of the French Wars', 189; Branch Johnson, *The English Prison Hulks*, 62.

20 Dye, 'American Maritime Prisoners of War', 300.

21 Garneray, *The Floating Prison*, 5.

22 Garneray, *The Floating Prison*, 225–6.

23 Rodger, *The Command of the Ocean*, p. 439.

24 Hawkins to Secretary of the Transport Board, 7 January 1813, WDRO: 413/1/12; Hawkins Journal WDRO: 413/1/14.

25 Abell, *Prisoners of War*, 92.

26 TNA: ADM 103/429; ADM 103/430; ADM 103/431.

27 Transport Board to Hawkins, August 1813, WDRO: 413/1/13.

28 James, *American Prisoners of War*, 3.

29 An ideal that was never achieved, as the emergency ships built at th e end of the Napoleonic Wars rotted faster than new ones could be built. Lambert, *Last Sailing Battlefleet*, viii.

30 Turner quoted in Smiles, *The Turner Book*, 142.

31 Log of the *Temeraire*, 20 and 21 August 1836, TNA: ADM 52/4632.

32 Quilley, 'The Battle of the Pictures', 134–6.

33 ADM 51/3742 and ADM 52/4016.

34 Beatson Accounts SLSL: MS 4639.

10. The Fighting *Temeraire*

1 Egerton, *Turner: The Fighting Temeraire*, 123.

2 Southey, *The Life of Nelson*, 258.

3 Stein, 'Remember the *Temeraire*', 176.

4 Hawes, 'Turner's *Fighting Temeraire*', 29.

5 Hawes claims the poem was written 1813–19, although the earliest copy I have been able to find is dated 1857. Hawes, 'Turner's *Fighting Temeraire*', 30.

6 Quoted in Hibbert, *Nelson*, 43.

7 Thackeray, writing as Michael Angelo Titmarsh Esq. in *Fraser's Magazine*, quoted in Finberg, *The Life of J.M.W.Turner, R.A.*, 372.

8 Finberg, *The Life of J.M.W.Turner, R.A.*, 372.

9 Quoted in Egerton, *The Fighting Temeraire*, 88.

10 Thackeray quoted in Hawes, 'Turner's *Fighting Temeraire*', 24.

11 Egerton, *Fighting Temeraire*, 76–8.

12 An 1886 engraving by T. A. Prior and published by Henry Graves and Co. also corrects this 'mistake'. Egerton, *Fighting Temeraire*, 91–2.

13 Cook and Wedderburn, eds., *The Works of John Ruskin*, XXXV, 576.

14 Egerton, *Fighting Temeraire*, 42–3.

15 An observation made by Wylie, quoted in Hawes, 'Turner's *Fighting Temeraire*', 38.

16 Butlin and Joll, *The Paintings of J.M.W. Turner*, II, 209.

17 Quoted in Tucker, *Handbook*, 51.

18 *Athenaeum* of 11 May 1839, in Butlin and Joll, *The Paintings of J.M.W. Turner*, II, 209.

19 Quoted in Rodner, 'Humanity and Nature', 463.

20 Fauré to Louis Aguettant 1902, J. Nectoux, *Gabriel Fauré*, 116.

21 Hawes, 'Turner's *Fighting Temeraire*', 33–5.

22 Stein, 'Remember the *Temeraire*', 180.

23 Quoted in Hawes, 'Turner's *Fighting Temeraire*', 36.

24 Hawes, 'Turner's *Fighting Temeraire*', 43.

25 Quoted in Stein, 'Remember the *Temeraire*', 177.

26 Cook and Wedderburn, eds., *The Works of John Ruskin*, XIII, 171.

27 Hawes, 'Turner's *Fighting Temeraire*', 43 n.2.

28 Egerton, Turner: *The Fighting Temeraire*, 121.

29 Uden, *The Fighting Temeraire*, 60.

30 Egerton, *The Fighting Temeraire*, 116.

31 Stein, 'Remember the *Temeraire*', 169.

BIBLIOGRAPHY

General Works

Egerton, J. *Turner: The Fighting Temeraire* (London, 1995).

Glete, J. *Navies and Nations: Warships, Navies and State Building in Europe and America 1500–1860*, 2 vols (Stockholm, 1993).

James, W. *The Naval History of Great Britain 1793–1827*, 6 vols (London, 1886).

Jenkins, E. H. *A History of the French Navy* (London, 1973).

Laird Clowes, W. *The Royal Navy. A History from the Earliest Times to 1900*, 7 vols (London, 1997).

Lavery, B. *The Ship of the Line*, 2 vols (London, 1983).

———. *Nelson's Navy: The Ships, Men and Organisation, 1793–1815* (Annapolis, 1989).

Rodger, N. A. M. *The Command of the Ocean: A Naval History of Britain 1649–1815* (London, 2004).

———. *The Wooden World: An Anatomy of the Georgian Navy* (London, 1986).

Tunstall, W. C. B. *Naval Warfare in the Age of Sail*, ed. N. Tracy (London, 1990).

Uden, G. *The Fighting Temeraire* (Oxford, 1961).

Winfield, R., and D. Lyon. *The Sail & Steam Navy List: All the Ships of the Royal Navy 1815–1889* (London, 2004).

Winfield, R. *British Warships in the Age of Sail 1714–1792. Design, Construction, Careers and Fates* (Barnsley, 2007).

———. *British Warships in the Age of Sail 1793–1817. Design, Construction, Careers and Fates* (London, 2005).

Chapter 1. The Escaping *Téméraire*

Aspinall-Oglander, C., ed. *Admiral's Wife: Being the life and letters of the Hon. Mrs. Edward Boscawen from 1719 to 1761* (London, 1940).

Beatson, R., ed. *Naval and Military Memoirs of Great Britain from 1727 to 1783*, 6 vols (London, 1804).

Callender, G. A. R. *The Naval Side of British History* (London, 1924).

Colomb, P. H. *Naval Warfare: Its Ruling Principles and Practice Historically Treated*, 2 vols (London, 1895).

Corbett, J. S. *England in the Seven Years' War: A Study in Combined Strategy*, 2 vols (London, 1907).

Dull, J. R. *The French Navy and the Seven Years' War* (London, 2005).

Edwards, P., ed. *Equiano's Travels: The Interesting Narrative of the Life of Olaudah Equiano or Gustavus Vassa the African* (Oxford, 1996).

Ekins, C. *Naval Battles from 1744 to the Peace in 1814, Critically Reviewed and Illustrated* (London, 1824).

Knox Laughton, J., ed. *From Howard to Nelson: Twelve Sailors* (London, 1899).

Lloyd, C., ed. *The Naval Miscellany*, Vol. IV (London: NRS Vol. 92, 1952).

Mackay, R. 'Edward, Lord Hawke, 1705–1781', in *Precursors of Nelson: British Admirals of the Eighteenth Century*, ed. P. Le Fevre and R. Harding (London, 2000), 201–23.

Middleton, R. *The Bells of Victory. The Pitt–Newcastle Ministry and the Conduct of the Seven Years War* (Cambridge, 1985).

Wilkinson, C. 'Edward Boscawen (1711–1761)', in *The Oxford Dictionary of National Biography*, eds. H. C. G. Matthew and B. Harrison (Oxford, 2004), 699–703.

Chapter 2. The Captured *Téméraire*

This chapter draws on a number of books used in Chapter 1 but the following were also useful:

Baugh, D. A. *Naval Administration 1715–50* (London: NRS Vol. 120, 1977).

Demerliac, A., *La Marine de Louis XIV: Nomenclature des Vaisseaux du Roi-Soleil de 1661 à 1715* (Nice, 1995).

Entick, J. *The General History of the Late War*, 5 vols (London, 1763).

Hervey, F. *The Naval History of Great Britain*, 5 vols (London, 1779–80).

Lacour-Gayet, G. *La Marine Militaire de la France sous le règne de Louis XV* (Paris, 1902).

Laughton, J. K., ed. *The Letters and Papers of Charles, Lord Barham*, 3 vols (London: NRS Vols. 32, 38, 39, 1906, 1909, 1910).

Laughton, J. K., and Pearsall, A. W. H. 'Thomas Brodrick (1704–1769)', in

The Oxford Dictionary of National Biography, eds. H. C. G. Matthew and B. Harrison (Oxford, 2004), 794–5.

Lavery, B. *The Arming and Fitting of English Ships of War 1600–1815* (London, 1987).

Lewis, M. A., ed. *A Narrative of my Professional Adventures by Sir William Dillon*, 2 vols (London: NRS Vol. 93, 1953; Vol. 97, 1956).

Oertling, T. *Ships' Bilge Pumps* (Texas, 1996).

Pritchard, J. *Louis XV's Navy 1748–1762* (Kingston, Ontario, 1987).

Villette-Mursay, Phillipe, Marquis de, *Mes Campagnes de mer sous Louis XIV*, ed. M. Vergé-Franceschi (Paris, 1991).

Chapter 3. The Amphibious *Temeraire*

Bonner-Smith, D., ed. *The Barrington Papers, selected from the letters and papers of Admiral the Hon. S. Barrington*. Vol. I (London: NRS Vol. 77, 1937).

Bullocke, J. G., ed. *The Tomlinson Papers* (London: NRS Vol. 74, 1935).

Charnock, J. *Biographia Navalis*, 6 vols (London, 1798).

Corbett, J. S. *England in the Seven Years War: A Study in Combined Strategy*, 2 vols (London, 1907).

Dull, J. R. *The French Navy and the Seven Years' War* (London, 2005).

Hackman, W. K. 'British Military Expeditions to the Coast of France 1757–61', Ph.D. thesis (University of Michigan, 1969).

Harding, R. *Amphibious Warfare in the Eighteenth Century: The British Expedition to the West Indies, 1740–2* (Woodbridge, 1991).

Hart, R. *The Siege of Havana* (1931).

Hebbert, J. F. 'The Belle-Isle Expedition of 1761', *Journal of the Society for Army Historical Research* LXIV (1986), 81–93.

Holbrooke, B. 'The Siege and Capture of Belle-Isle, 1761 from the Diary of an Officer Present at the Siege', *Journal of the Royal United Services Institute* 43 (1899), 160–83.

Keppel, T. *The Life of Augustus Viscount Keppel*, 2 vols (London, 1842).

Laughton, J. K., and R. Harding. 'Matthew Barton 1714/15–1795', in *The Oxford Dictionary of National Biography*, eds. H. C. G. Matthew and B. Harrison (Oxford, 2004), 207–8.

Mackay, R. F., ed. *The Hawke Papers: A selection 1743–1771* (Aldershot: NRS Vol. 129, 1990).

Marley, D. F. 'Havana Surprised: Prelude to the British Invasion, 1762', *MM* 78, no. 3 (1992), 293–306.

Middleton, R. *The Bells of Victory. The Pitt–Newcastle Ministry and the Conduct of the Seven Years War* (Cambridge, 1985).

Pocock, T. *Battle for Empire: The Very First World War, 1756–63* (London, 1998).

Smith, W. *An Authentic Journal of the Expedition to Belleisle and the Siege of the Citadel of the Palais 1761* (London, 1761).

Spinney, D. *Rodney* (London, 1969).

Syrett, D., ed. *The Rodney Papers*, Vol. 1 (Aldershot, NRS Vol. 148, 2005).

————., ed. *The Siege and Capture of Havana, 1762* (London: NRS Vol. 114, 1970).

Wareham, T., *Frigate Commander* (Barnsley, 2004).

Chapter 4. The New *Temeraire*

Albion, R. G. *Forests and Seapower: The Timber Problem of the Royal Navy, 1652–1862* (Annapolis, 2000).

Carr Laughton, L. G. *Old Ship Figure-Heads and Sterns* (London, 2001).

Coad, J. *Historic Architecture of Chatham Dockyard, 1700–1850* (London, 1982).

————. *The Royal Dockyards, 1690–1850* (Aldershot, 1989).

Defoe, D. *A Tour Through the Whole Island of Great Britain*, ed. P. Rogers (Harmondsworth, 1971).

Gardiner, R. *Navies and the American Revolution: 1775–83* (Annapolis, 1996).

————., ed. *The Campaign of Trafalgar 1803–1805* (London, 1997).

Goodwin, P. *Nelson's Ships: A History of the Vessels In Which He Served 1771–1805* (London, 2002).

————. *The Ships of Trafalgar: The British, French and Spanish Fleets October 1805* (London, 2005).

Gower, R. H. *A Treatise on the Theory and Practice of Seamanship* (London, 1808).

Hawes, L. 'Turner's Fighting *Temeraire*', *Art Quarterly New York* 35, no. 1 (1972), 23–48.

Laird Clowes, W. *The Royal Navy. A History from the Earliest Times to 1900.* 7 vols (facs. ed., London, 1997).

Laughton, J. K. 'The Journals of Henry Duncan', in *The Naval Miscellany Vol. 1*, ed. J. K. Laughton (London: NRS Vol. 20, 1902), 105–211.

Lavery, B. *Building the Wooden Walls: The Design and Construction of the 74-gun Ship Valiant* (London, 1991).

Leslie, R. C. *Old Sea Wings, Ways and Words* (London, 1890).

Morriss, R. *The Royal Dockyards During the Revolutionary and Napoleonic Wars* (Leicester, 1983).

Pritchard, L. A. 'Prisoner-of-War Bone Model of H.M.S. *Temeraire*', *MM* 36, no. 2 (1950), 111–16.

Webb, P. L. C. 'The Rebuilding and Repair of the Fleet 1783–93', *Bulletin of the Institute of Historical Research* 50 (1977), 194–209.

Chapter 5. The Blockading *Temeraire*

Bonner-Smith, D., ed. *Letters of Admiral of the Fleet the Earl of St Vincent*, 2 vols (London: NRS Vols. 77 and 81, 1922–7).

Crimmin, P. 'John Jervis, Earl of St Vincent (1735–1823)', in *The Oxford Dictionary of National Biography*, eds. H. C. G. Matthew and B. Harrison (Oxford, 2004), 67–75.

———. 'John Jervis, Earl of St Vincent 1735–1823', in *Precursors of Nelson: British Admirals of the Eighteenth Century*, ed. P. Le Fevre and R. Harding (London, 2000), 325–52.

Duffy, M. 'Devon and the Naval Strategy of the French Wars', in *The New Maritime History of Devon*, ed. M. Duffy, S. Fisher, B. Greenhill, D. J. Starkey and J. Youings (London, 1994), 325–52.

———. 'The Establishment of the Western Squadron as the Linchpin of British Naval Strategy', in *Parameters of British Naval Power 1650–1850*, ed. M. Duffy (Exeter, 1992), 60–81.

James, W. *Old Oak: The Life of John Jervis, Earl of St Vincent* (London, 1930).

Lavery, B., ed. *Shipboard Life and Organisation 1731–1815* (Aldershot: NRS Vol. 138, 1998).

Leyland, J., ed. *Dispatches and Letters Relating to the Blockade of Brest 1803–5*. Vol. I (London: NRS Vol. 14, 1898–9).

Lloyd, C. *The Health of Seamen* (London: NRS Vol. 107, 1965).

Morriss, R., ed. *The Channel Fleet and the Blockade of Brest 1793–1801* (Aldershot: NRS Vol. 141, 2001).

Ryan, N. A. 'The Royal Navy and the Blockade of Brest, 1689–1805: Theory and Practice', in *Les Marines de Guerre Européennes XVII–XVIIIe siècles*, ed. M. Acerra, J. Merino, J. Meyer (Paris, 1985), 175–93.

Steer, D. M. 'The Blockade of Brest by the Royal Navy 1793–1815', MA dissertation (Liverpool, 1971).

Thursfield, H. G., ed. *Five Naval Journals, 1789–1817* (London: NRS Vol. 91, 1951).

Trotter, T. *Medicina Nautica*, 3 vols (London, 1797).

Chapter 6. The Mutinous *Temeraire*

Anon. 'Trial of the Mutineers', *The Times*, 18 January 1802.

———. 'Trial of the Mutineers', *Gentleman's Magazine*, January 1802.

———. *The Trials of Fourteen Seamen for mutiny ... late of his Majesty's ship Temeraire ... before a court-martial held on board the Gladiator in Portsmouth Harbour January 6 1802* (London, 1802).

———. *Trial of the Mutineers, Late of His Majesty's ship Temeraire held on board his Majesty's ship Gladiator, Portsmouth Harbour* (London, 1802).

Bonner-Smith, D., ed. *Letters of Admiral of the Fleet the Earl of St Vincent*, 2 vols (London: NRS Vols. 77 and 81, 1922–27).

Brenton, E. P. *Life and Correspondence of the Earl St. Vincent*, 2 vols (London, 1838).

Gill, C. *The Naval Mutinies of 1797* (Manchester, 1913).

Goodwin, P. *The Ships of Trafalgar: The British, French and Spanish Fleets October 1805* (London, 2005).

Hughes, E. A., ed. *The Private Correspondence of Admiral Lord Collingwood* (London: NRS Vol. 98, 1957).

Lavery, B., ed. *Shipboard Life and Organisation 1731–1815* (Aldershot: NRS Vol. 138, 1998).

Mackesy, P. *War without Victory: The Downfall of Pitt 1799–1802* (Oxford, 1984).

Neale, J. *The Cutlass & The Lash: Mutiny and Discipline in Nelson's Navy* (London, 1985).

Nicol, J. *The Life and Adventures of John Nicol* (New York, 1936).

Owen, C. H. H., ed. 'Letters from Vice-Admiral Lord Collingwood, 1794–1809', in *Naval Miscellany VI* ed. M. Duffy (London: NRS Vol. 106, 2003), 149–220.

Owen, J. H., *Mutiny in the Royal Navy*, Vol. 1 1691–1919, Admiralty Publication: C.B.30327 (London, 1933).

Spinney, J. D. 'The Hermione Mutiny', *MM* 41, no. 2 (1955), 123–36.

Tucker, J. S. *Memoirs of Admiral the Right Hon. the Earl of St Vincent*, 2 vols (London, 1844).

Chapter 7. The Trafalgar *Temeraire*

Albion, R. G. *Forests and Seapower: The Timber Problem of the Royal Navy, 1652–1862* (Annapolis, 2000).

Anon. 'Fremantle and Trafalgar', *MM* 16, no. 4 (1930), 410–11.

Beatty, W. *Authentic narrative of the death of Lord Nelson: with the circumstances preceding, attending, and subsequent to, that event; the professional report on his lordship's wound; and several interesting anecdotes* (London, 1807).

Bourchier, J. *Memoir of the Late Admiral Sir Edward Codrington*, 2 vols (London, 1873).

Corbett, J. S. *The Campaign of Trafalgar*, 2 vols (London, 1910).

Cordingly, D. *Nicholas Pocock 1740–1821* (London, 1986).

Czisnik, M. 'Admiral Nelson's Tactics at the Battle of Trafalgar', *Journal of the Historical Association* CXXXIX, no. 296 (2004), 549–59.

Desbrière, E. *The Naval Campaign of 1805: Trafalgar.* Translated by C. Eastwick, 2 vols (Oxford, 1933).

Duffy, M. ' "...All was Hushed Up": The Hidden Trafalgar', *MM* XCI, no. 2 (2005), 216–40.

Fraser, E. *The enemy at Trafalgar: an account of the battle from eye-witnesses' narratives and letters and dispatches from the French and Spanish fleet* (London, 1906).

Fremantle, A. (ed.) *The Wynne Diaries 1798–1820*, 3 vols (Oxford, 1935–40).

Heathcote, T. A. *Nelson's Trafalgar Captains & Their Battles* (Barnsley, 2005).

Jackson, T. Sturges, ed. *Logs of the Great Sea Fights, 1794–1805*, 2 vols (London: NRS Vols. 16 and 18, 1899–1900).

Knight, R. J. B. 'The Fleets at Trafalgar: The Margin of Superiority', in *Trafalgar in History: A Battle and its Afterlife*, ed. D. Cannadine, 61–77 (London, 2006).

———. *The Pursuit of Victory: The Life and Achievement of Horatio Nelson* (London, 2005).

Laughton, J. K., ed. *The Letters and Papers of Charles, Lord Barham 1758–1813*, Vol. III (London: NRS Vol. 39, 1911).

Laughton, J. K., and Owen, C. H. H. 'Sir Eliab Harvey 1758–1830', in *The Oxford Dictionary of National Biography*, eds. H. C. G. Matthew and B. Harrison (Oxford, 2004), 652–3.

Lavery, B. *Nelson's Fleet at Trafalgar* (London, 2005).

Lewis, W. S. et al. (eds), *Horace Walpole's Correspondence*, 48 vols (London 1937–83).

Leyland, J., ed. *Dispatches and Letters Relating to the Blockade of Brest 1803–5*, Vol. I (London: NRS Vol. 14, 1898–9).

Lindsay, J. *J.M.W. Turner: His Life and Work* (London, 1966).

Mackenzie, R. H. *The Trafalgar Roll, containing the names and services of all officers of the Royal Navy and the Royal Marines who participated in the glorious victory of the 21st October 1805, together with a history of the ships engaged in the Battle* (London, 1913).

Morris, R. *Merchants, Medicine and Trafalgar: The History of the Harvey Family* (Loughton, 2007).

Morriss, R. *Cockburn and the British Navy in Transition* (Exeter, 1997).

———. *The Royal Dockyards During the Revolutionary and Napoleonic Wars* (Leicester, 1983).

Namier, L., and J. Brooke, eds. *The History of Parliament: The House of Commons 1754–1790*. Vol. 2 (London, 1964).

Nicholas, N. H., ed. *The Dispatches and Letters of Lord Nelson*, 7 vols (London, 1845).

Robinson, H. *Sea Drift* (London, 1858).

Rodger, N. A. M. 'Nelson and the British Navy: Seamanship, Leadership, Originality', in *Admiral Lord Nelson: Context and Legacy*, ed. D. Cannadine (London, 2005), 7–29.

Sakula, A. 'Admiral Sir Eliab Harvey of the *Temeraire*', *Journal of the Royal Naval Medical Service* 65 (1979), 153–64.

Steer, D. M. 'The Blockade of Brest by the Royal Navy 1793–1815', MA dissertation (Liverpool, 1971).

Thursfield, H. G., ed. *Five Naval Journals, 1789–1817* (London: NRS Vol. 91, 1951).

Tracy, N. *Nelson's Battles: The Art of Victory in the Age of Sail* (London, 1996).

Whitteridge, G. *William Harvey and the Circulation of the Blood* (London, 1964).

Wilton, A. *Turner in his Time* (London, 1987).

Chapter 8. The Baltic and Iberian *Temeraire*

Donaldson, J. *Recollections of the Eventful Life of a Soldier* (Staplehurst, 2000).

Esdaile, C. *The Peninsular War: A New History* (London, 2002).

Gardiner, R., ed. *The Campaign of Trafalgar 1803–5* (London, 1997).

Glover, R. *Britain at Bay; Defence against Bonaparte, 1803–14* (London, 1973).

Greenwood, D. 'James, Lord de Saumarez, 1757–1836', in *British Admirals of the Napoleonic Wars: The Contemporaries of Nelson*, ed. P. Le Fevre and R. Harding (London, 2005), 245–70.

Hall, C. D. *Wellington's Navy: Sea Power and the Peninsular War, 1807–14* (London, 2004).

Heathcote, T. A. ' "Serjeant Belle-Jambe" – Bernadotte', in *Napoleon's Marshals*, ed. D. G. Chandler (London, 1998), 18–42.

Munch-Petersen. 'The Secret Intelligence from Tilsit', in *Historisk Tidsskrift* CII (2002), 93–5.

Rees, A. *Naval Architecture* (Newton Abbot, 1970).

Rees, T. *A Journal of Voyages and Travels, by the Late Thomas Rees, Serjeant of Marines* (London, 1822).

Ryan, A. 'An Ambassador Afloat: Vice-Admiral Sir James Saumarez and the Swedish Court, 1808–12', in *The British Navy and the Use of Naval Power in the Eighteenth Century*, ed. J. Black and P. Woodfine (Leicester, 1988), 237–58.

———., ed. *The Saumarez Papers: Selections from the Baltic Correspondence of Vice-Admiral Sir James Saumarez 1808–12* (London: NRS Vol. 110, 1968).

Thursfield, H. G., ed. *Five Naval Journals, 1789–1817* (London: NRS Vol. 91, 1951).

Voelcker, T. 'Saumarez and the Role of the Commander-in-Chief Baltic, 1808', Papers Presented at the Twelfth Annual New Researchers in Maritime History Conference, University of Liverpool 2004.

Webb, P. L. C. 'Construction, Repair and Maintenance in the Battle Fleet of the Royal Navy, 1793–1815', in *The British Navy and the Use of Naval Power in the Eighteenth Century*, ed. J. Black and P. Woodfine (Leicester, 1988), 207–20.

Woodman, R. *The Victory of Seapower: Winning the Napoleonic Wars, 1806–14* (London, 1998).

Chapter 9. The Retired *Temeraire*

Abell, F. *Prisoners of War in Britain 1756–1815* (Oxford, 1914).

Anon. *Instructions for Agents under the Commissioners for conducting His Majesty's Transport Service, for taking care of Sick and Wounded Seamen, and for the Care and Custody of Prisoners of War, respecting the Management of Prisoners of War at Home . . .* (London, 1808).

Branch Johnson, W. *The English Prison Hulks* (London, 1957).

Cordingly, D. *Billy Ruffian: The Bellerophon and the Downfall of Napoleon* (London, 2003).

Czisnik, M. 'Commemorating Trafalgar: Public Celebration and National Identity', in *Trafalgar in History*, ed. D. Cannadine (London, 2006), 139–54.

Dickens, C. *Great Expectations* (London, 1994 ed.)

Duffy, M. 'Devon and the Naval Strategy of the French Wars', in *The New Maritime History of Devon*, ed. M. Duffy, S. Fisher, B. Greenhill, D. J. Starkey and J. Youings (London, 1994), 182–91.

Dye, I. 'American Maritime Prisoners of War, 1812–15', in *Ships, Seafaring and Society: Essays in Maritime History*, ed. T. Runyan (Detroit, 1987), 293–320.

Fraser, F. 'If You Seek his Monument: The Monuments to Nelson in Great Britain and Overseas', in *The Nelson Companion*, ed. C. White (Frome, 1997), 129–52.

Freeston, E. C. *Prisoner of War Ship Models 1775–1825* (Annapolis, 1973).

Garneray, L. *The Floating Prison: The Remarkable Account of Nine Years' Captivity on the British Prison Hulks During the Napoleonic Wars.* Translated by R. Rose (London, 2003).

Goodwin, P. *The Ships of Trafalgar: The British, French and Spanish Fleets October 1805* (London, 2005).

James, T. *American Prisoners of War at Dartmoor War Depot (1813–15)* (Chudleigh, 2007).

Joy, R. *Dartmoor Prison: A Complete Illustrated History*, 2 vols (Tiverton, 2002).

Lambert, A. *The Last Sailing Battlefleet* (London, 1991).

———. 'The Magic of Trafalgar: The Nineteenth Century Legacy', in *Trafalgar in History: A Battle and its Afterlife*, ed. D. Cannadine (London, 2006), 155–74.

Lloyd, C. *The Health of Seamen* (London: NRS Vol. 107, 1965).

McConville, S. *A History of English Prison Administration 1750–1877.* Vol. 1 (London, 1981).

Quilley, G. 'The Battle of the Pictures: Painting the History of Trafalgar', in *Trafalgar in History*, ed. D. Cannadine (London, 2006), 121–38.

Rees, T. *A Journal of Voyages and Travels, by the Late Thomas Rees, Serjeant of Marines* (London, 1822).

Smiles, S. *The Turner Book* (London, 2006).

Stein, R. L. 'Remember the *Temeraire*: Turner's Memorial of 1839', *Representations* 11 (1985), 165–200.

Tucker, S. C. *The Handbook of 19th Century Naval Warfare* (Stroud, 2000).

Chapter 10. The Fighting *Temeraire*

Butlin, M, and Joll, E. *The Paintings of J.M.W. Turner*. Vol. 2 (London, 1977).

Cook, E. T., and Wedderburn, A. eds. *The Works of John Ruskin*, 39 vols (London, 1903–12).

Finberg, A. J. *The Life of J. M. W. Turner, R.A.* (London, 1961).

Hawes, L. 'Turner's Fighting *Temeraire*', *Art Quarterly New York* 35, no. 1 (1972), 23–48.

Hermann, L. 'Turner, Joseph Mallord William (1775–1851)', in *The Oxford Dictionary of National Biography*, eds. H. C. G. Matthew and B. Harrison (Oxford, 2004), 632–47.

Hibbert, C. *Nelson, A Personal History* (London, 1994).

Nectoux, J. *Gabriel Fauré: A Musical Life* (Cambridge, 1991).

Rodner, W. S. 'Humanity and Nature in the Steamboat Paintings of J.M.W. Turner', *Albion: A Quarterly Journal Concerned with British Studies*, Vol. 18, No. 3 (Autumn, 1986), 455–74.

Smiles, S. *The Turner Book* (London, 2006).

Southey, R. *The Life of Nelson* (London, 1922).

Stein, R. L. 'Remember the *Temeraire*: Turner's Memorial of 1839', *Representations* 11 (1985), 165–200.

Tucker, S. C. *The Handbook of 19th Century Naval Warfare* (Stroud, 2000).

INDEX